AFGHANISTAN'S TROUBLED TRANSITION

Afghanistan's Troubled Transition

Politics, Peacekeeping, and the 2004 Presidential Election

Scott Seward Smith

Viva Books

New Delhi | Mumbai | Chennai | Kolkata | Bengaluru | Hyderabad | Kochi | Guwahati

First Indian Edition 2012

VIVA BOOKS PRIVATE LIMITED

- 4737/23 Ansari Road, Daryaganj, New Delhi 110 002
  E-mail: vivadelhi@vivagroupindia.net, Tel. 42242200
- 76, Service Industries, Shirvane, Sector 1, Nerul, Navi Mumbai 400 706
  E-mail: vivamumbai@vivagroupindia.net, Tel. 27721273, 27721274
- Jamals Fazal Chambers, 26 Greams Road, Chennai 600 006
  E-mail: vivachennai@vivagroupindia.net, Tel. 28290304, 28294241
- B-103, Jindal Towers, 21/1A/3 Darga Road, Kolkata 700 017
  E-mail: vivakolkata@vivagroupindia.net, Tel. 22836381, 22816713
- 7, Sovereign Park Apartments, 56-58, K. R. Road, Basavanagudi, Bengaluru 560 004
  E-mail: vivabangalore@vivagroupindia.net, Tel. 26607409, 26607410
- 101-102 Mughal Marc Apartments, 3-4-637 to 641, Narayanguda, Hyderabad 500 029
  E-mail: vivahyderabad@vivagroupindia.net, Tel. 27564481, 27564482
- Beevi Towers, First Floor, SRM Road, Kaloor, Kochi 682 018, Kerala
  E-mail: vivakochi@vivagroupindia.net, Tel: 0484-2403055, 2403056
- 232, GNB Road, Beside UCO Bank, Silpukhuri, Guwahati 781 003
  E-mail: vivaguwahati@vivagroupindia.net, Tel: 0361-2666386

www.vivagroupindia.com

Published by arrangement with

Lynne Rienner Publishers, Inc.
1800 30th Street, Suite 314
Boulder, Colorado 80301
USA

ISBN : 978-81-309-2067-2

Published by Vinod Vasishtha for Viva Books Private Limited, 4737/23, Ansari Road, Daryaganj, New Delhi-110 002. Printed and bound by Saku Printers, New Delhi.

For Susana

Contents

Acronyms

ACABQ	Advisory Committee on Administrative and Budgetary Questions
AIHRC	Afghan Independent Human Rights Commission
AREU	Afghan Research and Evaluation Unit
CLJ	Constitutional Loya Jirga
CSO	Central Statistics Office
DDR	Disarmament, demobilization, and reintegration program
DPA	Department of Political Affairs
DPKO	Department of Peacekeeping Operations
DSRSG	Deputy Special Representative of the Secretary-General
EAD	Electoral Assistance Division
ESOC	Elections Security Operations Center
EU	European Union
FEFA	Free and Fair Elections Foundation for Afghanistan
FPTP	First Past the Post system
IAEC	Independent Afghan Electoral Commission
IAPSO	Inter-Agency Procurement Service Organization
ICG	International Crisis Group
IDEA	International Institute for Democracy and Electoral Assistance
IDPs	Internally displaced peoples
IEC	Independent Electoral Commission
IED	Improvised explosive device
IFES	International Foundation for Electoral Systems
IOM	International Organization of Migration
IRI	International Republican Institute
ISAF	International Security Assistance Force
ISI	Inter-Services Intelligence
JEMB	Joint Electoral Management Body
MOSS	Minimum Operational Security Standards
NAM	Needs Assistance Mission
NATO	North Atlantic Treaty Organization

NDI	National Democratic Institute
NGO	Non-governmental organization
OCV	Out-of-country voting
ORB	Occasional Recuperation Break
OSCE	Organization for Security and Cooperation in Europe
PDPA	People's Democratic Party of Afghanistan
PR	Proportional representation
PRTs	Provincial Reconstruction Teams
SNTV	Single-non-transferable vote
SRSG	Secretary-General's Special Representative
UEC	UNAMA Electoral Component
UEU	UNAMA Electoral Unit
UNAMA	United Nations Assistance Mission in Afghanistan
UNAMET	United Nations Assistance Mission to East Timor
UNDEF	United Nations Democracy Fund
UNDP	United Nations Development Programme
UNHCR	Office of the United Nations High Commissioner for Refugees
UNOCHA	United Nations Office for the Coordination of Humanitarian Assistance
UNOPS	United Nations Office for Project Support
UNSMA	United Nations Special Mission to Afghanistan
UNVs	United Nations Volunteers
WFP	World Food Programme

1
Introduction

In a large bureaucracy it is rare to work in the area of one's specialty. My specialty, if I had one when I joined the United Nations in 1998, was Afghanistan. I had first visited the country in 1994, to carry out a short, three-week exploratory mission for a French Non-Governmental Organization (NGO), Solidarités. I returned the following year for eleven months, working for Solidarités again. In that first visit I had already discovered what many before me had discovered: Afghanistan, despite its manifest misery, is a dangerously addictive country to foreigners. There is something—perhaps the savage beauty of its landscape, perhaps the anachronistic dignity of its people, perhaps the culture of hospitality amid scarcity—that affects almost every foreigner who visits, and makes Afghanistan a place where one must always return. This was certainly the case for me. Between 1996 and 1998, while obtaining my Masters degree in international relations in New York, I obsessively sought to link every assignment I was given to Afghanistan so that I could read as much as I could about it. I had chosen my place of study—Columbia University—in large part because they offered a course in intensive Persian. In the summer of 2007, I returned to Kabul for a month to research my thesis on humanitarian work in Afghanistan. While all this helped satisfy my unending curiosity about the country, Afghanistan was, in terms of preparing a career, a fairly pointless obsession in the 1990s.

Indeed, my first posting for the United Nations was in Bougainville, Papua New Guinea. From that experience I developed a minor specialty in the South Pacific. In September 2001 I was en route to the Solomon Islands for a three month posting. My itinerary took me through Brisbane, Australia, where I breakfasted with a friend who I knew from my Bougainville days and who was also knowledgeable about the situation in the Solomons. Returning to my hotel room to pack and catch my flight to Honiara, a bit of news on CNN caught my attention. Ahmad Shah Massoud, the leader of one of the Afghan factions fighting the

Taliban, had been assassinated, apparently by members of Al Qaeda. Massoud was considered by many to be a brilliant strategist whose leadership was essential to the anti-Taliban coalition, known as the Northern Alliance. With his death, the defeat of the alliance was likely, and with it the takeover of the entire country by the Taliban. That would confront global policy-makers with the decision of whether or not to recognize the Taliban as the legitimate government of Afghanistan, but otherwise would not much disturb the world, which remained generally indifferent to that remote and unimportant country.

Later that evening I landed in Honiara and checked into my hotel. Around midnight, my friend in Brisbane called me to say that a plane had crashed into one of the towers of the World Trade Center in Manhattan. He knew that my wife was in New York and said that I might want to call her. Groggy from the long flights over the previous days, I simply assumed that it was one of those incidents where a single-engine Cessna lost control and hit the building. My wife was on the Upper West Side and was not likely to be affected by such an event, so I went back to sleep instead. The next morning, I did call my wife to report that I had arrived safely in Honiara, and asked, in passing, about this incident with the plane and the Twin Towers. That was when I learned what had really happened. I switched on the TV in my room and absorbed the events of the previous 12 hours. I was, perhaps, one of the last people on earth to learn the news of this horrific event that put Afghanistan, my obscure obsession, in the center of international affairs again.

When I returned to New York in December of 2001 I was assigned to the Afghanistan desk in the Department of Political Affairs (DPA). The Bonn Agreement had already been signed and the United Nations was preparing to expand its presence in the country in order to carry guide the political transition prescribed by the Agreement. One of the specific tasks assigned to the U.N. by the agreement was the registration of voters ahead of the general elections that were to be held in June 2004. In the late spring of 2003, I was assigned to the Electoral Assistance Division (EAD), specifically to work on the upcoming Afghan elections. This was the beginning of my involvement in the somewhat quixotic process that forms the subject of the following pages.

The 2004 Afghan presidential elections undoubtedly marked the high point of Afghanistan's political transition. But in the arduous process of making them happen, the seeds for the decline that followed were sown. Throughout the process, two points of view were in perpetual tension. The first, what might be called an institutionalist perspective, saw the legitimization of political structures as a long and incremental process, in which elections play a necessary but not sufficient role in assuring stability. It argues that "legitimacy is the key to building sustainable peace, and this legitimacy comes not from the timetable of donors with blueprints of postconflict reconstruction, but from the points of view of the population."[1] The second point of view, what might be called the political perspective, saw elections as a culminating event—a "punctuation point in a peacekeeping mission"[2]—whose political value resided more in the fact that they were held than on the conditions under which they were held.

My main contention is that the 2004 election was a success in both institutional and political terms, but the inattention to institutional aspects contributed, over the long term, to Afghanistan's present political crisis. In political terms, the election of Hamid Karzai in 2004 with more than 50 percent of the vote, in a process that was widely perceived as credible, not least by the Afghan people, fulfilled the primary purpose of the election—to legitimize the president. The secondary purpose was for the election to act as a referendum on the Bonn process; here the high turnout was correctly interpreted as a sign of popular support for the Bonn process. From the institutionalist perspective, the perceived credibility of the election was a major asset, as it allowed Afghan voters, many of whom were voting for the first time, to connect the act of voting with political change. The election therefore gave meaning to the process, as well as legitimacy to the government. The voter registration process that preceded the election had conferred a civic identity on a population that had, for the previous three decades, too often been the victim of politics. Finally, while international experts had played a large role in planning and organizing the election, enough Afghan capacity had been built to lay the foundation for a future Afghan electoral institutional framework.

After 2004, however, the institutional considerations were increasingly forsaken for short-term political concerns. This was the result of the pressure of time, the deteriorating security situation, an uncoordinated international community, and an Afghan political class whose members consistently and grossly put personal gain above the national interest. The difficult and contentious 2009 presidential election, was the logical result of the inattention to institutionalization that had characterized the previous half-decade. In many ways it undid the work of 2004, delegitimizing Karzai and signaling widespread discontent with the political process. Charles Tilly has noted that "democratization is a dynamic process that always remains incomplete and perpetually runs the risk of reversal—of de-democratization."[3]

Many now ask if we have reached in Afghanistan today the point of de-democratization.

While this is an attempt to write an objective history of the 2004 Afghan presidential elections, it cannot avoid the biases of its author. One of the charms of Afghanistan is how completely it captures its observers, so that in writing about it, it almost impossible to remain detached or impersonal.[4] At the same time, one of the temptations of writing a bureaucratic postmortem is the possibility of settling scores. This book suffers from a little of both that singular charm and that irresistible temptation. One hopes it is more interesting for both.

The book also contains chapters on the 2005 parliamentary election and the 2009 presidential election, to illustrate the consequences of the failure of institutionalization. The 2009 election was particularly contentious because of a dispute within the United Nations mission between the mission's head, Kai Eide, and one of his deputies, Peter Galbraith. In 2009 I was the Special Assistant to Eide and participated in many of the decisions taken during the very public controversy over how the electoral crisis was handled. I am necessarily less objective in my consideration of this dispute. My purpose is to elucidate the complexities that were too often glossed over in the heated press coverage, and to provide a defense of the approach taken by Eide.

As much as possible, I have used public sources to back-up my main contentions. These include official United Nations reports, papers issued by the myriad groups that offer policy advice for free—of which there are several devoted to Afghanistan—as well as published monographs. But the story cannot be fully understood without describing the more decisive policy discussions that took place within the United Nations. In these cases I have relied on memory, notes, and my journals, as well as internal documentation (such as budgets, operating plans, and so forth).

In writing this book, I owe an extreme debt of gratitude to José Maria Aranàz, a colleague during the 2004 election and a friend ever since. José Maria was based in Kabul while I was mostly based in New York during the preparations for the presidential election. Among many valuable contributions to my understanding of events in Kabul, José Maria also essentially wrote the first draft of Chapter 11 on the electoral law. Had there been, over the past five years, fewer elections in the world that required José Maria's even temperament and acute legal judgment, he would have been this book's co-author, and it would have been a better book.

I am also grateful to Richard Atwood, who was an early reader of the manuscript and a surprisingly supportive critic, given my own criticisms of the 2005 parliamentary election, on which he worked. I don't expect Richard to fully endorse my views of that election, but I hope my criticism is fairer for his comments. I am all the more grateful to him for the several embarassing mistakes he saved me from making. Those that remain are purely the result of my obduracy in continuing to perceive them as brilliant insights.

Finally, Professor William Maley has supported this project from the beginning. Ever since I met him at the U.N. bar in Kabul during the Taliban regime in 1997, he has been something of an unofficial mentor to me in my study of Afghanistan. Once, while still in graduate school in 1998, I sent him a snarky review I had published of a book on Afghanistan that had just come out. He gently admonished me, saying that the community of Afghan scholars was small and, for a group of academics, rather courteous, hinting that I had violated this decorum. Now fate and my foolish compulsion to write and be read has put me on the other side of the author-critic divide. I can only hope that the community of Afghan scholars, now far larger than it was before, will be indulgent and heed Professor Maley's long-ago advice to me.

---

[1] Shahrbanou Tadjbakhsh and Michael Schoiswohl, "Playing with Fire? The International Community's Democratization Experiment in Afghanistan" *International Peacekeeping* 15, no. 2, April 2008, p. 265.

[2] See Ben Reilly, "Elections in Post-Conflict Societies" in *The UN Role In Promoting Democracy: Between Ideals and Reality*, eds. Edward Newman and Roland Rich (Tokyo: United Nations University Press, 2004) p. 118.

[3] Charles Tilly, *Democratization* (New York: Cambridge University Press, 2007) p. xi.

[4] For example, Louis Dupree's sentimental account of Afghanistan's geology in the early chapters of his masterpiece, *Afghanistan* (Princeton: Princeton University Press, 1980), or Octavio Paz's wonderful comment that "I have seen the birth, the full flowering, and the decline of the Gothic style in rocks in the Valley of Kabul." *Alternating Current* (New York: Arcade Publishing, 1990) p. 28.

2
The Bonn Agreement

Most countries' fates do not hinge on a dentists' convention. Afghanistan's, for a moment, did. In late November 2001, Afghan political groups had gathered in Petersberg castle, near the German city of Bonn, to lay the foundations of their future state. The negotiations, under the auspices of the United Nations, took place in the wake of the rapid collapse of the Taliban regime. The immediate need was for the Afghan delegates at Bonn to agree on transitional governing arrangements and set out a "road map" to a more firmly-established and legitimate government. The delegates met for nine days without coming to a final agreement. A convention of dentists was scheduled to begin on the tenth day, when the Afghans would have to vacate the castle.[1] Recognizing that to leave Petersberg without an agreement would be a catastrophic failure, and a huge disappointment to the many Afghans who badly hoped for a political consensus that would put behind them decades of war, the delegates worked through the final night. They emerged at dawn on December 5 with an Agreement on Provisional Arrangements in Afghanistan Pending the Re-Establishment of Permanent Government Institutions.[2] The agreement specified that these "permanent government institutions" had to be democratic. Therefore a key provision of the agreement was the holding of elections two-and-a-half years later.

It would later be agreed by almost everyone with an opinion that the main flaw of the Bonn Agreement was not having included the Taliban in the negotiations. This narrative was endorsed, if not in fact begun, by Lakhdar Brahimi, the United Nations diplomat who oversaw the Bonn conference.[3] One must pay attention when the architect of an accord criticizes his own work. But in this case, the architect is perhaps excessively modest. Had the Taliban been involved in the Bonn negotiations, it is not at all obvious that there would have been an agreement; and had an agreement been reached, it surely would not have been as forward-looking as the one that emerged.[4] The absence of the

Taliban from Bonn allowed, but did not guarantee, the negotiation of an agreement that would return Afghanistan to the moderate and modernizing Islamic politics it had enjoyed for most of the twentieth century. Indeed, Brahimi recognized this at the time. Barnett Rubin, one of his advisors at Bonn, quoted him as saying that "no one would remember how unrepresentative the meeting had been if the participants managed to fashion a process that would lead to a legitimate and representative government."[5] Whatever their differences, the signatories to the Bonn Agreement were bound by a fairly strong consensus. That consensus would have been far more fragile had the Taliban been given a perpetual voice in the government that followed. The real error was in allowing the Taliban to re-emerge as a military force, not in refusing to grant them a permanent place in Afghan politics at the beginning.[6]

Who, then, did participate at Bonn? The conference included representatives from four Afghan groups.[7] The most important of these was the Northern Alliance, made up of a number of mostly non-Pashtun groups, many whom had fought each other during the civil war of the early 1990s, but who united against the Taliban after the fall of Kabul in September 1996.[8] The second most important group was the "Rome Group," representing followers of King Mohammed Zahir Shah (Zahir Shah had lived in Rome following his abdication after the 1973 coup against him by his cousin). The king's group was not overly powerful. The King himself had mostly stayed out of Afghan politics during the anti-Soviet resistance and the post-Soviet occupation civil war. But the royal dynasty was Pashtun, and the Rome Group therefore provided Pushtun representation to the conference, which was particularly important given the exclusion of the largely Pashtun Taliban.[9]

The other two groups were the "Peshawar Group," nominally led by Pir Sayed Ahmad Gailani, and the "Cyprus Group," associated with Homayoun Jareer, son-in-law of Gulbuddin Hekmatyar, leader of one of the most important anti-Soviet resistance groups. The Cyprus Group was backed by Iran, where Hekmatyar had fled following the fall of Kabul to the Taliban in 1996.[10] William Maley noted that the negotiators at Bonn were "a stellar group by Afghan standards," but also pointed out some notable absentees. One was Burhanuddin Rabbani, who was still recognized as the president of Afghanistan by most countries, except the three that had recognized the Taliban regime.[11] Another was Abdul Rashid Dostum, a powerful militia leader who was the figurehead of the Uzbek minority, and whose Junbesh party was aligned with the Northern Alliance.[12]

The negotiations at Bonn were held behind closed doors. They were chaired by Brahimi, a former Foreign Minister of Algeria, who had gained an international reputation for sagacity in the late 1980s for his role in negotiating the Taif Accords that ended the Lebanese civil war. Brahimi, outside the negotiation room, consulted regularly with diplomats of interested states who had sent representatives. One of these diplomats was the American, James F. Dobbins, who has written what is so far the most complete account of the conference. Dobbins conveys a sense of the drab atmospherics of the conference. It took place during a cold, wet, German December that happened to coincide with the Muslim fasting month of Ramadan. As Dobbins wryly noted, "from the Congress of Vienna in 1815 to the Dayton Peace Conference of 1995, many breakthroughs have been achieved over a good meal and generous measure of spirits. This Bonn meeting had to proceed without the benefit of either."[13] According to Dobbins, the actual design of the transitional arrangements was secured among the delegates with relative ease, as was the decision on Hamid Karzai to head the interim administration.[14] After the acrimonious 2009 election that pitted Karzai against Abdullah Abdullah, it is touching to read in Dobbins' account that "the unanimity of international support for Karzai was largely Dr. Abdullah's doing."[15] The more difficult and time-consuming part of the negotiation was the selection of ministers for the interim administration. That debate was far less relevant to the eventual conduct of elections than was the political process set up at Bonn that led up to those elections. But, rooted as it was in the contest of various personal ambitions, it did foreshadow one of the primary causes of the present crisis.

The Bonn Agreement, as J. Alexander Thier has written, "set two simultaneous processes in motion: a state-building process and a peace-consolidation process."[16] The holding of elections—the last step of the Bonn process—were critical to both. Elections would, in theory, provide legitimacy to the government, enabling it to extend its administration across the country and build durable governing institutions. At the same time, it was hoped that elections would allow for Afghanistan's infamously deadly political rivalries to be channeled through non-violent institutions. The oldest and most basic theoretical arguments for democracy—that it channels political conflict away from violence—was now being applied to the oldest and most basic problem of Afghan political order.[17]

The agreement set three specific tasks. First, it formalized an interim administration that was unrepresentative of the country as a whole but that reflected the balance of power in Afghanistan that obtained at the time. Twenty-nine ministries were created—far more than were needed to actually administer the country, but enough to allow sufficient inclusiveness to secure an agreement among the participants. Of these, 16 ministerial positions were given to the largely non-Pashtun Northern Alliance, which considered itself to have vanquished the Taliban.[18] This interim arrangement was intended to secure a window of stability in which to draft a constitution while beginning the reconstruction of the country.

Second, the Agreement laid out a step-by-step process, through increasingly representative mechanisms, to legitimatize the government. The first step was to hold a Loya Jirga, or grand assembly, within six months of the agreement to "decide on a Transitional Authority, including a broad-based transitional administration, to lead Afghanistan until such time as a fully representative government can be elected through free and fair elections."[19] This was termed an "Emergency Loya Jirga." Eighteen months later, a new constitution was to be ratified by another Loya Jirga. Lastly, general elections were to be held to create a new and fully-representative government.

The requirement of holding two Loya Jirgas demonstrated a grasp on the part of Bonn's drafters of the need to proceed in incriments while maintaining constant political engagement to maximize inclusiveness. Essentially, the "losers" at Bonn—those who felt that they had been unfairly excluded from political power—would be given a second chance at the Emergency Loya Jirga. The losers there would be given a third chance at the Constitutional Loya Jirga. Finally, credible elections would provide an even chance for all. It was expected that the constitution would provide for regular elections, institutionalizing the political pressure-release system for which the Bonn process provided a model. The fact that each step in the process was clearly laid out and dates for each step clearly indicated served to reduce political tensions throughout the process. Furthermore, each deadline that was met would increase confidence in the political process.[20]

The political process defined by the Bonn Agreement was well-designed. It also owed much to previous agreements that had attempted to end the Afghan civil war during the previous decade. (This familiarity perhaps helps explain why the transitional provisions were agreed to so easily during the Bonn negotiations.[21]) The most important examples were the Peshawar and Islamabad accords. The Peshawar Accord of April 1992, designed to fill the power vacuum left by the ouster of President Najibullah with a Mujaheddin-led state, called for a 51-member *shura*, or council, to be led by Sigbatullah Mojaddedi for four months. Mojaddedi would then hand over power to Rabbani, who would lead a Leadership Council for the next four months. Following that, he would hand over power to a Council for Supreme Popular Settlement which would have the task of organizing elections 18 months later.[22] The Islamabad Declaration of March 1993, signed by the main resistance groups following the collapse of the Soviet-backed Najibullah government,[23] also called for the election of a "Grand Constituent Assembly" (analogous to the Bonn Agreement's "Emergency Loya Jirga"), the drafting of a new constitution and the holding of general elections for a new president and parliament within 18 months.

The Islamabad Declaration has largely been forgotten. It is resurrected here for one important reason: to dispel the notion held by many that elections or "democracy" had been "imposed" on Afghanistan by the West. The holding of general elections was probably among the least contentious issue for the Bonn negotiators, not to mention the Afghan people in general. A study in the spring of 2002 on "Afghan Perspectives on Democracy" concluded that "by and large" Afghans favored democracy. "They want to have an elected government that is responsive to people's interests. They believe everyone should be equal under the law, and that even the highest government official should be held accountable."[24] If anyone had doubts about the wisdom of holding elections in Afghanistan, it seemed to be Western observers,[25] who wondered if the country was "ready" for democracy. Nor has this changed much, despite the evident problems of Afghan democratization, that elections are still seen as part of the country's political solution. In October of 2008, for example, Hekmatyar, an implacable foe of the Bonn Agreement, issued a statement saying that "The only solution to the existing crisis is the withdrawal of foreign troops, *the holding of fair elections*, the transfer of power to elected representatives and the establishment of an Islamic government in Afghanistan" (emphasis added).

The readiness of Afghanistan for democracy was not, however, an unreasonable question to ask. Afghan politics, because they are tribal, are both highly participatory and intensely local.[26] For these reasons, they are also deceptively sophisticated. Modern democracy, by imposing rules on political rivalry, tends to simplify politics around major interests. Non-institutionalized systems like Afghanistan's are often far more difficult to decode, since the loci of consensus are buried in tribal lore, family relations, financial connections, longstanding feuds and other considerations that are not easily penetrated by the modern political mind or organized by modern political institutions. Authority is instead earned or lost on strength of arms, sophistication of alliances, and use of money—what Josiah Harlan called "fiscal diplomacy" when he first observed it in the nineteenth century.[27] This has meant that Afghanistan, as a state, has never really been governed, at least in the sense of Mirabeau's formulation that "*administrer, c'est gouverner; gouverner, c'est régner; tout se réduit là.*"[28] The inability of any Afghan regime to impose power from the center consistently has prevented the development of modern political institutions capable of administering. State structures have always superficial, neither embedded nor autonomous.[29] Beyond the capital and the major urban areas, tribal structures rule. The most successful Afghan regimes have brought a minimum of stability across the national area not by defeating tribal and local institutions, but by managing them—in other words by trying to split or co-opt them.

An exclusive focus on the element of conflict within Afghan politics risks, however, overlooking the fact that for most of the twentieth century, when the great democracies of the West were murdering each other with the state-of-the-art technology, tribal and "backward" Afghanistan was largely peaceful and stable.[30] Furthermore, a degree of political modernization had been achieved in Afghanistan by the 1960s, under King Mohammed Zahir Shah.[31] This period, known as the New Democracy, saw the adoption of a new Constitution in 1964 and an elected parliament. Whatever promise the New Democracy might have contained was aborted by a 1973 coup against the King led by his cousin, Mohammed Daoud. Daoud could not control the modernizing political forces he had partly fostered and was assassinated five years later in another coup by Afghanistan's communist People's Democratic Party of Afghanistan (PDPA). The PDPA immediately began implementing a radical social and economic agenda. In response, uprisings began in rural Afghanistan. The inability of the PDPA government to contain these revolts prompted the intervention of Soviet troops.[32] That intervention sparked a massive resistance followed by civil war, Taliban rule, and eventually—two-and-a-half decades later—the Bonn Agreement and its promise of another new democracy.

The rapid historical sketch above suggests that democracy in Afghanistan was not as far-fetched a concept as it appeared to many Western analysts. It had been tried before in a limited fashion, and the years of the New Democracy had arguably been the most stable years in modern Afghan history. Furthermore, traditional decision-making in Afghanistan had always been consultative and participatory. Finally, the political economy of Afghanistan, determined in large part by its geography, had not allowed the development of large landholdings and feudal political structures like in the fertile flatlands of the Punjab to the south.[33] The inability to consolidate holdings meant that political power was fragile and fluid. The traditional politics of Afghanistan knew the concept of *altérnance*, even if it didn't come from the ballot box. But the historical perspective of the new experts was distorted by the West's highly refracted perceptions of what Afghanistan had become during the civil war of the 1990s and the Taliban era. Samuel Huntington has referred to the temptation during transitions to "pursue modernity at the expense of politics."[34] But there is enough evidence to suggest that democratization was not inconsistent with Afghanistan's political DNA. The key question was how the project would be implemented.

The international analysts weren't the only ones with blind spots. Many of the participants at Bonn were exiles who had not set foot in their country for decades. Perhaps they had not understood, when the document was signed, how destroyed Afghanistan really was and therefore how ambitious their political roadmap was. The war that had raged in Afghanistan between 1989 and 2001 had been a low-technology affair, fought with machine guns, rocket-propelled grenades, rockets, mortars, and very occasionally, Scud missiles and air-borne bombs.[35] The duration of the conflict, and its persistent intensity, had ensured a sort of patient and meticulous destruction of both rural and urban areas. In the countryside, the plumb-lined, square geometries of Afghanistan's traditional mud houses had been shattered by fighting and then eroded to an almost natural smoothness by weather, as if reclaimed by the loam from which they had been built. Every kilometer of road seemed to have been hit by a rocket or mortar, and the incessant traffic of buses and trucks, even through the worst of the war years, had created worn and winding paths around bomb craters. The capital, Kabul, was three-quarters destroyed by both street-to-street fighting in 1992, when Mujaheddin factions vied for control of the city immediately after Najibullah's fall, and then by a series of rocket duels over the next several years that characterized the period between the fall of Najibullah and the taking of the capital by the Taliban in September 1996.

Afghanistan's destruction was not only physical. Decades of war had decimated the educated class through assassinations, purges and exile. The PDPA, after taking over the country in 1978, immediately attempted to consolidate its authority by jailing and eventually the educated leaders that had previously run the state. Those who managed to escape to the refugee camps in Pakistan did not find refuge there for long. The anti-communist Islamist parties had based themselves in Peshawar and were equally hostile to the educated, urbanized elite. They were often able to prevail upon the Pakistani authorities running the camps to deny them assistance. Those who could, emigrated to the West.[36] The seizing of Kabul by the Taliban caused another exodus of the few remaining educated people.[37] Finally, the Taliban famously denied education to girls and persecuted intellectuals, particularly Dari speakers.[38]

Many of the Afghans who negotiated the Bonn Agreement were therefore either ignorant of the realities in Afghanistan or ignorant of the complexities of organizing an election—or both. While the notion of holding elections was not necessarily politically naïve, the timetable set at Bonn was unrealistic. The pressure to meet the timetable would undermine the effectiveness of the elections as a tool of consensus-building and a means of institutionalizing political rivalries. Those who called for more time in order to build this consensus and these institutions would be accused of obstructing the process; those who favored holding the elections on an unrealistic timetable would look like proponents of democracy.

The United Nations in Afghanistan

Given the immense complexities of organizing an election in an environment like Afghanistan's, it was assumed that the international community, and the United Nations in particular, would have to play a significant role. The Bonn Agreement contained an annexed provision that the United Nations should conduct the registration of voters. It was expected that it would have to play a large role in planning the elections as well. Over the previous decade, beginning with the 1989 referendum in Namibia and particularly in the 1992 elections in post-war Cambodia, the United Nations had gained a considerable amount of experience conducting or supporting postconflict elections.[39]

In addition to this electoral experience, the United Nations had a long involvement in Afghanistan. During the 1980s, Secretary-General Javier Perez de Cuellar's personal representative, the Ecuadoran diplomat Digeo Còrdovez, masterminded an intricate series of talks between the Soviet Union, the United States, and Pakistan that eventually led to the Soviet withdrawal from Afghanistan in 1989. In 1993, the Security Council authorized the establishment of the United Nations Special Mission to Afghanistan (UNSMA), which was based in Islamabad and mandated to mediate a solution to the civil war that had begun in 1992, with the fall of the Najibullah regime. UNSMA was still in place at the time of the signing of the Bonn Agreement. It is further relevant to note that between 1997 and 1999, UNSMA's mediation efforts had been led by Brahimi, who was then the Secretary-General's Special Envoy for Afghanistan.

When Brahimi was appointed as Special Envoy in 1997, the Taliban had just taken control of Kabul, were on the offensive militarily in the rest of the country, and seemed unlikely to negotiate away what they had achieved by arms. The momentum was in their favor. Furthermore, their unappeasable ideology would make any negotiated solution difficult. As Special Envoy, Brahimi was able to log some successes, including several rounds of intra-Afghan talks. But these were essentially theatrical interludes that were probably accepted by the parties to rest or consolidate gains—a demonstration of Ambrose Bierce's definition of peace as "a period of cheating between two periods of fighting."[40]

In July 1999, the Taliban launched a massive ground and air offensive, described as a decisive battle to defeat the Northern Alliance.. The alliance initially lost territory, and then regained it. The action and reaction reactivated fighting on a number of fronts across the country. Among the many casualties was the flickering hope that the rival Afghan factions were at all prepared to negotiate a real peace.[41] Brahimi must have sensed that he had become a superfluous man in Afghanistan. Theoreticians of conflict resolution speak of the "ripeness" for negotiations. In Afghanistan in late 1999, everything was rotten.

In November 1999, the Secretary-General informed the Security Council that, "Following a careful review of recent developments, my Special Envoy and I have reached the conclusion that given the lack of progress achieved so far, his activities should be 'frozen' until such time as circumstances change to justify his renewed intervention."[42] This was an unusual arrangement—to "freeze" but not terminate his mandate—but it was a reflection of Brahimi's realism. William Maley averred that "it was clear that [Brahimi] had not given up working on Afghanistan: rather, he was conserving his considerable personal authority for the moment when the conflict might somehow ripen for a settlement. As things turned out, he did not have long to wait."[43]

Secretary-General Kofi Annan, in the meantime, appointed Francesc Vendrell, a career United Nations diplomat who was then Assistant Secretary-General for Political Affairs, to lead UNSMA.[44] Vendrell, an outspoken (Catalan) Spaniard, had, throughout his career, nurtured an activist vision of the United Nations' capacity to solve international disputes. He had played an instrumental role in involving the organization in peace efforts from Central America to the South Pacific.[45] This talent had won him many admirers, inside and outside the United Nations, but was exercised with a sometimes-abrasive style that had also produced enemies, especially inside the United Nations.

Vendrell had inherited something of a poisoned mandate when he took over UNSMA. If the Secretary-General had withdrawn his favored mediator because the conflict was intractable, what did the Security Council expect Vendrell to achieve? Vendrell realized, as much as

Brahimi had, and for the same reasons, that resolving the Afghan situation looked like a hopeless task. A fairly new complicating factor was that the Taliban attitude toward foreigners was growing increasingly uncooperative and at times belligerent. In August 1998 the Taliban effectively forced international humanitarian organizations to leave Kabul by making the conditions for their staying intolerable. What was therefore probably expected from Vendrell was to hold the fort until the moment "ripened", and then cede way to Brahimi. This was not Vendrell's style. Upon taking over UNSMA, he focused his attention on attempting to begin a dialogue between the two sides. To do this, he used a rather unique tool within UNSMA—a "civil affairs" unit staffed by internationals, mostly recruited from humanitarian NGOs. UNSMA's recently hired civil affairs officers tended to have had a long experience in the country, a knowledge of local languages, and invaluable contacts, especially with the non-Taliban factions.

The civil affairs unit had originally been Brahimi's idea, sparked by the Taliban's expulsion of international aid workers. Realizing that UNSMA had no monitoring capacity of its own, Brahimi had convinced the Afghan factions, including the Taliban, to allow a few United Nations-appointed staff to operate inside the country in designated areas.[46] They were designated as "civil affairs officers" to mitigate suspicions that they were to play any political role. The stated objective of the unit was to "monitor the situation, promote and support respect for minimum humanitarian standards and deter massive and systematic violations of human rights and international humanitarian law."[47] But by their presence they would clearly be able to play a political role.

When Brahimi was withdrawn from UNSMA, recruitment of the new officers was just beginning. While all Afghan sides had agreed to the proposal, there were suspicions both among the Taliban and among the United Nations humanitarian aid workers about their real function.[48] In light of these suspicions, a mission sent from United Nations headquarters to Afghanistan in April and May 1999 stressed the importance of the civil affairs officers being "genuinely culturally sensitive" and aware of their environment.

Inheriting the concept from Brahimi, Vendrell was chiefly responsible for implementing it, especially for selecting the civil affairs officers. Eventually six separate offices were established at different locations within Afghanistan, staffed by a total of 11 civil affairs officers. Their "monitoring" included providing political information to Vendrell as he attempted to cobble together the basis of a peace agreement. In November 2000, the Secretary-General wrote in his report to the Security Council on Afghanistan, "It is only through the building of contacts and greater familiarity with the needs of the people that the United Nations can become more effective in pursuing its peacemaking activities."[49] This was precisely the role that Vendrell had set for his civil affairs officers.

Following the imposition of sanctions against the Taliban by the Security Council in October 1999, through the adoption of resolution 1267(1999), the Taliban insisted that UNSMA's offices inside Afghanistan, except the office in Kabul, be closed. The avenues for seeking any basis of accommodation were effectively barred. If there was any doubt about this, the Taliban erased it by destroying the two Buddhas of Bamyan in March 2001, an unnecessary and gratuitous act that shocked the consciences of even those who had not been paying attention to Afghanistan. (The Taliban professed to be shocked by the vastly negative global reaction, which they argued showed more concern for two stone Buddhas than for the humanitarian plight affecting millions of Afghans.) The destruction of the Buddhas convinced Vendrell that, as he put it in his farewell cable a year later, the Taliban movement was incapable of reform and no meaningful negotiations would be possible unless the military balance shifted against them.

That imbalance came with a more shocking and more violent act six months later—the destruction of the two World Trade Center towers in Manhattan on September 11. Within weeks, U.S. special forces were deployed to Afghanistan alongside Northern Alliance troops. The rapid collapse of the seemingly invincible Taliban from a combination of air power and fast-moving Afghan units accompanied by U.S. special forces was stunning.[50] At that moment, not only was the Taliban dispersed and defeated, but the other Afghan factions were too weak to renew hostilities among each other. The machine of perpetual war, maintained for decades by constant tactical realignments of armed factions being continuously rearmed, was stunningly over.

In a matter of weeks, Afghanistan had gone from hosting an obscure and supposedly unimportant civil war to being the center of global politics. Like most obscure wars, it had previously been relegated to resolution by the United Nations under a weak mandate by the Security Council. As a result, at the time of the collapse of the Taliban the U.N. was the only international (or even national) institution with detailed, current knowledge of contemporary Afghanistan and solid contacts within it. It was therefore accorded the central role in re-establishing political authority.

As predicted, Secretary-General Kofi Annan immediately reactivated Brahimi as his Special Envoy, turning Vendrell into Brahimi's deputy. This was a relationship unlikely to endure. Brahimi and Vendrell were men of immense capabilities and egos, but of totally different styles and possessing vastly different visions of the U.N.'s role in a post-Taliban Afghanistan. Those inside the United Nations who knew them both recognized that one would have to go and it was not likely to be Brahimi. Brahimi, of course, led the negotiations at Bonn, though Vendrell was present. And it was Brahimi who flew into a devastated Kabul with the newly-appointed members of the Interim Authority in mid-December 2001. The inauguration of the new governing authority occurred on schedule in Kabul on December 22. The first benchmark of the Bonn Agreement had been met, less than three weeks after the ink had dried. Attention immediately turned to the next stop on the roadmap—the holding of the Emergency Loya Jirga. The need to begin planning the seemingly distant elections seemed, at that optimistic moment, equally distant from anyone's mind.

---

[1] See James Traub, *The Best Intentions: Kofi Annan and the UN in the era of American World Power* (New York: Farrar, Straus and Giroux, 2006) p. 162.

[2] Ahmed Rashid, *Descent Into Chaos: The United States and the Failure of Nation Building in Pakistan, Afghanistan, and Central Asia* (New York: Viking, 2008) p. 104.

[3] Ahmed Rashid quotes Brahimi as saying, "The Taliban should have been at Bonn. This was our original sin. If we had had time and spoken to some of them and asked them to come, because they still represented something, maybe they would have come to Bonn. Even if none came, at least we would have tried." See Rashid, *Descent Into Chaos*, p. 104. Given the global aversion to the Taliban, and what appeared to be a convincing military defeat, this prospect was hardly even considered at the time.

[4] It is often overlooked that Kandahar, the Taliban capital, did not fall until after the Bonn Agreement had been concluded. Holding on to Kandahar while negotiating a role in the future government would have significantly strengthened their negotiating position, or perhaps have led to a de-facto partition of the country.

[5] Barnett Rubin, "Crafting a Constitution for Afghanistan," Journal of Democracy 15.3 (July 2004) p. 7.

[6] While it seems that almost every analyst now believes that excluding the Taliban from Bonn was a mistake, Thomas Ruttig notes that including them was politically implausible at the time. Including the Taliban was opposed by both Iran and the U.S., and the most powerful Taliban figures were also the ones who had the closest connections to Al Qaeda. See Thomas Ruttig, "The Other Side," Afghanistan Analysts Network Thematic Report (Kabul, July 2009): p. 8, footnote 18. On the question of letting the Taliban re-emerge, James Dobbins makes the same point, describing on the U.S. side a transfer of decision-making power from the CIA and State Department to a Department of Defense that was unconcerned with the necessity of projecting governance and security to the provinces. See James F. Dobbins, *After the Taliban* (Dulles, VA: Potomac Books, 2008) pp. 157-158 and 163-164. See also, for a similar argument, Michael E. O'Hanlon and Hassina Sherjan, *Toughing It Out in Afghanistan*

(Washington, D.C.: Brookings Institution Press, 2010) pp.22-24. Both Dobbins and O'Hanlon-Sherjan mention preparations for the upcoming invasion of Iraq as another factor in the diminishing attention paid to Afghanistan, despite the resurgence of the Taliban that was already perceptible in 2002. Finally, Rashid and Gilles Dorronsoro note the failure of the U.S. to insert ground troops in key areas following the collapse of the movement. See Rashid, *Descent into Chaos*, p. 241, and Gilles Dorronsoro, *Revolution Unending: Afghanistan, 1979 to the Present* (New York: Columbia University Press, 2005) pp. 325- 326.

[7] See Dobbins, *After the Taliban*, pp. 67-76. See also Ahmed Rashid, *Descent Into Chaos*, pp. 102-105. While in theory, Brahimi was the only international figure allowed inside the negotiation room, Rashid reported that, "several Western intelligence agencies had reportedly wired the hotel so they could listen in on the rooms. Serious conversations took place in the corridors." Rashid, *Descent into Chaos,* p. 103.

[8] Specifically, the Northern Alliance was made up by factions led by Burhannuddin Rabbani and Ahmad Shah Massoud (bothTajik), Muhammad Karim Khalili (a Shi'a Hazara), Asif Mohseni (a Shi'a Hazara whose followers also include some Qizilbash), Abdul Rab al-Rasoul Sayyaf (leader of the Ittehad-e-Islami small party, heavily supported by Saudi Arabia; while Sayyaf was Pashtun his Ittehad party remained attached to the Jamiat throughout the civil war), and finally Abdul Rashid Dostum's Uzbek militia. See William Maley, *The Afghanistan Wars* (New York: Palgrave Macmillan, 2002) p. 229.

[9] In fact, early in its existence, the Taliban was seen as both a Pashtun nationalist movement and an Islamic fundamentalist movement. The former explained the adherence of former communist Pashtuns such as General Tanai. The alliance with al-Qaeda in 1996 probably forced it into a much more Islamist direction.

[10] According to Thomas Ruttig, five moderate parties had been invited to Bonn but "the change at the head of the U.N. mission in late 2001 [from Francesc Vendrell to Brahimi] prevented these groups from fully participating as a joint fifth official delegation in Bonn at the last moment; they were instead reduced to an observer status." Thomas Ruttig, "Islamists, Leftists—and a Void in the Center: Afghanistan's Political Parties and where they come from (1902-2006)," Konrad Adenauer Stiftung, [undated] pp. 16 and 17.

[11] These were Pakistan, Saudi Arabia, and the United Arab Emirates.

[12] Maley, *Afghanistan Wars*, p. 269.

[13] Dobbins, *After the Taliban*, p. 81.

[14] Ahmed Rashid provides a detailed account of Karzai's actions in the days after 9/11, which contributed to the viability of his selection at Bonn. See Rashid, *Descent Into Chaos*, pp. 3-23.

[15] Dobbins, *After the Taliban*, p. 89.

[16] J. Alexander Thier, "The Politics of Peacebuilding" in *Nation-building Unraveled? Aid, Peace and Justice in Afghanistan*, eds. Antonio Donini, Norah Niland, Karin Wermester (Bloomefield, CT: Kumarian Press, 2004) p. 47.

[17] For a succinct and authoritative statement, see Giovanni Sartori: "If we manage to control power, this is largely because democracy works, in practice, as a device for slowing down, filtering, and decanting the processes of power."

The Theory of Democracy Revisited (Chatham, NJ: Chatham House Publishers, 1987) p. 430.

[18] Dobbins, *After the Taliban*, p. 96.

[19] Bonn Agreement, Article I.4.

[20] Ashraf Ghani and Clare Lockhart make a similar point. After describing the phases of the Bonn Agreement, they conclude: "At each stage teh agreement provided citizens with means by which to assess, participate in, and monitor progress." See Ashraf Ghani and Clare Lockhart, *Fixing Failed States: A Framework for Rebuilding a Fractured World* (Oxford: Oxford University Press, 2008) p. 182.

[21] See William Maley and Fazel Haq Saikal, *Political Order in Post-Communist Afghanistan* (Boulder, CO: Lynne Rienner, 1992) pp. 23-24.

[22] See Maley, *The Afghanistan Wars*, pp. 197-199.

[23] Among the many misconceptions about Afghanistan is that the Taliban emerged immediately after the withdrawal of the Soviet Union and the "abandonment" of Afghanistan by the United States. In fact, the sequence of events was as follows: The Soviet Union withdrew its forces in 1989. The Afghan Communist government that they had backed, led then by President Najibullah, remained in power until 1992, when the Mujaheddin forces took Kabul. A civil war broke out almost immediately afterwards between the main Mujaheddin factions who had agreed on an interim government. This fight centered on the capital city of Kabul, which was largely destroyed between 1992 and 1994, and which had been relatively untouched during the resistance to the Soviet occupation. In mid-1994, the United States ceased its cross-border assistance activities (though it continued funding some humanitarian relief operations). In late 1994, the Taliban emerged in Kandahar and gradually fought their way east, finally taking Kabul in September 1996. Maley, *Afghanistan Wars*, is an excellent reference, as is, Dorronsoro, *Revolution Unending*.

[24] Thomas O. Melia, "Afghan Perspectives on Democracy: A Report on Focus Groups in the Kabul Area on the Eve of the Emergency Loya Jirga," prepared for the National Democratic Institute for International Affairs, Washington, D.C., May 28, 2002, p. 2.

[25] In Dobbins' account, it was the head of the Iranian delegation who noted that elections were absent from an early draft of the Agreement, and suggested that they be included. See Dobbins, *After the Taliban*, p. 83.

[26] A subset, or perhaps a supra-set, of this debate is the question of the compatibility of Islam and democracy. Those disposed to the spread of democracy in Islamic countries are able to find appropriate references in the Koran and in Islamic customs. As I have done, many focus on the institution of the "shura"—mutual consultation—as a "means by which modern representative democracy can evolve out of traditional Islamic thought and practice." Timothy D. Sisk, *Islam and Democracy: Religion, Politics and Power in the Middle East* (Washington, D.C.: United States Institute of Peace Press, 1992), p. 20. See, also, John L. Esposito and John O. Voll, *Islam and Democracy* (Oxford: Oxford University Press, 1996). It is a pity that the contributions of Islamic scholars on this question are not more recognized. An interesting and detailed exegisis of Islamic doctrine sustaining the notions of

pluralism necessary for participatory democracy can be found in Abdulaziz Sachedina, *The Islamic Roots of Democratic Pluralism* (Oxford: Oxford University Press, 2001). A particularly vibrant discussion of the issue is contained in Fatema Mernissi, *Islam and Democracy: Fear of the Modern World*, trans. Mary Jo Lakeland (Cambridge, MA: Perseus Publishing, 2002). What is interesting about Mernissi's thesis is that she posits a nefarious association between political "reformists" of a nationalist bent who sought to consolidate their own political power, and Islamic traditionalists who accepted the association of Islamic legitimacy with nationalist constitutions to bolster their own political influence—in other words, an unholy alliance of democratic forms with Islamic traditions that led to the legitimacy of autocrats rather than true democracy. A defender of the tradition of Islamic rationalism, Mernissi asserts that nationalist movements in Islamic countries "introduced institutions and concepts of Western representative democracy, like 'constitution,' 'parliament,' and 'universal suffrage,' while yet failing to educate the masses about the essential point: the sovereignty of the individual and freedom of opinion that are the philosophical bases of these institutions and concepts. [...] Very quickly many reformers tried to link the concept of a constitution to the *shari'a*, that is, to law of divine origin. The politicians, on the lookout for arguments to extend their authoritiarianism, jumped at this opportunity to confuse the issue." p. 48.

[27] Josiah Harlan was an American who traveled to Afghanistan in the nineteenth century and ended up as an advisor to Dost Mohammad, one of the more effective Afghan kings. His remarkable tale is told in Ben Macintyre's *The Man Who Would Be King: The First American in Afghanistan* (New York: Farrar Straus Giroux, 2004). The fact that his insights—on Afghan politics as well as on the politics of Western intervention—remain more trenchant than the insights one might find on today's editorial pages is a tribute both to his clear-sightedness as well as to the endurance of Afghan political structures throughout the centuries.

[28] "To administer is to govern, to govern is to reign; everything is reduced to that." [My translation.] Ashraf Ghani, for example, writes that "the political history of the period under consideration [1747-1982] does not reveal a steady tendency towards administrative centralization or its opposite." Ashraf Ghani, "Afghanistan xi.Administration," *Encyclopedia Iranica*, Vol. I, 1985.

[29] These terms are of course taken from Peter Evans, *Embedded Autonomy: States and Industrial Transformation* (Princeton: Princeton University Press, 1995).

[30] Ahmed Rashid makes this point in, "In Afghanistan, Let's Keep it Simple" *Washington Post*, 6 September 2009.

[31] King Zahir Shah lived to see the signing of the Bonn Agreement. In the Constitution adopted in January 2004, he was given the honorary title of "Father of the Nation," though his descendents were deprived by that Constitution of any formal political role.

[32] Another common misconception about Afghan history is that popular resistance began as a reaction to the Soviet invasion. In fact, it preceded the invasion and was a reaction to the coup of the Communist government before

the Soviets intervened to defend it. See, for example, Louis Dupree, "The Democratic Republic of Afghanistan, 1979" (American Universities Field Staff Reports: Hanover, NH, 1979). Dupree's report, published three months before the Soviet invasion, speculated on the possibility of the Soviet Union sending forces to back the Afghan communist régime. He concluded that it would not happen, and quotes a Soviet diplomat as saying, "if there is one country in the developing world we would like not to try scientific socialism, it is Afghanistan." p. 7. Photos of resisters in to the PDPA regime in Kunar province in March 1979 can be seen in *Pascal Pugin, Reporters: Le Voyage Afghanistan, Regards Mosaïques* (Paris: Syros Alternatives, 1992), pp. 14-15.

[33] See Barnett R. Rubin, "Redistribution and the State in Afghanistan: The Red Revolution Turns Green" in *The Politics of Social Transformation in Afghanistan, Iran and Pakistan*, eds. Myron Weiner and Ali Banuazizi (Syracuse, NY: Syracuse University Press, 1994) p. 196.

[34] Samuel P. Huntington, *Political Order in Changing Societies* (New Haven: Yale University Press, 1968) p. 92.

[35] A number of books have been written about the tactics of the Afghan resistance. Four that were relied on in this writing are Ludwig Adamec, *Dictionary of Afghan Wars, Revolutions, and Insurgencies* (Landham, MD: Scarecrow Press, 1996), Maley, *Afghanistan Wars*; Stephen Tanner, *Afghanistan: A Military History from Alexander the Great to the Fall of the Taliban* (New York: Da Capo Press, 2002); and Mohammad Yousaf and Mark Adkin, *Afghanistan: The Bear Trap* (Havertown, PA: Casemate, 1992).

[36] An excellent account of the disappearance and marginalization of educated Afghans is in Grant M. Farr, "The new Afghan Middle Class as Refugees and Insurgents," in Afghan Resistance: *The Politics of Survival,* eds. Grant M. Farr and John G. Merriam (Colorado: Westview Press, 1987) pp. 127-150

[37] John Burns, "Afghan Professionals Fleeing Rule by Clerics" New York Times, 7 October 1996.

[38] Chantal Veron, "Nous Sommes Commes Morts" Les Nouvelles d'Afghanistan, Paris, No. 76, 1st trimester 1997, p. 8.

[39] See for example, Newman and Rich, *The UN Role in Promoting Democracy.*

[40] Ambrose Bierce, *The Devil's Dictionary* (New York: Dover Publications, Inc., 1958) p. 98.

[41] For a concise account in English of this period, see Maley, *Afghanistan Wars*, pp. 245-248.

[42] A/54/536-S/1999/1145, para. 4.

[43] Maley, *Afghanistan Wars*, p. 148.

[44] Brahimi had been a Special Envoy, but had not formally been the Head of UNSMA. During most of his tenure, UNSMA had been run by an "acting head," Andrew Tesoriere, a British diplomat. Vendrell, appointed on 1 February 2000, inherited the title of Personal Representative of the Secretary-General and Head of UNSMA, rather than the Special Envoy title, which Brahimi retained even though his activities on Afghanistan were "frozen."

[45] Vendrell had been a key player in the Central American peace processes of the late 1980s. In addition he had overseen the negotiations leading to the 1999 East Timor popular consultation and the set-up of the operation. He had also pushed for the United Nations to play a mediating role in resolving the conflict between Bougainville and Papua New Guinea in the early 2000s.

[46] See also Mark Duffield, Patricia Gossman, and Nicholas Leader, "Review of the Strategic Framework for Afghanistan" Afghanistan Research and Evaluation Unit, Kabul, 2001, p. 18. The authors of this study located the origins of the Civil Affairs Unit in "Brahimi's frustration with the inability of the UNHCHR [United Nations High Commissioner for Human Rights] to conduct credible investigations into the violation of human rights in Afghanistan."

[47]A/55/633-S/2000/1106, para. 19. This is the Secretary-General's summary of the unit's mandate. The Security Council, in resolution 1214(1998), further specified the tasks of the unit as follows: "to establish within UNSMA, without prejudice to its mandate and taking into account security conditions, a civil affairs unit with the primary objective of monitoring the situation, promoting respect for minimum humanitarian standards and deterring massive and systematic violations of human rights and humanitarian law in the future, and to send an assessment mission to Afghanistan, as soon as security conditions permit, in order to determine the exact mandate, composition and location of the civilian monitors" (operative paragraph 7).

[48] UNSMA's political activities took place at the same time and in the same space as humanitarian operations run by the United Nations Office for the Coordination of Humanitarian Assistance (UNOCHA). There was a basic conflict between these two mandates. On the one hand, UNSMA was attempting to negotiate a formal peace between the leaders of the major factions of the conflict. On the other hand, the humanitarian community was "building peace from below"—trying to use humanitarian assistance in a "principled" way to promote peace. These contrasting approaches undermined each other to the great frustration of both. See Duffield, Gossman, and Leader, "Review of the Strategic Framework for Afghanistan," for an excellent, in-depth review of this incoherence.

[49] A/55/633-S/2000/1106, para. 19

[50] Ahmed Rashid provides a concise description of the campaign, see *Descent Into Chaos*, pp. 61-83. The architect of the campaign, General Tommy Franks, described his strategy rather colorfully as follows: "The operation represented a revolution in warfighting. We would introduce the most advanced military technology in the world—TLAMs, JDAMs, Stealth bombers, laser target designators, and satellite communications—onto one of the world's most primitive battlefields. The Northern Alliance, with its tribal affiliates, a few broken-down Russian tanks and rickety transport helicopters, and thousands of horses, would move heavy weapons and munitions on the backs of donkeys and camels in a synchronized ballet, taking advantage of all that firepower and techno-sophistication. The Taliban and al Qaeda forces had twice as many troops as the Northern Alliance, and they were far better equipped. But I was confident that the balance of power was about to change." Tommy Franks,

American Soldier (New York: Regan Books, 2004) p. 262. See also Dorronsoro, *Revolution Unending,* pp. 315-328. Dorronsoro makes the interesting point that, "The war in Afghanistan, the first conflict of its kind, was exceptional because of the confrontation between three protagonists of different kinds. These were a state (the United States), a quasi-state unrecognized internationally (the Taliban), and a transnational movement (Al-Qa'ida)." (p. 320)

3
Signposts of Democracy: The Emergency Loya Jirga

As the Afghan Interim Authority moved into their broken government offices in Kabul in late 2001, Brahimi began to shape the future United Nations' presence in Afghanistan. His guiding principle was what he described as a "light footprint." He felt strongly that Afghans would never accept a United Nations transitional administration, such as the one that had administered Cambodia in the early 1990s or that was, at that time, governing East Timor. Vendrell felt equally strongly that Brahimi was wrong. He had submitted draft proposals that were inspired by the Paris Agreement that had ended the Cambodian conflict. Among them were to grant the Special Representative the power to "act as an umpire in case of disagreements within the cabinet, to override a decision taken by the Interim/Transitional Authority or even impose one to ensure compliance with the letter and spirit of the Bonn Agreement."[1] Vendrell's advice at Bonn was ignored. A few months later, Vendrell was informed that Brahimi would be named as the Special Representative of the Secretary-General (SRSG), the normal designation for the head of a U.N. peacekeeping mission, and would oversee the organization's new mission in Afghanistan. While still in Islamabad as the head of UNSMA, he was asked to tender his resignation. (Shortly thereafter, Vendrell was appointed as the European Union Special Representative for Afghanistan, a post which he held until 2008.)

The U.N. leadership in Afghanistan was now clarified beyond any doubt. Brahimi immediately began setting up the new United Nations headquarters in Kabul in the cramped and oddly shaped rooms of the former Goethe Institute, located in the center of the city. The first task was to attend to the myriad details of what the new mission would look like. An Integrated Mission Task Force at United Nations Headquarters in New York ensured that all of the usual bureaucratic stakeholders within the U.N. system were involved. Some of these had to be accommodated, but overall, Brahimi had a fairly free hand in designing the mission structure as he saw fit. This was in many ways a unique moment for the world organization: it was playing an indispensable—and generally independent—role on an issue that was central to the interests of its most powerful members. The blink of a geopolitical eye in which Afghanistan was transformed from a sleeper conflict to the highest item on the international agenda assured the U.N. a role in a manner that had never occurred before. Brahimi's recommendations were presented in the form of a report by the Secretary-General.[2] The report was endorsed and the United Nations Assistance Mission in Afghanistan (UNAMA) was created by Security Council resolution 1401 on March 28, 2002. UNAMA supplanted both UNSMA and the UNOCHA humanitarian assistance program, which was to be subsumed under the new "integrated mission."[3]

Brahimi and his political team, made up mostly of UNSMA's civil affairs officers, meanwhile began the work of preparing the Emergency Loya Jirga, scheduled to take place in June of 2002. At that time, Brahimi did not yet have a political deputy, but his political affairs department was headed by Anders Fange, a level-headed Swede who had spent two decades in Afghanistan, first as a journalist and then as the head of an NGO. Fange spoke Dari and knew the country and its main protagonists thoroughly. He began to lay the groundwork for the first test of the Bonn Agreement.

Loya Jirgas

Much about the Emergency Loya Jirga had to be invented from scratch. The Loya Jirga was a traditional mechanism for consensus and decision-making on a national scale in Afghanistan. It had been somewhat institutionalized during Afghanistan's modernizing period to ratify important decisions, including constitutions. But it was still more tradition than institution, and therefore lacked formal rules on composition and procedure.[4] As Leon Poullada describes, jirgas are "quasi-judicial and quasi-parliamentary in function."[5] They were generally convened to deal with specific issues (as opposed to *shuras*, or councils, which last longer and generally deal with multiple issues).[6] The key criteria of a jirga is that its members are selected according to the consent of the disputing parties and that it is empowered to implement its decisions. This empowerment generally comes from the requirement that each side provide a financial guarantee (*mechelgha*); should one side refuse to accept the jirga's decision, the guarantee is forfeited.

The local jirga thus provides the basic framework for the Loya Jirga—or grand council. Loya Jirgas are exceptional events that bring together all tribes of Afghanistan to decide on issues of national importance. Unlike the local jirgas, the Loya Jirgas tended to decide matters of policy, rather than to arbitrate disputes. It was a Loya Jirga held in 1747, at which the Pashtun tribes selected Ahmad Shah Abdali, recognized as the first modern ruler of Afghanistan.[7] Loya Jirgas were also convened in 1915, to ratify King Habibullah's decision to remain neutral in the First World War; in 1919, to declare independence from Britain after the Third Anglo-Afghan War;[8] in 1941, to ratify the country's neutrality in the Second World War; and in 1964 to approve the new Constitution that was the foundation for Zahir Shah's New Democracy period. The Loya Jirga of 1747 was in some ways the first expression of Afghan national unity—though that expression was of course formulated in the idiom of tribal politics rather than Weberian notions of statehood. All subsequent Loya Jirgas have exhibited the same characteristic.[9]

If local jirgas presented the basic model for Loya Jirgas, the latter were fundamentally different in one important aspect. As Vartan Gregorian has written, "with its democratic spirit and tenets, the jirga defied political centralization, and its constant accommodation of regional interests made it a particularly divisive force in the drive to form a modern and unified state."[10] The role of the Emergency Loya Jirga in 2002 was, according to the Bonn Agreement, to unify the state by accommodating "regional interests" in a "democratic spirit." As with much of the rest of the Bonn Agreement, it was in some sense called upon to defy recent history.

Organizing the Emergency Loya Jirga

UNAMA's initial working conditions were initially extremely uncomfortable. The Kabul-based team worked out of small spaces demarcated by thin screens amid the Goethe Institute's creaking staircases and uneven floors. Tensions were high due to the physical proximity of stressed political officers, Bonn's tight deadlines, and Brahimi's exacting management style. Eight regional offices were quickly established around the country in a mammoth and rapid logistical effort.[11] These offices would soon bear the brunt of the action, as selection of delegations to the Emergency Loya Jirga began to take place. Vendrell's civil affairs officers would become indispensable in traveling throughout the regions to explain to local leaders how the process was supposed to work, answering questions and criticisms, and goading their Afghan contacts to participate in a cooperative spirit in the vital attempt to found a new political order.

In Kabul, Brahimi's first efforts were focused on helping Karzai put together a 21-member Emergency Loya Jirga Commission. There is an art to creating commissions in Afghanistan, and Brahimi was a master of it. His experience in Lebanon, where some 20 major confessional groups needed to be satisfied with appropriate representation through an expert command of sectarian mathematics, was undoubtedly useful. In Afghanistan, the five major ethnic groups in particular had to be accommodated. It was equally important, and politically necessary especially for the international community, for several women to be included in the commission. The effectiveness of any post-Bonn commission also depended on the inclusion of political moderates, though this had to be balanced with jihadi[12] party members, who felt strongly that they had borne the brunt of Afghan's long national tragedy, and had a perhaps exaggerated sense of their role in the defeat of the Taliban. Finally, each commission also needed some people of a certain level of education and competence, and these were frequently those who had fled during the war years and hence had little legitimacy in the eyes of the jihadi members.

Democratic Features of the Emergency Loya Jirga

The Emergency Loya Jirga Commission, once formed, had to first decide how the members of the Jirga would be selected. Brahimi's advice had a great deal of weight at this early stage of the process. UNAMA's Afghan experts made the case to Brahimi that the Jirga needed to be demonstrably representative, and therefore some form of election was required for at least a portion of the delegates. Brahimi accepted this argument, as did the Commission, which proposed that approximately two-thirds of the delegates be chosen by indirect election.[13] The remaining third would be selected by the Commission itself in consultation with civil society groups, nomads, refugees and other defined constituencies.

The Commission's discretion in making appointments would ensure that the main power-holders participated—implicitly anticipating that not all those who held de facto power would actually be elected. This accommodation was criticized from the start, especially by Western human rights groups. Brahimi defended the decision on the logic that peace could not be secured without the participation of those who had the means to restart a war. Brahimi, the negotiator, understood how fragile the peace he had crafted was. He understood enough about the country, its history, and its leaders to sense that the deep-seated animosities accumulated during two-and-a-half decades of war would constantly threaten that fragile peace.

The Commission published its composition procedures in early April 2002, revealing a two-stage "election" process. Representatives of communities within a single administrative district would select in their own manner a college of electors for the district. This college would number between 20 and 60 members depending on the size of the district. There were no set rules for how the selection would be made, though it was assumed that local consultative mechanisms would be used. The college would then travel to one of UNAMA's eight regional centers where they would, by secret ballot, choose between two and seven members—again, predetermined according to population[14]—from amongst themselves to go to Kabul to represent the district in the Emergency Loya Jirga.

The organization of the Emergency Loya Jirga would, in addition, demand an immense amount of logistical planning and support, most of which had to be provided by the United Nations. The Interim Authority simply did not have the capacity, or even perhaps the credibility, to manage such a complex and expensive operation particularly given the broken nature of Afghanistan's infrastructure and the tentative legitimacy of its new governing institutions.

Unfortunately, the United Nations bureaucratic machinery was not geared to work as quickly as the Bonn timeline demanded. Despite decades of peacekeeping, U.N. hiring and procurement procedures were still slow and cumbersome by design—in order to reduce corruption—as well as error-prone and lackadaisical in implementation. It took all of Brahimi's considerable prestige within the United Nations system to get what he needed when he needed it. Even so, the system failed him on crucial occasions. There was, for example, an urgent need for helicopters to transport both United Nations staff to remote regions and to bring the delegates to the eight regional centers. The World Food Programme (WFP) was able to provide eight helicopters almost immediately, certainly much faster than the Department of Peacekeeping Operations (DPKO) would have been able to.[15] The helicopters that were delivered, however, had internal fuel tanks. Ever since a helicopter crash in Bosnia in the 1990s killed all of its passengers when the internal fuel tanks exploded, DPKO staff members were prohibited from flying in aircraft with internal tanks. These rules did not apply to WFP, however. Since UNAMA staff members were on DPKO contracts, they were, in effect, prohibited from flying in the WFP helicopters that had been provided. Weeks away from the Emergency Loya Jirga, Brahimi therefore had eight helicopters that bizarrely he could not use to transport his staff. In a tense meeting with his senior managers, a livid Brahimi ordered that UNAMA staff should travel on the helicopters regardless of the regulations.[16]

The indirect election for representatives of a district in the isolated province of Nuristan[17] provided an interesting forewarning of the difficulties of grafting a modern democratic process onto Afghanistan's traditional political culture, as well as the thrill of the attempt.

Nuristan's indirect election took place in Jalalabad, UNAMA's regional center for the eastern region. The representatives selected by the district *shuras* trooped down from the mountains and arrived at the somewhat-refurbished Polytechnic in Jalalabad. It was amazing enough that the message concerning the rules had gotten out to the far corners of the country and that the delegations had complied with them. At the Polytechnic, each district had been assigned a classroom to hold their secret ballot election for the two representatives who would go to Kabul. Suddenly, there was turmoil in the classroom assigned to one of the Nuristani districts. The Emergency Loya Jirga Commission staff rushed to ascertain the cause. It turned out that the Nuristanis were baffled by the single ballot box. They explained that there should be two ballot boxes, one for each of the two candidates that they would elect. They explained that on their march down from the mountain they had already decided among themselves the two representatives they would send to Kabul. They were expecting an electoral system where there would be a box with each candidate's name, and they would insert slips of paper into one or the other.[18] In other words, they had expected a system that would ritualistically ratify the decision made by negotiation and consensus during the several-day trek to Jalalabad.

The one-box, secret ballot option that the officials tried in vain to explain baffled them. Not the least of the problems was that not everyone in the delegation could write (although the Emergency Loya Jirga Commission's rules had specified that all delegates should be literate). They were thus confronted with the theoretical possibility that the secret ballot, one-man-one-vote system, could violate the consensus they had achieved among themselves. This was actually a problem identified by Louis Dupree in his discussion of the 1965 parliamentary elections: "One objection to the secret ballot is culturally oriented. In the *jirgah* [sic] system all voting is open, and participants raise their hands (or rifles) to vote on issues; but under the secret ballot, as many expressed it, 'a man can talk one way in public and vote another in private."[19] After much discussion and explanation, the Nuristanis agreed to hold the vote according to the Commission's procedures. The result was astounding—the two candidates who had been previously selected by communal consensus won the election, each receiving thirty votes. There had hardly been time in the chaos to collude amongst themselves who would vote for whom, so the voting probably broke down along clan lines, with each clan knowing for whom they were to vote. All over Afghanistan this procedure, and perhaps variations on this strange reaction to it, took place. In this way, the 1,051 semi-elected delegates were chosen and then were transported to Kabul for the main event.

Another foreshadowing of the election process was the insecurity around the event. The Emergency Loya Jirga selection process took place in an environment that was far from calm. Clashes were ongoing in the Hazara-dominated Central Highlands as well as in the Pashtun south and south-east. The Pashtuns, in particular, were said to feel "alienated" by the interim government set up in Bonn, which they considered included too few Pashtuns.[20] While some, naturally, sought to increase their influence in Kabul through the Emergency Loya Jirga, others objected to the process itself and actively undermined it.

Lessons for the Future

The Emergency Loya Jirga was held in the Kabul Polytechnic, on the north-eastern outskirts of the city, near where the old front lines used to divide the Massoud-led Northern-Alliance from the Hazara Hezb-i-Wahdat during the battles for Kabul in the mid-1990s. The International Security Assistance Force (ISAF)[21] and the U.S.-led Coalition[22] troops provided perimeter security. Guns were prohibited from the Polytechnic itself—another "modern" decision that did not sit well with some participants. But everyone understood that a successful attack against the Jirga would perhaps fatally cripple the new government's legitimacy. For the most part, the tight security measures were respected.

The event opened on schedule, on June 10, to the relief of all and probably to the surprise of many. The process of selecting delegates and preparing the event had been hurried and exhausting, and at every moment fraught with the possibility that something could go wrong. But on June 10 the "tent" was erected and air-conditioned, the delegates were present from all parts of the country, and a tremendous sense of optimism prevailed. The second benchmark of the Bonn process had been met.

The logistical element had gone as well as could be expected. The real test of the Emergency Loya Jirga was political. This was Afghanistan's first representative and deliberative gathering in decades, and the controversies that arose within it would provide early notice of the kinds of issues that would harden and divide the Afghan political community during the drafting of the constitution, and that would drive much of the posturing and alliance-making prior to the presidential election scheduled to be held two years later.

The first issue was the inclusion in the Emergency Loya Jirga of so-called "warlords", in particular those who had gained and exercised power during the resistance and the civil war, in the jirga tent and in the government that emerged from it. Brahimi disliked the term and insisted that the U.N., in its reports, use the term "factional leaders" or some other euphemism. Brahimi's sensitivity on this stemmed from the pejorative connotations of the term that, he believed, contributed to an overly simplistic analysis of Afghan political dynamics. Giustozzi, in his far-from-superficial analysis, described "warlords" as "military leaders who emerge to play a de facto political role, despite their lack of full legitimacy."[23] Brahimi recognized that, as the de facto power holders, the so-called warlords could not be immediately sidelined without putting the entire peace process at risk. The strategy that he devised was to tender the offer of political legitimacy in exchange for concessions to the Kabul government and demilitarization, or threaten political marginalization if they refused.[24] This would be a long and complex process whose precise calibrations would demand a great deal of diplomatic skill. Its success was by no means assured, especially since other major players, such as the U.S. military, were simultaneously creating new "warlords" by arming or re-arming factions that claimed to be able to help them fight terrorists. Brahimi's approach recognized that the "warlords" not only possessed real power, but in some cases commanded allegiances in their communities that stemmed from deeper sources of solidarity, and even legitimacy, than pure coercion.

The warlords were, as Giustozzi noted, adept at playing a political role as well as a military one. In their own view, their legitimacy was rooted in the fact that they had remained in Afghanistan and fought the Soviets, defending Afghanistan's independence, while many others had fled. This perception was strong enough in the immediate aftermath of the Taliban that a paragraph had been inserted in the preamble to the Bonn Agreement, expressing "appreciation to the Afghan Mujaheddin who, over the years, have defended the independence, territorial integrity and national unity of the country and have played a major role in the struggle against terrorism and oppression, and whose sacrifice has now made them both heroes of jihad and champions of peace, stability and reconstruction of their beloved homeland, Afghanistan."[25]

Brahimi's strategy was condemned by the international human rights community and parts of the Afghan Diaspora. The judgment of the International Crisis Group (ICG) on the Emergency Loya Jirga, for example, was curt and cutting: "Having gathered Afghans from great distances, some of whom took considerable risks in standing for election, key Afghan and international decision-makers failed to harness their potential. For Afghanistan to move beyond the Kalashnikov culture, its warlords must begin to perceive, and respect, the power of popular representation. They will not have from this exercise."[26]

In his own report to headquarters on the event, Brahimi did not hide his frustration with this point of view, sarcastically noting that some, among the Afghan Diaspora in Europe and the United States, believed that the process in post-war Afghanistan would be more democratic than in the countries where they had sought refuge, and that the "warlords" would vanish into thin air.

In the two-and-a-half years between the Emergency Loya Jirga and the presidential election, the legitimization-marginalization strategy against the warlords would be put into effect with varying degrees of success[27]—and a reasonable judge could conclude that it had been put to effect with *more* success than could have been expected. But these powerful figures would never entirely disappear nor entirely give up the extra-legal power that they held, especially when they were able to combine it, through elections or appointments, with legitimate authority. And even when some warlords would appear to convincingly embrace the political game and abandon their military power, there would remain the complaints that the blood already on their hands should have perpetually barred them from any role in Afghan political life.

There was much blood on many hands in Afghanistan. There had been slaughters and counter-slaughters throughout the decades of resistance and civil war. The cycle of atrocity and vendetta went far deeper even than the post-9/11 champions of human rights in Afghanistan realized. Such abuses were tragically, but indelibly, stained into the fabric of Afghan life at every level. Even among the members of the Interim Authority, there were unresolved feuds that might otherwise demand vengeance, but that were being overlooked or suppressed for the sake of this chance at peace. The new Afghanistan could not be founded on an immediate accounting of past transgressions.[28] The fragility of the ruling coalition and the ongoing capacity within it for armed violence simply did not allow too much public truth too early. The new Afghanistan, instead, had to be built by momentarily ignoring these transgressions, by making 15 million separate peaces with them, and by re-founding political life on a series of rules that channeled political conflict into non-violent forms.[29] This would be as true for the elections as it was for the Emergency Loya Jirga.

The second theme that emerged during the Emergency Loya Jirga, and that would recur during the preparations for the elections, was what William Maley refers to as a "Pashtun-Panshiri schism."[30] The "Panshiris" referred to the followers of Ahmad Shah Massoud, who came from the Panshir valley, which he successfully defended from the Soviets and the Taliban until he was killed by al Qaeda suicide bombers on September 9, 2001. The Panshiris were ethnically Tajik, Afghanistan's second largest ethnic group, but had gained an inordinate amount of power in the Interim Authority due to the specific circumstances of the post-Taliban era.

The circumstances that led to this unusual dominance were the result of a combination of events and decisions just before the Bonn Agreement that were then sealed into Afghan politics as a result of that agreement. According to Steve Coll, only days before Massoud's death, the George W. Bush administration had authorized the CIA to covertly assist Massoud in his resistance to the Taliban. This decision altered a policy of neglect of Afghanistan that had been in place since 1994, when the Clinton administration, frustrated with the ongoing Afghan civil war, decided to virtually cease cross-border assistance to Afghanistan. At the time of Bush's decision, Massoud and his forces were basically limited to defending a sliver of territory in northeast Afghanistan from an increasingly confident Taliban. Most analysts thought that a Taliban victory was a matter of time, with only Massoud's tactical and organizational genius holding together the Northern Alliance-led coalition that stood between the status quo and total Taliban victory. Upon hearing of Massoud's death on September 9, U.S. analysts reportedly concluded that the anti-Taliban alliance was now neither politically nor militarily viable.[31] Two days later, of course, lower Manhattan was a smoking ruin and the situation in Northeast Afghanistan had radically changed. U.S. support became overt rather than covert, and intensive rather than probing.

When the Taliban were routed with the help of U.S. special forces, the Northern Alliance seized their unique political opportunity. Mohammed Fahim, Massoud's successor, led the Panshiri-dominated Northern Alliance into Kabul, despite a specific and public request from the President Bush not to advance beyond the Shamali Valley, several dozen miles east of Kabul. Claiming credit for the defeat of the Taliban, the Panshiris converted their military hold over Kabul into a political advantage at the negotiating table in Bonn. In the interim administration that emerged from Bonn, the three most important ministries—defense, interior, and foreign affairs—were given to Panshiris.[32]

One of the unstated goals of the Emergency Loya Jirga was therefore to reduce the Panshiri predominance in the interim administration and increase Pashtun representation. As the International Crisis Group stated: "The key expectation for the Loya Jirga on the part of most Afghans and the international community is that it will correct the ethnic imbalance produced at the Bonn conference that has created an Interim Authority dominated by ethnic Tajik members of the Northern Alliance."[33] The Panshiri triumvirate was broken when Yunis Qanuni, under severe pressure from Karzai, reluctantly agreed during the Emergency Loya Jirga to give up the Ministry of Interior for the Ministry of Education. The negotiations behind this abdication were messy and clumsily conducted by Karzai. They left Qanuni, one of the most astute of the Mujaheddin leaders, feeling betrayed by both Karzai and fellow-Panshiri Fahim, who had managed to hold onto the powerful defense ministry.

Replacing Qanuni at the Interior Ministry with a Pashtun was not enough to satisfy expectations, however, and in the end Karzai finessed or fudged the question of Pashtun participation by increasing the size of his cabinet to over 30 ministries, as well as creating two vice presidents, several national advisor positions, and a number of national commissions. These additional posts provided sinecures to accommodate additional Pashtuns. Brahimi reported to New York that even as Karzai entered the tent to announce parts of his cabinet at the final session, he was cornered by various leaders and, apparently, making last-minute changes to his list.

The cabinet that emerged was not much different from the one that had been formed at Bonn. The Pashtuns were still unsatisfied with the result (though their expectations had probably always been unrealistically high). Their display of dissatisfaction gave them cover to maintain a reserved position towards the Bonn process in general, from which they could later attempt to exchange additional participation in government for future concessions. In this sense, rather than quelling the question of ethnicity, the Emergency Loya Jirga accentuated it while also deepening specific political rivalries, such as that between Karzai and Qanuni.

The third theme that emerged was the leadership of Karzai himself. Most observers considered that he had mishandled his role at the Emergency Loya Jirga, making maladroit, unprepared public appearances and missing opportunities to demonstrate decisive leadership. The event could never have lived up to the expectations of its most optimistic and sometimes naïve observers, but with better stage management Karzai could have made it seem a less cynical and more democratic exercise. Between his autocratic mien and his lack of appreciation for the value of political theater, he allowed the event to become a convention showcasing the leaders of Afghanistan's bitter past, rather than the beginning of a new era that so many Afghans had been waiting for. Brahimi faulted Karzai in particular for not being able to intuit the pulse of the event, the designs of potential spoilers, and the expectations of the people of Afghanistan. His political team, dominated at that time by newcomers from the Afghan Diaspora, probably contributed to the overall lack of strategy and misreading of the political moment.

None of this prevented Karzai from being elected as interim head of state by the Emergency Loya Jirga delegates, receiving 1,295 of the 1,911 votes cast. The other bit of good news, especially for the international community and Afghan progressives, was the second-place finish of Dr. Massouda Jalal, a woman, who earned 171 votes. For all its flaws, therefore, the Emergency Loya Jirga was at least, in the words of the International Crisis Group, "a small but critical step in Afghanistan's political development."[34] If it failed to meet the democratic expectations of many within Afghanistan and their international supporters, the extent of disappointment could be spun more positively as a sign that Afghans truly wanted democracy, recognized what democracy was, and were frustrated at not seeing more of it.

Brahimi was more optimistic in his overall assessment of the Emergency Loya Jirga than the ICG, describing it to New York as "Afghanistan's first experiment with democracy."[35] He noted that Afghans had elected their first leader after 23 years of conflict, in what was widely considered to be the nearest thing to a free and fair ballot, with a significant participation of women. He added that in these respects, Afghanistan was already ahead of many other countries in the region.

Democratic or not, small step or large step, the key achievement was that the event had taken place and the fragile peace had held. For those with longer political memories this was of overwhelming significance. The last attempt at peace, in 1992, had broken down when President Rabbani had refused to hand power over after completing his six month term as specified in Peshawar Accord. A decade later, Rabbani was present in the Emergency Loya Jirga tent, along with many others who had participated in the subsequent and devastating civil war. This time the "warlords" may have, as the International Crisis Group complained, "sat in the front row of the Loya Jirga," but the front row was still better than the front line. At a minimum, the Bonn Agreement had survived its first big test.

The Emergency Loya Jirga delegates, meanwhile, returned to their far-flung valleys to report to their people on this new transition process. The next test would be the drafting of a new constitution and the convening of another Loya Jirga in 18 months to ratify the constitution. In Kabul attention turned to the creation of yet another commission—the Constitutional Drafting Commission. Around this time, at United Nations headquarters in New York, the Electoral Assistance Division (EAD) began to lay the groundwork for the elections themselves.

---

[1] This quote is taken from Francesc Vendrell's August 2008 final report to the European Commission when his appointment as the European Union Special Representative for Afghanistan ended. The report, leaked to the media, documented a number of disagreements Vendrell had with Brahimi at the end of 2001 and the beginning of 2002.

[2] United Nations document S/2002/278.

[3] The concept of an integrated mission was formulated by Brahimi himself, who in the two preceding years had chaired a high-level panel to modernize United Nations peacekeeping. The panel's recommendations were contained in the "Brahimi Report": i.e. the Report of the Panel on United Nations Peace Operations (United Nations document A/55/305 - S/2000/809). Brahimi therefore had the bad bureaucratic luck of being the first person to implement the recommendations of his own panel.

[4] This description of jirgas and Loya Jirgas is heavily indebted to an unpublished paper by Shahmahmood Miakhel, "The Importance of Tribal Structures and Pakhtunwali in Afghanistan: Their role in Security and Governance." Miakhel was a deputy to Ali Ahmad Jalali, when he was Minister of Interior (between 2003 and 2005) and later joined UNAMA as a senior political officer.

[5] Leon B. Poullada, "The Pashtun Role in the Afghan Political System," Occasional Paper Number One, The Afghanistan Council of the Asia Society, 1970, p. 11.

[6] According to Thomas Ruttig, *shuras* are deliberative and give advice to the leader, who may accept it or not, whereas jirgas are more egalitarian and make binding decisions—though he adds that "many Pashtuns use both terms, jirga and shura, interchangeably now." See Thomas Ruttig, How Tribal Are the Taliban? Afghanistan's Largest Insurgent Movement between its Tribal Roots and Islamist Ideology," Afghan Analysts Network, Thematic Report 04/2010, Kabul, June 2010, p. 2.

[7] As with every apparent fact in Afghanistan, there is scholarly debate over whether or not Abdali should be credited as the father of modern Afghanistan. But this is among the least controversial assertions of Afghan history.

[8] Afghan "independence" is a paradoxical thing. Great Britain never effectively colonized Afghanistan, but maintained a powerful, if not always decisive, influence over its politics through the provision of subsidies to Afghan leaders. What "independence" ultimately meant for Afghanistan was freedom to make its own foreign policy.

[9] This common interpretation of the role of Loya Jirgas is contested by M. Jamal Hanafi, who provides a post-modern interpretation of the phenomenon. Hanafi argues that, "The template of the 1924 Loya Jerga [sic] was woven out of Western colonial distortions of local categories by Afghan rulers and their intellectual collaborators in civil society to produce the appearance of consensus through blatant manipulation and deceit. We have come full circle. The falsehood of the 1747 assembly, the 'coronation' of Ahmad Khan Abdali, and his 'election' as king in a borderless context subsidized by external resources is reenacted in the 2002 neocolonial government of Kabul, imposed by outsiders on a handpicked assembly of Afghans, guarded by international armed forces, all underwritten by international donations." See Hanafi, "Editing the Past: Colonial Production of Hegemony Through the Loya Jerga [sic] in Afghanistan," *Iranian Studies* 27, issue no. 2, June 2004, p. 321.

[10] Vartan Gregorian, The Emergence of Modern Afghanistan: Politics of Reform and Modernization, 1880-1946 (Stanford: Stanford University Press, 1969) p. 40.

[11] The offices were in Kabul, Herat, Kandahar, Gardez, Mazar-i-Sharif, Jalalabad, Bamyan and Kunduz. In other words, the six offices that UNSMA had established plus Gardez and Kunduz.

[12] "Jihadi" is from the same root as "mujaheddin," the name applied to anti-Soviet rebels fighting a "holy war." There were eleven main jihadi parties, seven based in Pakistan and four in Iran. Little united them, as the civil war in the 1990s proved, except for the fact that they fought against the Soviets and that they considered themselves to be legitimized by Islam. The formation of the resistance parties in Peshawar is dealt with comprehensively but succinctly in Dorronsoro, *Revolution Unending*, pp. 137-172, and Olivier Roy, *Islam and Resistance in Afghanistan* (Cambridge: Cambridge University Press, 1995) pp. 110-126.

[13] In the end, 1,051 delegates were selected by indirect district elections. The rest of the composition was as follows (with seats for women in parentheses): members of the Interim Administration 30 (2); members of the Loya Jirga Commission 21 (3); religious personalities 6; credible individuals 30 (10); civil society members 51 (12); professional and scientific organizations 39 (6); nomads 25; refugees 100 (25); Internally-Displaced Persons (IDPs) 6 (2); other women, distributed geographically 100. For further details see "The Loya Jirga: One Small Step Forward?" International Crisis Group Asia Briefing Paper, 16 May 2002, pp. 7 and 8.

[14] The Loya Jirga Commission aimed at one participant per 25,000 people. The process was complicated by the "discovery" of additional districts during the process. See Chapter 7 on the difficulty of defining districts and even provinces in Afghanistan.

[15] At the time, the logistics for all U.N. Secretariat field missions were handled by the Office of Mission Support (OMS) within the Department for Peacekeeping Operations (DPKO), regardless of who the "lead department" for the mission was. In 2002, the lead department for UNAMA was the Department of Political Affairs (DPA). In 2003 responsibility for UNAMA shifted to DPKO, in part to correct what was percieved as inusfficient attention to

UNAMA's logistical needs when it was a DPA mission. When Ban Ki-moon became Secretary-General in 2007, OMS was severed from DPKO and became a a separate Department, the Department of Field Support (DFS), ostensibly to service equally all peace operations, whether headed by DPA or DPKO.

[16] In the end, a complicated compromise was found, where tanks were removed from some of the helicopters, allowing staff to fly in them. On long trips, another helicopter with the internal tanks would accompany those with tanks removed and refuel them. This allowed the rules to be respected but cut in half the actual number of helicopters available.

[17] Nuristan is one of the more isolated provinces of Afghanistan, in the northeast corner, barricaded by mountains. It was once known as "Kaffiristan," or "land of the infidels," as it was one of the last areas of Afghanistan to be Islamicized. It was renamed Nuristan, or "Land of Light," once its inhabitants had been converted to Islam by the "Iron Emir," Abdul Rahman Khan, in 1896. Its inhabitants are proud blue-eyed Afghans, said to be a race founded by the descendants of Alexander the Great. See Vartan Gregorian, *Emergence of Modern Afghanistan*, p. 36. It is also not accidental that Kipling located in Nuristan his tale about two British veterans who decide to become emperors of a remote corner of the Empire, *The Man Who Would Be King*. If Ben Macintyre, however, in correct in his own recent book of the same name, then the actual person who inspired Kipling was an American and had in fact sought—and been granted—a kingdom in Ghor, at the northwestern edge of the Hazarajat. See Macintyre, *The Man Who Would Be King*.

[18] Such systems have in fact been used until recently in places like the Solomon Islands and in some parts of Africa.

[19] Dupree, *Afghanistan*, p. 587.

[20] For a more detailed discussion of this phenomenon, see International Crisis Group, "The Problem of Pashtun Alienation" Asia Report No. 62, Kabul/Brussels, August 5, 2003.

[21] ISAF was an international force, initially led by the United Kingdom, that was authorized by U.N. Security Council resolution 1286 of 20 December 2001 to provide security in Kabul. It operated separately from U.S. forces carrying out counter-terrorism operations at the time. From the beginning, Brahimi argued that ISAF needed to expand beyond the capital. Security Council resolution 1510, adopted on 13 October 2003, authorized the expansion of ISAF to "areas outside of Kabul and its environs." This expansion was slow, however, and generally one step behind the increase in insurgent activities.

[22] The coalition was carrying out the counter-terrorist "Operation Enduring Freedom."

[23] Antonio Giustozzi, "'Good' State vs. 'Bad' Warlords? A critique of State-Building Strategies in Afghanistan" Crisis States Programme Working Papers no.51, October 2004, p. 5. Olivier Roy offers a consistent definition based on different criteria: "A warlord is a commander who has been able to extend his authority beyond his own solidarity group and to build on a wider identity (tribal in the South, geographic or ethnic in the North) to establish a regional leadership." Olivier Roy, "Afghanistan: Internal Politics and Socio-

economic Dynamics and Groupings" WriteNet Paper, March 2003, ISSN 102-8429, p. 6.

[24] The implementation of this strategy was complex. In general, warlords who fought the state were to be marginalized, and those who professed allegiance were to be legitimized (and eventually disarmed). Punishment for fighting the state was normally carried out by the U.S. forces, which, unlike ISAF, could operate all over the country. In the first year of the Bonn Agreement, however, some of the warlords fighting the state were also providing, or pretending to provide, assistance to U.S. forces hunting Bin Ladin. The U.S. was thus reluctant to punish them. An interesting game could then be played by the warlords by pitting the two American priorities—finding Bin Ladin and supporting the new Afghan government—against each other.

[25] Bonn Agreement, preamble.

[26] International Crisis Group, "The Afghan Transitional Administration: Prospects and Perils" Afghanistan Briefing, Kabul and Brussels, July 30, 2002, p. 4. In this paper, the ICG noted the problem of defining a "warlord," adding that: "A definitional battle is being played out that will be central to the process of reconciliation and military reintegration." It also introduced a distinction between "warlords," such as Dostum Gul Agha, and Karim Khalili, and "strongmen," such as Mohammad Fahim, then Minister of Defense. Beyond providing these examples, it did not develop a typology to reliably distinguish between the two.

[27] See Chapter 12 for a more detailed description of how this strategy was implemented.

[28] This was demonstrated several years later, in 2007, when the publication by Human Rights Watch of a report on past atrocities led the recently-elected parliament to adopt a law amnestying those who had been involved in the previous wars from criminal prosecution. The Human Rights Watch report in some ways arguably set back the possibility of a proper accounting for years.

[29] It was nonetheless significant that a number of courageous delegates, women especially, used the Loya Jirga to denounce the crimes that warlords had committed.

[30] William Maley, *Rescuing Afghanistan* (Sydney: UNSW Press, 2006) p. 36.

[31] Steve Coll ends his *Ghost Wars* with the dramatic account of the authorization of covert assistance and the death of Massoud. See Steve Coll, *Ghost Wars* (New York: The Penguin Press, 2004) pp. 567-576.

[32] Fahim was Minister of Defence, Yunis Qanuni was Minister of the Interior, and Abdullah Abdullah was Minister of Foreign Affairs.

[33] ICG, "The Loya Jirga" p. 1.

[34] ICG, "The Afghan Transitional Administration" p. 1.

[35] This was not technically true given the New Democracy period under King Zahir Shah in the 1960s, but it was true enough in that the New Democracy elections never reached as far into the Afghan hinterland as the Loya Jirga process had. As Dupree wrote, "Few Afghans participated in the 1965 election." Dupree estimated a turnout of around 15 percent. See Dupree, *Afghanistan*, p. 589.

4
Plans and Personalities

The Emergency Loya Jirga had been part of the strictly political element of the Bonn process. Brahimi and his political team in UNAMA had been the masters of it, as far as the United Nations was concerned. He had reported to New York but had not sought advice from headquarters. Elections, however, were a different matter. In the United Nations system, all electoral assistance activities are approved and overseen by the Electoral Assistance Division (EAD), which is part of DPA. EAD reports directly to the Under-Secretary-General of DPA, who is also the United Nations "focal point" for electoral assistance. Both the focal point and EAD are fairly recent creations in the U.N.. They reflect global changes and possibilities caused by the end of the Cold War and the wave of democratization that followed.

In the era that emerged following the collapse of the Soviet Union, some member states, the U.S. in particular, proposed that the U.N. should be more active in helping member states improve the effectiveness of their democratic institutions. At the 1990 General Assembly, U.S. President George H.W. Bush proposed the creation of "a United Nations electoral commission that would attend member states' requests for electoral observation and other kinds of electoral assistance."[1] This was unprecedented because it was a potential infringement on the domestic jurisdictions of member states. During the first 50 years of the United Nations' existence, the few electoral activities undertaken by the organization had been mostly limited to areas where it had a clear mandate to intervene in the internal political affairs of a member state. These were mostly cases of decolonization, where the Charter granted a certain amount of oversight to the world body (and the General Assembly had asserted the right to even more).[2] In the late 1980s, the United Nations began to involve itself in postconflict elections where it had a specific mandate, as a guarantor of the peace processes that ended these conflicts. Two early cases were Nicaragua and El Salvador, where the Security Council endorsed the respective peace agreements and the U.N. Secretariat was given a role in implementing them, including helping to organize elections. It was obvious to some member states, as reified in President Bush's proposal to the General Assembly, that this newfound expertise could be of use to other member states, should they request it.

At the same time, a number of member states were wary of this new role for the United Nations. Article 2(7) of the United Nations Charter prohibits the organization from interfering in "matters which are essentially within the domestic jurisdiction" of a member state. There are few exercises more inherent to national sovereignty, or "domestic jurisdiction," than national elections. Apart from states' understandable jealousy over their sovereignty, there was also the prohibiting factor that, "liberal democracy is still not an uncontested right even at the level of normative theory."[3] The foundational texts of the United Nations are clear enough about democracy as far as they go; Article 21 of the Universal Declaration of Human Rights states that "the will of the people shall be the basis of the authority of government [and] shall be expressed in periodic and genuine elections which shall be by universal and equal suffrage," and Article 21 of the International Covenant on Civil and Political Rights states that "every citizen shall have the right [...] to vote and to be elected at genuine periodic elections which shall be by universal and equal suffrage and shall be held by secret ballot, guaranteeing the free expression of the will of voters." Still, even conceding these premises, discussions about democracy that go beyond these basics have, as Barrington Moore has written, "a way of leading away from real issues to trivial quibbling."[4] Finally, these premises themselves can be debated. As Tom J. Farer notes, "a number of consequential U.N. members—China, Cuba, and Saudi Arabia prominent among them—openly and categorically reject the equation of legitimacy with triumph in electoral competition."[5]

In order to balance both the post-Cold War hope of greater democratization and the corresponding fear that this would open the door to breaches of sovereignty—establishing precedents that could be the beginning of a slippery slope—the General Assembly in 1990 adopted twin resolutions: one on "enhancing the effectiveness of the principle of periodic and genuine elections,"[6] and the other reasserting the "respect for the principles of national sovereignty and non-interference in the internal affairs of States in their electoral processes."[7] An inexorable dynamic had been unleashed, however, by the resolution on electoral assistance, and it is not without irony that one of the country's most jealous of guarding its sovereignty against U.N. intervention, the United States, was also the driving force behind the organization's involvement in elections. The following year, the General Assembly adopted another resolution establishing the Under-Secretary-General for Political Affairs as the "focal point" for electoral assistance.[8] The next year the General Assembly created the Electoral Assistance Unit. In 1994 the Electoral Assistance Unit became a full-fledged division, initially as part of the Department of Peacekeeping Operations, but shortly thereafter it was moved to the Department of Political Affairs.

One of the main functions of EAD was to evaluate requests for electoral assistance and provide recommendations to the focal point on how to answer these requests. Over time, EAD also became the guardian of what it termed "system-wide coherence" or "consistency." Consistency was, in effect, a proxy for "standards." But the word itself was avoided because there were no internationally-agreed upon standards to define whether a country is democratic or not. As Farer notes, "potential controversy [in democracy promotion] has also been avoided most of the time by the U.N.'s flexibility in defining democracy, more precisely by not insisting in particular cases on any single contested conception."[9] Consistency, on the other hand, as defined by the Secretary-General,

> ensures that key factors, such as the widest possible enfranchisement of voters and the existence of a free press, are respected in democratic processes. And while the design and implementation of each electoral assistance project takes into account the particularities of the local context, it does not do so at the expense of global consistency.[10]

Given the divergent attitudes of member states towards electoral assistance, a certain amount of circularity in the definition was required. On a practical level, however, it meant that the political officers in EAD had to strive to ensure that decisions taken on electoral assistance in the field would not create precedents that undermined certain basic tenets without which the notion of democracy was meaningless.

In practice, this meant defending certain points of doctrine that were either extrapolated from General Assembly resolutions or had become precedents in the practice of U.N. electoral assistance. For example, the General Assembly had established that technical assistance must be requested by a member state and an evaluation of that request must be made by EAD. The standard methodology that was developed for evaluating the requests ensured a consistency in analyzing various electoral systems and practices. The General Assembly also established a roster of electoral experts, managed by EAD, from which all experts working on U.N. electoral projects had to be selected. By controlling the quality of experts on the roster, EAD was able to control the consistency of assistance provided. The advantage of the roster, whose creation was approved by the General Assembly, was that individuals could be selected from it by EAD without having to go through the cumbersome candidate selection process required for most U.N. recruitment. The price for that flexibility was, however, that there had to be a fairly rigorous vetting process for those placed on the roster. The experts selected were generally technical specialists who had worked for EAD before and understood its underlying philosophy of democratization as well as the sensitive political context in which the U.N. provided electoral assistance. The fact that their professional destinies depended more on EAD than on the management of whatever mission EAD placed them in helped to provide professional insulation, allowing experts to make independent recommendations that safeguarded electoral consistency.

EAD's defense of these principles often put it at odds with the rest of the United Nations system, and in particular its main implementing partners: the Department of Peacekeeping Operations, which was responsible for most postconflict elections, and the United Nations Development Programme (UNDP), which carried out electoral assistance projects in developing countries. In postconflict elections there was always a strong temptation by the heads of peacekeeping missions to cut electoral corners for understandable political reasons. EAD was concerned that whatever corners were cut would contribute to a global erosion of democratic consistency, as well as to the credibility of the specific process concerned. These conflicting interests set up numerous bureaucratic contests.

At the time of the Bonn Agreement, the Director of EAD was Carina Perelli, an assertive Uruguayan who had worked in elections with the United Nations for several years, mostly with UNDP. She was a rare combination of bureaucrat, activist, and intellectual. When she was hired to head EAD in 1998, she became one of the youngest directors in the U.N. system. While a teenager she had been a member of one of the most radical Marxist groups committed to violently overthrowing the military junta that ruled Uruguay. Her commitment to the ballot box emerged unexpectedly when the military junta risked submitting a constitutional referendum to a popular vote. The junta gambled that the population was sufficiently intimidated to endorse the proposed constitution. When the ballots were counted they discovered that the population had gambled that the ballot would actually be secret and had rejected the draft constitution. This ignited a string of events that eventually led to the downfall of the military government and a transition to democracy. For Perelli, this was a powerful demonstration that democracy could be more effective than violence in promoting enduring political change, leading her to become a student of and believer in democratic transition processes.

Shortly after assuming the directorship of EAD, Perelli was confronted with her first major challenge. The Indonesian president had unexpectedly decided to allow a referendum on independence in East Timor, the half-isle that had been under contested Indonesian control since 1975. The time frame to arrange the "popular consultation" was extremely short—the agreement had been finalized in May 1999 and called for the referendum in August. EAD had plan the election, hire experts, and set up of the operation on the ground, where there was no existing U.N. presence. Perelli worked closely with Vendrell, who was at the time the Director of the Asia and Pacific Division of the U.N.'s Department of Political Affairs.

The numerous acts of violence that occurred as the date of the referendum approached led many inside the U.N. to recommend that it be postponed. It was increasingly clear that the expected outcome, a vote in favor of independence, would provoke a bloodbath by the Indonesians in Timor. The Timorese argued that the referendum could not be postponed. They had endured 25 years of resistance to reach this unexpected moment, they might never be given a similar opportunity again, and they were willing to risk whatever bloodshed might ensure. Perelli and Vendrell backed the Timorese position within the United Nations. The referendum was held, the independence vote won, and the predictable wave of violence ensued. Dili, East Timor's capital, was burned to the ground and about 1,500 Timorese were killed.[11] But when the fires were doused and the dead were buried, the Timorese had gained their independence.

Perelli's combative personality earned her many enemies in the organization in the years after the Timor operation. But her effectiveness had gained her the full confidence of the Under-Secretary-General for Political Affairs, Kieran Prendergast. With this backing, Perelli pursued her bureaucratic battles with a sense of impunity that pearned her more enemies than she actually needed. At the same time, few understood the notion of consistency in electoral practice that she zealously defended. As she stated in an unaired interview,

> the first thing we do is have a frank discussion within the [United Nations] and with the member states about whether the plan they foresee makes sense in electoral-political terms, try to share our hard-

> earned lessons. Sometimes that leaves wounds because many actors prefer expediency over sustainability. It is often my job to be the voice of dissent in terms of how these processes are conducted."[12]

It is critical that the function of this "voice of dissent" is understood. It was, within the bureaucracy, a necessary brake on the sort of "expediency" that was the inevitable result of the organization's inherent and understandable tendency to compromise. Compromises for the purpose of striking deals that end wars are understandable and necessary, but undue compromises in the conduct of electoral events can undermine the political function of elections and the U.N.'s own legitimacy in promoting democracy. Perceptions of lack of credibility in one operation would affect future operations. Perelli saw EAD's role as being a bulwark against this tendency for expediency and compromise. She knew, furthermore, that no other part of the organization would play this function—that her voice would often be a lonely one. She therefore decided that it had to be a ferocious one. As long as it was heard—and backed up by the focal point—she was able to win what she considered to be the most important battles. In this way it could be said that the system worked, though painfully.

Initial Electoral Planning Options in Afghanistan

In early 2002, EAD in New York began anticipating the electoral demands required of the United Nations by the Bonn Agreement. In March 2002, Perelli asked her staff to prepare a brief analysis of the requirements for holding an election in Afghanistan. The EAD analysis zeroed in on the tight timetable for elections in the Bonn Agreement, the problem of identifying who was an Afghan,[13] the lack of a legislative framework, and the need to create a credible and impartial institution to conduct the elections. The paper concluded that an electoral Needs Assessment Mission should be dispatched as soon as possible to Afghanistan and that an electoral expert should be attached to UNAMA to advise on "decisions that may impact intentionally or inadvertently on the subsequent electoral process." This latter point echoed a common refrain from EAD, which often found itself having to organize elections in a context defined by previous political decisions that had "inadvertently" made those elections more difficult to organize. The recommendation to deploy an electoral expert was turned down by Brahimi, who was then focused on the Emergency Loya Jirga.

A few months later, in July 2002, Brahimi met with Perelli in New York. The main question discussed was the possibility of combining the census (also required by the Bonn Agreement) with the voter registration exercise. Perelli argued against this, saying that the two operations would, if conducted together, undermine each other. Voter registration exists to compile the minimum amount of information required to positively and exclusively identity a given voter, while a census exists to provide as much information about an individual without revealing his or her identity. If potential voters were simultaneously asked census-like questions about income, education levels, ethnicity,[14] and other private information, they might doubt the secrecy of their eventual vote. Brahimi accepted this rationale.

Perelli raised, in addition, a number of other technical issues of which she felt Brahimi needed to be aware. Brahimi noted them, and understood through them that it would probably be impossible to hold elections within the Bonn timetable. Brahimi and Perelli agreed, however, that the U.N. at that point needed to be seen to be making every effort possible to meet the deadline, if only to maintain the momentum of the process. They also agreed that Perelli would visit Afghanistan in the near future to develop her own more detailed assessment.

Perelli's assessment mission took place in late October and early November 2002, when she traveled to Afghanistan with her Chief of Operations, Sean Dunne. Perelli and Dunne focused on the lack of an institutional and legal framework for holding elections, noting that these would be time-consuming to set up and were therefore a priority. They proposed three options. The first option was to allow the constitution, which according to the Bonn Agreement was to be adopted by December 2003, to determine the legislative framework. In other words, the electoral law would be written in conformity with the relevant constitutional provisions. Perelli's report advised against this, primarily because the six months between the adoption of the constitution and the scheduled holding of elections were insufficient to address the many operational issues that would not be able to be determined until the law was drafted.

Typically, an electoral law sets deadlines, such as the number of months before an election that the election date has to be set, that candidates must submit their applications, and that the voter register must be finalized. In addition, the type of election (presidential and/or legislative) and the electoral system affected the design of the ballot, the number of ballots required, the layout and size needs of the polling station and the number of polling station workers required. A particularly complex electoral system would require additional resources to be devoted to ensuring that the count was accurate. A law, for example, establishing a two-round electoral system in case no candidate earned 50 percent of the vote in the first round (as would be the case in Afghanistan) created logistical consequences that had to be anticipated long in advance.

Perelli and Dunne also suggested that there was a political advantage in separating the drafting of the electoral law from the drafting of the constitution. This was the fear that electoral politics would affect constitutional deliberations, making it both harder to achieve consensus on the constitution and potentially skewing decisions made by the constitution's drafters toward short-term electoral prospects rather than the long-term interests of the country.

These considerations led to the second option, which they described as the "legislative approach." Here the proposal was to promulgate electoral legislation by decree prior to and irrespective of the adoption of the constitution.[15] This would allow greater time to prepare the election, but would also suffer from the same conflict of interest—that those making the laws, Karzai in particular, were also likely to be electoral contenders.

The final option—recommended by Perelli and Dunne—was what they called a "one-time" modality. Like the legislative approach, a decree would be issued prior to the constitution, thus gaining a significant amount of time for preparations. Unlike the "legislative approach," the "one-time modality" would not simply be decreed by Karzai's administration, but would result from a process of negotiation among the major electoral actors, including those who were not part of the administration and those who felt alienated from it. Perelli favored this approach. It embodied her theories about using elections not simply to distribute political power, but to build consensus in postconflict environments. It would also improve the quality of the election by reducing the risk of potential disputes over their results. If the main actors accepted the rules at an early stage because they had participated in shaping them, they would have fewer grounds on which to complain about the results later. Finally, it would provide an opportunity to bring into the Bonn process those political actors who resented the fact that they had, so far, been excluded from power.

The second major issue, apart from the law, was the need to create an electoral management structure. Perelli's Needs Assessment Mission report proposed the creation of both an "Independent Electoral Commission" to oversee and verify the process, and an interim "Afghan Electoral Authority," which would be the executive body that managed and organized the elections. The Authority would benefit from a "support secretariat" staffed by international experts to provide the technical knowledge that few in Afghanistan had. This infrastructure was fairly standard for this type of postconflict operation, and the report stressed the need to begin establishing these bodies as soon as possible, in particular to begin training the Afghans. Perelli's report was approved by Prendergast and sent to Brahimi in December 2002, in a cable signed by the Under-Secretary-General of DPKO, which had in the meantime taken the lead for UNAMA from DPA.[16]

Within UNAMA there had also been some thinking about elections. A UNAMA political affairs officer had been tasked to write a "discussion paper" on electoral issues. Unlike Perelli's focus on how to establish a system and institutional structure that would allow Afghan political actors to take electoral decisions, the UNAMA paper adumbrated what those decisions should be. It is useful to compare these two approaches, because they are indicative of the vastly different thinking between EAD and UNAMA's political department. The UNAMA paper was a fairly typical example of a field of electoral scholarship that relies on the design of electoral systems to promote political goals that the designers consider beneficial for the polity in question. In this case, UNAMA's paper argued for an electoral system that would "prod non-Pashtun jehadi parties to broaden their appeal," provide the smaller Northern Alliance parties with enough political representation to "stay in the political game," while limiting the influence of local military commanders on the outcome of the election. To accomplish these goals, the paper proposed a complex system through which a national assembly would be elected by both a national list system and direct geographical representation.

For Perelli, the paper was a work of political amateurism that had the unfortunate effect of disrupting the serious debate that should have taken place over the options she had proposed. While this sort of "electoral engineering" in postconflict situations was becoming a well-practiced and increasingly documented art,[17] it too often yielded to the temptation to *over*-engineer—to create, in T.S. Eliot's words, "systems so perfect that no one will need to be good."[18] It is undeniable that every electoral system presents a set of incentives that affect the behavior of political actors. It follows that some systems are preferable to others in a given situation, and these systems can be identified (and in fact a large body of scholarly work has been devoted to this, as will be described later). At the same time, the tendency to over-engineer often leads to a systemic complexity that can be self-defeating. The first principle of postconflict elections, especially where there is scant electoral tradition, should be simplicity. If democracy is to be at all sustainable, voters must understand what they are doing and how their choices in a voting booth translate into the political arrangement that results from their votes. As Perelli argued in a note to Prendergast, contesting the UNAMA paper,

> in a country just engaging with democracy, a complex and opaque system is most likely to draw credibility away from the election [...] any proposed electoral system should strive for simplicity, to ensure that the election is as transparent and comprehensible to the average member of the public as possible.

A further problem with the temptation of electoral engineering is that the designs created tended to reflect the political cultures of the engineers—generally foreign experts—rather than the political realities of those being engineered.[19] An incentive that a foreigner may feel would induce an Afghan towards cross-ethnic solidarity, might not have that effect at all to an Afghan. The ironclad law of unintended consequences was always downplayed by the electoral engineers, while their ability to perfectly anticipate how political actors will react to the incentives they set were always assumed to be ironclad.

A significant, if arcane, debate—which would have implications for everything that followed—had now been engaged between New York and Kabul. It was to some degree an expression of the tension referred to earlier between the supposedly political "realists" and the electoral "purists." But these tags misrepresented the actual terms of the conflict, which was between those who took a long-term institutionalist view of electoral processes and those who saw elections as political events that were important especially for their immediate results.

It was easy to dismiss the institutionalist approach as being politically naive on the grounds that electoral "standards" could not be expected to be upheld in the complex and messy world of postconflict peacebuilding. But this easy dismissal was based on a superficial reading of EAD's approach. There was in fact a profound political realism that undergirded the promotion of institutions. No one in EAD was arguing for the maintenance of the highest possible standards—for "free and fair" elections as the terminology went—in situations where those standards could not possibly be met. The point was rather that, with sufficient planning and competent negotiation, a higher standard of elections could be obtained than was immediately apparent, and that higher standard would contribute to both short-term stability and long-term democratization.

Perelli in fact had a strong distaste for the term "free and fair" to describe elections. As Eric C. Bjorlund has pointed out, "free and fair" has become a "rhetorical touchstone" that has "encouraged international election assessments to make categorical, 'bottom-line' judgments that fail to take nuances and context into account."[20] Perelli considered "free" and "fair" to be normative notions ill-suited to describe the realities of politics, whether in postconflct or more normal situations. EAD political officers were instructed to use the term "credible" instead of "free and fair" when commenting on drafts of official U.N. documents prepared by other departments. (DPKO and DPA political affairs officers, on the other hand, continued to resort automatically to the term "free and fair" in drafting official reports.)

The intensifying debate between what may be termed the electoral and political approaches to the election began to define the context in which Brahimi considered EAD's Needs Assessment Mission report. In late January 2003, Brahimi proposed several amendments to Perelli's recommendations. First, he suggested combining the "legislative" and "one-time" approaches by convening a working group of independent personalities, rather than representatives of existing political groups, to develop an outline of the electoral process. Representatives of political parties, he proposed, would be brought on board afterwards. The justification for this approach was the perceived political stigma attached to parties in Afghanistan.[21] Brahimi also suggested the establishment of an "Electoral Cooperation Board" combining the "Afghan Electoral Authority" with the electoral unit that would need to be established within UNAMA.

At this point, the debate was academic. The U.N. had not yet been formally requested by the Afghan government to provide assistance on organizing the elections (the Bonn Agreement only referred to the U.N. organizing voter registration). With Brahimi's encouragement, Karzai wrote U.N. Secretary-General Kofi Annan, requesting that "UNAMA be entrusted with the mission to help prepare and organize the electoral process and to coordinate international electoral assistance." Normally a request initiated a Needs Assessment Mission. But given that the assessment mission had already taken place, and that discussions had already begun between UNAMA and headquarters on how to address the elections, Karzai's letter merely ratified a process that was already underway. Nonetheless, it gave a green light to UNAMA to proceed with establishing an electoral unit and beginning preparations for a larger electoral assistance role. The wording of Karzai's request was, however, vague in terms of who was responsible for which functions, and in particular what would be the limits of the UN's responsibility. Since no local electoral institutions existed, it was impossible at that time to obtain a greater level of clarity. The task now fell to EAD,

UNAMA, and the Afghan transitional administration to define what was meant by "help prepare and organize."

The issue began to be clarified a month later, when the Secretary-General issued a report on Afghanistan which included a section on the electoral process.[22] The report, largely drafted by UNAMA, said that "UNAMA will work with the Electoral Assistance division [...] to define the appropriate modalities for electoral assistance." The Secretary-General requested the Afghan government to "urgently appoint a national electoral body to oversee the organization of the elections." The report further noted that, given that the constitution was not likely to be completed until the end of 2003, "specific and limited electoral and political parties' laws may have to be promulgated for the purposes of the 2004 elections only. Laws for subsequent elections would draw upon the new constitution." EAD's idea of a "one-time modality" was still alive and, if not fully endorsed yet by Brahimi, it had been at least openly accepted as a possibility. Finally, the report recommended the creation of an electoral support unit within UNAMA, "headed by an internationally recognized senior expert supported by an appropriate team in Kabul and in the provinces."[23]

The main lines of electoral support had therefore been set, and two immediate priorities had been identified: the appointment of an Afghan electoral commission and the recruitment of a senior electoral expert to head UNAMA's electoral support unit. The Security Council endorsed the Secretary-General's proposals by adopting resolution 1471 (2003).[24] The United Nations' electoral involvement now entered a new, more intense, phase.

Assembling the Electoral Team

Unknown to Perelli, Brahimi already had a candidate in mind to head the electoral unit: Reginald Austin, a Zimbabwean, who was then serving as the Director of Elections of the Stockholm-based International Institute for Democracy and Electoral Assistance (International IDEA). Austin was indeed an "internationally-recognized senior expert." He had headed the electoral operation in Cambodia in 1992, the U.N.'s first major postconflict election, which had in many ways established the template for such operations.

The Cambodian elections had been a massive operation, implemented primarily by the United Nations Transitional Administration in Cambodia (UNTAC), which was the interim government of the country at the time. In other words, the country, during the transition period, was being administered by the United

Nations. Over 500 international staff working on the elections alone, from writing the electoral law to organizing the logistical operation to hiring over 50,000 Cambodians and 1,000 internationals to man polling stations on the day of the election. The logistics had been complex, the politics murderous, and the security environment extremely unstable. Nonetheless on election day, Cambodians voted in large numbers, and accusations by political parties of fraud and electoral irregularities were deftly and convincingly refuted by Austin and his team. Austin's Cambodian operation was generally seen by observers and analysts as a success, and many experts on the United Nations electoral roster had cut their professional teeth while working on it. There had only been one operation after Cambodia where the United Nations had conducted the election itself, as opposed to assisting national authorities to organize electoral operations. That exception was the popular consultation in East Timor in 1999.

Austin, on paper, was therefore an excellent choice. Furthermore, Brahimi had worked with Austin in 1994, when Brahimi had headed the United Nations Observer Mission to the post-*apartheid* South African elections that elected Nelson Mandela. Given Brahimi's personalized management style, it was important that the chief electoral adviser have his confidence. Without consulting Perelli, Brahimi had asked Austin if he would take the job.

Perelli knew Austin well and respected his work in Cambodia. She had doubts, however, that he was the right person for Afghanistan. Unlike Cambodia, where the U.N. had a massive presence due to the fact that it was, in essence, running the country, the U.N. footprint in Afghanistan was explicitly "light." Support for the elections would inevitably come not only from UNAMA, which Brahimi controlled, but from other parts of the system, such as UNDP, that had separate lines of authority. Perelli considered that the Chief Electoral Officer would also have to be something of a bureaucratic battler to obtain the necessary resources from the various parts of the organization that would be involved. She was not convinced that Austin possessed that specific mix of qualities or had enough experience within the U.N. system to recognize its traps. On a bureaucratic level, Perelli resented the fact that Brahimi had offered the position to Austin without consulting her, thus violating the principle that EAD select the international experts who work on U.N. election projects.

Austin, meanwhile, accepted Brahimi's offer and moved to Kabul from Stockholm in late February 2003 with a small advance team of three experts. The clock had begun ticking and Austin's team began to survey the enormity of the task ahead. If the Bonn Agreement was to be kept, over the following 14 months millions of voters would have to be registered and elections would have to be held. On the logistical side, this would require the procurement of tons of equipment, the hiring of thousands of staff—Afghan and international—all according to a pace that would test the cumbersome bureaucracy of the organization. In the meantime, there was no budget, no legislation, no tradition of elections, and the attention of the Afghan Government and its international partners was focused elsewhere.

Establishment of the UNAMA Electoral Unit

On election day in any country virtually the entire resources of the state are focused on the electoral event. Administrative resources are deployed to ensure that polling takes place, security forces are directed to provide order, and government policy-making essentially stops. In some countries, the electoral commission is vested with the legal control of the state's security services on election day; in others it is given partial control over the national budget. In countries where elections are held regularly, these efforts become familiar and are exercised without a second thought. In Afghanistan, not only was the holding of elections unfamiliar, a state apparatus to organize them could hardly be said to exist. At the same time, the holding of these elections was of primordial importance for the international community and for the consolidation of the Bonn process.

Securing the budget for the UNAMA Electoral Unit became the first priority for Austin and his small team in Kabul, backed by EAD in New York. Most electoral experts on the EAD roster were painfully familiar, from experience, with the dissonance between the insistence at a political level among interested member states that elections be held on time and according to the highest possible standards, and the reluctance to provide the necessary resources in a timely manner to bring this about. This dissonance was not expected to occur in Afghanistan. In early 2002—prior to the U.S. invasion of Iraq and less than six months after the September 11 attacks—Afghanistan was at the center of the world. Significant international attention was directed to its transition process and resources were being pumped into the country. For the United Nations, Afghanistan was similarly a center of attention. It had been given a key role in the political transition, and the Secretary-General had entrusted the task of implementing this mandate to his most able diplomat.

Despite all of this, UNAMA was administratively short-changed from the beginning by U.N. member states and by the organization's own administration. Member states decided in late 2001 that the new mission should be funded out of an existing budget envelope that was used for small "Special Political Missions," such as those in Bougainville (Papua New Guinea), Burundi, Somalia and Tajikistan, rather than as a peacekeeping mission. Special Political Missions tended to be either the downsized results of successful peacekeeping missions (Burundi and Tajikistan), or operations dedicated to conflict mediation (Bougainville and Somalia). The budget for Special Political Missions was part of the organization's "regular budget," which was limited to zero-growth due to longstanding pressure from the U.S. Congress.[25] Peacekeeping missions, on the other hand, were funded from a separate "assessed budget" that required, once the mission was approved by the Security Council, additional funds from each member state according to an agreed-upon scale.[26] Peacekeeping missions were therefore not restricted by the zero-growth provisions of the regular budget. (This meant, in theory, that any increase in the budgets of political missions would have to be found from cuts elsewhere. In the decade since the creation of UNAMA, the special political budget has grown from around $100 million to around $1.2 billion, generating an increasingly acerbic debate in the budgetaring Fifth Committee between developing countries who complain that most of this is devoted to missions, like Afghanistan and Iraq, where the "West" has an interest, while the concerns of developing countries are increasingly short-changed.)

UNAMA's first annual budget was $57 million. This was easily financed from the special political envelope, but only provided for the mission's core activities. Ancillary activities that were nonetheless essential to the mission's mandate—such as the disarmament, demobilization and reintegration (DDR) program, support to the Constitutional Commission, and voter registration and elections—required additional funding that had to be provided voluntarily from donors. The costs of the Afghan electoral operation—both registration and elections—was initially estimated at around $100 million.[27] It also was known from previous experience that voluntary funding would be provided at a voluntary pace. The need to secure such a large sum within the tight timelines of the Bonn Agreement created a major vulnerability to the process.

Apart from undermining the predictability of operations in the long term, in the immediate term, the need for voluntary contributions yielded an administrative complexity. The financial contributions would have to be received by a fiduciary entity, which would have to be able to work in effective partnership with UNAMA. The most flexible option was a UNDP trust fund.[28] Since its creation in 1965,[29] UNDP had developed two powerful instruments that made it indispensable to the United Nations system as a whole. The first was a network of offices in over 130, mostly developing, countries. The second instrument was an array of financial tools that made it convenient for donors to contribute funds for development projects implemented by the program's country offices. In 2003, UNDP was spending $2.55 billion around the world, of which $978 million was in cost-sharing arrangements or trust funds—money provided by donors over and above established programs that were part of UNDP's regular budget.[30]

Another advantage of UNDP was that it charged a lower management fee for its trust funds than other U.N. system funding vehicles. The Secretariat, which also administered trust funds through its Controller's office, charged an overhead of 13 percent that was hardly ever negotiable. The Controller's byzantine procedures for disbursement required approvals for every minor deviation from the budget—even deviations that saved money—making Secretariat-managed trust funds notoriously cumbersome and therefore unsuitable for time-sensitive operations such as elections. UNDP's overhead could be negotiated to as low as three percent, and allowed much greater flexibility in shifting budget lines. This latter feature would be essential for an operation that would need to constantly adjust its plans and spending to adapt to discovered realities. Nonetheless, UNDP procedures had their own idiosyncrasies. Often the quality of a project's implementation depended on the ability of the project manager to know which rules could be stretched and by how far.

While the main funding for the election would be from voluntary contributions channeled through UNDP, UNAMA and U.N. Headquarters in New York agreed that the need for early planning in face of the uncertainty of voluntary funding would best be met by the creation of a core electoral unit within UNAMA. Since the unit would be part of UNAMA, it could be financed by the regular budget, and would not depend on the whims of donors. On the other hand, it meant that the Secretariat would have to exceptionally approach the budgetary committees to secure additional financing outside of the regular budget cycle. Austin's first task, working closely with EAD, was to design his expanded unit and justify it to the committees that made decisions on the use of the organization's resources. This core unit would be responsible for planning the main lines of the electoral operation at a time when donor interest was focused on DDR, the constitutional process, and other more current priorities, and in the absence of an Afghan counterpart. In May 2003, a supplemental budget of $12.3 million for the UNAMA Electoral Unit (UEU)[31] was approved, allowing for the immediate recruitment of 39 international staff, 112 national staff, and 32 United Nations Volunteers (UNVs).[32] With the budget now secured, Austin was able to begin to put his team together. Electoral preparations had moved finally from notional debates to a financed structure on the ground.

Initial Plans

Austin's next challenge was the lack of information about Afghanistan that was required for planning nation-wide elections. This included basic information such as population densities, the existence and condition of roads and transport infrastructure, the administrative capacity of the state at the sub-national level, and the pool of literate Afghans to staff the operation. Austin lamented that, compared to Cambodia in 1992, where a massive, detailed assessment had already been carried out by a research team before election planning even began, no such work had been done in Afghanistan. Twenty-five years of war had left a vast information vacuum. Whatever knowledge did exist was often fragmented, decentralized, and unreliable. To complicate matters, the ongoing military clashes in parts of the country meant that the facts on the ground—particularly concerning population locations—were constantly changing.[33]

In Cambodia, the United Nations had been the administering authority and therefore had the prerogative of drafting laws. In Afghanistan, the legal framework would depend on decisions taken by Karzai and his cabinet. There was no way to anticipate when or what decisions they would take, nor whether they would accept the recommendations of international experts. Finally, there was still no sense of who Austin's Afghan counterparts would be or how much training they would need. Inevitably, the first decisions would have to be taken by Austin's team, and then adjusted, and perhaps reversed, once the Afghan counterparts became more engaged. There seemed no end to the uncertainty of critical elements of the operation, and the only certainty was the impossibly short timeline.

Austin's team presented its first draft plan for voter registration to Brahimi in early June 2003. The plan, while a competent beginning that covered the major issues, reflected the lack of information about the electoral environment. It did not, for example, address the problems of dealing with gender sensitivities in Afghanistan, and it glossed over the logistical challenges that would be caused by the winter snows that made some provinces inaccessible. The plan's weaknesses were partly due to the overall lack of knowledge, but they were also due to the lack of frequent contact between Austin's fledgling electoral unit and UNAMA's political officers, who possessed some of the knowledge required. Austin's electoral staff, overestimating their self-sufficiency on electoral matters and underestimating Afghanistan's particularities, did not make enough of an effort to seek them out. At the same time, the mission's political management, did not sufficiently understand the need to begin paying attention to election planning at as early a date possible, and allowed the political team to remain fully focused on the constitutional process.

Accompanied by Brahimi, Austin briefed Karzai's cabinet in early June on the preliminary registration plan. He sensitized ministers to the need to enact legislation, highlighted the immense logistical challenges, and noted that the ongoing insecurity could jeopardize the operation. In his report on the briefing to U.N. headquarters, Brahimi added that he had himself taken the floor to inform the cabinet that, while the constitution would outline the basic electoral system, the details of that system would probably have to be *further* articulated in an electoral law. In New York, Perelli was taken by surprise. What this off-hand addendum meant was that the one-time modality was no longer under consideration. Perelli again was irked that a key policy decision had been taken by default rather than made after a full consideration of its merits, that EAD had been left out of whatever discussion had taken place, and that it had been informed of the decision in an almost accidental manner.

In the cabinet room, the first reaction to Austin's briefing was a discussion on when to schedule the elections. Everyone acknowledged that meeting the June 2004 date prescribed by Bonn was becoming increasingly unlikely. Karzai, however, felt that the date should be respected as much as possible. His reasons were personal and political. He argued that the last time an Afghan president had overstayed his mandate, civil war had ensued.[34] Brahimi argued that a three- to five-month delay would not present a significant danger to the process, noting that a number of Afghans were already beginning to talk of a delay, and even of the possibility of holding the presidential election first, followed later by the legislative ones (assuming of course that the constitution prescribed a directly-elected legislature).

The final issue dealt with at the cabinet meeting was the electoral authority. After Austin's presentation, Karzai proposed the creation of an Afghan Electoral Commission. Austin had responded to this initiative by saying that, if this were to happen, it would be extremely important to find commissioners who would be perceived as independent and impartial, and that this would have to take place quickly. Karzai's proposal had taken everyone by surprise. EAD's concern, upon reading Brahimi's report of the meeting, was that the creation of an Afghan commission at that point would have a large impact on the validity and usefulness of the operational planning, budgetary submissions and logistical preparations undertaken thus far. Perelli, who had received no reaction to her earlier proposal to create an Afghan Electoral Authority, was worried that the introduction of an Afghan commission at such a late stage would slow the timeline—major decisions would have to await the creation of the Afghan commission and then their consent. A minimum amount of training would be required to ensure that the Afghan commissioners understood what they were approving. This capacity-building requirement added an entirely new assistance requirement that, up to then, had not been budgeted for nor taken into account in the formulation of timelines.

At the same time, EAD acknowledged that the introduction of an Afghan body would provide some advantages. It would increase Afghan "ownership" of the process and it could reduce the costs of the operation by allowing the Afghan commission, rather than the United Nations, to hire staff at Afghan government salaries, rather than the rates that U.N. paid for national staff.

For Perelli this was another policy decision that needed to be examined on its merits. The partnership between the United Nations and an Afghan body could take a number of forms. For example, the U.N. could be fully responsible for some sub-aspects of the process, such as voter education, while the Afghan authority would be responsible for all other elements. Alternatively, the United Nations could provide "shadow" advice on all issues for which the Afghan authority would be otherwise responsible. Perelli's main concern was to avoid a situation where the United Nations would be given responsibility for the election but would have no real authority when it came to major decisions. Given her mandate to maintain global "consistency" for electoral operations, she felt that if the U.N. were not provided with the authority to ensure certain standards, then this lack of authority should be explicit in order to protect to organization and, implicitly, EAD. She therefore requested from Brahimi written confirmation that the planning assumptions had changed.

Brahimi dismissed Perelli's request and began to implement the new arrangements on the ground. Communications between UNAMA and EAD began to break down, with information provided to EAD officials haphazardly by phone from the electoral team in Kabul. But even the electoral team was not fully informed as Brahimi had delegated the task of negotiating the composition and powers of the new Afghan commission to his political staff. The lack of a clear, written statement on what the United Nations' role and responsibilities would be increasingly led to a sense by Austin and his team that this crucial issue was being decided without them even as it would seriously affect their work. Austin informed EAD of his concerns, namely that a number of important issues were being rushed. He felt that Brahimi was riding a momentum of interest in the electoral process that had been generated by the June 10 cabinet meeting, but feared that decisions were being made without their technical consequences being fully understood by the political officers who were now making them.

Bringing the Afghans Back In

Austin was flustered by another decision made by UNAMA, on the recommendation of Brahimi's deputy for political affairs, Jean Arnault, who was increasingly involved in the electoral process. This decision was to delegate the recruitment and payment of Afghan electoral staff to the United Nations Office for Project Support (UNOPS). UNOPS was a self-financing spin-off of UNDP, and was essentially an implementing agency that had more flexibility than either the Secretariat or UNDP in hiring and procurement practices. UNOPS had a huge operation in Afghanistan, spending nearly a million dollars a day on project contracts it had won from the Afghan government, USAID, and other donors. The involvement of UNOPS meant that the project could avoid DPKO's notoriously slow recruitment system[35], a particularly important advantage given the short timeline before the elections, and would be even faster than UNDP. Austin, however, was worried that the involvement of UNOPS would cause him to lose even more managerial control of the operation.

Perelli took these concerns seriously. If Austin was losing operational control, then so was EAD. If EAD had no operational control, it had no leverage to ensure electoral consistency. Perelli, who was traveling at the time but had received the note of EAD's conversation with Austin, requested that it be sent to the Under-Secretaries-General of DPA and DPKO, Prendergast and Jean-Marie Guéhenno respectively. A cover note entitled "Concerns Regarding the Electoral Process in Afghanistan" summed up EAD's misgivings and was signed by EAD's Deputy Director, who explicitly wrote that it was written on Perelli's instructions.

The cover note highlighted that UNAMA had still not responded to cables requesting written confirmation on the change of institutional arrangements. It complained that the process of delineating responsibilities between the proposed Afghan electoral commission and UNAMA had been rushed and that EAD might not even have a chance to look at the final version of the relevant decrees. It argued that the change in assumptions meant further delays in preparing the voluntary budget and hence in securing financing for the operation. It concluded with EAD's concern that the UNAMA electoral unit was not always fully consulted by the UNAMA leadership on matters pertaining to the electoral exercise.

On July 10, UNAMA sent a cable acknowledging that adjustments would have to be made to the electoral plan given the re-emergence at the cabinet meeting of the idea of an Afghan electoral commission. UNAMA described the "joint venture" system it had been developing on the ground. This would be operationally led by UNAMA, but policy responsibilities would be shared by UNAMA and the Afghan Independent Election Commission (AIEC). The mechanism for making policy would be the JEMB, which would be a combination of Afghan election commissioners appointed by Karzai and international experts appointed by Brahimi. The precise responsibilities of the JEMB would be elaborated in a forthcoming presidential decree.

It was precisely those responsibilities on which Perelli insisted on having a say. UNAMA's vague proposals on "joint ventures" were meaningless if the specific responsibilities were not clear. A theological impasse had been reached. For Perelli, her key function in the United Nations system was to keep electoral devils at bay, and details were her tools of exorcism. UNAMA now acted as if those details were beyond her jurisdiction.

The rift between Perelli and Brahimi was made clear to all in a blistering cable on July 14 by Brahimi, who had recieved UNAMA's note of "electoral concerns" in a separate channel from DPKO. Brahimi provided substantive rebuttals to the points made in the note, but was absolutely withering with regard to EAD's lack of consultation with UNAMA leadership before sending its note, which he regarded as unjustified and unacceptable. He then provided, in writing, precisely the clarifications on substance the EAD had been requesting for the previous five weeks. But the damage was done. Brahimi asserted that the UEU did not need advice from EAD. He essentially refused to accept EAD's role as a firewall against expediency. Brahimi was too powerful a figure in the United Nations system, and Afghanistan remained too important an issue for the organization, for Perelli to prevail. The direct link between EAD and the electoral team in UNAMA had been broken.

---

[1]Arturo Santa-Cruz, *International Election Monitoring, Sovereignty and the Western Hemisphere Ideal: The Emergence of an International Ideal* (New York: Routledge, 2005) p. 200.

[2] See Chapter XI and XII of the U.N. Charter on non-self-governing territories and trusteeship territories respectively. Namibia was the emblematic case where the U.N. essentially ran the election. See *The Blue Helmets: A Review of United Nations Peace-Keeping*, Third Edition, (New York: United Nations Department of Public Information, 1996).

[3] Tom J. Farer, "The Promotion of Democracy: International Law and Norms" in *UN Role in Promoting Democracy*, p. 38

[4] Barrington Moore, Jr., *Social Origins of Dictatorship: Lord and Peasant in the Making of the Modern World* (Boston: Beacon Press, 1967) p. 414.

[5] Farer, "The Promotion of Democracy" p. 38.

[6] See United Nations General Assembly resolution 45/150. In the resolution, the Assembly "Affirms the value of the electoral assistance that the United Nations has provided" (operative para. 8) and "Believes that the international community should continue to give serious consideration to ways in which the United Nations can respond to the requests of Member States as they seek to promote and strengthen their electoral institutions and practices" (operative para. 9).

[7] General Assembly resolution 45/151.

[8] General Assembly resolution 46/137.

[9] Farer, "The Promotion of Democracy" p. 52.

[10] Report of the Secretary-General to the 58th session on "Strengthening the role of the United Nations in enhancing the effectiveness of the principle of periodic and genuine elections and the promotion of democratization" (United Nations document A/58/212, para. 11)

[11] Michael G. Smith notes that "On this issue there was common agreement between the UN and the [CNRT] (as well as the core group of interested nations) that to postpone the ballot indefinitely would be to jeopardize it occurring at all." See Michael G. Smith with Maureen Dee, *Peacekeeping in East Timor: The Path to Independence*, (Boulder and London: Lynne Rienner, 2002) p. 44. Smith and Dee also stress EAD's role in organizing the ballot: "But much of the credit for the electoral success went to the excellent preparatory work done by the DPA's Electoral Assistance Division, under the capable direction of Carina Perelli from Uruguay" (p. 43). See also, Ian Martin, *Self Determination in East Timor: The United Nations, the Ballot, and International Observation*, International Peace Academy Occasional Paper Series (Boulder and London: Lynne Rienner, 2001).

[12] Transcript of an interview with U.N. radio (never aired).

[13] This multifaceted problem included the lack of documentation among Afghans, the flows of population during the war, the traditional movements of nomadic populations, and the potential voting rights of the refugee population (which then numbered some five million).

[14] U.N. standards on census-taking prohibit asking direct questions about ethnicity, but census-takers can approximate this information through proxy questions such as the language that one uses most often. In Afghanistan, in particular, language closely correlates with ethnicity, as each of the major ethnic

groups has their own language, even as the all mostly also speak Dari, the common language of administration.

[15] During the transitional period—in other words before a legislature was elected—all laws were promulgated by President Karzai with the agreement of his Cabinet.

[16] In November 2002, the Secretary-General decided to shift the "lead" on Afghanistan from DPA to DPKO. The official reasons for this transfer were that the mission had grown too large for DPA to handle. Unofficially, the reasons are less clear. Brahimi was frustrated at the lack of administrative support he was receiving for UNAMA. DPKO was then responsible for administrative and logistic support to all peace operations, whether they were led by DPA or DPKO. Brahimi felt that if the mission was placed under DPKO, the administrative support to UNAMA would improve.

[17] See for example, International IDEA, *Electoral System Design: the New International IDEA Handbook* (Stockholm: IDEA, 2006), and Pippa Norris, *Electoral Engineering: Voting Rules and Political Behavior* (Cambridge: Cambridge University Press, 2004).

[18] From Canto VI of "Choruses from 'The Rock'" in T.S. Eliot, *The Complete Plays and Poems: 1909-1950* (New York: Harcourt, Brace & World, 1971) p. 106.

[19] Huntington makes the following perceptive point concerning Americans in particular: "When an American thinks about the problem of government building, he directs himself not to the creation of authority and the accumulation of power but rather to the limitation of authority and the division of power. Asked to design a government, he comes up with a written constitution, bill or rights, separation of powers, checks and balances, federalism, regular elections, competitive parties—all excellent devices for limiting government. The Lockean American is so fundamentally anti-government that he identifies government with restrictions on government. Confronted with the need to design a political system which will maximize power and authority, he has no ready answer." Huntington, *Political Order*, p. 7. Zalmay Khalilzad, the U.S. Ambassador to Afghanistan during the constitution-drafting process, described this effect in practice: "At the Constitutional Loya Jirga, delegates were more concerned with creating an effective national government than they were with curtailing its power." Zalmay Khalilzad, "Lessons from Afghanistan and Iraq" Journal of Democracy, Vol. 21, No.3, July 2010, p. 44.

[20] Eric C. Bjornlund, *Beyond Free and Fair: Monitoring Elections and Building Democracy*. (Woodrow Wilson Center Press: Washington, D.C., 2004) pp. 96-97. The United Nations increasingly, uses the terms "credible and transparent" rather than "free and fair," under the logic that an election that is not entirely fair but that is still accepted by the population and political actors is sufficient for its legitimacy. (Although, "free and fair" has so engrained itself in the democratization discourse that is relflexively reverted to as a convenient shorthand, especially by senior officials.) In fact, "credible and transparent" and "free and fair" should not be seen as opposing concepts. Rather, the first emphasizes political realities and the second emphasizes ideal qualities. The idea of credibility, rather than "free and fair" also better reflects the language in

United Nations political rights documents. Article 25 of the International Covenant on Civil and Political Rights, for example, refers to "genuine and periodic elections which shall be by universal and equal suffrage and shall be held by secret ballot, guaranteeing the free expression of the will of the electors." In a competing school of thought, however, much has been written on what makes an election literally "free and fair"; see: Inter-Parliamentary Council of the Inter-Parliamentary Union, Declaration on Criteria for Free and Fair Elections, Paris, 26 March 1994; Guy S. Goodwin-Gill, *Free and Fair Elections: International Law and Practice*, new expanded edition, (Geneva: Inter-Parliamentary Union, 2006); Jorgen Elklit and Palle Svensson, "What Makes Elections Free and Fair?" Journal of Democracy, vol. 8, 1997, pp 32-46; Elklit, "Free and Fair Elections" in Richard Rose (ed.) *International Encyclopaedia of Elections* (Washington, D.C.: CQ Press, 2000).

[21] The political party stigma was a widespread perception in the post-Bonn period. The theory was that political parties in Afghanistan would be associated by Afghans with the "parties," known in Dari as *tanzims*, that had conducted the civil war, in particular the seven Peshawar-based parties that had been responsible for most of the fighting. This perception had a great effect on the determination of the electoral system, and is discussed in much greater detail in Chapter 11.

[22]United Nations document S/2003/333, March 18, 2003, paras. 15-18.

[23]United Nations document S/2003/333, March 18, 2003, paras. 15-18.

[24] Adopted on March 28, 2003. The Council's endorsement allowed the Secretariat to request supplemental funding of about.$ 13 million for the new electoral unit.

[25] In 1984, the United States Congress unilaterally voted to reduce its contribution to the United Nations general budget from 25 percent to 20 percent. The United Nations viewed assessments as legally binding and therefore considered the difference to be a debt. But since the organization could not take out loans, the practical effect of Congress' action was very real and very limiting. Secretary-General Perez de Cuellar had to implement a hiring freeze and essentially maintain a "zero growth" budget. See Joachim Müller, ed., *Reforming the United Nations: The Quiet Revolution* (The Hague; Kluwer Law International, 2001) p. 26, for a brief discussion of these reform efforts.

[26] The 1999 Helms-Biden law adopted by the U.S. Senate required, in exchange for the U.S. paying its arrears, that the U.S. contribution to the regular budget be reduced from 25 percent to 22 percent, and that its contribution to the peacekeeping assessed budget be reduced from 30 to 25 percent. Eventually, in 2001, the U.S. agreed to repay its arrears following a regular budget contribution that was reduced to 22 percent, as in the Helms-Biden law, and the assessed contribution at 26.5 percent—slightly higher than what was required in Helms-Biden (and in a 1994 law that said that the U.S. should not pay more than 25 percent of U.N. peacekeeping) but which was ultimately accepted by Congress. During the George W. Bush administration, the zero-growth principle was essentially abandoned, in part because of the perceived need for the organization to become more involved in Afghanistan and Iraq. See Brett D.

Schaefer, "Time to Reign in the U.N.'s Budget", Heritage Foundation's Backgrounder, No. 2368, Washington D.C., February 3, 2010.

[27] This figure was determined by looking at the per-voter cost of analogous post-conflict elections and multiplying it by the estimated number of voters in Afghanistan. This, obviously, was a very rough way of estimating the total cost, given in particular that the number of voters in Afghanistan was a wild guess.

[28] UNDP was already managing, in Afghanistan, three trust funds that paid for the salaries of the national police, reconstruction activities, and the payment of government salaries.

[29] UNDP was the result of a merger between the Special United Nations Fund for Economic Development and the Expanded Program of Technical Assistance. The merger married a technical branch of the United Nations that had a small financing capacity with a fund that had been established at the behest of the poorer countries but had little implementation capacity.

[30] See "Information on United Nations system technical cooperation expenditures, 2003, Report of the Executive Board of the United Nations Development Programme and of the United Nations Population Fund," United Nations document DP/2004/37, para. 11.

[31] The name would be changed to the UNAMA Electoral Component in September 2003; perhaps the consonantless UEU sounded too much like wind blowing through emptiness.

[32] The United Nations Volunteers (UNV) program was created by the U.N. General Assembly in 1971. UNVs, who receive a stipend but no salary, are supposed to be technical specialists who lend a few years of their lives to the U.N. to support its activities. The program has, however, also become an entry-point into the U.N. system for many staff members. Given the UNVs have become the infantry of U.N. electoral projects that require large number of internationals; the use of UNVs keeps the overall cost of the project down.

[33] The electoral team would soon discover other complicating population issues besides internally-displaced peoples. For example, the return of refugees in the first years after the fall of the Taliban regime had been significant, but there was no reliable data on where they had resettled. Second, there is a significant nomadic population in Afghanistan that migrated on yearly cycles. They needed to be tracked and their total population identified. How the electoral planners dealt with these issues is described in more detail in the following chapter.

[34] Karzai was referring to President Burhannudin Rabbani's holding on to power in 1992. See also footnote 17 in Chapter 12.

[35] This weakness had been pointed out by Brahimi himself, when he chaired a panel on peacekeeping operations following his departure from the Afghan scene in 1999. Brahimi's report had noted that, "To date, the Secretariat has been unable to identify, recruit and deploy suitably qualified civilian personnel in substantive and support functions either at the right time or in the numbers required. Currently, about 50 percent of field positions in substantive areas and up to 40 percent of the positions in administrative and logistics areas are vacant, in missions that were established six months to one year ago and remain in desperate need of the requisite specialists." See Brahimi Report, para.

127. In testimony to the U.N. Fifth Committee, which deals with budgetary matters, Dileep Nair, the Under-Secretary-General for Internal Oversight Services, noted in 2004 that the average time of recruitment for peacekeeping operations was 347 days. See United Nations document GA/AB/3616 (Press Release on the Fifth Committee's 58th General Assembly meeting, May 13, 2004).

5
Budgets and Donors

Brahimi and UNAMA had prevailed on the modalities of electoral management. On July 26, 2003, the Joint Electoral Management Body (JEMB) was established by two separate presidential decrees. The first created the Afghan Independent Election Commission (AIEC) that Karzai had proposed during the July 10 cabinet meeting; the second created the JEMB itself, which was the combination of the six Afghan members of the AIEC and five international commissioners appointed by the SRSG.[1] Given that decisions in the JEMB would be made by consensus, the international commissioners would have a de facto veto over decisions. This was an important safeguard that Austin welcomed, particularly given the lack of electoral experience of the Afghan commissioners.[2] On the other hand, it was unfortunate that the selection of the Afghan commissioners had not been particularly transparent. Instead, instead they were the product of negotiations between Karzai and Brahimi according to the required arithmetic of Afghan commissions.[3] Finally, the tight timeline now did not allow much time to try to train the commissioners on election basics.

By this time, the UNAMA Electoral Component (UEC), heady by Austin was almost fully-staffed. The unit had been assigned a compound on Jalalabad Road, on the outskirts of Kabul, where offices were being hastily built. Per Arnault's recommendation in June, UNOPS had been tasked with supporting the Afghan commissioners, who insisted on being housed in a more central location in Kabul. A building was found for them, but it was a half-hour drive in Kabul's heavy traffic from the UEC.

The immediate problems facing the JEMB were not yet the big questions of policy and planning, but the intricate management challenges that resulted from the lack of intra-operability within the U.N. system and from the new requirement of supporting the unexpected Afghan partners. Karzai had created his commission, but he expected the international community to fund and equip it.

Austin continued to harbor reservations about the role of the Afghans and how it would affect his own responsibilities. He was a man of great moral authority and credibility, which he had demonstrated in Cambodia and South Africa. He had the demeanor of a kind professor and sometimes appeared overwhelmed by the challenges facing the Afghan electoral process, especially compared to the meager resources at his disposal and the diminishing authority granted to him. He was committed to holding elections of a certain quality and he had invested his professional reputation behind this goal. But the more the electoral team learned about their environment, the more unattainable this goal appeared. And if the Afghan environment was difficult enough, it seemed that the decisions being taken by the mission were designed to make it even harder. Despite the fact that Brahimi had personally selected Austin, even that relationship began to crack. Brahimi and Arnault were under growing pressure from the international community, and the U.S. in particular, to demonstrate progress on registration, which was scheduled to start in October 2003. They began to interpret Austin's careful enumeration of problems as a lack of will to solve them. At the same time, their own failure to properly understand the obstacles facing Austin's operation hindered a coordinated, rational, and informed process of finding ways to overcome them.

Neither was Austin always well-served by his management team. The challenges seemed initially to overwhelm most of the section heads, none of whom were particularly dynamic in seeking solutions. Many of the electoral team had been pulled from the recent 2001 elections in East Timor. They were slow to recognize the differences between Timor and Afghanistan as well as between the United Nations mission in East Timor and UNAMA.

Electoral experts are a peculiar breed of international technocrat. They tend to exhibit a defensiveness about their work that can be perceived as arrogance. This was summed up by the attitude of one of the new experts who, arriving for the first time in Kabul from East Timor remarked, "elections are going to be the main game in town, and the political people will have to get out of the way, just like in Timor." The difference in Afghanistan was that the "political people," especially in the regions, still tended to be the civil affairs officers recruited by Vendrell, who had close ties to local leaders and intimate knowledge of the country. UNAMA's new electoral officers tried create a necessary perception of independence and impartiality from UNAMA by establishing distinct relationship with local leaders, bypassing UNAMA's political officers. Local Afghan powerbrokers did not understand the need for electoral impartiality. Their currency was trust, and hence they continued to rely on the political officers in UNAMA as their main interlocutors on electoral issues as on any other issues. The disfunctionality of the relationship between UNAMA's electoral and political officers began to have consequences. Not only were electoral officers deprived of valuable insights from those on the ground who understood the situation far more deeply, but the dominating intermediary position of the political staff meant that the electoral component was not able to enjoy a perception of autonomy from the political office, which would be required when operations really began.

The need for such a perception was understood by neither the local authorities nor the UNAMA political officers, who jealously guarded their relationships. At the same time, the electoral team underestimated the amount of sensitization that was required to make their point. The UNAMA political office was actively, explicitly, publicly, and properly trying to advance the effectiveness of the Karzai administration; this was its mandate. If Karzai were to run for president, which was nearly a certainty, there would inevitably be a perception of a conflict of interest between the part of the United Nations that was actively working to support Karzai's administration and the part of the United Nations that was supposed to organize an election in which Karzai and his opponents would compete on a level playing field. It was to avoid this perception that EAD and the UEC had tried to separate the electoral part of UNAMA from the rest of the mission.

There was a further intra-U.N. relationship that was problematic. This was between the electoral unit and UNAMA administration. In any United Nations mission, "administration" or "mission support" is responsible for the staffing, procurement, and logistics required to run a mission, from air operations to air conditioners. Administration staff were perhaps looked down upon by the so-called "substantive" professionals, but their domination of the myriad and complex series of rules in the United Nations system gave the administrative staff a power to make life agreeable or hellish for political officers, and a power to make something happen or not happen.

The arrogance of some UEC staff-members combined with its own weak logistics section infuriated UNAMA's administration chiefs. UEC's demands tended to be vague but always urgent. The UEC logistics staff expected the administration to ignore the other mission priorities to cater to electoral needs.

In any circumstance, the United Nations system is not geared towards flexibility and speed. Decades of perceived corruption and cronyism have led to the creation of procurement and recruitment rules that are so complex that they almost must be broken in some way in order for anything to happen in time. Every "reform" process seemed to have added to the complexity of administrative arrangements and undermined the goals of reform. The fact that administration managers are deemed personally liable for precise adherence to these rules makes those managers extremely conservative in their interpretation of the rules. The system only really works when there is a detailed planning process that anticipates as many problems as possible, the setting up of a constant feedback loop, close communications between all actors, and the preparation of contingency plans. None of this was happening in Kabul in the summer of 2003. The UEC had neither provided a detailed plan nor demonstrated a bureaucratic understanding of the need to get the administration on their side.

The breakdown of this relationship was revealed in the almost comical attempt to set up the data center in the UEC compound. The registration plan called for all registration data, which would be recorded by hand, to be returned to Kabul and inputted into a computer database. The data center where these inputs would be made would require about 80 computers being operated simultaneously and constantly. This in turn required the construction of a dedicated building in the electoral compound that had to be maintained within a tight range of temperatures so that the machines and the data would not be damaged. The operating environment was particularly important in Kabul, where winter temperatures are below freezing and summer temperatures are above one hundred degrees Fahrenheit. As the launch of the registration approached in the fall of 2003, it was important to ensure, for both the computers and the staff, that the heating system was installed. But problem followed problem as the electoral logistics staff complained that UNAMA administration weren't giving them priority, and the UNAMA administration complained that they lacked necessary information from the UEC's logistics unit. The heating units were finally fully operational in mid-February 2004, as winter was ending. Then the battle began for the air-conditioners.

Preliminary Budgets

The question of administrative support was further complicated by the non-UNAMA entities now involved in the election. The core international planning and management functions would be carried out by the UEC, financed from UNAMA's supplemental budget secured in May, and supported logistically by DPKO. Expanded international staff required by the UEC would be funded from the voluntary budget under the UNDP trust fund. UNDP would therefore be responsible for the hiring, procurement, and logistical support of this expanded international section, which worked alongside the DPKO-supported team. The Afghan counterpart institution, the AIEC, would be funded from voluntary contributions that came through the UNDP trust fund, but would be supported logistically by UNOPS. In other words, UNDP would transfer funds to UNOPS to carry out the recruitment, procurement, and logistics required by the Afghan side.[4]

In mid-July, the UEC estimated that $55 million would be required for the expanded UNDP-supported international component and $22.2 million for UNOPS to support the Afghan component of the project. Each of the main UN entities involved had their own administrative systems and their own reporting lines. Making these components work together would be a major challenge. As Brahimi once told the Security Council, with exasperation and wit, "I thought that dealing with the Afghan tribes was difficult, but that was easy compared to dealing with the tribes of the U.N."

The challenges to making all of this work were often petty and always exasperating. For example, most of the expanded international staff members were to be sent to the regional offices to support the registration activities. Given that they were hired by UNDP, they were hired under different conditions from the heads of the regional electoral offices, which were UNAMA staff. This meant, among other things, that their Occasional Recuperation Break (ORB)[5] cycle was once every six weeks, as opposed to once every 12 weeks for UNAMA staff.[6] Then there was the problem of who was responsible for the induction of new staff—they were formally UNDP staff, but would be working under UNAMA's authority. Were their radios supposed to be issued by UNDP or by UNAMA? Logically, UNDP should be responsible, but UNDP programmed their radios differently from UNAMA. But if UNAMA issued the radios, how could it ensure that it could recover them at the end of the mission, since UNDP controlled the payroll of the staff from which the costs of missing equipment is usually deducted? Finally, there was the problem of how to pay UNDP-hired staff in the field for their local expenses. UNDP did not have any field offices outside of Kabul, but UNAMA administration officers in the regional offices were prohibited by UNDP's rules to issue cash to UNDP staff.

A steering committee involving all of the actors was established in August 2003, and a working group was assigned by the committee to resolve these issues. After painstaking negotiations, what emerged was a complex series of "treaties" between the various organizations on handling the multitude of areas where cooperation was required. As is frequently the case in such circumstances, the personalities involved were crucial, and on this score the operation finally ran into some good luck. UNAMA's head of operations was Kiplin Perkins, an American with a military background and a long history with the United Nations. Perkins made it clear to his team—already antagonized by the UEC's arrogance and laziness on the logistical side—that the registration process was a key United Nations mandate and everyone was responsible for making it a success. Many in UNAMA administration had felt that the introduction of UNDP into the equation made the electoral process a "UNDP project" and therefore their responsibilities ended with the servicing of the UEC. Perkins impressed upon them that their objective was the registration of voters and the holding of elections, not merely servicing the UEC.

The project manager for UNDP's side of the operation was Jerome Leyraud, a Frenchman with a private sector background. Leyraud had handled logistics for elections in East Timor. He had a manic capacity for work and an almost monastic patience with bureaucratic frustrations. He knew UNDP regulations thouroughly, but was not a career UNDP staffer and was also dedicated to the larger goal. UNOPS was run by Gary Helseth, an American who had grown up in Afghanistan as a teenager, where his father was a diplomat. Helseth spoke Dari and was unafraid to travel to the remotest regions. He was also, perhaps to a fault, willing to overlook bureaucratic pettiness for the sake of the common objective of holding elections. The steering committee met regularly to resolve those problems that had not been anticipated, and allowed the project to begin to move into its operational phase with greater managerial coherence.

Registration of Exceptional Populations

The June plan for registration was, as described, vague and unreflective of Afghanistan's many complicating factors. As the months went on, new information was processed and the plan began to more accurately address the complexities of Afghanistan's geographical, infrastructural, political and institutional environments. The creation of the JEMB had been messy, but having Afghan input in the planning process was a benefit.

Planning could only go so far without having a legal framework. On November 11, 2003, Karzai finally issued the necessary decree on registration, which had been drafted with inputs from the JEMB. The decree stated that "the United Nations Assistance Mission in Afghanistan (UNAMA) shall conduct the voter registration process, under the oversight of the Joint Electoral Management Body." It set the voting age at 18, stated that a voter's card would be issued, provided for a public exhibition of the provisional list, and allowed for observation of the process by political parties. It also stated that the "registration of qualified women who wish to register shall be separate from men." ("Qualified" here meant women who met the legal requirements of being a voter.)

Austin's planning team now had to estimate the number of eligible voters. The last census, in 1979, had estimated the Afghan population at around 15 million, but this was something of an extrapolation since the census had not been completed. As always in Afghanistan, there was no real data, only combinations of guesswork, rumor, and politically-influenced conjectures and assertions. Even if the exact population size were known, it would have to be broken down into those who were above 18 years old and those who were below. In a country subjected to a quarter-century of war, it was extremely difficult to estimate the shape of the population pyramid. Back-of-the-envelope calculations in EAD led to a population estimate of around 21 million, and a voter population of around 10.5 million. This was nothing more than a very rough planning assumption.

The registration of women created an immense logistical problem. The separate registration required by the decree made sense given Afghan cultural sensitivities, but it meant that literate female registrars would have to be identified and then trained. No one had any idea if there were enough literate women, given both the effects of war and of the Taliban's policy against educating girls. Also, the educated women who were available tended to be from urban centers. Their ability to travel depended on the consent of their families, which often came only if provision was made for a male family member to travel with them.

The next problem was the specificity of registration information. In a perfect world, when a voter is registered, he or she is assigned to an individual polling station. This greatly simplifies the planning of an election by allowing planners to know exactly how many ballots are required per polling station, while improving an election's quality by making it much easier to control against multiple voting. The utter paucity of information in Afghanistan about who lived where meant that, from the beginning, it would be impossible to assign registrants to polling places. In fact, the decision of where to locate polling places would end up being a by-product of the registration process.

Another significant planning problem was the weather. The central and eastern parts of Afghanistan are snow-bound in winter, precisely when the registration process would need to take place if elections were to be held the following June. The problems of accessibility did not end with the winter: in the spring, snowmelt flooded rivers, closing off fording spots (there were few bridges), and creating a separate accessibility challenge lasting into the late spring.

A fourth challenge was the need to register "vulnerable populations". These were "Kuchis" (nomads), refugees, returnees, and internally-displaced peoples (IDPs). The particularity of these populations in electoral terms was that there was no guarantee that they would vote in the same place where they registered. Since the register had to include at least a provincial affiliation for potential legislative elections, they had to somehow be linked to a province or given a special category. The UEC's original registration plan had developed basic strategies for each of these groups. For example, returning refugees were normally processed through the 11 United Nations High Commission for Refugees (UNHCR) encashment centers around the country, where they were given identity cards and assistance packages to help them resettle. The United Nations would establish registration sites within these centers to allow them to register to vote at the same time they were processed as returning refugees. Similarly, there were an estimated 350,000 IDPs, of whom 200,000 lived in established camps, while the rest were integrated within communities. The latter would be registered as part of the community with which they were living, though they would be asked if they intended to move before the election date, in which case their registration card would contain a mark indicating their IDP status. IDPs living in camps would be registered with the name of the camp as the name of their "village."

The nomadic Kuchi population was estimated at two to three million. They moved in generally predictable patterns according to the seasons, herding livestock. Usually their migration was from the highlands to the lowlands during the fall, and back to the highlands in the spring. The precise pattern was, however, unpredictable as it was affected by security and climatic conditions. Some migrated into and out of Pakistan, while others remained within Afghanistan's borders; still others had begun to establish semi-permanent settlements, though they were more prone than other Afghans to migrate if climate conditions became unfavorable. For Kuchis, the plan was to deploy mobile teams to locate and register these groups, and to indicate in their registration documents their nomadic status, allowing them to vote in the province where they happened to be during the election.

All of these were necessarily imperfect solutions, but were deemed sufficient for a first election. The main problem was the possibility that a non-indigenous population could skew the results of a legislative election in any given province. But since the actual date of the election had not been set, it was impossible to even guess who would be where and when. The only solution was to place these groups in a special category and allow them to vote wherever they were at the moment of the election.

The refugee population outside of Afghanistan posed an even greater challenge. Since nobody knew, at the time of registration, whether there would be a provision in the electoral law to allow them to vote, there was no provision for refugee registration in the original plan.[7] At the same time, the numbers of refugees in neighboring Pakistan and Iran was so significant—an estimated five million[8]—and the international precedents for holding out-of-country voting were well-established, that there was some pressure from Afghan and international interest groups to allow them to vote in their countries of residence.[9] The planning team ignored this element in June, assuming that if a decision was later taken to allow out-of-country voting, a separate registration process would have to take place with a separate budget and a separate plan.

The Role of the Afghan Commissioners

The Afghan members of the JEMB had not been intimately involved in the technical aspects of the plan because the basic planning parameters had been set before the creation of the AIEC. They began to assert themselves, however, during the preparation phase. This proactive attitude was positive in that it demonstrated they were taking interest in and ownership of the project. One of the commissioners, Suleiman Yari, the old Hazara former Senator, often rejected international advice by saying that, "The owner of a house always knows the house better than the visitors." The AIEC's decision-making process, however, was extremely slow and influenced by cultural traditions. For example the opinions of Zakim Shah, the Chairman, and Yari, as the oldest men, were always given greater weight given traditional Afghan respect for "white beards." The status-conscious Afghan Commissioners were also focused, almost inordinately, on getting their offices set up and ensuring that they all had cars and drivers. This process was slower than it should have been due to the lack of voluntary contributions to the UNDP trust fund and to the expanding demands of the Commissioners. These demands began to compete with other demands of the process, such as the procurement of vehicles or the hiring of local staff to actually carry out the registration.

The highly deliberative pace of the Afghan Commissioners in approving the most basic of decisions began to threaten the tempo of the project. The Commissioners were particularly focused on personnel issues and spent their first several weeks approving the layout of the application format for potential registrars. They also wanted to personally review all applications for the registration staff, the numbers of which would be in the tens of thousands. The internationals, under constant pressure from Brahimi and Arnault to demonstrate progress, had been shoe-horned into an impossible position; they had been instructed by Brahimi and Arnault to work with the Afghan body, but they were blamed when things were delayed because of the commissioners' desire to not merely act as an Afghan rubber stamp for international decisions.

Donor Difficulties

By early September, the electoral components of UNAMA's regional offices were staffed and were able to suggest refinements to the operational plan down to the regional and provincial levels. A great deal of progress had been made, but it was still progress on planning alone. Implementation required money, and in the fall of 2003, hardly any money had been deposited into the UNDP trust-fund.

Clausewitz famously remarked that no plan survives contact with the enemy; the Afghan voter registration plan was not even surviving contact with its allies. The first problem was a disconnect between the political representatives of embassies, who make the decisions to support a given project, and the treasury officials, who ensure that the money reaches the project. Treasury officials work to a different set of priorities; political "emergencies" do not really concern them. This meant that there was no way of knowing when money promised by diplomats would actually be provided.

The electoral team began to classify the flow of money into three different phases. "Pledges" referred to the sums of moneys that diplomats had promised, often orally; commitments referred to signed letters saying that the money would actually be provided; and "disbursements" referred to money that was actually in the project account and could be spent. According to its rules, the United Nations could not spend money that it did not have, nor could it borrow from other sources. Therefore, the issuing of contracts could only be based on disbursements—the commitments and pledges were worthless in practical terms. It took, on average, three to four weeks for pledges to become commitments, and another two to three weeks before the money was actually deposited in the UNDP trust fund. Given the several weeks it took to ship goods or travel new staff, a lag of two to three months had to be assumed for planning purposes between the pledging of funds for a certain end and its obtainment.

Another complication in funding was the tendency of donor's to earmark their pledges for specific uses. Some donors required that their funds only be used for paying salaries, not for purchasing equipment, or vice versa. Others required that their monies be used for the rental but not the purchase of equipment, or vice versa. Others had time limits on their funds—for example that they had to be spent before the end of their fiscal year. It fell to Leyraud to juggle these demands and ensure that all donor conditions were satisfied, at least ex post facto, and the project received what it really needed when it was needed. Since money is fungible, this sometimes required spending it on what was needed and hoping that enough un-earmarked funds would arrive at a later date to justify a postdated accounting of earmarked funds. It was an additional frustration to the project managers that, while the lack of donor support was the main obstacle to demonstrating results, Brahimi and Arnault considered this very real constraint to be an excuse for inaction.

In August 2003, Austin and his Chief of Operations, Peter Spelman, met with Brahimi and Arnault to explain why, due to the lack of funds, it was unlikely that any real registration would begin until January 2004. "How much do you need?" Brahimi asked them. "Three million? I'll get it from Ashraf Ghani." Ghani, a western-educated technocrat who was then the Afghan finance minister had an excellent relationship with Brahimi. Brahimi turned back to the electoral team. "There. You have your three million. Start hiring people." In this case, Brahimi's strength as a diplomat was his weakness as an administrator: he compelled people to say "yes" to him. Nobody had the courage to tell Brahimi that staff could not be hired on the basis of a promise of three million dollars that he claimed would be provided by the Afghan finance minister.

Leyraud inevitably bore the brunt of the criticisms from Brahimi's office. He returned to his spreadsheets, trying to reconfigure expenditures so that the project would get what it needed while satisfying the donors' specific conditions on how the money they had already provided had been spent. Given that Afghanistan was everyone's priority, it seemed absurd that donors' conditions and the project's needs were so frequently in conflict.

Perhaps because it had assumed that the political interests of donor countries would drive their financial contributions, one of the UEC's major weaknesses was its diffidence towards the donor community. From the start, it overestimated the understanding within the donor community about the importance of the registration process. As it turned out, donors needed to be convinced that a registration process was essential to the election before they released funds for it. Diplomats in Kabul tended to be, even more than the UNAMA political section, slaves to the Bonn calendar, and many felt that if the delays in the registration risked delaying the electoral date, the solution was to skip the registration process. The diplomatic community clung for too long to the strange logic that if elections—any sort of elections—were not held in June 2004, the entire Bonn process would be in jeopardy. It was as if they believed that everything that had been achieved up to then—the transitional administration, the Emergency Loya Jirga, the ongoing constitutional process—would evaporate if elections were held on July 1 instead of June 30. The failure of the UEC to communicate early and effectively the political and technical reasons for registering voters cost valuable months in terms of securing funds, and allowed the fetishism over the Bonn timeline to endure for far too long.

Confusion—whether from an inability of diplomats to follow the process, or from poor communications by the U.N.—led to some almost comical mishaps. For example, in mid-October 2003, Arnault informed the registration project's steering committee that the Americans had informed him that they were under the impression they had fully funded the voter registration project. When Leyraud replied that this was far from true—hardly any American money had been provided—it was discovered that the U.S. embassy in Kabul had confused the registration of delegates for the Constitutional Loya Jirga with the registration of voters for the election. Unfortunately, the mistake had been passed on to the Europeans, who therefore saw no reason to mobilize funds because the U.S. had supposedly already paid for registration. Silliness like this added more weeks to the funding process, adding to everyone's anxiety about when registration would start.

By late October, around $9 million had been deposited with UNDP. This was not enough to fund the increase in operational tempo that was needed. The registration steering committee immediately faced a difficult decision. Should the entire amount be used to begin procuring the equipment that was needed—especially vehicles (Russian jeeps), aircraft, and registration kits[10]— and hope that money to hire staff would come soon afterwards? Or should the funds be split among jeeps, kits and staff, and then order additional jeeps, kits and staff when more funds arrived. The second solution would cost the project more in the long run, because it would forgo savings achieved through bulk purchases, but it would ensure that some fully equipped and staffed teams existed to start registration by December 1. According to Leyraud's calculations, the $9 million would support 70 registration teams, but these would have to shut down in mid-February if no further funds were received. According to the plan, 305 registration teams would be required register the estimated 10.5 million voters in time for a June election. In the end, the conservative decision was taken to use the $9 million to field 70 fully-equipped teams, while everyone crossed their fingers that more funds would be provided before mid-February. The anticipated uncertainties of the voluntary funding modality had begun to manifest themselves in a very concrete way.

These uncertainties were somewhat allayed when UNDP agreed to loan $11 million of its own funds against future donor financing. With this decision, things began to move more quickly. The registration kits arrived, registration teams were recruited and trained, and the civic education campaign got off the ground. After months of planning, the project was finally becoming visible.

---

[1] The AIEC was chaired by Zakim Shah, an Afghan technocrat who had previously been the Deputy Minister of Finance. The other representatives were Faqir Bahram, Zahida Ansari, Gothai Khawrai, Qaeym Qudbuddin, and Suleyman Yari. (Ansari and Khawrai were women). The international members of the JEMB were, originally, Reginald Austin (Zimbabwe), Ray Kennedy (USA), Barbara Reinhardus (Canada), Irfan Abdul Rahman (Madagascar) and Maarten Halff (The Netherlands).

[2] Suleiman Yari, the oldest member, had been elected to the Afghan legislature during the "New Democracy" period in the 1960s.

[3] This deal-making can be unfavorably compared with the transparent process of open applications and vetting by an independent international committee that was used, a year later, to select the electoral commission in Iraq.

[4] Except under very specific circumstances, which did not obtain for the Afghan electoral operation, UNOPS is not allowed to raise funds directly from donors.

[5] This is essentially a rest-and-recreation break of one week that U.N. staff members in difficult missions are entitled to. The SRSG of each mission sets the periodicity of the break but the U.N. agencies in the same mission area do not necessarily have to follow the SRSG's decision.

[6] It also did not help that UNDP paid for the travel of its staff members when they went on ORB, whereas UNAMA staff had to pay for their own travel. In fact, UNDP conditions of service were significantly better than DPKO/UNAMA conditions, which raised understandable resentments among the staff of the two organizations performing the same work.

[7] In a review of postconflict elections, Jeff Fischer found that in the seven cases where refugees made up a significant amount of the electorate (Namibia, Western Sahara, Angola, Cambodia, Mozambique, Bosnia and Herzegovina, Liberia, Eastern Slavonia, and Kosovo), in almost every case repatriation, whether organized or spontaneous, preceded voting. See Jeff Fischer, "Elections and Peace Operations: Analysis and Case Studies, 1989-2000" IFES Center for Transitional and Postconflict Governance, Washington, D.C., March 2005.

[8] A 2007 Congressional Research Service report, basing itself on UNHCR statistics, noted the return of 2.1 million Afghan refugees in 2002 alone—1.7

million from Pakistan and 400,000 from Iran in 2002 alone. A total of 3.6 million had returned by the time of the presidential elections in 2004. Nonetheless, the report noted that 2.46 million refugees remained in Pakistan and 900,000 in Iran. This meant that the original estimates of 5 million refugees understated the reality, and in fact there was probably a total of around 8 million refugees in those two countries, with much of the difference probably accountable to births within the refugee population during their two decades of exile. See Rhoda Margesson, "Afghan Refugees: Current Status and Future Prospects" Washington, D.C.: Congressional Research Service, January 26, 2007.

[9] There is no worldwide standard practice regarding out-of-country voting. As International IDEA points out in a publication produced in 2007, attention to out-of-country voting is a recent phenomenon that "derives from the worldwide political changes of the 1990s." The study also notes that "there is currently no likelihood of general, global, common electoral stardards or guidelines being developed" in this area. See *Voting From Abroad: The International IDEA Handbook*, (Stockholm and Mexico City: International IDEA, 2007) pp. 1-3. For a more skeptical look, see Claudio Lopes Guerra, "Should Expatriates Vote?" *Journal of Political Philosophy*, vol. 13, issue 2, June 2005.

[10] These kits contained the cameras, papers, glue, scissors, laminators etc. to make the low-tech registration cards.

6
Security and the Baghdad Effect

Afghanistan's worsening security situation had always hung menacingly over the planning process. The defeat of the Taliban in late 2001, which had initially appeared decisive, looked rather less so in late 2003. Analysts began to refer to the emergence of a "neo-Taliban"[1] movement, though it was understood that part of the increasing insecurity was generated by factions dissatisfied with the Bonn Agreement and not necessary ideologically aligned with the Taliban.

The renewed violence was particularly evident in the Pashtun south, where the sense of political marginalization was especially strong. Another source of insecurity was Gulbuddin Hekmatyar's Hezb-i-Islami movement. Hekmatyar had been one of the major Mujaheddin figures of the 1980s and a key rival to Massoud's Northern Alliance in the 1990s. He fought against the Taliban between 1994 and 1996. But when the Taliban took Kabul in 1996, Hekmatyar fled to Iran. He returned to Afghanistan after the Bonn Agreement, but, opposing the presence of foreign troops in Afghanistan, he allied himself with the Taliban in 2002. Since then he maintained a skirmishing presence, especially in the east, northeast, and areas adjacent to Kabul.[2] Jalalludin Haqqani, a minister in the former Taliban government, and a leader of the Zadran tribe, located around Khost, also joined the fight against the government in a loose alliance with the Taliban.

Another source of instability was fighting between groups that formally accepted the Bonn Agreement but that jockeyed for position within the government. The governor of Herat, Ismail Khan, was engaged in a simmering conflict against local rivals to retain total control over the lucrative border city, through which about 80 percent of Afghan imports were then flowing. A similar rivalry was playing out in the northern city of Mazar-i-Sharif, between Generals Rashid Dostum and Mohammed Atta, both of whom pledged allegiance to the Bonn Agreement while continuing a pre-Bonn struggle to control the city. The fact that the government and international community had some influence over the protagonists of these grievances, however, made it possible to address them and mitigate their consequences.[3]

In October 2002, in a report to the Security Council, the Secretary-General cited attacks that had occurred against members of the Afghan Transitional Administration and the United Nations, including a September assassination attempt against Karzai himself in Kandahar, as evidence of "a renewed vitality and commitment on the part of those groups that are hostile to the peace process."[4] By mid-2003, at a time when the planning of the registration effort was well-advanced, the situation had worsened. In a report issued in July, the Secretary-General referred to "terrorists said to be aligned with the Taliban, al-Qa'idah and Gulbiddin [sic] Hekmatyar have stepped up their activities."[5] For the first time, Hekmatyar was described as having joined forces with the Taliban—an indication that the so-called neo-Taliban were becoming a viable force. Ominously, the Secretary-General reported that "attacks against the assistance community have intensified significantly over the past three months, jeopardizing the safety of both international and national staff."[6] In March 2003, an international staff member of the International Committee of the Red Cross was killed in Uruzgan province. This was the first assassination of a foreign aid worker in Afghanistan since 1998.

A pattern of attacks began to appear, centered on the Taliban's former capital, Kandahar. By the summer of 2003, it appeared that the insurgent movement was attempting to surround the city, often referred to as its "spiritual capital," and seal it off from the rest of the country. To the northeast of Kandahar, they were attempting to block the road to Uruzgan, the home base of Mullah Omar, the spiritual head and military leader of the Taliban, who was still alive and widely presumed to be living in the Pakistani city of Quetta.[7]

Most of the attacks were carried out on the main roads. The planners of the registration operation were, however, acutely aware that the registration teams, when deployed, would present tantalizing targets for the Taliban. It was feared that the electoral process might represent a particularly attractive target for its political symbolism: the elections were seen as the culminating point of the Bonn process. To frustrate them was to undermine the Bonn process and Karzai's government. The registration teams would also be quite vulnerable. Numerous teams traveling with minimal security to remote areas along minor roads would be susceptible to ambush.

The security situation presented another dilemma, this one affecting the politics of the election. The fact that the insurgency was most active in the south, where the vast majority of the Pashtun population lived, meant that the voters register might be ethnically imbalanced. The inability to register Pashtuns due to poor security would exacerbate the sense that they were under-represented in the transitional administration and excluded from the political process and foster further resentment and withdrawal, if not outright opposition.

Brahimi therefore ordered that an enhanced security component to the registration project be prepared. According to the security plan that was hastily drawn up, newly-trained and armed Afghan police officers would accompany each registration team in jeeps (which would have to be procured) with radios that would allow calls for reinforcements. These police would receive additional training in the registration and electoral process to ensure that they functioned as elements to defend the registration teams but not to intimidate the population. Their training would focus on the rules of registration as well as on basic elements of crowd control. The security component would add an additional $11 million to the cost of registration.

Like the registration plan, the security project raised innumerable logistical problems—should provincial police be brought to Kabul for training or trainers sent to the provinces? How would the per diems of provincial police be paid in the absence of a proper banking system?[8] Should national police be coupled with provincial police? Given that there would be female registration teams for female voters, it was also necessary to recruit and train female police officers, which up to then, had not been envisaged. In fact, the first female Afghan police officers emerged from the voter registration security project.

The Afghans were only supposed to provide the first "ring" of security. The U.S.-led military Coalition, in cooperation with ISAF, which was now led by the North Atlantic Treaty Organization (NATO), was expected to provide the outer rings. The Coalition, which had been tasked by the Pentagon to do everything possible to ensure that the political process moved forward on schedule, agreed to provide the United Nations with threat assessments and some protection.[9] In the summer of 2003, the Coalition agreed in principle to provide air assets. They stated that their current assets were stretched but, if the United Nations' needs were presented clearly and were found to be compelling the Coalition would make the case to Central Command in Tampa[10] to augment its capacity to support the constitutional, electoral and DDR processes. This marked a shift in the thinking of the U.S. military, which now seemed to recognize that its exit strategy depended upon the successful implementation of the three main political tasks. This support would prove to be indispensable.

The Canal Hotel Bombing in Baghdad

On August 23, 2003 an event occurred in Baghdad, Iraq, that greatly increased the attention to security in Afghanistan. A truck bomb exploded in the compound of the Canal Hotel where the United Nations mission in Iraq was housed, killing 21 staff and injuring many more. This was a physical, moral and psychological blow to the United Nations system. To take these in order, on the "physical" side, a great deal of the devastation had been caused due to poor security planning. The first internal United Nations report of the incident, led by Martti Ahtisaari, a former President of Finland, was brutal: "The main conclusion of the Panel is that the current security management system is dysfunctional. It provides little guarantee of security to United Nations staff in Iraq or other high-risk environments and needs to be reformed." The Ahtisaari report prompted an immediate re-evaluation of security measures in Kabul, which was considered to be a likely future target. This meant increased restrictions on movement and additional safety requirements for residential and office buildings used by United Nations staff.[11]

The bombing of the Canal Hotel was a moral blow because it made clear that the United Nations was considered by Islamic terrorists to be a legitimate target. The sky blue flag, to the dismay of those who worked under it, appeared not to be considered neutral in this strange new war. For all the care that, over the decades, had gone into ensuring respect for the principles of humanitarian neutrality, humanitarianism itself was one of the enemies as far as the other side was concerned. While indications that this was true had been building during the 1990s, the Baghdad bombing was an incontrovertable confirmation.

Finally, the bombing was a psychological blow because one of its victims was the United Nations mission in Iraq, Sergio Vieira de Mello, one of the most widely-admired figures in the U.N. system.[12] He was admired, especially, by a cadre of young officers who had known him while he was heading the United Nations transitional administration in East Timor between December 1999 and May 2002, and had overseen the transition of Timor from a U.N. administered entity to an independent country. Many who had worked for him then had migrated to UNAMA, which was being staffed around the time that the Timor mission was being downsized. Even those in UNAMA who had never known "Sergio" felt in the collective anguish a sense of irreparable loss, accentuated by the question asked in hushed tones among UNAMA staff: Are we next?

A few months later, in November 2003, a bomb exploded outside the United Nations electoral office in Kandahar, blowing out the blast-resistant windows but luckily injuring no one. A few days after that, a French UNV working for UNHCR, was shot and killed while driving through the southern city of Ghazni, on the main road between Kabul and Kandahar. The Taliban claimed responsibility for her murder. This caused the United Nations to suspend its activities in four southern provinces. Wherever one looked, there was no good news on the security front.

Registration Begins

By the time the registration process began in December 2003, security had worsened even more than expected. In fact, the expectations had been that security would gradually improve as the Coalition began to deploy their Provincial Reconstruction Teams[13] (PRTs) around the country. Many PRTs, however, were deployed to the safer areas of the country, where they made little difference. Others, set up in more difficult areas, became targets of attack, rather than the nodes of radiating security that they were intended to be. As registration began, it was more clear than ever that the process itself would be a target of the insurgents.

As will be discussed in more detail below, voter registration began finally on December 1, as scheduled, in all eight regional capitals, with the exception of Kandahar, where it started on November 30, and Gardez, in the difficult southeast, where it began on December 5. This was really only a token beginning, however. Registration sites were only open where elections were taking place for delegates to the Constitutional Loya Jirga, and the process was hardly visible to the general population. But Brahimi had promised donors that he would meet the deadline and, in however minimal a way, he had. The launch added a bit of confidence to those who wondered if the U.N. was capable of getting the process off the ground. As 2004 began, it began to expand. But the lack of financing and procurement delays meant that registration was, in its initial stage, restricted to the major city centers. This was described as "Phase I" of the registration project, operating at only about 20 percent of the number of teams that would eventually be required. Phase II was scheduled to begin on May 1, 2004, though this was still contingent on receiving sufficient funds.

By early March 2004, the funding situation was still dire. The 8,840 registration kits required for Phase II had not yet been ordered; orders had been placed for only 400 of the 1,000 required Russian jeeps; and 62 UNVs (acting as Provincial Field Coordinators, Logistics Officers, Training Officers, and Civic Education Officers) still needed to arrive in the country and be trained and deployed. At this point, the cash shortfall of the project was $60 million, though $45 million had at least been "committed."

The new security requirements arising from the Baghdad incident provoked other delays: 20 of the 33 provincial office sites had been identified, but only 14 of these were certified as complying with the Minimum Operating Security Standards (MOSS) that the U.N. had designated for Afghanistan. In six provinces, vehicles had to have ballistic blankets fitted, but only one company in Afghanistan been licensed to carry out this sort of refitting. The lack of armored vehicles prevented international staff from carrying out preparatory activities in the all-important south, southeast and eastern regions. None of the security officers required for each regional and provincial office had yet been recruited.[14]

The Baghdad bombing had at least forced those responsible for security in Afghanistan to take a hard look at the arrangements that were in place. The counter-measures hastily implemented by those responsible for the security were necessary and sound, but they had not been considered by the electoral planners. They added to the costs and stressed the timelines. The political pressure to implement the Bonn Agreement did not, however, abate.

---

[1] As Amin Tarzi notes, "The term *neo-Taliban* first surfaced in a 2003 article in *The Economist* and has been gaining currency among Afghan observers. What it conveys is that the opposition maintains certain characteristics of, and links to, the old regime but also points to important differences. Whereas use of the word *Taliban* may limit understanding of the motivations and makeup of the varied actors that have surfaced since 2002 to oppose the post-Taliban order, the category 'neo-Taliban' better characterizes an opposition that has evolved beyond the old regime to encompass new groups with new agendas." See Amin Tarzi, "The New Taliban" in *The Taliban and the Crisis of Afghanistan*, eds. Robert D. Crews and Amin Tarzi (Cambridge: Harvard University Press, 2008) p. 276 (emphasis in original). As the title of his book implies, Antonio Giustozzi in *Koran, Kalashnikov, and Laptop: the Neo-Taliban Insurgency in Afghanistan* (New York: Columbia University Press, 2008), also adopts the designation. In a subsequent book he even refers to "'old' Neo-Taliban" suggesting that there might now be "new Neo-Taliban." See Antonio Gustozzi, ed, *Decoding the New Taliban: Insights from the Afghan Field* (London: Hurst & Company, 2009) p. 293. Thomas Ruttig argues that

there is greater continuity between the Taliban of the 1990s and the Taliban today. See Ruttig, "How Tribal Are the Taliban?" pp. 19-22.

[2] See Giustozzi, *Koran Kalashnikov, and Laptop*, pp. 129-130 and Rashid, Descent into Chaos, p. 244.

[3] In the case of Ismail Khan, the government, backed by U.S. force, was able to use those arrayed against him to force him eventually to accept a government post in Kabul. The dispute between Dostum and Atta was eventually reduced through a UNAMA mediation effort led by Jean Arnault, then the Deputy SRSG of UNAMA responsible for political affairs. These rivalries, and how they were managed, are discussed in more detail in Chapter 12.

[4] United Nations document S/2002/1173, para. 29.

[5] United Nations document S/2003/754, para. 23.

[6] United Nations document S/2003/754, para. 23.

[7] See, for example, Carlotta Gall, "At Border, Signs of Pakistani Role in Taliban Surge," *New York Times*, January 21, 2007.

[8] The difficulty of paying policemen serving outside their areas of residence continued. In 2007, following the establishment of branches of some Afghan banks around the country, direct-deposits could be used. Many policemen, upon receiving their salaries, reportedly thought they had been given a raise. The difference, of course, was the cut that their supervisors were unable to take when the salaries when directly from the payroll to the policeman's account.

[9] The Coalition was sometimes *too* helpful: they offered for example, to assist in the distribution of draft copies of the Afghan constitution during the popular consultation process. Nothing said "puppet government" more than the image of an American soldier handing to Afghans copies of a constitution they were eventually expected to vote on; this assistance was rejected.

[10] Tampa Bay, in Florida, is the headquarters of the U.S. Central Command ("CENTCOM"), which oversaw the Coalition's Operation Enduring Freedom.

[11] The U.N. sets, in each operating area, "Minimum Operating Security Standards," which include, for buildings, such measures as blast-proof film on windows, walls of a certain height and thickness, sandbagged entrances, barbed wire, and other similar measures.

[12] Samantha Power both records and reflects this admiration in her biography, *Chasing the Flame: Sergio Vieira de Mello and the Fight to Save the World* (New York: The Penguin Press, 2008).

[13] Provincial Reconstruction Teams (PRTs) were joint military and civilian units that were intended to provide a measure of security in their area in which development projects could be carried out. Initially, the intention was for the PRTs to establish a zone of security that would provide a peace-dividend that would redound to the credit of the Afghan government. In fact, they have become targets—in other words, they have in many cases created nodes of increasing insecurity.

[14] Recruitment of these specialized personnel was a function of what was then called the U.N. Security Coordinator's Office (UNSECOORD). As a result of the post-Baghdad reform, the structure and mandate of this office was changed and it became the Department of Safety and Security (DSS). The point

remained, however, that the registration operation became completely hostage to another branch of the U.N. service that did not necessarily feel the same urgency or political imperative.

7
Drafting the Constitution

We have described the Bonn process as a machine designed to convert a politics of violence into a stable and democratic order by through a series of valves where Afghanistan's political energies, which tended towards violence, could be released. At the same time, the designers knew that the pressure would be so great at each of these valves that it could potentially destroy the machine. The Emergency Loya Jirga had proceeded about as well as could be expected. It had not succeeded in dissipating all of the violent political energy that existed among those who accepted Bonn—Pashtuns were still disaffected, the Jihadi power brokers still had disproportionate control, and state administrative institutions had not sufficiently improved—but neither had it broken the machine. Furthermore, while the insurgency continued to be a factor of increasing concern, no Afghan political figure of great importance had yet defected from the process, and the Kabul government had gained an incremental element of legitimacy through the somewhat democratic nature of the Emergency Loya Jirga.

At the back of many minds, however, was the sense that the Emergency Loya Jirga had succeeded in part because the memories of war were still fresh, making it politically costly for any party to threaten the only viable infrastructure of peace. Furthermore, the United States and the international community still had their full attention on Afghanistan, and the perception of U.S. military omnipotence, formed by the rapid and overwhelming campaign against the Taliban in October 2001, remained vivid. Finally, the jirga had only addressed the minimum fundamental questions of political order in Afghanistan, deferring the most contentious questions to the next stage—the Constitutional Loya Jirga. One of the reasons that the actions of the Emergency Loya Jirga valve had not destroyed the machine was that it had channeled much of the political pressure to the next valve.

In the 18 months between the end of the Emergency Loya Jirga and the convening of the Constitutional Loya Jirga a lot had changed. The war in Iraq, which began in March 2003, diverted attention and resources from Afghanistan. The lengthy process, described below, of drafting the constitution, discussing it, and preparing the Constitutional Loya Jirga allowed a number of deep-seated political disagreements within Afghanistan to be brought to the fore. This was necessary for the process to advance, but no less dangerous for being necessary. If the Emergency Loya Jirga had tinkered with the leadership of Afghanistan, the constitutional process addressed its soul. As William Maley wrote:

> A country's constitution, whether codified or uncodified, is best seen as its fundamental law, identifying the actors and institutions that craft, execute and interpret laws, and defining the limits of their powers. Constitutions are important at a symbolic level [...] But constitutions are also important as a source of order. The challenge for their makers is to devise a constitution that will prevent power from being so concentrated that it facilitates dictatorial government, while also preventing power from being so fragmented that it leads to ineffectual and unworkable government.[1]

These challenges are difficult enough under the best of circumstances. In Afghanistan the challenges were accentuated by the deep divisions within the country over what Afghanistan should be, based on different conceptions of what it had been. The political actors who would meet to consider the draft constitution had all played roles in Afghanistan's political experiments of the previous decades—experiments that had gone from a political order based on communism's "new man" to one based on the Muslim figure of the "perfect man."[2] Wilfred Cantwell Smith has noted the "profound and crucial distinction that while communism treats ideals as instruments for attaining political power, Islam treats political power as instruments for attaining ideals."[3] Afghanistan had seen, in the previous few generations, a monarchy, a constitutional monarchy, republican dictatorship, communism, anarchy, and theocracy. The Constitutional Loya Jirga would include powerful abusers of ideals, idealistic abusers of power, and everything in between.

Furthermore, the deliberations in December 2003 would differ in important ways from any previous constitutional discussion in Afghanistan.[4] The rise of the Mujaheddin in response to the Soviet invasion had created a current of political Islam[5] that had not previously existed. It was an ideology that went far beyond the conservative versus modern debates that had, for example, characterized the administration of King Amanullah Khan at the beginning of the twentieth century, where the debate had centered on mostly symbolic issues such as the wearing of the veil by women.[6]

Another new dimension to the constitutional debate was the relationship of the central government to the periphery.[7] The long years of civil war had led to an awakening of ethnic identities in a manner not seen before in Afghanistan. Previously, Pashtuns had almost always held the seat of power, but had understood that retaining that seat of power depended on negotiating with, and sometimes subjugating by force, non-Pashtun tribes.[8] The resistance to the Soviets had led to the significant arming of factions of all ethnicities in Afghanistan by a variety of foreign patrons, including the U.S., Pakistan, Russia, and Iran. The combination of armed, ethnically defined solidarity groups with the long duration of the civil war had deepened the sense of ethnic identities throughout the country. The new constitution, in other words, would have to set rules to a game that was in some sense already far advanced. It was understood that the constitution's success would depend on balancing Afghanistan's deeply rooted political characteristics with the more recent and more ideological developments. At the same time, those ideological developments had generated new interpretations of what Afghanistan's deeply rooted political characteristics were. A pact for long-term stability needed to be fashioned at a moment deeply affected by short-term political perspectives.

Finally, because the international community had such a huge investment in Afghanistan, it also had a stake in the constitution. This meant that certain basic rights—those enshrined in the Universal Declaration of Human Rights, for example—would also have to be included.

The Constitutional Drafting Process

Speculation about when Brahimi would leave Afghanistan had been ongoing among the gossips and prognosticators in Kabul for some time. This speculation intensified after the successful conclusion of the Emergency Loya Jirga in June 2002. Many expected him to leave on this high note. He was, after all, 70 years-old, and had worked at a pace that would be punishing for someone three decades younger. He had famously said that diplomacy "was a twenty-four hour job,"[9] and anyone who worked closely with him knew that he lived this maxim fully. No one would have accused him of opportunism had he chosen to leave in 2002. Those who knew him well, said that he felt a distinctive sense of obligation to the Afghans. To his credit, he remained after the Emergency Loya Jirga, and continued for another 18 months, shepherding the Constitutional Loya Jirga to its conclusion in January

2004. Brahimi had proved himself to be something of a political magician; the Constitutional process would be his hardest trick.

As with the Emergency Loya Jirga, Brahimi, on the advice of his political affairs team, decided that the constitutional process had to be as inclusive as possible. This would take place through three mechanisms. First, an ethnically-inclusive drafting committee, overseen by a similarly composed Constitutional Commission, would prepare a first draft of the document. Second, a public consultation process would take place in all provinces of Afghanistan. Third, a representative Constitutional Loya Jirga would finalize the text and ratify the document.

The first step was to appoint the drafting committee. This was headed by Vice President Neamatullah Shahrani (an ethnic Uzbek), and made up of nine Afghan jurists and scholars selected by the president. It was another balancing act that required not only the usual mix of ethnicities and women (there were two) but also people of a certain intellectual caliber and understanding of political systems. It was difficult to be overly "democratic" about the selection of such a group. Nonetheless, the International Crisis Group made much of the "suspicious" manner by which the Committee was created:

> The selection of the drafting body occurred through a series of private negotiations between the U.N. and the Transitional Administration. No criteria were ever published. [...] The absence of a decree that laid out the commission's obligations also facilitated the gradual lengthening of the drafting period, increasing the delay in the formation of the full commission.[10]

The report also noted the comparatively high salaries of the nine commissioners ($2,000 per month) and their "conflicting interests," and complained about the lack of consultation during the drafting process. The extent to which the Afghan populace could have meaningfully contributed to the initial draft was probably exaggerated by the ICG and other international critics. The issue was not simply the lack of education on the part of most Afghans and the broken state in which Afghan society found itself. The question was how to replace the worst of traditional Afghan politics by a new, but recognizable, model that would allow powerless Afghans to escape the visceral and violence-prone political combinations that had fueled the civil war. This had to be achieved by elites—it is a fact of political power and of the design of political transitions.[11]

The drafting committee completed their preliminary draft on April 24, 2003. The 35-member Constitutional Commission, which included seven women, was inaugurated two days later, with the goal of shepherding the draft through a popular consultation process and organizing the Constitutional Loya Jirga.

Notwithstanding the ICG's complaint of an opaque process led by overpaid Afghans burdened with conflicts of interests, public consultations on the constitutional question formally began on June 6, 2003. Teams of commissioners began traveling to all provinces of Afghanistan, as well as to refugee communities in Iran and Pakistan, to discuss the main issues with Afghans. Curiously, the Commission, in holding these consultations, decided not to release the actual document prepared by the drafting committee. They justified this decision by saying that they did not want to limit the discussion to a draft that only covered some issues. This was, in the end, probably an error—it distorted public discussions over possible constitutional options and contributed to a sense that the process was, in fact, only superficially "popular" and democratic.

By mid-July, UNAMA estimated that 335 meetings had been organized with over 70,000 participants, around 20 percent of whom were women. UNAMA international staff attended as observers and noted a generally free atmosphere, though it was also clear that some local power-holders were able to control the participation and the direction of some of the debates. UNAMA's reports of these consultations revealed a number of trends that were probably an accurate reflection of the thinking of the Afghan population at large at the time.

Two of these trends involved the elections and are therefore worth mentioning here. First, there was strong support for a woman's right to vote. Second, there was a general feeling that the Kabul government should be strong enough to enforce the rule of law and bring the Bonn process to completion (though some areas in the north and the Hazara-dominated Central Highlands favored a federal system with regional autonomy). On the basis of these consultations, the Commission began the process of compiling popular observations and including them in the revised draft, which was supposed to be available in early September in order to allow a month of additional review and comments before the Loya Jirga began in October.

The drafting process also benefited from the advice of several international consultants. The main international experts were Barnett Rubin, a well-known American expert on Afghanistan; Yash Ghai, a Kenyan who had been involved in the drafting of a number of constitutions around the world, and was then the chairman of Kenyan constitutional reform commission, and a French professor of law, Guy

Carcassone.[12]. During the early drafting stage, however, the advice of the international consultants was not particularly welcomed by the Afghan commissioners. As Cornelia Schneider wrote, "One consultant who had been present in Afghanistan for years described the [Constitutional] Commission as 'generally wary of outside input' and the handful of foreign advisers as 'all extremely frustrated at various points'."[13] In addition, despite the presence of Austin's team in Kabul, UNAMA's electoral experts were not consulted on the electoral provisions of the constitution. This unfortunately meant that a number of problematic technical provisions concerning elections did not even appear to have been discussed.

The Commission's final draft was published five weeks before the scheduled opening of the Loya Jirga and after it had been reviewed by the National Security Council. The Constitutional Loya Jirga convened on December 14, 2003, at the same site as the Emergency Loya Jirga 18 months earlier. It was in some ways a more tumultuous gathering than the Emergency Loya Jirga as the stakes were perceived to be higher. The main debates were over a presidential versus a parliamentary system, the national language, and the role of religion and Islamic Law. The Jirga lasted 22 days, with the national language question continuing to threaten the process down to the final day. On January 4, 2004, after some last minute amendments to resolve the language issue, the 504 delegates voted by standing up to unanimously approve the new constitution.

The debate over a parliamentary or a presidential system had been so contentious that Karzai, in his closing remarks to the Constitutional Loya Jirga, sought to justify the adopted presidential system by saying that the years of war and division had weakened the state to such an extent that it required a strong executive, and at the same time tried to placate the pro-parliament delegates by suggesting that, in ten years, if stability was achieved and political parties had developed, a new Loya Jirga could amend the Constitution and provide for a parliamentary system. So far so good—this is how political compromises are wrought, though as a concession this was not huge. Whatever the behind-the-scenes machinations were, the Afghan political class gave a decent accounting of itself, given the stakes and the wide divergence of views. One perceptive foreign observer, however, noted the dangers that lurked within the achievement:

> Presidential systems come in diverse forms, but can be a recipe for disaster where societies or political elites are deeply divided: a pure presidential system effectively permits only one winner, while

> potentially generating many disgruntled losers. Karzai's non-confrontational personality may have hidden this problem for the moment, but it is lying buried just below the surface in Afghanistan's new political framework, like a bomb waiting to explode. Ultimately, what the Loya Jirga produced was not a constitution for all time, but a constitution for Karzai.[14]

The Electoral Provisions of the Constitution

There was a far more immediate problem with the new Constitution than its winner-take-all apportionment of executive power. This problem arose from the details in the document that affected the design of the electoral system—constitutions are, after all, "designs for democracy."[15] With so much energy spent on the big, controversial issues, it is surprising in hindsight how little thought went into the details that would give those decisions meaning through elections—or how poor was the quality of that thought.

It was in retrospect a rather large mistake to have not had technical electoral expertise available to the Constitution's drafters, whether that expertise was provided by Austin's team or by others. That advice would probably have been accepted by the Afghan commissioners since the issues were technical and did not touch on the main fault lines of Afghan politics. Instead, what confronted Austin's electoral team when the Constitution was ratified was how inept the provisions governing elections were. They could not have been better designed had their intention been to complicate the upcoming elections and frustrate long-term democratization in Afghanistan. Let us consider them in some detail.

The first error was to give in to the temptation of excessive political engineering. The International Crisis Group, in its report on the constitutional process, had issued an interpretation of the Constitution's role that was echoed by many. It argued that:

> A new architecture of governance, both within the central administration and between national and sub-national units, can provide respected and accepted channels for the resolution of political conflict. More importantly, a period of constitutional change conducted under the glare of international attention can empower moderate and progressive leaders, consolidating what peace there is and furthering development of a democratic political culture.[16]

The constitutional engineers—Afghans and their international advisors—had apparently accepted the debatable view that the central historical problem in Afghanistan was an imbalance of power within formal state structures between the center and the periphery. More accurately, the real problem was an imbalance of power between the state, which ruled from the center, but whose authority extended outwards with diminishing effect, and a decentralized society, which from various sources of traditional authority had always negotiated its relationship to the state. Balancing formal state institutions would have little effect as long as local power mostly acted beyond state institutions. Proceeding from a flawed premise, the constitutional engineers attempted to create an inappropriate solution. This solution was to create a legislature whose upper house was made up of three classes of members: one-third of the upper house (Meshrano Jirga) was made up of members elected by each provincial council; a second-third was elected, one delegate per province, from among all the District Councils in that province; the final third was selected by the President.[17] This supposedly addressed the problem of an imbalance of power between Kabul and the regions.

This "new architecture of governance" was fatally flawed because it was impossible to implement. The first reason for this impossibility was rooted in the reality of districting in Afghanistan.[18] Administrative boundaries in Afghanistan in 2003 were a palimpsest that marked the various ebbing and flowing of reform and war over the previous decades.[19] In 1963, the government carried out an administrative reform just prior to the planned "New Democracy" reforms. The fact that a number of new provinces were created in the Pashtun areas led many to believe that this administrative reform was nothing more than gerrymandering.[20] As R. Gopalakrishnan has suggested, "the concentrating of provinces along the eastern and to a lesser extent in the northern Afghanistan [sic] indicated the latent influence of the Pashtun and non-Pashtun elements in the state's politics."[21] Confusion was added in the 1990s, during the Rabbani presidency, when 14 new districts were added to Rabbani's home province of Badakhshan. Additional districts were reportedly created during the resistance either as means of governing territories that conformed to the realities of who held what ground, or as rewards to smaller commanders. In other words, by 2003, unofficial districts existed in reality alongside official districts. The unofficial districts were often acknowledged by the provincial governors, who allocated money to them and recognized their heads.[22] In March 2004, three separate district lists were being used, or had been used, for three official exercises: the UNAMA electoral unit was using a list of 32 provinces and 387 districts for its planning, the Central Statistics Office (a government agency) was using a list of 32 provinces and 391 districts, and the Emergency Loya Jirga of 2002 had used a list of 32 provinces and 465 districts.

This confusion created two knotty electoral planning problems. First, it became impossible to draw district electoral boundaries without antagonizing de facto power holders. Second, if, during the voter registration process, registrants were asked to which district they belonged, their answers would not necessarily be consistent.[23] In other words, residents of a single area might provide different answers to the question of what district they belonged to, depending on what regime they remembered or what faction they favored. Until the districting question—a highly controversial issue—was resolved, it would be impossible to hold district elections and, therefore, impossible to constitute the upper house of the legislature as called for by the Constitution.[24]

Another significant problem created by the Constitution was its electoral calendar. The presidential and Wolesi Jirga terms were set at five years, the term of Provincial Councils at four years, and term of District Councils at three years. This meant that nation-wide elections would have to be held in three out of every five years. For a country emerging from conflict, where organizing elections is expensive and their political effect is potentially divisive, this punishing schedule was not only impossible to implement, it was almost a recipe for constant political conflict.

The electoral calendar contained another stupefying provision. The dates for the expiration of the presidential and lower house terms were set as May 22 and June 22 respectively, with elections needing to occur within 30 to 60 days prior to those dates. This meant that, if presidential and lower house elections were held together, which the Consitution intended, then there was only one date, April 22, on which both elections could be held together—30 days before the expiration of the presidential term and 60 days before the expiration of the legislative term. This meant that elections in Afghanistan always had to occur during the spring, which, for reasons of weather and accessibility was hardly ideal.

Finally, the Constitution called for proportionality in the electoral system—in other words, each representative should be elected by roughly the same number of electors—as well as a quota for the representation of women. The Constitutionn specified that the lower house should have at least twice as many women as the number of provinces.[25] The system that best fulfilled these two criteria was a proportional representation (PR) system that used closed party lists, and prescribed that women be placed near the top of the list or placed alternately with men. As will be discussed in much greater detail later on, the cabinet, and Karzai in particular, argued against proportional representation because it required the existence of parties, which were perceived by many to be artificial in Afghanistan and not trusted by Afghans. This virtually forced the option of the single-non-transferable vote (SNTV)—a notoriously unrepresentative voting system, that most experts deemed particularly noxious for Afghanistan. Here the constitutional exercise again clashed with a proper understanding of political realities in Afghanistan.

It has been argued that the Constitution had to embody long-term solutions for Afghanistan, and therefore that some of the decisions, while not convenient in the short term, were appropriate for the long term and therefore necessary to include in the document. This argument would be more convincing had another provision of the Constitution been used to mitigate the negative impact of the articles governing elections. The Constitution included a chapter (Article 159) on transitional arrangements, giving the transitional government the power to adopt "necessary measures to prepare the ground for implementing provisions of the Constitution." This could have been used for precisely the purpose advocated by EAD two years earlier—the creation of a one-off electoral modality that would have allowed the first post-Bonn elections to have been both constitutional and more realistic.

In the short term, the implementation of the Constitution was constricted by realities such as the districting problem and the spring calendar. In the long term, the electoral process designed by the Constitution was unsustainable due if nothing else to the immense costs of holding three elections every five years. The result was that the nascent state, which was supposed to be founded on the rule of law, was forced into an immediate dilemma—hold elections as called for by the Bonn Agreement, or wait until they could be held according to the terms set by the Constitution. Afghanistan was caught between two incompatible regimes, each equally valid on its own terms, and both midwifed by the international community.

In the long-term, however, the electoral provisions would prove extremely costly. It is especially unfortunate that they appear to have been more the result of carelessness than of difficult political compromises. The periodicity of elections, election dates, or district-level representation in the upper house were not fundamental issues for most participants at the Constitutional Loya Jirga; they were technocratic. They did not engage notions of identity, as the language debate did. They were not issues that factions had been fighting for over the preceding decades.

These negative effects were not immediately realized upon ratification. The immediate relief in January 2004, especially among the international community, was that the Constitution had been ratified without a return to violence, and that the contentious political issues had been finessed. The Bonn process had survived its most important test. The political valves emitted a bit more smoke, trembled and hissed, but the machine continued to turn.

On the note of constitutional success, Brahimi finally decided to leave Afghanistan. In his speech at the conclusion of the Constitutional Loya Jirga, he congratulated the delegates on their achievement and reminded them that the Constitution was "just words on a page that needed now to become a living reality." He spoke of the insecurity that continued to plague Afghanistan and reminded the audience that much of the insecurity was caused by local strongmen who were backed by powerful figures in government. In other words, insecurity was not simply a problem of the then low-level insurgency, but of the lack of a "rule of law," which could only be addressed by those who had just ratified the supreme document of law. In an unexpected gesture, Brahimi paid tribute to the women of Afghanistan, speaking of their sacrifices, warning of the struggles ahead, and urging them to continue their struggle "with dignity and courage." Exiting the stage, he would leave to others the task of implementing the Constitution. The first test of course would be that of holding elections—a task which had just been undermined by the careless provisions of that very same Constitution.

---

[1] Maley, *Rescuing Afghanistan*, pp. 43-44.

[2] See the interesting discussion in Olivier Roy, *The Failure of Political Islam*, trans. Carol Volk (Cambridge: Harvard University Press, 1994) p. 100.

[3] Wilfred Cantwell Smith, *Pakistan as an Islamic State* (Preliminary Draft) (Lahore: Shaikh Muhammad Ashraf Publisher, 1951) p. 28.

[4] There were three categories of earlier constitutions in Afghanistan. The first category was the "monarchical" constitutions of 1923, 1931 and 1964. The latter, adopted under King Zahir Shah, was notable for its liberalism and for excluding the members of the royal family from holding ministerial posts, though it retained a great deal of power for the king himself. The second category was the Republican, or "Royal Republic" constitution of Daoud in 1977, following his coup d'état against his cousin, the king. The third category comprised the two constitutions adopted under the Communist regime, in 1980 and 1989. See S. H. Amin, *Law, Reform and Revolution in Afghanistan* (Glascow: Royston Publishers, 1993) pp. 39-53, for a more detailed discussion.

[5] The most comprehensive analysis of this change is in Roy's *Islam and Resistance in Afghanistan*. See also, Roy, "The New Political Elite of Afghanistan," in *The Politics of Social Transformation*, pp. 72-100.

[6] "Because Amanullah was obsessed by the image of modernity rather than by modernity itself, he attached considerable importance to appearances and in

particular to clothing. [...] The symbolic value of appearances was to function not only for the modernists but also for the adversaries of modernization, who opposed the signs of modernization with those of modesty (ample clothing, the veil, the turban) and treated partsans of change as agents of licentiousness and immorality." This is from Micheline Centlivres-Demont, "Afghan Women in Peace, War, and Exile," in *The Politics of Social Transformation*, eds. Weiner and Banuazizi, p. 336.

[7] The (far from completed) history of the modernization of Afghanistan is in many ways a catalog of tribal resistance to central rule. Gregorian, noted that "Despite the attempts of the Afghan monarchs to broaden their political base and to pursue a policy of centralization, their dependence on the strength of the Afghan tribes committed them to defending the feudal tribal social structure" Emergence of Modern Afghanistan, p. 40, and that "The tribes vigorously resisted any regulation that threatened their traditional privileges, especially their property rights." ibid p. 42. Attentive students to the ongoing insurgency in Afghanistan have noted that some tribes have allied with the so-called Taliban movement not because they share its aims or desire it to win, but simply because in the short term in helps them stave off central government authority over their "traditional privileges." See Giustozzi, *Koran, Kalashnikov, and Laptop*, pp. 52-69.

[8] See for example, M. Nazif Shahrani, "Taliban and Talibanism in Historical Perspective," in *The Taliban and the Crisis of Afghanistan*, eds. Crews and Tarzi, pp. 155-181. Shahrani locates the seeds of the Taliban in the "internal colonialism" of Pashtun-dominated regimes. The most effective of these regimes, in terms of subjugating non-Pashtun peoples, and especially the Hazaras, was that of Abdul Rahman Khan. See M. Hasan Kawun Kakar, *Government and Society in Afghanistan: The Reign of 'Abd al-Rahman Khan* (Austin: University of Texas Press, 1979).

[9] He reiterated this with his characteristic dry wit at a lecture on 27 January 2003 at Georgetown University, while receiving the Jit Trainor Award from the Institute for the Study of Diplomacy: "In the long years that I have been involved in diplomacy, I have often been asked by people outside the field about what diplomats actually do. Many, of course, are convinced that all we really do is talk at meetings and mingle at receptions. This is not entirely wrong, but one might add, however, that the work of a diplomat is a 24-hour job, because a good diplomat must always be thinking of the potential problems and opportunities developing out of the political environment he or she is faced with."

[10] International Crisis Group, "Afghanistan's Flawed Constitutional Process" Asia Report No. 56, Brussels, 12 June 2003.

[11] Even the American Constitution was drafted by elites and later adopted following a long process of persuasion, according to extensive literature on this subject. One need not be a devotee of Charles A. Beard's argument that the U.S. Constitution was drafted by wealthy elites for wealthy elites to subscribe to the general point that the document did not emerge from some perfect distillation of popular will through a magical alembic, but was the product of a deliberate design by a small group of men whose vision was by no means universally

shared at the time. Despite this, the U.S. Constitution came, over time, to embody an almost sacred status among Americans. This topic is far from the topic of the present study, but a nice representation of views is contained in Robert A. Golwin and William A. Schambra, eds., *How Democratic is the Constitution?* (Washington and London: American Enterprise Institute for Public Policy Research, 1981. Michael Parenti's article in this volume, "The Constitution as an Elitist Document," makes the argument quite succinctly.

[12] A French constitutional professor had also provided advice to the Afghan commission that drafted the 1964 constitution. At the time, Dupree reported, this caused great mirth among western observers in Kabul who joked: "Afghanistan is seeking stability in government, so why choose a French adviser? [...] Since 1789 France has had two monarchies, two empires, five republics, the Vichy interlude, and fifteen constitutions." See Dupree, *Afghanistan*, p. 566.

[13] Cornelia Schneider, "The International Community and Afghanistan's Constitution," *Peace, Conflict and Development: An Interdisciplinary Journal*, Vol. 7, July 2005, p. 187. See also Rubin, "Crafting a Constitution for Afghanistan."

[14] Maley, *Rescuing Afghanistan*, p.46.

[15] G. Bingham Powell, Jr., *Elections as Instruments of Democracy: Majoritarian and Proportional Visions* (New Haven and London: Yale University Press, 2000) p. 20.

[16] ICG, "Afghanistan's Flawed Constitutional Process."

[17]This structure to some degree replicated the Constitution of 1964, but with a crucial difference. In 1964, the upper house was also made up of equal thirds: one-third selected by the King, one-third elected by provincial constituencies, and the remaining third were the chairmen of the Provincial Councils. The 2004 Constitution added to the complexity of this by creating District Councils and, crucially, putting the election of District Councils on a different cycle from that of provincial councils and of the Wolesi Jirga For an detailed description of the 1964 constitution, see Richard S. Newell, *The Politics of Afghanistan* (Ithaca and London: Cornell University Press, 1972) pp. 104-107. See also Dupree, *Afghanistan*, p. 587.

[18] Given the creation in April 2004 of two new provinces (Daikundi and Panshir), even provincial boundaries were initially fluid.

[19] As Frédéric Roussel and Marie-Pierre Caley note in their fascinating paper, "Les 'Manteqas': Le Puzzle Souterrain de l'Afghanistan" (photocopy), districts in Afghanistan are not so much territorially-defined entities, but rather human settlements loosely associated with a district center; the district center is normally close to a bazaar, connected to the center by a telephone line, from which the authority of the state is weakly enforced by the presence of a district chief (the woloswal), a judge, and a gendarmerie (kumandan-e-amania) of ten or twenty soldiers. While the district was how the state imagined the administrative division of the country, that division was not necessarily recognized by those who lived in the district.

[20] Xavier de Planhol, in *Les Nations du Prophète* (Paris: Editions Fayard, 1993) pp. 632 – 635, argues that the new provinces were required by the number

of towns created as a result of the construction of the Kabul-to-Kandahar road. (Cited in Roussel and Caley.)

[21] R. Gopalakrishnan, *Geography and Politics of Afghanistan* (New Delhi: Concept Publishing, 1982) p. 178. Until 1963, Afghanistan was divided administratively into four major provinces, four minor provinces, 10 districts, 97 prefectures, and 158 cantons. The 1963 reforms split the country into 28 provinces, 174 districts, and 118 sub-districts.

[22] See Anne Evans, Nick Manning, Yasin Osmani, Anne Tully and Andrew Wilder, *A Guide to Government in Afghanistan* (Kabul: The World Bank and the Afghanistan Research and Evaluation Unit, 2004) pp. 94-97, for a more detailed discussion of "proliferating districts."

[23] For example, from a study just before the Communist revolution: "Foremost among the problems was the fact that the villagers' conception of a village differs from that of the government personnel who compile village lists. Government officials, depending on the jurisdiction in which they resided, often grouped discrete settlements under one village. Villagers, on the other hand, are cognizant of subtle differences in rural society, and therefore break grouped villages' designations down into their own categories. The result is that I was confronted by many villages having names which did not appear on the formal villages lists." Nigel J.R. Allan, *Tribe and Village Agrosystems in the Hindukoush* (Syracuse: University of Syracuse Press, 1979) p. 6. (Cited in Roussel and Caley, "Les 'manteqas'.")

[24] See Chapter 12 on how this dilemma was eventually resolved—or finessed. Interestingly, this problem also occurred in 1964. In the 1964 constitution, the Meshrano Jirga was made up as follows: one-third appointed by the king, one-third directly elected by the constituents (senators), and one-third elected from the Provincial Assemblies. As Dupree wrote, "since the constitution required that one-third of the Upper House come from the Provincial Councils (one from each of the 28 provinces), some constitutional authorities argued that the entire nine year period was unconstitutional." Louis Dupree, "The New Republic of Afghanistan: the first twenty-one months" Special Paper, Afghanistan Council of the Asia Society, 1976. p. 3.

[25] According to Brahimi, in a conversation the author long after the event, this provision came about in a rather remarkable way. Progressive civil society groups backed by international advocates wanted the parliament to have a quota of at least 15 percent for women; more conservative members of the CLJ balked at more than 5 percent. Arnault, his political deputy at the time, suggested as a compromise that instead of focusing on percentages, there should be at least two women per province. This sounded reasonable and was agreed to. It was only later that delegates realized that with the total size of the lower house set at 249, this led to a women's quota of more than 25 percent, one of the highest in the world. Given the arithmetic of seat allocation, in provinces with a small population, the entire parliamentary delegation could conceivably be made up of women.

8
Resetting the Electoral Clock

When the new Constitution was adopted in January 2004, voter registration had been underway for less than a month. The election date set by Bonn, June 2004, was less than six months away. As the new Constitution was printed and distributed around the country, attention in Kabul swung ponderously to the voter registration process and the now rapidly approaching elections.

As with all logistical processes, there is an inescapable relationship between time, money and quality. If time is fixed, then more money is required to increase quality. In Afghanistan, with the election set for June, time was the only constant. The flow of funding remained unpredictable due to its voluntary nature. If the required resources were not forthcoming, then quality would suffer. From a political point of view, however, quality should have been the primary variable—if the elections were not acceptable to the population, the entire exercise would be a waste of both time and money.

The idea that the credibility of the Bonn process depended entirely on meeting its timetable continued to retain its fetishistic dominance over the thinking of the international community. A close reading of events suggests that Brahimi, at least, had tried to loosen this hold. In the final months of his tenure he had begun a carefully prepared campaign to condition Afghan and international actors to the idea that the elections might have to be postponed.

This should not have been a surprise to any student of postconflict elections. Nearly half of all such elections have had to be postponed. The phenomenon was common enough that an electoral expert, Horacio Boneo, who had been EAD's first director, had written an unpublished paper entitled "The Rules of Postponement." Boneo argued that it was better to hold credible elections on a postponed schedule rather than poor elections simply to maintain an ultimately arbitrary timetable. He claimed that political actors would generally accept postponement if three simple rules were followed: the postponement should be announced as soon as possible after it is understood it is required; the reasons for the postponement should be clearly explained; and these reasons should be demonstrably of a purely technical nature—in other words not designed to favor any given political group.

In Afghanistan, Brahimi was not the only one preparing the ground for a probable delay of the elections. The Afghan Research and Evaluation Unit[1] (AREU) published a paper in November 2003 entitled, "Afghan Elections: the Great Gamble." AREU argued that "holding national elections in Afghanistan seems to be more oriented to satisfying international expectations, rather than address Afghans' need for positive change." The report correctly described conditions of insecurity and the weakness of political institutions in Afghanistan—underlining in particular that the "newly formed Independent Afghan Electoral Commission will have neither the experience nor the know-how to orchestrate the event." It pleaded for the international community to "support a new approach that combines a new interim political framework and timeframe with long-term funding commitments," reasoning that:

> The stakes for holding elections are high on all sides and the pressure to use elections as an incentive for pushing reform and keeping stakeholders engaged are significant. But policy makers need to take a step back and ask themselves whether gambling on Afghanistan's future is really worth the risk.[2]

After the June 2003 cabinet meeting on elections, Brahimi had informed United Nations headquarters that Afghans had already begun to internalize the possibility of an electoral delay, and had raised the possibility of a presidential election first, followed by a legislative election. Brahimi understood that elections, if they were to be the crowning achievement of a state-building process, would need to be based on a number of pre-conditions. An article in *The New York Times* as early as February 2003 quoted Brahimi as saying:

> If the support of the international community is there for another couple of years, and if our ideas concerning the national army are really moved forward," and then if a police force and judiciary are created, then success is possible, [Brahimi] said. "And if to put—as it were—the roof over the house, we manage to organize a credible, fair, free election 18 months from now, you will have your state.[3]

Brahimi also understood, as Boneo had, that if elections had to be postponed, the ground for that postponement would have to be carefully prepared. In his briefings to the Security Council, he had increasingly begun to note the possibility, and then the probability, of a postponement of the election date. It was clear, however, that there were limits to how far the date could be postponed. He felt that the elections would have to be held at some point in 2004, the calendar year in which they were originally planned, and they would have to be held before the winter set in. (The political necessity of holding elections in 2004 was where Brahimi's short-term postponement differed from AREU's proposed longer-term postponement.) In addition, in 2004 the Muslim fasting month of Ramadan began in November. The election would have to be largely concluded before then for practical reasons. The timeline, finally, had to take into account the constitutional requirement for a run-off election if no candidate received 50 percent of the votes in the first round.

Brahimi had told the Security Council, on May 12, 2003, that even if resources were provided and security was assured, the June 2004 timetable for elections might not be met for technical reasons. He noted that it could slip to September without any major political repercussions. Certain issues could simply not be rushed if the election was to be meaningful. For example, since this was arguably Afghanistan's first full suffrage election, voter education was particularly important. Candidates also needed time to organize and conduct their campaigns.

This message was not easily swallowed by Security Council members, who had also embraced the Bonn timeline fetishism. In his final briefing to the Council on January 15, 2004, Brahimi did not raise the issue of the election date. On the other hand, the United States representative, supported by France, emphasized the importance of sticking to the Bonn deadline. The U.S. representative argued that the Constitutional Loya Jirga had interpreted the will of the people to determine that the legislative and the presidential elections should happen at the same time,[4] and that it was the responsibility of the international community to meet those deadlines. In response, Brahimi reiterated his earlier comments that elections were only useful on the condition that they took place at the "right time" and with the "right preparation." He added that, for this reason, he was of the view that not even the presidential election could take place in June 2004. Furthermore, while it was desirable to have both presidential and legislative elections together, he doubted it could be done in 2004. The choice was therefore between holding the presidential election in 2004 and legislative elections later, or postponing both. The option of having both in 2004, let alone having both in *June* 2004, was simply not realistic.

This was a strong defense at a high political level for the integrity of the electoral process. Just as Brahimi had used his farewell message to the Afghans at the Constitutional Loya Jirga to underscore the importance of the rule of law and women's rights, he had used his last political capital in the Security Council to make clear that the presidential election would have to be postponed beyond June, and in all likelihood, legislative elections would have to be postponed even further. For all the frictions with the UNAMA's electoral unit and EAD, Brahimi had evidently understood their arguments and reiterated them to the Council. He made this point again, publicly, in his final interview with *The New York Times*: "There is now a very well-meaning and welcome Western interest in supporting democracy everywhere, but they want to do it like instant coffee. It doesn't happen that way."[5] This series of public comments appeared to be a well-calculated attempt to gradually inject some realism into the perceptions of the international community. It was also a gift to his still-unidentified successor, who would be able to hide behind the credibility of Brahimi's pronouncements in the likely event that it would become necessary to postpone one or both of the elections.

Planning for the Best

When Brahimi left Afghanistan, his deputy for political affairs, Jean Arnault, was named the interim head of UNAMA, pending identification of a successor to Brahimi. Arnault was well-placed to play this interim role. He had been intimately involved with the electoral operation from the beginning, he knew UNAMA intimately, having been appointed as deputy in early 2002, and he was a long-time U.N. insider with a reputation for possessing a brilliant political mind. Some had suggested that if too much time passed without finding a replacement for Brahimi, Arnault should in fact become the next SRSG. In the meantime, registration had to continue, along with preparations for the elections.

If, in his final public statements as SRSG, Brahimi had laid the ground for a postponement of the elections, giving a gift of political capital to his immediate successor, Arnault either did not see it or did not accept it. Assuming Brahimi's mantle in January 2004, he immediately rejected the idea of holding elections later than the June date set at Bonn. There were likely two reasons for this position. The first was his genuine belief, which he would enunciate later, that the success of Bonn really did depend on meeting the timelines. The second was U.S. pressure to hold the elections on time. Not only did the U.S. share the view that the timelines had to be met, but the American ambassador in Kabul, Zalmay Khalilzad, was among those pushing the Secretary-General to nominate Arnault as Brahimi's replacement.[6]

On February 1, 2004, Arnault informed New York by cable of a meeting he had had with President Karzai on the electoral process. Attached to the cable was a note on the 2004 elections that he had shared with the president. The note essentially presented a concept of how the elections could be held by June 2004, identifying a series of benchmarks that would have to be met in the coming weeks and months by the Afghan government. These included the delineation of district boundaries, security improvements, the disarmament of still-armed factions and cantonment of their heavy weapons, and the adoption of an electoral law. Arnault argued that while every effort should continue to be made by the government and the international community to hold the presidential and parliamentary elections simultaneously, no commitment to simultaneous elections should be made until it was clear that they could be held successfully. He added, rather optimistically, that the simultaneous holding of presidential and parliamentary elections could, however, not yet be excluded, and he instructed that planning proceed on this basis.

A prudent rule of politics is to hope for the best, but to plan for the worst; in this case, the UNAMA electoral team was instructed to hope and plan for the best—combined presidential and legislative elections in June 2004—no matter how unrealistic the prospect. Given the slow pace of registration, the lack of funds and continued unreliability of their disbursement, the recent adoption of the Constitution, the non-existence of an electoral law, the logistical challenges presented by a country whose geography and lack of development hindered easy accessibility, the notion that holding combined June elections should be the basis for electoral planning was becoming irresponsible. One could, in defiance of Boneo's rules of postponement, pretend that elections could happen in June for as long as possible. But to actually plan for that outcome risked wasting time and resources.

In terms of logistics, planning for a process to take place in six months, to which a three-month extension is appended half-way through, is far inferior to knowing that one will have nine months to complete an operation. The former case would force a compression of training programs and of the public information campaign. It would force corners to be cut and increase the risk of a "catastrophic" logistical complications.

EAD reacted to Arnault's cable by noting that the U.S. position on maintaining the June deadline was most likely a tactic to force the United Nations to be more active in its preparations. The slow pace of registration still caused many to believe that the U.N. was dragging its heels. This was a reasonable expectation but an unhelpful tactic. Ultimately, EAD believed that the U.S. would not object to an election that was delayed several months, especially if those months allowed for an improved process, and the case was made clearly. EAD also noted that there were signs that U.S. pressure for June elections was abating. Not only had UNAMA reported in February that Karzai was comfortable with an election being held as late as the beginning of August, but a *New York Times* article a week later reported that "the Bush administration has begun suggesting that Afghanistan's elections scheduled for June may have to be postponed because of security problems and the failure to register enough voters."[7]

There was, EAD argued, a real risk in planning for June elections knowing that the plan had little chance of succeeding and would probably have to be revised much later in the operation. Any such revision could raise distrust among political actors involved in the process. From both a political and technical point of view, therefore, EAD argued that it was a mistake to abandon Brahimi's more realistic position on election timing. The electoral division recommended that a lucid evaluation be made of the earliest possible realistic date for elections, both presidential and parliamentary. Arnault, however, continued to instruct the electoral team in Kabul to plan for combined presidential and legislative elections in June.

Losing the policy argument once again, EAD and the UEC managers complied with the new directive, spending the last week of January coming up with a new "plan" to fit the June timetable. Assuming the most optimistic assumptions, they came up with a series of timetables by which elections could be held by June. This required that 2.5 million voters be registered in the eight regional centers by the first week of April. The remaining eligible population (eight million) would then have to be registered in a massive three-week registration campaign in 4,200 locations in the first three weeks of May in order to allow a week-long "exhibition and challenges" period.[8] In other words, within a three-week period, three times more voters would have to be registered than had been in the previous four months. This, in turn, depended upon an "acceptable level of security throughout Afghanistan from March to June, and a high-level commitment from donors and others to meet the plan's needs promptly"—hardly realistic planning assumptions if recent history was any indicator. The compression of time would also increase the cost of the registration project from $78 million to $105 million.[9]

In other words, if all the money required was available immediately, and the Taliban cooperated with the registration plan, and the snowcap disappeared, and millions of Afghans quickly learned to read and write, and nothing that could go wrong did go wrong, the proposed timelines could possibly be met. Only in the best of all fictional worlds was the plan feasible. The "plan," in fact, was not really a plan but a mathematical exercise in which a number of estimated voters who remained to be registered was divided by the number of weeks that remained before the election. It wasn't a plan, it was arithmetic.

"Co-Responsibility"

The other significant policy decision that Arnault made during his period as interim head of UNAMA was to alter the management structure of the elections. In the February 1 cable to New York, he advocated a "co-responsibility" approach to the elections. The thrust of his argument was that the end of the Constitutional Loya Jirga, and the availability of experienced Afghan staff from the jirga's secretariat, offered an opportunity to retool the institutional arrangements for organizing the election, increasing the Afghan role.

This "retooling" was presented to the UEC in a hastily-arranged meeting on January 24. Arnault arrived late to the UEC compound, directly from a meeting with the U.S. ambassador. In his articulate and convincing manner, he began by describing the historical dimension of the UEC's work. The elections were the largest challenge in the history of Afghanistan. He conceded that there had not been much thinking at Bonn about elections, but noted somewhat ominously that if the elections failed, it would force a review of the Bonn process.

Austin replied by outlining his concerns about the credibility of elections in the current security climate. Arnault answered that "the question was not credibility but opportunity." This brief exchange distilled the great issues that both sides had been skirmishing over for months. Arnault was undoubtedly correct that the security situation, as bad as it was getting, did not justify calling off the elections, which represented an unprecedented opportunity for Afghans to break out of the cycle of violence that had defined their political condition for the past three decades. Austin was undoubtedly right to point to the fact that if elections were to play this role, then they needed to be perceived as credible. The question was, in fact, about *both* credibility and opportunity, but once again the electoral and political masters had spoken past each other.

Arnault, aware that his comments might have gone beyond the taste of an audience of electoral technocrats, reassured them that if there were doubts about the credibility of the process, he would not support the elections. At the end of his speech, he informed the electoral team that there would be a brainstorming session the next day to discuss the operational plan and necessary preparation for elections.

The meeting the next day took place in UNAMA's Compound B, in the center of Kabul. The UEC managers were surprised to find themselves outnumbered at the brainstorming by representatives from the U.S. Embassy, the National Democratic Institute[10] (NDI), the U.S. military, Global Risk Incorporated (a private company that had helped with the logistics of the Constitutional Loya Jirga), The Asia Foundation, and Farooq Wardak, who had recently been the head of the Constitutional Commission Secretariat, as well as Wardak's top aides from the Constitutional Loya Jirga operation.

Arnault began by talking about the need for "free and fair elections" in Afghanistan. Then he gave the floor to a young American, Larry Sampler. Sampler, a former Special Forces soldier, had previously been seconded to UNAMA by the U.S. to assist in the complex logistics of the Emergency Loya Jirga and the Constitutional Loya Jirga. These were challenging tasks which he had handled with great competence and diplomatic sensitivity, earning him a reputation as someone who could get things done under pressure in Afghanistan, working with Afghans but not ruffling them.

As Sampler began speaking, it became clear that the meeting's real purpose was to compare the existing UEC plans with plans that had been prepared in parallel—and without the UEC's knowledge—by Global Risk. The UEC's Chief of Operations, Spelman, then went through the electoral calendar, stressing the planning phases and resource requirements. Wardak countered with an exposé of how he had worked with the 500 Constitutional Loya Jirga delegates and 20,000 tribal leaders. The implication of Wardak's presentation was that the problems Spelman laid out were easily surmountable. One of Wardak's aides additionally made a passionate case that there was no time to build confidence in the process, and the elections had to go ahead as close to schedule as possible. In order for this to happen, the Global Risk operational plan identified the need for an "aggressive management style," which in turn required changes in the existing management structure.

No one at the meeting was there by accident. It soon emerged that one of the ulterior motives for the proposed management changes was the need to do something with the Secretariat of Wardak's

Constitutional Loya Jirga commission, whose employees had gained a certain amount of experience but faced unemployment now that the Constitution had been adopted. Arnault proposed merging the Constitutional Loya Jirga Secretariat with that of the JEMB. Zakim Shah, the JEMB Chairman, expressed doubts about this proposal. He accepted the logic of benefiting from the experience of the Constitutional Loya Jirga Secretariat staff, but said that they should at least be vetted prior to joining his own Secretariat. The quality of the Secretariat staff was mixed. Some were excellent, others were unqualified, and some were known to be corrupt. These concerns were dismissed by Arnault and Wardak, and the decision was made to put the merger in motion. A further element of the new plan was to make Wardak the head of the JEMB Secretariat. On this, Austin and members of his management team had larger doubts. Wardak, described by Arnault as "one of the best managers the country has to offer," was also very close to Karzai, raising a potential conflict of interest.

The JEMB Secretariat, up to now, had been unambiguously headed by Austin, though working under the authority of the Afghan and international JEMB commissioners. Arnault's proposal effectively introduced an Afghan management structure that would shadow the existing international structure that Austin had put in place. At the top, Austin and Wardak would share responsibility. Each department under them would similarly be headed by an Afghan and an international. Arnault stressed in a note on the new structure "the need to accelerate the training of Afghan experts and managers who will have to support the future 'Independent Electoral Commission' in the organization of elections, as prescribed by the Constitution." He continued: "This argues in favor of bringing more Afghan staff into the JEMB Secretariat Headquarters." It did—but it also didn't. As always, there was a need to find the appropriate balance between holding the 2004 elections under the best possible conditions and building Afghan capacity to hold future elections. Clearly, the objective of training a new cadre of electoral administrators on the job added a major burden to the already significant challenge of holding the first real election in Afghanistan's history. Arnault's sudden interest in capacity building at the very least conflicted with his earlier instruction to do everything possible to hold both elections in June. The concerns raised about about how this would affect the timing of operations were also dismissed. On February 18, Karzai signed a decree reifying the new management structure, specifying the following role for the United Nations: "The United Nations staff serving with the Electoral Secretariat shall provide advice and support in the implementation of all its functions. The United Nations may take all necessary measures to observe and verify the implementation of the decisions of the Joint Electoral Management Body."

Again EAD requested clarifications from UNAMA on how the structure would work. Its fundamental concern was the same as those evinced with the creation of the JEMB: that the respective responsibilities under the "co-responsibility" model were not clearly defined. The point, for EAD, was not to demand excessive refinement of essentially practical details, nor was it to undercut decisions taken in the field, many of which were perhaps the least-bad solutions to complex problems with a limited solution set. The point was to prevent, as much as possible, the organization from being held accountable for the results of an exercise over which it actually had very little operational control. The new management structure appeared to EAD to institutionalize that worst-case scenario.

These concerns were shared by the UEC managers, who believed that the co-responsibility concept could work in theory, but should not be applied to the 2004 election, which was still, officially, less than half-a-year away. The UEC managers argued that shifting to the new structure would be extremely disruptive at a time when the revised registration plan had to be implemented, and the election plan had to be refined. Both EAD and Austin had specific reservations regarding the ambiguous relationship between Austin and Wardak, as well as, at the middle-management level, the relations between the international experts and their new Afghan counterparts. There was reason for concern that, when faced with a choice between expediency and upholding electoral practice, expediency would win due to the significant political pressure for early elections and the eroded formal role of electoral experts. There was also concern that another form of pressure, from the presidential palace, would be exerted through Wardak.

This highlighted once again the great divide between EAD's conception of electoral management and that of UNAMA and Arnault. EAD considered that the rules of the relationships should be clearly defined and communicated. UNAMA preferred the inclusion of ambiguities to allow more flexibility of maneuver. This difference in conception, in fact, extended to elections themselves. EAD had argued that the rules of the game should be transparently formulated in consultation with the main actors, and then the political contest be fought according to those rules. The ultimate defense of any electoral result was that the process was credible in large part because the rules of the process were clear and had been agreed to by the major players before the process began. Arnault and DPKO were less focused on credibility as a central issue, and more worried about timetables and outcomes, in particular the desire of the international community to see Karzai elected, and hopefully in the first round.

This debate in fact went back to the United Nations' first massive electoral operation in Cambodia in 1992. In his analysis of the Cambodian operation, Stephen Ratner made the following comment about the head of UNTAC, under whom Austin had worked, Yasushi Akashi:

> Akashi's preference for mediation over assertive executive action resonated clearly with the career UN officials serving in UNTAC. They came from a tradition that places a premium on diplomatic discourse and proper relations with host authorities; in conference settings, UN officials, like many diplomats from member states, prefer to avoid confrontation through compromise, delay, or obfuscation (such as use of ambiguous phrasing in UN documents). This behavior reflects the need to interact with states with sharply contrasting political views and interests. The UN civil servant thus starts any relationship with foreign officials by trying to establish a smooth rapport. [...] This attitude, however, entails significant costs in new peacekeeping operations, where executing and guaranteeing a settlement assume primary importance. Defiance or hesitancy by one party does not always, or even often, merit utilization of the traditional tools of the UN civil servant.[11]

EAD felt that this behavior was recurring now in Afghanistan, that nothing had been learned from the past. Austin, who had been in charge of the Cambodian operation, must have sensed the parallels, and indeed his reticence to the co-responsibility model was possibly driven by a need to avoid them. But by this point, relations between EAD and UNAMA had so badly soured that no serious discussion was held on the restructuring issue. Arnault was acting-SRSG, with full powers over the mission. Understanding the pressure he was under to fill Brahimi's large footprints, nobody in the U.N.'s senior management in New York wanted to undermine his confidence by second-guessing him at such a delicate moment. As the new structure was put in place, UEC staff nervously followed the rumors surrounding the selection process of a new SRSG, hoping for an ally or at least someone with electoral experience who would give more weight to their concerns. The rumors, however, increasingly indicated that Arnault himself would be confirmed as SRSG, as the search outside the U.N. was yielding few results. This was an outcome that the UEC dreaded—it would mean that the co-responsibility model would be irrevocable, and that the UEC would be in a powerless passive position during the planning of fantastical June elections "co-managed" by an Afghan Secretariat whose head was one of the most trusted advisors of the leading candidate for the presidency. The issue for the UEC was no longer credibility, but incredulity. This was an election rapidly ceasing to resemble any they had previously experienced.

---

[1] AREU was a Kabul-based research organization funded by international donors and led by international staff. It prepared highly intelligent research papers on all the major components of the Afghan transition and reconstruction process.

[2] Christina Bennett, Shawna Wakefield, and Andrew Wilder, "Afghan Elections: The Great Gamble," Afghanistan Research and Evaluation Unit, Kabul, November 2003, p. 16.

[3] "UN Representative Warns That Afghan Peace Is Fragile," Carlotta Gall, *New York Times,* 24 February 2003.

[4] Under the constitution's chapter on Transitional Provisions, Article 162 states, "Multilateral efforts shall be made to hold presidential as well as National Assembly elections concurrently and simultaneously."

[5] Carlotta Gall, "With Future Charted, U.N. Envoy Departs," *The New York Times*, January 6, 2004. The reference to "instant coffee" uncannily echoes Dupree's criticism of the 1960's New Democracy. Dupree reported that most Afghans "knew little and cared less about the new Constitution and 'New Democracy,'" but the intelligentsia in the urban areas "chafed at the slowness of the government [...] in moving towards 'true' democracy." Dupree editorializes: "What these dissident intellectuals (usually Western-trained) wanted was 'instant democracy': take dry Constitution, continue with fluid elections and stir, and *voilà*, 'instant democracy'—without the agony of generations of development." Dupree, *Afghanistan,* p. 587). The Brahimi report also dealt with this issue: "Elections need the support of a broader process of democratization and civil society building that includes effective civilian governance and a culture of respect for human rights, lest elections merely ratify a tyranny of the majority or be overturned by force after a peace operation leaves." Brahimi Report, para. 38

[6] There was still, at the time, an assumption by most that Brahimi would be replaced by someone besides Arnault. The main candidate at the time was Abdul-Ileh al-Khatib, then the Jordanian Deputy Foreign Minister, who had been recommended by Brahimi, and who had gone as far as to visit Kabul before deciding on the job, but who ultimately declined the offer.

[7] Steven Weisman, "U.S. Aides Hint Afghan Voting May be Put Off" *New York Times,* 16 February 2004.

[8] Allowing the population to see the voter lists, verify that their names were on them if eligible, or point out others who should not be on them, was considered standard practice, especially when it was the first time that such a list had been produced. Nonetheless, given the quality of the data, and the fact that the lists would not be able to be broken down per polling station, this would be a largely superficial exercise.

[9] The increase was due to a variety of factors, including the need to use air transport more than land and sea in order to get materials on time.

[10] NDI was a U.S. non-profit organization loosely associated with the U.S. Democratic Party. It carried out pro-democratization activities around the world. In Kabul, it had mostly focused its activities on strengthening political parties and civil society.

[11] Steven R. Ratner, *The New UN Peacekeeping* (New York: St. Martin's Press, 1995) pp. 200-201.

9

Voter Registration: Turning Victims into Citizens

In December 2003, the registration process had begun with a gimmick that allowed Brahimi's self-imposed December 1 deadline to be met. The UEC established registration centers in the eight major cities where elections were taking place for delegates to the Constitutional Loya Jirga. The results were negligible—only the 19,000 delegates attending the indirect Loya Jirga elections in the eight regional centers were targeted for registration. The beginning of registration took place with little fanfare; most of the attention was addressed to the constitutional rather than the electoral process. If the fact of a December beginning to the electoral registration gave confidence to the international community, then the token start was a success. From the perspective of democratic institution-building, however, it was meaningless. The real issue was to register as many of the estimated 11 million eligible voters as possible, not 20,000 members of the political elite.

The challenge was to bring the registration process to the population at large. The uncertainty of donor financing continued to be a major worry into 2004, but there were two more immediate concerns for the UEC, both related to the deteriorating security situation. First, UNAMA's head of security issued a directive in November 2003 not to use schools as registration sites in the south, southeast and eastern regions of Afghanistan while schools were still in session. The logic was that registration activities could expose schools—and therefore teachers and students—to terrorist threats. This was a blow to the UEC; in many communities, rebuilt schools, with their solid infrastructure and multiple rooms, were the only appropriate places to conduct registration, especially in the winter when teams and their equipment would need to be shielded from the elements.

The second significant concern was that UNV headquarters in Bonn decided to halt the deployment of volunteers to Afghanistan until it was confirmed that MOSS-compliant accommodation could be found for them. This decision was prompted by the discovery that many UNVs were being lodged in a guesthouse that was deemed insecure. This decision prevented the deployment of about 60 UNVs assigned to the registration project. It was a serious blow since most of the internationals carrying out registration were UNVs, acting as a sort of electoral infantry who were essential to extending registration to the regions. Frantic efforts were made to locate a MOSS-compliant facility in Kabul that would be able to temporarily house UNVs from the moment they arrived in-country until they were deployed to the regions. Facilities in the regions also had to be MOSS compliant, which was not always the case. There were, at the time of the decision to halt the deployment of UNVs to Afghanistan, 25 UNV Registration Supervisors in Kabul waiting to travel to the regions. The decision to halt deployment backed everything up, jeopardizing the next phases of the registration project, when an estimated additional 250 UNV supervisors were expected to be deployed. (It should be noted that all of this took place in late 2003, before the decision to Afghanize the operation and when it was still expected that the United Nations would bear the brunt of the registration exercise, hence the reliance on low-cost UNVs.)

The security concerns that led to these decisions were real. In November 2003, a car bomb detonated in Kandahar directly opposite the United Nations electoral office. Luckily, no staff members were inside at the time, and there were no injuries. But the incident suggested that the Taliban had identified the registration process as a strategic target and had sufficient intelligence to know which buildings and other assets were crucial to the operation. Practitioners of the grim art of war accounting knew that one or two losses of life could jeopardize the entire operation—the psychological impact of dead internationals could have a devastating effect, especially on UNVs, who weren't paid enough to justify the risk.[1]

Small mercies saved the project. The issue of MOSS-compliant residences for the UNVs was resolved by spending money to upgrade the accommodations, and United Nations security officials allowed the process to move forward despite the immense security risks that were being courted by these staff. The schools remained off-limits, however, and the registration teams had to find creative alternatives.

By mid-December, registration began to expand slowly across the country, beginning in the major cities. Turnout was particularly heavy in Jalalabad, Herat, and Bamyan. Because of the restriction on using school buildings as registration sites, the process was halted entirely in Kunduz and Mazar-i-Sharif, where classes continued until later in the month. Unfortunately, the end of classes coincided with the beginning of winter.

Heavy snows—occurring earlier than expected in the winter of 2003 and 2004—forced the closing of several sites in Bamyan. This foretold the problems ahead.

Registering Women

The registration plan included a number of specific provisions to encourage the registration of women. The need to register women was self-evident from a political rights perspective. It was equally self-evident for reasons of political representation. Paradoxically, the extra efforts to register women helped the conservative Pashtun population. The lack of reliable up-to-date figures on Afghanistan's population meant that, over the previous decades, each major ethnic group had an inflated sense of its own importance. Pashtuns, who considered themselves a majority of the population, already felt "alienated" by the Bonn process,[2] particularly after the Emergency Loya Jirga, where they felt they had not been accorded a role commensurate with their numbers and their historical political domination of the country. The combined perceptions of political alienation and demographic overestimation created a minefield into which the registration process was forced to march.

The data from the registration process would inevitably be seen as a proxy census in Afghanistan.[3] Its results would therefore be politically contentious. The results would also have to be taken into account, directly or indirectly, in what many feared would be a fervid political battle over the allocation of seats per province for the lower house.[4]

These two factors made the registration of women in Pashtun areas essential to Pashtuns in general. They were, however, more conservative than most other ethnic groups in Afghanistan and, therefore, much more reluctant to allow their women to vote. On the other end of the scale were the Hazaras, who comprised the main Shia population in Afghanistan, who were far more relaxed about allowing women to register. The combination of security problems in the south, and the contrasting attitudes toward women, meant that there was a real risk that the numbers of Pashtuns and Hazaras registered would be distorted relative to each other, risking an even deeper alienation of the Pashtuns. The point was not to engineer a result that conformed to the Pashtun's own view of their numerical superiority, but to encourage maximum enfranchisement in accordance with human rights norms.

The discrepancies became apparent early in Phase I of the registration process. They were noted by Arnault in a report to U.N. headquarters at the end of February. At that moment, women represented 27 percent of the total number of registered voters. The good news was that the weekly rate of women's registration had begun at about 14 percent and had risen to over 30 percent, suggesting a demonstration effect was at work—the more women registered, the more they incited others to register. UNAMA presented the following breakdown, however, which showed significant divergence between the main regions of Afghanistan. In the Central Highlands, 42 percent of registrants were women—the highest in the country. The western and northern regions were not far behind, with women's registration at 37 percent. The south and southeast, however, were at 14 and 13 percent respectively, and the east, at 17 percent. Forty-two percent of all registrants were from the central region where Kabul was located (reflecting the urban targeting of Phase I); here 27 percent of registrants were women.

Special incentives were put in place to try to increase the overall participation of women, especially in the south. The Washington-based International Foundation for Electoral Systems (IFES) had funded a study on the best ways to target women in rural areas of Afghanistan. Among the more creative ideas was to provide small, useful items for distribution at female civic education and registration venues, such as basic hygiene products like washing soap, combs, shampoo, and baby powder. In addition, civic education messages were crafted to appeal not only to women, but to the men who retained a significant influence over the women in their families. The electoral unit had provided for women-only civic education teams and voter registration teams to be hired throughout the country. These teams were also made mobile and sent to locations where women gathered, such as mosques and clinics. The fact that women would be registered only by women reduced the reluctance of men to allow them to register—but there were fears that there would simply not be enough women registrars for when the program had to be ramped up during Phase II. Literacy, of course, was a major factor, as was the insistence of many families that women registrars be accompanied by a male relative.

Nonetheless, as the process continued, both statistical and anecdotal evidence began to suggest that the Afghan public, and especially men, had begun to understand the relationship between registered women voters and political influence for their areas. Furthermore, political leaders had begun to compete among themselves to register more voters, for example, by providing transportation for women, as was done by the Mayor of Kabul.

Flaws in the Voter Registration Database

The positive attitudes of political leaders towards the registration exercise in general had a great mobilizing effect. On January 18, President Karzai registered to vote in a televised ceremony intended to help boost public interest. By the end of January, the total number of registered voters reached half a million. At that time, 200 teams were operating in 50 sites, but all of these sites were within the eight regional centers—none had reached the other provincial capitals, let alone the more remote districts, where awareness of the electoral process and the importance of voter registration were far weaker.

As planning for Phase II intensified, two immediate problems presented themselves. The first was the need to make the data center fully operational. This need increased as registration accelerated. Registered voters were presented at the moment of registration with a laminated card containing a Polaroid photo[5] and their name, their date of birth, their father's name, as well as their province and district (or municipality and municipal district). The same data was entered into a counterfoil that replicated the registration number as on the card. The counterfoil was sent back to Kabul for entry into a national database. The idea was to be able to have at least a breakdown for planning purposes of the number of voters by province. (For reasons already explained, it was impossible to be sure of the accuracy of district identification or to assign voters to polling stations.) Also, in theory, each voter would be identified by a single registration number, and his or her individual information would be in the database in Kabul. (Embarassingly, these individual numbers, it was later discovered, were not coded by province.)

The database was based on software that the Australian Electoral Commission had developed for Pacific island states. The delays in building and equipping the data center, and then in recruiting and training national staff, meant that a backlog of counterfoils built up as the pace of registration increased. This backlog had to be reduced prior to Phase II, when the amount of data coming in would increase exponentially. The data center began work on January 26, with 17 operators. The plan called for 30 to 40 applicants to be tested and interviewed, with the goal of hiring 15 to 20 operators per week. The intermediate target was to have at least 50 operators by the first week of February, and 100 as soon as possible after that.

The second problem was the quality of the data. The operators at the data center—mostly young Afghans who had learned computing as refugees in Pakistan—quickly realized that the counterfoils contained a significant amount of errors. These ranged from omission of vital data on the forms (for example, the name of father), misspelling of names, and poor handwriting. Many of the registration team members were quite old—two generations of Afghans in Afghanistan, after all, had been deprived of an education, particularly in rural areas. Older Afghans were more likely to be able to read or write, but many of these also had bad eyesight or tired quickly. These were unavoidable realities of the Afghan context—the unforeseen details that were the products of years of war.

The immediate consequence of the flawed data was that it undermined the whole idea of a central database. If, for example, a name in the electronic register was, because of poor calligraphy, spelled differently by the data operator than it was on the card, then the connection between the data entry and the card-holder was broken. Additionally, if part of the data was omitted, then possible corroborating keys were lost, further sundering the connection.

The quality of the Afghan voter register would be correctly criticized by all of the post-election auditors, evaluators, and observers.[6] The register—though not the cards—was essentially useless as a means of ensuring electoral integrity and electoral planning, as its critics later charged. But few of these critics were aware of the particular constraints of the Afghan environment, and especially of the fact that the timelines imposed simply did not allow these constraints to be addressed.

Phase II and Funding Woes

January 2004 saw the departure of the UEC Chief of Operations, Peter Spelman. Spelman had earned a sterling reputation for his work overseeing the 2001 elections in East Timor. Afghanistan, of course, was an entirely different challenge in scale and scope, and these challenges had frustrated Spelman. Unlike Timor in 2001, where the United Nations had an existing electoral team whose roots reached back to the 1999 popular consultation, the Afghan operation had to be built from nothing and quickly. The political, security, and social complexities of Afghanistan were far more intricate than those of Timor. Spelman had not responded convincingly to mounting criticisms of the registration process by the UNAMA political team as well as from the outside experts embedded in groups such as the Asia Foundation and interested embassies. The relationship between Arnault and Spelman, in particular, had reached a point of almost perpetual conflict, with Arnault's frustration easier to justify than Spelman's irritation. At the end of January, Spelman was temporarily replaced by Kerry Heisner, a more dynamic operator with experience with the United Nations in the East Timor elections and in Afghanistan with IFES, until a full-time Chief of Operations could be identified. Heisner's personality and thicker skin fit better with the nature of the mission and he was able quickly to impose some order on the UEC.

Heisner's main task during his interim period was to move the registration process beyond the major cities and plan for the June elections that Arnault and the Americans continued to insist upon. As February drew to a close, the June deadline appeared increasingly fantastical. Even more unrealistically, the project was still expected by its political masters to run on goodwill rather than hard cash. At the end of February, $71.2 million had been pledged out of the budgeted $98.4 million for registration, but only $31.4 million had actually been received in cash. Donors perversely maintained that they were unconvinced the United Nations was doing a satisfactory job, and therefore, had not yet put their money in the trust fund.[7] They did not seem to understand that the main factor in the United Nations' unconvincing performance was the funding that donors still refused to provide.

Given that June was still the official date for the election, every day counted. A major problem from the lack of funding was the inability to procure essential big ticket items, such as the Russian jeeps that were required to transport the registration teams into the hinterland. As long as registration teams were operating in major cities, teams could find other means of transport—for example rented vehicles or taxis. Once the project moved beyond the cities and into the provincial capitals, they would need the full complement of jeeps for the transport of registration teams and their equipment as well as for the police teams that would accompany them. Once the jeeps arrived, it took about several weeks for them to clear customs. Then they had to be fitted with the appropriate radios, logged, and given license plates—adding more weeks to the process. These lags would be repeated in some form or other for every major purchase—voter registration kits, ballots, election materials, and so forth. The delays bothered the donors, who continued to withhold funding. In a frustrating vicious circle, donor ambivalence was adding to the cost of the project and causing less-than-optimal results, both of which increased donor ambivalence.

Lines of Control

In the month following Brahimi's January 2004 departure, Arnault had been operating in an interim capacity as SRSG. The search for

Brahimi's successor gradually wore down without result. On February 6, 2004, Secretary-General Annan abandoned the search and appointed Arnault as SRSG and head of UNAMA.

Arnault happened to be in New York when his appointment was announced. One of his first acts as SRSG was to ask EAD in New York if Austin could be replaced. Austin, he argued, had alienated many Afghans by suggesting that they did not have the capacity to run an electoral operation. Perelli now found herself having to defend Austin. Twelve months earlier she had questioned his appointment by Brahimi, but now she shared Austin's concerns, which had been frequently communicated to EAD by Austin and his team, about an increasingly unclear United Nations role which disconnected the organization's authority from its accountability. Whatever Austin's weaknesses were as a bureaucratic warrior, he had consistently defended the need for credible elections.

EAD was aware of the growing tensions in Kabul between Austin and AIEC chair Zakim Shah on one side, and Arnault and Farooq Wardak on the other, over the implementation of the co-responsibility model. The informal e-mails from UNAMA's electoral team to EAD had begun to suggest that some key staff members were sufficiently concerned about the credibility of the election that they were considering leaving the project if their roles under the co-responsibility model were not clarified. Many complained that Arnault was attempting to sideline the U.N. international electoral professionals, in part encouraged by advice he was getting from the Asia Foundation. They feared that the goal of holding elections according to the timetable was being pursued at a cost that was too high in terms of the credibility of the process. They also feared that, on the Afghan side, the same move was being made by Wardak, who had managed to bring in his Constitutional Loya Jirga staff without any vetting process. In other words, the fault lines were not between Afghans and internationals, but between electoral and non-electoral staff.

The uncertainty among international staff regarding their role under Arnault's now-confirmed leadership was matched by an uncertainty in general of working in Afghanistan. On January 28, 2004, a suicide bomber in a vehicle exploded himself while targeting an ISAF convoy on Jalalabad Road. The incident occurred in front of the UEC compound. Shockwaves from the blast broke office windows and damaged doors; debris and body parts were thrown into the compound yard.

The professional doubt, metaphysical questioning, and physical insecurities generated an extreme pessimism among international electoral staff. At the same time, they were increasingly criticized at the working level by important donors who had begun to question, at cocktail parties and at the U.N. bar, the ability of the team to deliver registration. All of this was included in an e-mail from Austin—who shared many of these doubts, questions, fears, and pessimism—to EAD around that time. Austin described "a state of uncertainty amongst the international staff, which is not helped by the fact that this and associated processes tend to 'move' in unpredictable ways." He added that he had discussed these concerns with individual staff members and had reassured them that "in all the circumstances they are entitled to assess their professional and personal security concerns in these radically changing circumstances." This solicitude may have been misinterpreted by some staff as an invitation to leave; certainly, it reflected the authentic doubts of many on the team about whether they would be able to fulfill their professional goals with the integrity they felt they required. EAD had already received several emails from staff members who wanted to know if the United Nations would still consider them for future electoral work if they decided not to renew their contracts in Afghanistan.

The electoral team certainly had its faults—a tendency towards defeatism in face of Afghanistan's difficult context, an insufficient dynamism, and too often an undiplomatic or dismissive attitude towards other colleagues in the mission who better understood the political context. (Their critics, especially donors, had their faults as well—a similar incomprehension of the environment, an inability to deliver funds, and a primitive understanding of the role elections play in postconflict transitions in general, and in Afghanistan in particular.) But for Perelli, the electoral experts were professionals with significant experience. Given her own battles with the U.N. bureaucracy over similar issues, she sympathized with their Kafkaesque torment—on the one hand being called upon to organize elections according to certain norms of credibility, and on the other hand being denied first the means and then the authority to do so.

EAD addressed this situation by sending a detailed note to Prendergast on March 2, 2004. The note recommended that the Arnault needed to provide more clarity on exactly how the international and Afghan roles were supposed to be divided. EAD's main fear was not of a "sub-par" election—that was a given and always had been. It was of having to accept responsibility for an election over which it had no real control.

At the same time, EAD sent an email to Austin laying out what it understood to be the main concerns of electoral staff and proposing ways to resolve them. Among the proposals was that if guarantees could not be provided that the United Nations would have the means to defend its essential norms, then EAD would propose that a purely technical assistance mission be established, where it was clear that the Afghans would be ultimately responsible for the electoral exercise, and it was equally clear that the U.N. role was to provide non-binding advice.[8] The e-mail was also intended to assure the electoral team that EAD was defending their position, given that no one else in the system seemed to be, and that their expertise remained essential to the success of the operation. A copy of the email was given to Arnault by one of its recipients. He immediately called EAD to complain that it was acting as a "wedge rather than a bridge" between UNAMA and its electoral component. He followed this by writing his own email, addressing the same concerns that EAD had attempted to address. Meanwhile, in a separate email, Austin wrote his own response to EAD. These separate but simultaneous communications by Arnault and Austin, reacting to the same issues, demonstrated the distance that remained between the SRSG and his Chief Electoral Officer. Arnault's point was that "you cannot be a control freak in postconflict peacebuilding these days." He insisted that the implied or informal "agreements" with the Afghans would ensure that the U.N. maintained sufficient control. For Austin, it was important to clarify what could be clarified, even while understanding that not *everything* could be clarified. For Austin, the "grey zones" created by Arnault's implicit agreements would "only increase the possibility of denying us the control needed to avoid 'unelectoral' decisions, while having to bear the responsibility of being the implementors of what we would regard as 'wrong' decisions."

On an operational level, EAD had hoped that by addressing the concerns of electoral staff—who spoke a different language than Arnault's political team, but a language that EAD understood—it would be able to prevent a potentially catastrophic departure of the electoral staff. In doing so, EAD had misjudged the amount of bad blood that ran between Austin's team and Arnault's. The net result of the initiative was to ensure that the UNAMA-EAD rift that had been created under Brahimi would continue under Arnault. The divide between the UEC and the rest of UNAMA would also deepen. The irreconcilable positions on how to manage the United Nations' electoral role was now affected more deeply by irreconcilable personalities.

Austin, for his part, tried to clarify his practical concerns in a detailed e-mail to Wardak at the end of February. Wardak's view of his own role, in his reply to Austin, was clear, almost arrogantly so:

> As Director of the Secretariat, I am responsible for the process and will be held responsible by the Afghan nation and the international community for whatever goes wrong, therefore, I need to make sure that an adequate management structure is put in place,[the] right people are put in the right jobs at the right time, comprehensive and reader friendly rules of procedures are put in place, all staff members are trained in the [rules of procedure], and then we let them do the job.

This was undoubtedly a competent and confident response of a manager. What it did not do, however, was allay the fears of the internationals regarding the credibility of the election. This was especially important given Wardak's close relationship with Karzai. Whatever misgivings Perelli and EAD might have had about Austin at the beginning, he was doing exactly what EAD would have expected of him—fighting for guarantees of a credible electoral process. Knowing, surely, that he was at the losing end of the battle, Austin nonetheless sent a reply to Wardak that attempted at least to explain the substance of his concerns. It was a *cri de coeur,* and perhaps, a valedictory warning. Austin had surely understood by then that he would be able to do very little against the combined weight of Arnault and Karzai, who both stood solidly behind Wardak:

> Here, as at every stage of your work as Director, you will be under enormous pressure to satisfy a range of important interests which may not coincide with the credibility of the Secretariat as an objective, neutral and professional organization. It must be a body clearly and exclusively dedicated to the achievement of an electoral process which will result in elected bodies, from Central Government downwards, which are perceived by people everywhere, as legitimate. The pressures will come from many whom you respect, from those who may seem to have the power to ruin you or to make your life much better. You will be faced with the choice between your commitment to the electoral process and self-interest, which one can quite easily rationalize as less than that. It is for this reason that the various procedures and processes surrounding all good electoral practices are put in place: to ensure transparency. This makes it more difficult for us, as electoral officials (from the registration/polling officer upwards) to succumb to the pressures and temptations we will certainly and constantly be faced with. And if we do succumb to them, to make our error transparently obvious and thus capable of rectification.

For better or for worse, by late February, Arnault's co-responsibility electoral management structure was in place. On February 18, Karzai signed a decree revising the composition of the JEMB.[9] Now, the six members of the AIEC and the five international members appointed by the SRSG[10] still had voting rights, while the Director of the Electoral Secretariat (Wardak), appointed by the president, and the Chief Technical Advisor of the United Nations (Austin) would be members without the right to vote. The second decree also contained a far more detailed lists of "tasks" for which the JEMB would be responsible.

The decree additionally created the "Electoral Secretariat," which was the implementation arm of the JEMB. The Secretariat was headed by Wardak and his managers from the Constitutional Commission were appointed to head the substantive units. The decree, interestingly, stated that the "Secretariat shall, under the supervision and instruction of the Joint Electoral Management Body, and in consultation with UNAMA, perform the following tasks [...]."[11] The concerns of the international electoral team, now reduced to a consultative status, about political interference were hardly allayed. Most of them, nonetheless, stayed on.

Around the time that the decree on the new JEMB was issued, one of the more experienced members of the JEMB, who had worked a great deal on behalf of EAD in other countries, was in New York. Meeting with EAD's Afghanistan team, he confirmed the perception that had emerged through the various e-mails: that Arnault was ignoring electoral advice, that morale among the UEC had "tanked," and that other actors—such as the Asia Foundation and IFES—were taking over electoral activities and decisions.

Still, with all its ambiguities, implied agreements, internal contradictions, and external interference, the new electoral structure had to get quickly to work. Phase II of the registration project was looming and the elections themselves had to be planned, especially if they were to be held in June, which was still the official position.

Distraction and Opportunity: EAD and Iraq

Perelli had lost another battle in Afghanistan with the implementation of the co-responsibility model despite her cautions. Her attention to the process in Afghanistan was, in any case, further attenuated by events to the west, in Iraq, where she was called upon to play an unexpectedly significant role. In fact, the Afghan electoral process was beginning to intersect with Iraq in illuminating ways that were only beginning to be perceived, and that would bring her into conflict again with Brahimi.

An Iraqi parenthesis is here required. In late 2003, the prominent Iraqi Shia cleric, Ayatollah Ali Sistani, had rejected an American plan for caucus-style indirect elections for the new Iraqi government to which it intended to hand sovereignty in June 2004. Sistani insisted that direct national elections must be held prior to the planned handover of sovereignty in June. Hundreds of thousands of his followers filled the streets of Baghdad, demonstrating his capacity to mobilize the Shia community, and by implication, to undermine any political formula that he did accept. Sistani further stated that the only way he would accept a postponement of direct national elections was if the United Nations determined that these were not technically possible by June. In February 2004, Perelli was instructed by the Secretary-General to go to Baghdad to assess the feasibility of Sistani's conditions.[12]

This put the U.S. in an illogical position. In Afghanistan, the administration was requesting that elections be held by June, no matter what EAD said about the feasibility of holding credible elections under that timeline. In Iraq, the ability of the U.S. to extract itself from the occupation with a minimum of legitimacy and without provoking a political crisis depended on the assessment of the head of EAD. In other words, in Iraq they depended on the same United Nations advice on the credibility on elections that they appeared willing to ignore in Afghanistan.

---

[1] Regular U.N. staff were fairly well remunerated, receiving on top of their salary and living allowance a hazard pay of a thousand dollars per month. The UNVs received a minimal stipend rather than a salary. Since they were volunteers, however, they could opt out of the Afghanistan effort. Given the surge of electoral operations the United Nations was conducting around the world at the time, they had a number of other employment options. (In 2004, the U.N. was also heavily involved in preparing elections in Burundi, the Democratic Republic of the Congo, Iraq, and Liberia.)

[2] The real issue, initially, was perhaps less "Pashtun alienation" in general, than alienation of those Pashtuns who felt that they had been insufficiently rewarded or included by the Karzai Government, such as many Ghilzais, which were the rival tribe to Karzai's Durranis. There was, at the time, an ongoing debate as to whether the Neo-Taliban phenomenon was a Ghilzai reaction to the dominance of Karzai's Durrani tribe. Giustozzi provides a compelling argument that the Ghilzai leadership of the Taliban did not necessarily make it a Ghilzai movement: "Clearly, the Taliban did not want to present themselves as aligned with a particular tribe or community. This made it easier for them to move across tribal territories without antagonizing the locals, but at the same time was also a way of advertising the Movement as above inter-community rivalry." See Giustozzi, *Koran, Kalashnikov and Laptop,* pp. 47-48.

[3] The voter registration teams of course did not ask people's ethnic identities, but with the exception of Kabul, which was very ethnically mixed, geographic areas served as a sufficiently credible proxy for ethnicity.

[4] The UNAMA electoral team successfully opposed a proposal to base the apportionment on registration figures, in part because the registration process

would only measure eligible voters, rather than total population, and in part because of problems of access and variations of tradition mentioned above that would inevitably distort even the numbers of voters registered.

[5] It did not help that, after nearly five hundred Polaroid cameras had been sent to the field, technicians from Polaroid identified several problems with the cameras and determined that all of them were likely to fail sooner or later. The cameras had to be recalled and representatives from Polaroid were dispatched to Kabul to find a solution.

[6] Ashraf Ghani and Clare Lockhart are particularly harsh critics, arguing that instead of helping Afghanistan to "leapfrog history and create a unified database of the country's citizens based on reliable biometrics that would have enabled the state to function and increase citizens' access to certification of their own identities," the U.N. "blocked this innovation by instead insisting on an expensive manual method that allowed significant fraud to take place." Ghani was Minister of Finance at the time and indeed introduced UEC experts to representatives of a private firm that was attempting to sell a biometric database. The UEC team felt that Ghani underestimated the logistical problems of making such systems work in a place like Afghanistan. In fact, an effort to implement a high-tech biometric registration system in Timor Leste had almost derailed the election. A similar system in the more infrastructurally-developed Balkans have also proven extremely problematic. Ghani and Lockart's account is in *Fixing Failed States,* pp. 77-78.

[7] The electoral team knew that U.S. embassy staffers in particular were openly criticizing the U.N. U.S.-U.N. relations were at a low point in general, given the Iraq war. The U.S. was, however, the major donor to the project and its support was critical.

[8] This was the model adopted for the 2009 and 2010 elections. See Chapter 16 below.

[9] Decree No. 110 of 18 February 2004.

[10] On 22 January 2004, the SRSG appointed the following to the JEMB: Mr. Irfan Mohamed Abdool-Rahman (Mauritius), Mr. Jose Maria Aranaz (Spain), Mr. Reginald Austin (New Zealand), Mr. Ray Kennedy (USA), and Ms. Barbara Reinhardus (Canada). Mr. Aranaz replaced Mr. Halff (see Chapter 5, footnote 1) as legal advisor. Eventually, as 2004 wore on, Ms. Reinhardus would be replaced by Lily Munir (Indonesia), Mr. Abdool Rahman by Mr. Surinder K. Mendiratta (India). Mr. Svante Renstrom (Sweden) became the fifth international member when Austin, as head of the JEMB Secretariat, became a non-voting member.

[11] Decree of the President of the Islamic Transitional State of Afghanistan on the Elements of Convening Elections during the Transitional Period, 18 February 2004, Decree No. 110, Article 3(2). Emphasis added.

[12] In a further twist in this tale full of twists, when she arrived in Amman, Jordan, on her way to Iraq, Perelli learned that Brahimi would in fact be "leading" the U.N. "fact-finding" mission to Iraq, a detail that had been kept from her until the last minute.

10
Democracy and the Durand Line

Spring in Afghanistan presents a wondrous awakening from the bleak dreariness of its winters. The snows melt, the rivers swell, the rains leave behind a stubble of green on the brown hills, the still-white caps of the highest mountains glisten stark and clean against deep turquoise skies, while the more remote valleys fill with red and yellow poppies and their tragic but lucrative harvest.

UNAMA's electoral team felt little of this charm as they took stock of the situation. They were still under orders to hold elections in June—only several months away—yet there was no electoral law, few funds, and only about ten percent of estimated eligible voters had been registered. They remained, as experts, unsure of their role within the new management structure that had been established in haste and with confusion and controversy. For them, spring signified no rebirth, only the relentless hammering of time and the oppressive reminder that too much remained to be done in too few days.

In mid-March, Heisner, the temporary chief of operations, left Afghanistan as planned. David Avery, another former official of the Australian Electoral Commission, with over 20 years experience including in international operations, took over the vital post of Chief of Operations. Avery was, like Heisner, energetic and unintimidated by the Afghan environment. To some, he was too blunt and too insensitive to Afghan leadership. To others, this characteristic was necessary given the huge time constraints on the operation. Upon arriving in Kabul, he continued Heisner's efforts to tighten up the operation and respond to the unforeseeable issues that continued to complicate the mission.

One of his first concerns was to address the constantly deteriorating security conditions. As the registration process moved beyond the main regional centers, the registration teams became increasingly vulnerable. The registration security project, which oddly proved much easier to secure international funds for than the elections themselves, provided the teams with police escorts. But these would be insufficient against well-organized ambushes or improvised explosive devices, the increasingly preferred tactics of the growing insurgency. In February 2004, Mullah Dadullah, a Taliban commander thought to be responsible for killing a Red Cross worker the previous year, as well as for massacres against Afghans during the Taliban's period in power, publicly warned Afghans not to vote. Chris Patten, the European Union's External Relations Commissioner, happened to be in Kabul when Dadullah's announcement was made. Patton stated publicly that NATO would have to take a bigger security role in Afghanistan if the elections were to be held on schedule.

One of Avery's first moves was to establish, in early April, an Elections Security Operations Center (ESOC) to coordinate the activities of the security agencies involved in securing the election. ISAF, the U.S.-led Coalition, the Afghan National Army, and the Afghan Ministry of Interior were requested to send liaison officers to the ESOC. Each officer would be responsible for ensuring direct communications with their organization to provide accurate and timely communications between military and police organizations and the JEMB. The ESOC was established inside the JEMB compound and maintained 24-hour operations.

Avery made, early in his tenure, another decision that would have an important impact in the months that followed. He contracted a medical evacuation company with air support to deal with potential injuries that could occur during the process. UNAMA had up to then a minimal evacuation capacity from its single Cessna Citation executive jet, which served as transport for the SRSG but could be converted into a flying ambulance.

The poor security conditions, which had begun to prevent United Nations access to some areas of the country, also forced the introduction of a new set of actors into the electoral process. The United States government, through a grant to the Asia Foundation, had provided funds for an outside security company to carry out the important work of scouting and setting-up registration sites in areas that were off-limits to the U.N. The Asia Foundation, in turn, contracted a private security firm, Global Risk, to perform this task. Global had previously been contracted in Afghanistan to support the Emergency Loya Jirga. The approximately 100 employees hired for the electoral project tended to be former soldiers with significant logistical capabilities but with little linguistic, political or cultural training, and scant electoral expertise. Global deployed 33 two-man teams to the difficult provinces (except Uruzgan and Zabul, which were judged too dangerous even for them).

An additional 16 regional managers (two in each regional office) and six headquarters staff were attached to the JEMB Secretariat.

While the role of Global personnel was supposed to be limited to logistics support, it was obviously impossible for them to travel to remote areas to scout possible registration sites without explaining to locals what voter registration was and, therefore, what the election was. They consequently and unavoidably had to conduct basic civic education activities. This was not an ideal practice from the point of view of electoral credibility, but even EAD recognized that it was a necessary concession to the increasingly insecure realities of Afghanistan. With the Global teams filling the gap left by the U.N., Phase II was becoming a reality: the registration process was finally moving from the urban centers to the winding valleys of the country, where many people had not only never experienced an election, but, as it was later reported, some did not even know that the Taliban had fallen, the Bonn process had occurred, or that a man named Karzai was now the interim president of Afghanistan.

In the last week of March, reality began to impose itself on the June election date, especially within the JEMB. Phase II had not yet begun and, even if the exhibitions and challenges process for the register was eliminated, three weeks would not be enough to register the remaining millions. Furthermore, other elements on the critical path, especially the electoral law, were not yet in place. The JEMB therefore proposed, citing technical reasons, that the presidential election be held in September of 2004, and the far more complex parliamentary elections be postponed until 2005. Discussions were held with international stakeholders who, initially, continued to remain irrationally committed to a June election. The UNAMA electoral team (now part of the JEMB Secretariat but for all intents and purposes still carrying out the operational and financial planning) noted that, even for the September scenario to hold, all remaining funding would have to be in place by May 1, and the electoral law would have be adopted as soon as possible.

The Secretary-General, in his report to the Security Council on March 19, nonetheless continued to maintain, on Arnault's advice, that "the simpler process of presidential elections is deemed to be feasible in June or early July," though the report conceded that "parliamentary elections cannot be held so soon." The Secretary-General concluded that "Two basic options are therefore open: a presidential election within the Bonn time frame and a parliamentary election later this year or next year; or simultaneous elections held outside the Bonn time frame."[1] This position accepted one reality—the impossibility of legislative elections by June—but continued to advocate the fiction of holding presidential elections "within the Bonn time frame."

Consequences of the 2004 Berlin Conference

At the end of March, the German government hosted a major international conference on Afghanistan in Berlin. The conference was a sort of political coming-out party for Arnault, as the new SRSG, as well as an opportunity to reassess the overall status of the implementation of the Bonn Agreement. The upcoming elections—in particular the date and the need for financing—was a major theme.

The Berlin conference yielded three decisions that were of consequence for the Afghan elections. First, the participants agreed that the first phase of the DDR process—covering 40,000 soldiers—needed to be completed before elections could be held.[2] Second, the question of out-of-country voting for Afghan refugees was raised seriously for the first time.[3] On this topic, the conference's communiqué delicately concluded: "The Government of Afghanistan welcomes the support of the Governments of Pakistan and Iran to allow participation of Afghan refugees in their countries in the elections." While somewhat noncommittal, this wording implied an international endorsement of the idea of out-of-country elections. This was disappointing to the UEC international experts, who were afraid that conducting such a complicated operation at such a late date could undermine the already difficult in-country election. Third, the participants at Berlin specifically endorsed the provision in the new Afghan Constitution concerning transitional arrangements, namely that "multilateral efforts shall be made to hold presidential as well as National Assembly elections concurrently and simultaneously."[4] Except for the decision on DDR, which, if implemented, would help to improve the security environment, the Berlin decisions were greeted with dismay by the electoral planners. They seemed to institutionalize, publicly and at a high level, the lack of seriousness with which the process' major backers viewed the practicalities of the election.

Phase II of Registration

April 2004 was consumed by preparations for Phase II of voter registration, which was scheduled to begin on May 1. The Global teams had begun their work in the difficult provinces. The large numbers of UNVs—who had been requested the previous November but put on hold because of inadequate security arrangements—began to arrive in Kabul in April and were sent on to their field postings. Over 4,000 registration kits arrived and were ferried by truck and helicopter to Afghanistan's provinces. Spurred by the Berlin conference, the donors had finally become serious. By mid-April, $86.2 million had been received in cash or kind, and an additional $10 million had been committed. The shortfall for the registration project had been reduced to a manageable $4 million.

The famous Russian jeeps were finally arriving in bulk. There were now also sufficient funds to purchase 6,000 Thuraya satellite phones—essential security items in case of ambush. The number of registrations in the urban regional centers began to dwindle as a saturation point was reached. The JEMB Secretariat reduced the approximately 400 registration teams operating in the regional centers to about 250, and reconfigured the rest of the teams for deployment to the provinces with the new Russian jeeps. The hiring and training of additional registration staff began: provincial trainers instructed the 1,200 Afghan field coordinators, who in turn trained the approximately 35,400 registration staff at the provincial and district levels. Tons of civic education materials were flown in from Dubai, where they had been printed, and began making their way to the regional centers and then the provincial capitals. The data center, in the meantime, had finally begun to reduce its backlog. The additional staff required for the mountain of data that would come in as Phase II geared up were hired and trained. As spring temperatures began to rise in Kabul, the data center operators kept up their valiant fight with UNAMA administration for air conditioners.

The success of both the registration and the election would depend on people being aware of both processes—how they related to each other and how they could be accessed. There were two general types of messages: civic education, which roughly answered the question of "why vote?" and public information, which answered the questions of when, where, and how to vote? The usual challenges applied: the remoteness of the population, the forbidding terrain, and the lack of literacy among the targeted groups. In the absence of the written word, the two main methods of communication were radio, of which an estimated 80 percent of Afghans listened to daily, and the thousands of posters distributed throughout the country that conveyed in visual cartoons the importance of voting. Other techniques such as mobile theater, cinema, and flip-charts for face-to-face meetings were also used.

The civic education and public information unit had commissioned a number of local artists to paint either thematic scenes, such as the "road" from war to peace that passed through the electoral process, or more pragmatic information, such as the stages of the registration process or the fact that there would be separate registration and voting facilities for women. These posters were reproduced in the thousands and sent all over the country. It was especially important that these information campaigns begin as soon as possible to give time to sensitize people to what was ahead. Given that, at the time the materials were produced, so much about the election was unknown—its date or whether it would presidential *and* parliamentary or only presidential—the civic education team either had to be vague on certain issues or guess how decisions would ultimately be made. The information campaigns were like a massive game of charades, except that the contestants were not actually familiar what was being described. Despite these lacunae, the launch of the civic education and public information campaign had laid down a noticeable gauntlet—it provided a colorful and hopeful promise across the country that the elections *would* be held.

Following the overall intensification of activity in the spring of 2004, Phase II of registration began on schedule and generated a much-needed wave of optimism. By May 10, the total number of Afghans registered was over two million. The weekly total was more than 200,000, the highest ever. The daily average in the first weeks of Phase II was 45,000 per day, compared to 15,000 during Phase I. The target was 100,000 voters per day using 9,200 registration teams at 4,600 sites. Registration was proceeding in 30 of 34 provinces—Zabul, Nuristan, Paktika and the newly-created province of Dai Kundi were the exceptions, due to remoteness and insecurity. There were 343 operational registration sites and 664 teams, and the number was growing each week. Registration increased significantly in the northeast once the teams expanded beyond the regional center of Kunduz. Registrations in the Central Highlands increased in absolute terms, but declined as a percentage of the national total, given the massive increases everywhere else.

The expansion beyond the regional areas led to an immediate adjustment of the data trends. The proportion of women registering in the first weeks of Phase II was 35 percent, and was strong even in areas where it had been weak during Phase I. Nowhere in Afghanistan was the rate of women's registration lower than 20 percent, and the southeast, south and east registered 26, 29, and 34 percent respectively. The political incentives and the civic education efforts were combining to create numbers far superior to even the most optimistic estimates.

A harbinger of a more negative trend also occurred in early May. In Nuristan, two international staff from Global and their Afghan interpreter were killed while scouting registration sites in that remote and unruly province. The Taliban subsequently claimed responsibility for the assassinations. It was never clear if their claim was opportunistic—taking credit for an essentially criminal act—or if they had actually committed the murders. It was another demonstration, however, that to the Taliban election activities were a legitimate target. Farooq Wardak immediately visited Nuristan to discuss and explain electoral preparations with the tribal elders and, by his presence, attempted to demonstrate that electoral personnel would be safe.

No matter how much one wanted or needed to believe that attacks against registration assets were incidental, the vulnerabilities of the process were clear, and all evidence suggested that more attacks would occur. The Taliban understood as much as the international community how important the electoral process was to the creation of a viable state. The state that would ideally emerge from the transition process would be one in which there was little room for Taliban-style governance. The stakes had been raised for both sides.

The Initial Debate over Out-of-Country Voting

With Phase II underway and registration proceeding according to schedule, the JEMB Secretariat in Kabul had to focus on planning the elections themselves. In early May, the draft electoral law was still being formulated[5] though it was scheduled for cabinet consideration on the 16th of that month.

While the most contentious issues in the draft law were being ironed out, the JEMB was confronted with the still-lingering question of out-of-country voting in Iran and Pakistan. There were strong political rights arguments against excluding the Afghan refugee populations in these two countries. According to UNHCR, in September 2001 there were approximately 1.5 million Afghan refugees in Iran and 2 million in Pakistan. By the end of 2003, UNHCR had reported the return of 2.5 million refugees, mostly from those two countries. While there was a case that the remaining millions should be registered and allowed to vote, the existing plan did not cover them given the absence of a political decision on out-of-country voting (OCV). A decision to carry out OCV this late in the process would add huge costs to the operation and divert time and energy from the central goal of holding elections in Afghanistan.

The complications were much greater in Pakistan than in Iran. In Iran, Afghan refugees were provided identity documents (*amayesh* cards) by the Iranian government and were, therefore, easy to corroborate. In Pakistan, large refugee camps had been established for Afghans in the 1980s, and hundreds of thousands still lived in these camps. During the two-and-a-half decades of occupation and war, many

Afghans had also settled outside the camps, in the Pakistani cities of Peshawar and Quetta especially, but also as far south as Karachi. Some had been registered by UNHCR, but even many of those did not necessarily have identification papers. The issue was further complicated by the fact that Pakistani Pashtuns ("Pathans", as they were known in Pakistan) were ethnically identical to Afghan Pashtuns.

Here again, modern notions of identity cut across tribal ones, and old historical polemics began to matter. Pakistan's motives in pushing for OCV most likely had to do with the political imperative of stressing these spatially-mapped identities, rather than concern for the rights of Afghans in Pakistan. Coincidentally, between January 2004 and January 2006, Pakistan happened to be a member of the U.N. Security Council, where it was able to argue strongly for out-of-country voting.[6] (The Security Council was the U.N. organ charged with giving UNAMA its mandate and its guidance.) The historical fact behind Pakistan's position is related to the long and complicated story of the line drawn, but never fully demarcated, by Sir Henry Mortimer Durand between Afghanistan and British India in 1839. The line had been drawn before the existence of Pakistan, as a border between British India and Afghanistan. It had been accepted as a border by the Afghan Emir Abdur Rahman in the late nineteenth century, though Rahman later retracted this, arguing that he had accepted it "under duress," while he was weak and heavily pressured by Britain. Rahman's reticence was due to the fact that the line split the ethnically homogenous Pashtun population, which was his tribe. At one time, Peshawar, in present-day Pakistan, had been the winter capital of Afghan emperors. The Durand line was nonetheless inherited as an international border by Pakistan when that country was created following the partition of British India.

Prior to partition, the Afghan government and Pashtun nationalists had demanded a referendum offering those Pashtuns living in territories within the Raj the option of voting for independence—not simply the choice that they *were* offered between joining India or Pakistan. This third option of independence, which had been given to the princely states within the Raj, had been denied to the Pashtuns (as it had been to the Kashmiris, creating another, enduring international dispute). The "Pashtunistan" issue became a thorn in Afghan-Pakistani relations from the moment that Pakistan was created. It was one of the reasons that Afghanistan was the only country to vote against Pakistan's entry into the United Nations in 1947, and it helped to justify Pakistan's suspicions towards any government in Kabul that was not explicitly friendly to Islamabad or reassuringly weak.[7]

What this meant for the electoral process in 2004 was that, unless real safeguards were in place, Pakistani Pathans might be able to register as Afghan Pashtuns. Non-Pashtun groups in Afghanistan were quite aware of this and, in the event of a close election where a Pashtun narrowly beat out a non-Pashtun, the lack of safeguards in the out-of-country registration could be used as a strong argument not to accept the results. At the same time, there was a compelling intrinsic reason based in human rights and international practice to allow Afghan refugees to vote. In addition, the pace and pattern of refugee returns in 2003 and 2004 suggested that many who voted in 2004 would return before the next election; therefore they had a strong stake in the composition of Afghanistan's first democratic government.

While UNAMA's electoral experts used the possibility that out-of-country voting could undermine the credibility of the vote in-country, Pakistan's adroit diplomats turned the argument on its head. In meetings in Islamabad in late April with Arnault, Pakistani diplomats argued that the political process had to match the perceptions of Afghans—if too low a number of Pashtuns were registered to vote, the process would be considered by many, especially Pashtuns, to be flawed. Seen from that perspective, out-of-country voting could compensate for both security problems in the south and a lower rate of registration among Pashtun women.

There was a clear element of realpolitik in the Pakistani position. For many years, out of concern over the Pashtunistan issue, Pakistani policy towards Afghanistan was characterized by an attempt to co-opt Pashtun groups. Pakistan had channeled U.S. support during the Soviet occupation, for example, mostly to Pashtun groups, especially Hekmatyar's Hezb-i-Islami.[8] As Barnett Rubin wrote just prior to the emergence of the Taliban in 1994, the "resentments and fears that the Pashtunistan issue aroused in the predominantly Punjabi rulers of Pakistan, especially the military, continue to affect Pakistan's perceptions of interests in Afghanistan."[9] After the collapse of the Soviet Union, Pakistan saw a role for itself as a trade outlet for the newly-created central Asian states, and to complete that role it needed a pliant government in Kabul. Following the failure of Hekmatyar to gain a decisive advantage in Afghanistan after the collapse of Najibullah in 1992, Pakistan saw an opportunity in the Taliban.

When the Taliban emerged in 1994, supported by elements within the Pakistani government,[10] they offered the hope of pacifying enough of the country to open a transit corridor to Central Asia. In addition, the Taliban was, as has been noted, essentially a Pashtun movement in terms of ethnicity. Supporting the Taliban therefore fit the grand historical lines of Islamabad's policy towards Afghanistan. Finally, the fact that the anti-Taliban factions were supported by India, Pakistan's geopolitical, and perhaps even existential, rival added a further geopolitical dimension to the equation.[11]

A final reason for Pakistan's insistence on OCV might have been its reluctance to continue hosting the Afghan refugees. If these refugees voted as Afghans, they would have to admit to being Afghans. If they so admitted, then they would essentially renounce any long-term claim to remain in Pakistan.

Whatever the real reasons were for its support of OCV, in 2004 Pakistan was able to use its fortuitously-timed membership in the Security Council to insist that a March 26, 2004 resolution include an operative paragraph encouraging "Afghan authorities to enable an electoral process that provides for voter participation that is representative of the national demographics including women and refugees."[12] The word "refugees" brought Pakistan clearly into the Afghan electoral process.

A major problem in actually taking a decision on OCV, however, resulted from the uncertainty over the type of election to be held. Technically, it would be much easier to plan for refugee participation if only the presidential election was held in 2004. OCV for parliamentary elections, on the other hand, imposed huge costs and even more complications. First of all, a method would have to be defined to determine in which province refugees could be registered. Did it have to be their province of origin? If so, what sorts of documentation—if any—would have to be provided to prove this? Or would they be allowed to register for any province they wished? This latter option opened a possible opportunity for electoral manipulation—Pashtuns could be organized to register in non-Pashtun provinces where they could play a decisive role in determining who the winning candidates would be. Even if this didn't actually happen, it could always be claimed by those who disliked the result in a given province, and believed by those who wanted to believe it. The logistical complications were also immense. Ballots for multiple provinces would have to be provided in each polling station, according to the provinces for which voters in Pakistan and Iran registered. As long as the presumption remained that legislative elections would be held at the same time as presidential elections, the technical arguments against OCV remained compelling.

In February 2004, in anticipation of this question, the JEMB Secretariat had sent missions to Iran and Pakistan to look at the feasibility of out-of-country voting. On the basis of information gathered during these visits, the Secretariat estimated that out-of-country registration and elections would cost an additional $86 million—a high cost partially dictated by the tightening timeframe for elections. If a credible registration process were to take place in Pakistan, in particular, the bulk of this funding would have to be provided almost immediately. This exorbitant figure initially dampened enthusiasm for out-of-country voting among donors, whatever the objective arguments were, and whatever had been agreed to at Berlin and by the Security Council. This hesitation at the cost of the process contributed to the lack of appetite on the part of any party to take a decision or to insist that a decision be taken.

Through most of the spring of 2004, the out-of-country option was therefore debated without resolution and without a great deal of seriousness. The high costs and daunting complexities were dissuasive. But each day that passed without a decision raised the costs and increased the complexities. Ultimately, the decision was forced, rather than taken.

By the end of May, the results of registration had one politically worrying aspect: with a total of three million Afghans registered, and taking regions as proxies for ethnicity, Pashtuns only amounted to about 25 percent of registered voters. Given that the lowest estimates of the Pashtun share of the population were between 40 and 50 percent, the low rate of registration signaled a possible disaffection with the electoral project among Pashtuns, and laid the grounds for Pashtun complaints in the future. There were three explanatory variables for the low turnout. First, the registration figures took the south, south-east, and eastern regions as proxies for Pashtun voters, but didn't count Kabul. The population of Kabul was estimated to be around two million, most of whom were probably Pashtun. Since registration figures were not disaggregated by ethnicity, it was impossible to know for certain. The other two qualifications were the previously-discussed issues of women and security. The Pashtun areas tended to be less secure and, therefore, had fewer registration teams with reduced access to remote areas. The presumed reluctance to allow women to register for cultural reasons further decreased Pashtun registration numbers.[13] Even with these caveats, the low numbers of Pashtun registrants became a worrying variable for the international community, which expected and desired a Karzai victory in the election.[14] A strong Pashtun turnout would be critical to ensuring this result. Given these calculations, the prospect of registering an estimated 1.4 million Pashtun refugees in Pakistan suddenly became attractive for political reasons, as dangerous as it was for technical reasons. Once again, the political trumped the technical, and once again the main decision-makers failed to grasp the connections between the political and the technical.

UNAMA's electoral experts in Kabul had long assumed that the issue of out-of-country voting was dead. Its resurrection was swift, surprising, and clumsy. In late May, Arnault traveled to New York to brief the Security Council on developments in Afghanistan, a pre-scheduled event. Electoral preparations were, of course, the focus of interest. The JEMB had, at Arnault's request prior to his departure for New York, formally begun deliberating on out-of-country voting on the basis of a paper prepared by its Secretariat. The Secretariat's paper encapsulated the views of UNAMA's electoral experts—it was essentially pessimistic about OCV for technical and financial reasons.

The JEMB's deliberations were, however, suddenly confused by the introduction of a new paper, presented to it after Arnault's departure, that presented a far more optimistic scenario. The new paper suggested that out-of-country voting could be accomplished to a sufficient degree of technical correctness within the short time period remaining. The JEMB believed the second paper to be a revision by the Secretariat of its previous paper. In fact, it had been prepared by Arnault's office and was presented to the JEMB by his new chief of staff, Larry Sampler, formerly of the Asia Foundation. Deliberately or inadvertently, Sampler did not specify the origin of the new OCV paper. After presenting the paper, Sampler told the JEMB that a decision needed to be taken within the following two hours. His aim was to have a decision on the issue before Arnault addressed the Security Council. This would allow the SRSG to announce the decision in New York to the Council. The JEMB's Afghan commissioners had, by now, gained sufficient understanding of the importance of the issue and resisted the time pressure. They continued to discuss the issue long past Sampler's deadline.

By the time Arnault returned to Kabul, the JEMB still had not taken a decision. Arnault then played his trump card—he leaned on the international members to vote in favor of OCV, despite their strong reservations on technical grounds, by reminding them of the clause in their terms of reference that required them to "implement the strategies of the SRSG." This clause had been drafted during the time of Brahimi. Its intention had been to insulate international JEMB members against possible pressure from the Afghan government. Now it was being used by the SRSG to pressure the international experts into taking a decision that they did not agree with. Even the Afghan members of the JEMB, however, had misgivings on OCV, and the JEMB's final directive, issued on May 30, reflected the messiness of the circumstances in which the decision was made. The first part of their written decision presented the following premises: (i) It is essential to include refugees in Pakistan and Iran in the electoral process; (ii) Voting for refugees should be limited to participation in the presidential election; (iii) Out-of-country voting must take place simultaneously with the in-country voting; and (iv) The registration and election processes must meet minimum international standards.

The second part of the directive presented six "deep concerns" about holding OCV. These included the risk that the entire election might have to be postponed, that the additional funding suddenly required "will jeopardize the planning for and proper execution of in-country registration and voting activities," and that the different standards in Pakistan and Iran might be "unacceptably unfair." The JEMB concluded by noting that the decision in favor of holding OCV was made "based on political concerns rather than technical considerations." It was a decision that was not decisive, essentially saying: we'll do it, though it probably can't be done, and if it can be done, it will be at the expense of the in-country election.

The immediate effect of the decision was to turn funding into a major problem once again. The registration process was finally fully funded, and a new round of fundraising was underway for the elections themselves. The estimated budget for the elections was $70 million, for which no funds had yet been received. The revised cost for out-of-country voting was $27 million, of which $5 to $10 million would be required immediately for start-up operations.[15] Given the priority of beginning registration in Pakistan, and the typical slowness of the donor response, the start-up funds for out-of-country elections would have to come from the first contributions to the electoral project, justifying the worries of the technical experts that out-of-country voting would divert resources from the essential project of in-country elections.

Attacks Against the Registration Process

By the end of May 2004, more than 60,000 voters were being registered per day; 904 sites were operational with 1,627 registration teams. The teams were traveling to increasingly remote areas, where communications and infrastructure were poor, to locate voters. The process was becoming picturesque, with donkeys conveying registration teams and equipment over high passes to reach areas inaccessible by vehicles. The media picked up on these stories and the registration process was gradually becoming good news. The image of donkeys carrying electoral materials would provide striking stories for journalists—and be recycled in every election afterwards.

There was more good news. The proportion of women registered reached 33 percent and was rising. The percentage of women registered in the final week of May was 42 percent. In the west, the Central Highlands, and the north, the rate of registration of women began to equal and exceed that of men. In the Central Highlands, the *total* number of women registered exceeded that of men.

On the other hand, events were justifying previous concerns about security. In early June, a daylight ambush was carried out against a clearly marked JEMB vehicle containing United Nations international staff. The staff members, who had jumped from the vehicle into a culvert along the road, called the security operations center with their Thuraya phones. The quick reaction system worked surprisingly well. The Coalition liaison officers within the ESOC alerted their command and air support was scrambled and directed to the location of the attack. The level of responsiveness was highly unusual and a clear demonstration of the U.S. desire to see the elections happen. Everyone understood how costly any international deaths would be to the process.[16]

At the end of June, however, two terrible incidents occurred. In Jalalabad, the driver of a bus containing female national voter registration workers slowed down for a speed bump and then leapt from the bus. Seconds later, the bus exploded killing three and injuring 13 more. The medical evacuation and coordination structures worked well again, but they could not prevent the loss of life. This was clearly a deliberate targeting not only of the electoral process, but of one of its unexpected successes—the registration of women.

The same week, reports reached Kabul that 14 people were murdered by Taliban insurgents who had set up a checkpoint along a road in Uruzgan. The insurgents stopped a bus and forced its 17 passengers to exit and empty their pockets. The majority of the passengers were carrying voter registration cards. The Taliban lined up the passengers with cards and shot them. One of those killed was a registration team leader. Three passengers managed to escape and inform authorities of the incident. It was, as terrorist attacks go, a very well-designed and intimidating operation. It made people fear not only attacks at the moment of registration, but also the fact of having registered. It clearly illustrated the difference between the rival projects of the international community and the Afghan government on the one hand, and the Taliban on the other. The former were trying to convey an identity of citizenship and ownership over the country's destiny through the act of providing a voter registration card. For the Taliban, possession of such a card was a death warrant. Remarkably, these sorts of attacks did little to dissuade the Afghans, who continued to register to vote despite the evident risks.

The End of Registration

Phase II of registration would continue through June and into first half of July. In mid-July registration sites began to close, marking the beginning of the saturation of the process. The final phase was a concentration of registration and security assets in the most insecure provinces, generally in the south, and a focus on finding and registering nomads. These teams remained operational until mid-August.

Data entry continued until September 23, with the data center operating in two shifts between seven in the morning and eight-thirty in the evening to clear the backlog, entering approximately 600,000 records per week. On September 24, the data center closed its operations and delivered the voters list to the JEMB, bound in 300 books containing 9,716,413 names, 41.3 percent of whom were women. Again, taking provinces as rough proxies for ethnicity, and excluding Kabul, the percentage of assumed Pashtuns registered had risen above 30 percent. Printed and bound voter lists were also sent to all provinces for display, in order to comply with the "exhibitions and challenges" requirement. While this conformed with the letter of the law, it was, in practice, a meaningless exercise. The lists were only displayed at the provincial capital and only for two weeks. The vast majority of the affected populations would not have the opportunity to ensure that their names were on the lists, or protest that ineligible names were on the list.

The quality of the registration data was so flawed, for reasons already mentioned, that the database could not be used to confidently eliminate double registrations. At the same time, there was anecdotal evidence of significant multiple registrations. Some people registered more than once with the intention of voting more than once; others, according to news reports, had re-registered because they had erroneously been informed that their registration cards would be used for food rations. There was absolutely no way to prevent those who registered from registering again. Efforts, instead, would have to be focused on preventing those who had registered more than once from voting more than once. The main mechanism for accomplishing this would be the use of indelible ink to mark the fingers of voters.

Another significant flaw in the register—though one not uncommon in first postconflict elections[17]—was that voters could not be assigned to specific polling stations. But despite these flaws, the registration exercise had succeeded in bringing about the psycho-political effect that had always been one of its main rationales—the transformation of people who had been buffeted by political decisions made by others into political decision makers themselves. Nearly ten million people, almost none of whom had ever voted before, were now prepared to participate in the ultimate political decision of their country. It was something of an achievement, and perhaps surprised even those who had been working on it for over a year, whose optimism had been repeatedly battered by the daily unexpected problems and by the constant criticisms of others.

The criticisms, at least, ceased with the undoubted success of registration. The American diplomats who had previously wanted the international election staff fired for incompetence were now congratulating the JEMB and its Secretariat in the Security Council, and even President Bush publicly praised the results. An *Economist* article[18] cited the registration of nearly ten million Afghans as "the biggest reason for optimism" amid a situation where the "introduction of democracy has had to contend with terrifying security and logistical problems, the threat of murderous power struggles between warlords, worries about intimidation, and attacks on government and election officials." The goats of the UNAMA electoral compound had become, briefly, the toast of the town.

---

[1] Report of the Secretary General to the Security Council on the Situation in Afghanistan and its implications for international peace and security, 19 March 2004 (A/58/742-S/2004/230) para. 15.

[2] International Crisis Group, "Disarmament and Reintegration in Afghanistan," Asia Report No. 65, Kabul/Brussels, September 30, 2003.

[3] The Security Council resolution renewing UNAMA's mandate, adopted a week before, included the following language on out-of-country voting: "*Encourages* Afghan authorities to enable an electoral process that provides for voter participation that is representative of the national demographics, including women and refugees." SC Resolution 1536 (2004) para. 4 [italics in original].

[4] Constitution of Afghanistan (2004), article 160.

[5] The process of drafting and approving the electoral law is described in some detail in the next chapter.

[6] The ten non-permanent members of the Security Council are essentially elected by their regional blocs to the Council. This amounts, in some reasons, to a rotational system. It was mostly a coincidence that Pakistan was on the Council while the main decisions on the Afghan electoral process were being made.

[7] For a brief account of the Durand Line and the "Pashtunistan" claim, see Adamec, *Dictionary of Afghan Wars,* pp. 181-182 or Victoria Schofield, *Afghan Frontier: Feuding and Fighting in Central Asia* (New York: Palgrave Macmillan, 2003) pp. 59-61. For a more comprehensive treatment, see Dupree,

Afghanistan, pp. 485-494. Omrani and Ledwidge argue that the Durand Line was never meant as an international border. See Bijan Omrani and Frank Ledwidge, "Rethinking the Durand Line: The Legality of the Afghanistan-Pakistan Frontier," *Rusi Journal*, vol. 154, No.5, October 2009, pp. 48-56.

[8] The literature on this is voluminous. The most accessible account is perhaps Steve Coll, *Ghost Wars*.

[9] Barnett R. Rubin, The Fragmentation of Afghanistan: State Formation and Collapse in the International System (New Haven: Yale University Press, 1995) pp. 63-64.

[10] Interestingly, the Taliban are often perceived as being the creatures of Pakistan's Inter-Services Intelligence. Olivier Roy, however, argued in February 1995 that the Taliban were supported by the then Minister of Interior, General Nasrullah Babar, as a *counter-weight* to the ISI's influence over Hekmatyar. Afghanistan Info. No. 36. February 1995 (mimeograph). Ahmed Rashid confirms the decisive role of Babar, but emphasizes the Pakistani desire for an open trade corridor to Central Asia, rather than the Babar-ISI rivalry. See Ahmed Rashid, *Taliban: The Story of the Afghan Warlords* (London: Pan Books, 2001) p. 27.

[11] Ahmed Rashid argues that the Taliban had many contacts across the Pakistani government, and that, as a result, they were not, as is commonly thought, the pure instrument of Pakistan's intelligence services, nor did they consistently act in Pakistan's interests. He also notes, however, that the "shared Pashtun culture of this border region has never been better reflected than in the phenomenon of the Taliban." See Ahmed Rashid, "Pakistan and the Taliban" in *Fundamentalism Reborn*, ed. William Maley (New York: New York University Press, 1998) p. 72.

[12] SC resolution 1536 (2004).

[13] The numbers of women registered in Pashtun areas would eventually climb, but at the end of May, the rate of women's registration was 26 percent, compared to 33 percent in non-Pashtun areas.

[14] As much as Karzai has been criticized recently, Zalmay Khalilzad, in a 2010 article, correctly identifies the impression of Karzai held by the international community nearly a decade before: "In the early years after the Taliban regime fell, [Karzai] was heralded as an effective leader who forged political unity and progress to a degree that few had thought possible." Khalilzad, "Lessons from Afghanistan and Iraq," p. 48.

[15] The reduction from the initial $86 million projected in February was due in part to a more sober calculation and to the decision that registration would not have to be undertaken in Iran, where voters would be able to vote on the basis of their *amayesh* cards.

[16] During the same period, the French NGO Médecins sans Frontières, which had been working in Afghanistan for nearly two decades, ended its operations in the country after five staff, including three internationals, were killed during an attack in Badghis province on 2 June.

[17] For example, South Africa in 1995 and East Timor in 1999. In addition, for all the complaints that the 2005 parliamentary election team made about the

voter register not being able to link voters to polling stations, it was still not possible to do in 2005—or, for that matter, in 2009.

[18] *The Economist,* "Confounding the doomsters," London, July 24, 2004, vol. 372, p. 56.

11
Drafting the Electoral Law

The decision to link the electoral law to the adoption of the Constitution had been taken by default. It was the result of the non-decision regarding EAD's 2002 recommendation to adopt a one-off electoral law prior to the Constitution being adopted. One of the reasons that EAD had recommended a one-off law was to avoid a rushed legislative process where pressing deadlines would eliminate desirable options because there was not enough time to implement them. With the Constitution adopted in January 2004, and the elections still scheduled for June, the timelines for drafting and approving legislation were horrendously tight. They precluded not only the consideration of desirable options, but also any consultation with political actors beyond the president's inner circle.

The legislative process began in mid-January 2004, when senior UNAMA staff, including Austin and some of his experts, were summoned to the presidential palace to determine the steps required to hold elections. The new Constitution had been approved two weeks earlier and all attention was now focused on the elections. Karzai had therefore requested a briefing from the United Nations on the voter registration project and upcoming election plans.

The President, sitting at the head of the long table in the small meeting room beside the cabinet's chamber, was surrounded by, his legal adviser, Enayat Qazimi, along with Farooq Wardak and three representatives from the U.S. Embassy. Karzai began by requesting an update on the registration, which at the time of the meeting had hardly advanced. Asking why the registration numbers were so low, Austin explained the reasons for the delays, including the decision to introduce the Afghan component. Karzai reacted positively to this, approving the "Afghanization of the operation." Around the table there was a consensus that if the recruitment of Afghan staff took place on time, the voter registration process could expand more quickly to all areas of the country and the pace of registration would accelerate.

Austin cautioned that the challenge was not only to increase the number of electors but to produce a reliable voters list that would not undermine the credibility of the upcoming elections; this would take time. Reacting to Austin's statement, one of the U.S. embassy representatives stressed the need to have an election in June 2004, as prescribed by the Bonn Agreement. When Austin quoted Brahimi's estimate that the conditions for holding elections by June were not propitious, the same U.S. official interrupted to make clear that this "was not the view of the new head of the UN mission." (Arnault at that time was, in fact, still acting in an interim capacity as SRSG.) Karzai settled the dispute diplomatically, but in a way that was not helpful operationally, by saying that the June date should be aimed for, with the possibility of reviewing it if necessary."

The meeting, and the stark U.S. position that had been laid down, made it clear that the upcoming elections were a political priority not only for the Afghan government but also for the U.S. administration. George W. Bush was himself facing re-election in November 2004, and many speculated that he needed a "success" in Afghanistan, given the increasingly bleak news from Iraq. The elections would be that success. The U.N. electoral experts left the meeting fearing that this factor would mean that the legal mandate of the "independent" JEMB would soon be subjected to pressures from a source of significant power.

If elections were to be held in June, then the electoral law had to be submitted to the cabinet before March 1, 2004 and approved by the cabinet as soon as possible thereafter. With less than six weeks to prepare a draft, the President instructed that a working group be created, composed of representatives from the JEMB, the Ministry of Justice, and the President's legal advisor. The working group was given four weeks to prepare a draft, after which it would be sent for comments to a consultative group, which originally was envisaged to include the Constitutional Commission, technical experts from IFES, and the Indian Electoral Commission (the Indian government had offered its technical expertise as an in-kind contribution to the process). Following that review, it would be sent to the Ministry of Justice for a judicial review. The last step would be submission to the cabinet for approval. This was a far cry from wide consultations with all political parties that Perelli had recommended back in 2002. (To be fair, an earlier plan for drafting the law included a "consultative committee" to gather opinions from the provinces. But the tight timelines meant that this step—which would have strengthened the legitimacy of the law beyond the constricted set of Karzai's cabinet—was the first to be dropped.)

It took several weeks to appoint the members of the working group. The group finally met on February 12. The JEMB, the Ministry of Justice, and the U.N. were represented. Karzai's representative, his legal advisor Qazimi, did not show up at the opening meeting or at any other drafting session. This would have consequences later on. At its first meeting, the group decided to structure the draft law into 13 chapters as follows: General Provisions and Definitions, Electoral Administration, Electoral Boundaries, Voters, Presidential Elections, Parliamentary Elections, Provincial and District Elections, Preparation for Elections, Polling, Results, Observers, Agents and Media, Electoral Offences, Enforcement of Electoral Laws and a final chapter, Miscellaneous.

In order to accelerate its proceedings, the group divided itself into sub-committees. Each chapter was drafted separately by different sub-committees and later distributed to the group as a whole for comments. The work was slowed by the need to produce all the draft chapters and comments in both Dari and English, and by the fact that the Afghan participants had only a vague idea of the requirements for competitive elections. Some members remembered the elections conducted under the Communist régime of Najibullah, but this was not necessarily the most useful of references for democracy-builders.[1] They therefore had to learn as they went, and it took time to explain the less obvious, but nonetheless important points.

The most problematic chapter was the one covering parliamentary elections. The Afghan Constitution had adopted ambiguous language calling for the lower house to be elected by a system that would produce a "fair representation of the people of Afghanistan." This was interpreted by all electoral experts involved to indicate a form of proportional representation (PR). Among other things, PR was the best suited system to accommodate the women's quota also required by the Constitution. Furthermore, a broad consensus had formed over the years in the electoral community that, in postconflict countries where there is ethnic polarity, some version of proportional representation is the optimal method of generating consensus across ethnic groups which was seen as essential to maintaining political stability at that frail moment in the transition.

There were many forms of proportional representation systems—it was, in fact, more of a genus of electoral system than a species. What differentiated most forms of PR from other systems was that electors voted for parties rather than candidates. Each party established a list of candidates for each constituency. The lists could be "open" or "closed." In the former, voters were able to vote for a specific candidate on a list; in that case their vote went to the party's overall tally, but the preference for the individual candidate was also taken into account. Under a closed list system, the party established the ranking of the list. Once the votes were tallied seats were allocated to parties in proportion to the percentage of votes received.

There was an entire science devoted to different formulas of how to distribute seats so that the distribution was either as proportional as possible,[2] or that it favored or disfavored fringe parties, or that it encouraged coalition-building.[3] The underlying point behind proportional representation was, however, that a party earning around 20 percent of votes should get about 20 percent of the seats in the legislature. This was not the case in a first-past-the-post system, which could generate highly disproportionate results and therefore a high number of what were considered "wasted votes."[4] Since proportional representation was based on party lists, it required political parties. It was therefore also seen as a useful vehicle to promote the development of parties. Normally this was seen as something desirable in a representative democracy; it was not seen as desirable by President Karzai.[5]

During the debate over the system, a number of international experts appeared in Kabul to provide advice,[6] the most well-known of whom was Dr. Jorgen Elklit, a Danish professor of political science who specialized in electoral systems. Elklit held a number of meetings with the working group, with Qazimi, and with the president, and recommended a system by which 219 seats (the Constitution called for a lower house of less than 250 seats) would be elected through a proportional representation formula in multiple member provincial constituencies elected from closed party lists,[7] and individual candidates would be elected to an additional 30 seats allocated as "compensatory seats."[8] The formula would simplify the provisions for women's representation and would produce generally proportionate results. Following the discussions of the working group this formula was accepted. Other organizations such as IDEA, IFES and NDI also submitted comments pertinent to the text, but without challenging the system proposed by Elklit. On February 28, the deadline established by the President, the Chairman of the JEMB, Zakim Shah, submitted the draft to the for review by the Ministry of Justice.

Nothing happened for the following three weeks. The electoral Secretariat staff members involved were glad for the break in this intensive and time-consuming process. A number of decisions related to voter registration still had to be made, as well as preparations for Phase II. This period also coincided with the adjustment to the new co-management arrangement of the JEMB Secretariat. But while these dramas played out, unbeknownst to them the most important decisions governing the elections were taken elsewhere.

The Cabinet Debate

On March 26, following the Ministry of Justice's review, the draft was distributed to the cabinet for the first time. In the cabinet meeting, many ministers criticized the proportional representation system which, in their view, was more appropriate for developed democracies than for Afghanistan's first postconflict election. This was followed by a bitter exchange between Abdul Rahim Karimi, the Minister of Justice, and Qazimi. Karimi began by asking who had written the draft. Qazimi replied that he had. Then Karimi requested an explanation of the formula for allocation of the compensatory seats. For a tense moment Qazimi hesitated, and then admitted with embarrassment that he could not explain the formula. Karimi submitted this as proof that the draft had been produced by the "international advisers" and not by Qazimi. In the absence of an adequate response from Qazimi, Karzai postponed the debate until someone was able to explain the compensatory seat allocation formula to him.[9] This episode had an end more appropriate to a soap opera than to a cabinet session: in the corridor outside the cabinet room, Karzai's bodyguards had to stop Qazimi from trying to punch the Minister of Justice.

A few days later, the draft was transferred back to the Ministry of Justice. Minister Karimi had been tasked with ensuring a proper briefing for the cabinet. Karimi requested several meetings with the electoral experts about the details of the system, in particular the advantages and disadvantages of the compensatory seats. At the end of these briefings, even he was convinced that proportional representation was an appropriate formula for Afghanistan.[10]

On April 19, the cabinet convened again to discuss the law. They listened to a detailed explanation by Karimi of the proportional representation system and awaited Karzai's reaction. That reaction was sudden and unequivocal. Karzai began by saying that he was not convinced that Afghanistan was ready for a democracy based on political parties. Afghans mistrusted political parties as these, in the past, had either been communist or Islamist, and had only brought war and destruction to Afghanistan. Following his lead, most ministers, with the exception of the female Minister of Education and the Minister of Finance, spoke against PR, arguing that citizens would not know who they would be voting for if they voted for lists rather than individuals, that unpopular candidates in the party tickets would benefit from the support of popular candidates, and that political parties would be unfairly advantaged compared to individual candidates.[11]

Karzai then stated that, while he favored democracy, he wanted a democracy that was in accordance with the traditional values of the Afghan society. He argued that Afghanistan was a traditional society where people wanted to vote for candidates they knew and trusted. He said he wanted to avoid creating superficial representatives, especially given that the parties were not mature in Afghanistan. Above all, he wanted to ensure that the law neither depended on political parties nor gave any advantage to political parties against individual candidates. Resting on these criteria, Karzai asked whether there was a system by which individuals could be elected individually and still meet the constraints posed by the Constitution. He tasked the JEMB to explore the different options and to prepare a new presentation.

There were only two systems that could effectively accommodate Karzai's conditions. The first was a single-member district, such as that in the United States, where states are sub-divided into electoral districts, the number of districts depending on the population of the state, from which one candidate is elected. U.S. Ambassador Khalilzad favored this system for Afghanistan. The only problem was that the delineation of districts was politically contentious and geographically difficult. For reasons already described, the precise location and naming of villages and districts was still at best unclear, and at worst contested. Population figures were not sufficiently known to ensure that districts would be more or less equal in population—another constitutional requirement. There was no way that the extremely complex process of drawing electoral boundaries within provinces could be done in the short time that remained for a June election. Nobody, furthermore, wanted to risk the political Pandora's box that it would open. The option that remained was the deceptively-simple Single Non-Transferable Vote (SNTV).

SNTV and the Exclusion of Political Parties

Karzai's aversion to political parties was a pity in that it closed off what might have been the most appropriate electoral system and it prevented any concerted effort to build political parties which are essential to democratization. "The principle institutional means for organizing the expansion of political participation are political parties and the party system," Huntington, for one, has noted.[12] The aversion to parties, however, was not necessarily unique to Karzai. This aversion had, furthermore, occurred previously in Afghan history. During the constitutional period between 1964 and 1973, Dupree noted that "several members of the 1964 Constitutional Committee have informed me that it was generally agreed in the Committee that it would be better if no political parties should function during the elections for the Twelfth and Thirteenth Parliaments."[13] Nor was this aversion unique to Afghanistan or Karzai. It is a common conceit among founders of nations, who see themselves as embodiments of the nation and parties as unnecessary divisions at a moment that called for unity, no matter how often history has dictated that competing interests take the form of factions, and factions become parties. A system whose institutional framework is sufficiently strong can not only endure these political schisms but benefit from them; few founders, however, are willing to bet that the nascent political institutions they are nurturing can withstand that pressure.[14]

Politically, Karzai's concerns were not without foundation. At that early point of Afghanistan's democratic development, an encouragement of parties may well have meant a consolidation of political forces around fault lines that were already quite entrenched and that had done a great deal of damage in the past: communists, jihadis, royalists, Islamists and Pashtun nationalists. These would have allowed little space for the emergence of moderate democrats, and above all, constitutionalists, and could have risked creating a political order that refought the wars of the past—first with words and then, perhaps, returning to arms.[15]

Under the circumstances, however, the only other option was SNTV. This was a dismaying development to most electoral experts, inside and outside of Austin's team.[16] SNTV was deceptively simple.[17] Like proportional systems, it was based on multi-member constituencies. That is, for each electoral constituency (in Afghanistan's case, the province), there was more than one seat at play. In the seat allocation that would eventually be made for Afghanistan, the number of seats per province would vary from two to 33. Each voter under SNTV had one vote;[18] after polling, the votes were counted and the candidates who received the most votes were elected. This meant that, in a lightly-populated province like Zabul, with two seats, the two candidates with the most votes would be elected; in populous provinces like Kabul, with 33 seats, the 33rd highest vote-getters would be elected.

There were several dangers of using this system in Afghanistan, particularly in constituencies where seats-per-constituency ("district magnitude") were high, as in Kabul. The first problem was Afghanistan's tribal make-up. Consider, for example, a province with five seats, where 40 percent of the population was aligned behind a single tribal leader. That would mean that one candidate would absorb 40 percent of the votes; the remaining 60 percent would be divided between the rest of the candidates, of which four would be elected. Mathematically, the highest possible number of votes that could be obtained by the remaining four candidates, if each received the same percentage of the electorate, would be 15. In practice, however, the results were likely to be far more uneven than that, and the fourth vote-getter could quite conceivably receive less than five percent.

The second criticism applied to detribalized urban provinces where district magnitudes were particularly high. In Kabul, for example, with its 33 seats, it was likely that the difference between the last elected candidate and the first non-elected candidate (i.e. between the 33rd and 34th vote-getter) would be so trivial that it would amount to a virtual lottery. This would put an enormous amount of pressure on the credibility of the electoral process itself. For example, should the 34th vote-getter complain that, for a few votes more, he would have been elected, would the electoral process be of sufficient quality that the electoral authorities could defend the result? Few of the electoral experts were willing to subject the process or the authorities to that test at that time.[19]

The third criticism was that, due to the above two factors, the electoral results would be extremely fragmented and would thus complicate the building of enduring coalitions in parliament. In all likelihood, a large majority of the parliament would be elected by a small minority of their constituency. Provincial interests were hardly likely to be articulated, let alone the national interest. Instead, tribal or highly parochial issues would dominate parliamentary deliberations.

These weaknesses were very much on the mind of the JEMB when it met following the April 19 cabinet meeting. Zakim Shah gave his version of the cabinet discussion before the JEMB began to examine the six different options that were under consideration. These options were: proportional representation with closed lists, closed list PR with compensatory seats, PR with open lists, PR with open list and compensatory seats, the bloc vote, and SNTV. Zakim Shah, understandably, put great emphasis on the Karzai's criteria and his bias against political parties. Karzai's opinion was a red line that few of the supposedly independent Afghan commissioners dared to challenge. Gothai Khawarai, a female Pashtun, stated that the JEMB should not contradict the President's views. Yari, the elderly Hazara, also felt that the JEMB should not undermine the President, adding that the proportional representation system with compensatory seats, which had originally been proposed, was far beyond his understanding. Fakir Bahram also supported SNTV. The two commissioners who had taken most time to understand the options, Zahida Ansari (the other female member) and Qayem Qudbuddin, argued in favor of proportional representation. The three international commissioners voted for proportional representation. Zakim Shah was the last one to express his opinion and he supported SNTV. The divided opinion of the JEMB could not, however, be conveyed beyond the JEMB's conference room. From then on the JEMB views would be conveyed through its chairman, Zakim Shah, who would represent the body to the cabinet.

On 2 May, a consultative meeting took place with representatives of the international community under the auspices of the United Nations. Again, the electoral experts from UNAMA, NDI and IFES described the dangers of SNTV. Ambassador Khalilzad, like Zakim Shah, stressed the importance of accommodating the President's reservations against political parties. Khalilzad added that first-past-the-post worked perfectly well in the U.S. and he could not see why it could not also be adapted to Afghanistan. When the impossibility of drawing 249 equitable single-member electoral districts in the current timeframe was explained, he conceded that SNTV should prevail for the first Wolesi Jirga elections. However, he added that for the future elections the law should be amended to a first-past-the-post system. The United Kingdom Ambassador agreed with the U.S., though he proposed holding separate elections for women—an idea advanced by Harvard Professor Pippa Norris, who claimed it had worked very well in Pakistan.[20] The European Union representative, still Francesc Vendrell, also agreed, apparently reluctantly, to throw his support behind SNTV.[21]

If there was consensus on anything, it was to recommend that the electoral law apply only to the upcoming Wolesi Jirga elections and should be amended after these had taken place—in other words that it be a one-time provision. Arnault, on behalf of the U.N. addressed concerns that SNTV could be used by strongmen to increase their chances of being elected: the question was not to exclude warlords from participating, but to make sure that the warlords could not exclude others from participating. This statement was simply a recognition of the policy that had been initiated by Brahimi and accepted since Bonn. The unanswered question, however, was what would be done to prevent warlords from excluding others from participating? From the point of view of the electoral experts, however, the SNTV system's weaknesses went far beyond how easily it could be manipulated by strongmen. Even if it worked as designed, it was likely to undermine democratization for the reasons outlined above. The meeting concluded with a strong sense of defeat among the electoral experts. It was clear that, again, an expedient reading of immediate political considerations would prevail over the longer-term considerations for building democratic institutions in Afghanistan.

The next day, May 3, another meeting was convened in the presidential palace. Karzai was presented with the results of the discussions held over the previous days. Instead of a presentation of divided views, he was given a sense of support from the JEMB as expressed by Wardak and Zakim Shah. Khalilzad repeated his contention that SNTV could be used for the first elections but that subsequent elections should be held under a first-past-the-post system. It was, of course, academic what Khalilzad thought about subsequent elections. The rules governing those elections would be decided by whatever parliament was adopted under SNTV. But Khalilzad's comments essentially closed the debate on the electoral formula. The way forward was clear, and the drafters of the electoral law would have to reflect the conclusion in the new draft.

In the post-Taliban context, the adequate representation of women was a sensitive one as, on one side, women's and human rights groups were demanding proactive steps after the marginalization women had endured under the Taliban; on the other side, some members of the cabinet were well-known jihadi's and ideologically not very far from some of the Taliban positions on women and human rights. The new Constitution required, as described above, that "at least two female delegates should be elected from each province." The implementation of this constitutional requirement would affect the choice of the electoral formula. Since the beginning of the discussions on the electoral law, there were two interpretations on the issue: those who supported having two seats reserved for women in each province and those who supported a number of female candidates integrated in the lists at appropriate intervals. (For example, the original draft of the law, which had assumed a proportional representation system with closed lists, had simply included the provision that every third candidate in each party list had to be a woman. This was later modified so that women had to be placed sequentially, in the second, fifth, seventh, and eleventh positions, and so forth, with basically the same effect.) Supporters of the reserved seats for women argued that this formula was used in other Islamic countries like Sudan, Pakistan, Morocco, Jordan, and Bangladesh. Against these precedents it was argued that reserved seats could end up turning the constitutional requirement for *at least* two women per number of provinces into a limitation of *only* two women per number of provinces. In addition, reserved seats presented a potential problem of legitimacy, as women representatives would likely be elected with considerably less numbers support than their male peers. It was also argued that reserved seats would segregate women instead of forcing parties to integrate them into political parties. The counter-argument was that, traditionally, politics in Afghanistan were a man's affair.

The question of women's participation was complicated by the conflicting provisions between two paragraphs within Article 83 of the Constitution. One paragraph said that that the number of seats should be proportional to the population in each province. This meant that some of the least populated provinces, such as Nimroz and Nuristan, would have only two seats. The other stated that at least two women from each province should be elected. This meant that the least populated provinces would be represented only by women. This was clearly unacceptable to the political powers in those provinces. In the end, it was agreed to interpret the Constitution's provision in the electoral law as requiring that the total number of women in the lower house had to be equal to twice the number of provinces. Again, a political arrangement had to be made to cover an inept constitutional provision governing elections.

Even under SNTV, the population of the country would have to be divided by province, and from that division there would need to be a determination of the number of seats per province. Due to the lack of accurate information on population, this was bound to be a politically contentious exercise. The drafters of the law eventually agreed that Central Statistics Office (CSO) should provide the population data. The CSO, which was receiving a great deal of technical support from the United Nations, was in the middle of carrying out a pre-census household survey that, while not exact, was yielding the most accurate population data available thus far. It was not certain, however, that the survey would be completed prior to the election date—in part because the election date itself was not certain. The relevant provision of the law (Article 19) therefore read, "At least 90 days prior to each election, the Central Statistics Office will provide the official population figures or estimates for each province to the AIEC." The phrase "or estimates" was inserted in case the survey wasn't finished in time.

The law reverted to the cabinet on May 16, and for the first time, the discussion was not controversial. Karzai obtained what he wanted—SNTV—and the ministers supported the resulting text. The draft was then sent back to the Ministry of Justice for the final technical adjustments. Karzai signed the law on May 27, 2004, almost three months after the cabinet received the first draft, and three days before the beginning of the month in which presidential elections were supposed to be held.

Much speculation would occur later on the role played by Ambassador Khalilzad and by extension, President Bush, in the decision to adopt SNTV. According to one account, Khalilzad "intervened brusquely at a meeting with United Nations officials and diplomats in Kabul to declare that he had just spoken to President Bush, who said 'SNTV is the choice. SNTV is going to happen.'"[22]

What had been missed in the many accounts of how SNTV was adopted was that, like so many decisions in the process, it was not *taken* following deliberations, but was *accepted* following the elimination of other options. As Andrew Reynolds wrote: "Afghanistan ended up with SNTV not as a result of extensive deliberation and careful evaluation of its pros and cons, but rather by a fairly random process of elimination. [...] It is important to note that Karzai did not choose SNTV with any understanding of its consequences or history."[23]

Unfortunately, the sequencing of the ratification of the Constitution and the drafting of the election law, as well as the artificial pressure applied by maintaining the unrealistic June election date, ran against the grain of Afghan political realities. In a well-designed process, the electoral system ought to have been a link between political realities of the existing order and the political goals of the new order. If this fundamental point had been understood, the design of the electoral system would not have been decided so late in the process, and a wider menu of options would have been on the table. It is possible that President Bush may, as some seemed to contend, have cracked open his edition of David Farrel's *Electoral Systems,* made his own analysis of Afghanistan's needs, and concluded that SNTV was the best system in Afghanistan because it was "consistent with U.S. interests in a strong presidential system."[24] But the reality is that as long as the tight deadlines precluded the delineation of electoral districts for single-member constituencies, and as long as Karzai held on to his founder's fear of parties, there were simply no options besides SNTV.

Perhaps the key to understanding the debate about the electoral system was more clearly exposed in one of AREU's recommendations after Karzai had prevailed on SNTV:

> Functioning parliamentary democracies need strong and effective political parties. Under the SNTV voting system Afghanistan is heading for a fragmented parliament with small parties that do not represent national constituencies. The generally bad reputation of political parties should not lead to the conclusion that they should be kept weak and ineffective, but rather they should be supported and strengthened to do a better job in the future than they did in the past. There needs to be more investment and support from both the Afghan

government and the international community to develop political parties that can unite the country and become the backbone of parliamentary democracy in Afghanistan.[25]

In other words, the real debate was not about the choice of electoral system, but about what would be the pivotal institution of the new Afghan democracy: the parliament or the presidency. President Karzai had put—inadvertently or not—his prestige behind the electoral formula most likely to deliver a weak parliament that could not threaten presidential authority. In this imbalance lay the seeds for a future political crisis, confirming William Maley's prophecy following the Constitutional Loya Jirga, that presidentialism lurked beneath Afghanistan's new legal framework "like a bomb waiting to explode."[26]

---

[1] A fairly common misperception at the time was that the 2004 elections were the first elections in Afghan history. The 1964 Wolesi Jirga was also elected, though from a mostly urban electorate. Nonetheless, according to Louis Dupree, "Most observers agree that the elections were as fair as any they had seen in Asia, or in some parts of Alabama—or in Cook County, Illinois." Dupree, *Afghanistan*, p. 589. In April 1986, President Najibullah conducted one of the few elections known to be rigged by a government to *increase* the opposition representation (in an attempt to legitimize his regime). See Henry S. Bradsher, *Afghan Communism and Soviet Intervention* (Oxford: Oxford University Press, 1983) p. 166. Also of interest in looking at Afghanistan's early democratic development were the university politics in the 1960s and 1970s, unleashed by King Zahir Shah's "New Democracy." These parties, on both the left and the right, soon became radicalized. They formed the seeds of both the Communist and Islamist parties that would vie for power in the decades after the 1970s. See Antonio Giustozzi, "Between Patronage and Rebellion: Student Politics in Afghanistan" (Kabul: AREU, February 2010) pp. 1-4.

[2] While most European democracies use proportional representation, and look down on the U.S.'s single-member plurality system, it is of passing historical interest that the two most popular means of assuring proportional outcomes were devised by Americans. The "highest average" method was devised by Thomas Jefferson, and the "largest remainder" method was devised by Alexander Hamilton. Their purpose was not, however, to determine the allocation of seats won according to a PR election, but to determine the allocation of seats in the House of Representatives based on the populations of the states.

[3] See, for example, Norris, *Electoral Engineering*; Benjamin Reilly, *Democracy in Divided Societies: Electoral Engineering for Conflict Management*, (Cambridge: Cambridge University Press, 2001); Andrew Reynolds, *The Architecture of Democracy: Constitutional Design, Conflict Management, and Democracy*, (New York: Oxford University Press, 2002), as well as the more theoretical and broader *Democracy, Accountability and Representation*, eds. Adam Przeworski, Susan C. Stokes, and Bernard Manin (Cambridge: Cambridge University Press, 1999).

[4]David Farrell provides a number of examples from different countries on the disproportionality of first-past-the-post elections. See David Farrell, *Electoral Systems: A contemporary Introduction*, (New York: Palgrave, 2001) pp. 21-44. On the other hand, while there is a consensus among most academics on the superiority of PR, especially for ethnically-riven postconflict countries, Guy Lardeyret offers a compelling critique. In discussing electoral politics in Africa, and the tendency for elections to "degenerate into ethnic contests over legslative seats and public offices," Lardeyret conludes: "The best way to counteract these propensities is to oblige members of each group to run against one another on (transethnic) political and ideological grounds in single-member districts. The worst way is to adopt PR, which tends to reproduce ethnic cleavages in the legislature." See Guy Lardeyret, "The Problem with PR," in *The Global Resurgence of Democracy,* eds. Larry Diamond and Marc F. Plattner (Baltimore and London: The Johns Hopkins University Press, 1996) p. 180. Lardeyret's article is a response to Arend Lijphart's article, "Constitutional Choices for New Democracies" in the same volume (pp. 162-174). The practical application of this debate in Afghanistan is discussed in Chapter 15. Finally, G. Bingham Powell Jr.'s *Elections as Instruments of Democracy* is entirely devoted to this discussion.

[5] For the international experts, steeped in their own electoral traditions, the need to promote political parties was axiomatic. But Afghanistan is not the only country where leaders have shown skepticism about parties. Sam Huntington, points out that "Cliques and factions exist in all political systems. So also do parties in the sense of informal groups competing with each other for power and influence. But parties in the sense of organizations are a product of modern politics." He further notes that the shift "from the politics of status to the politics of opinion" led to the creation of the political party as an institution. The designers of the U.S. Constitution in 1789 believe that their document would control the effects of "factions." (Their wise practicality prevented them from attempting to *prevent* the occurrence of factions, merely to limit their influence.) See *The Federalist Papers,* Ed. Roy P. Fairfield, Second Edition (Johns Hopkins University Press: Baltimore, 1981) pp. 19-23. George Washington, however, according to Huntington, warned that "'self-created societies' were 'laboring incessantly to sow the seeds of distrust, jealousy, and of course discontent' about the country and that if not stopped they would destroy the government of the country." See Hungtington, *Political Order,* p. 403. Huntington also cites leaders such as Ayub Khan, Franco, and Singman Rhee as Bolingbrokian "Patriot Kings" who avoided the development of parties. In the French revolution—another founding moment—Camus , more philosophically, notes: "To paraphrase Saint-Just, no one is virtuous innocently. From the moment that laws fail to make harmony reign, or when the unity which should be created by adherence to principles is destroyed, who is to blame? Factions. Who compose the factions? Those who deny by their very actions the necessity of unity. Factions divide the sovereign; therefore they are blasphemous and criminal." Albert Camus, *The Rebel: An Essay on Man in Revolt,* trans. Anthony Bower (New York: Vintage International, 1991) p. 124. Finally, of course, there

was another great founder, Saint Paul, who urged the Corinthians as follows: "Let there by no factions; rather be united in mind and judgment."

[6] IFES deployed Elklit and Lopez Pintor. AREU deployed Andrew Reynolds, from the University of North Carolina and co-author with Elklit of the *International IDEA Electoral Systems Design Handbook.* Pippa Norris' paper was also widely circulated in Kabul.

[7] "Closed" lists mean that people would vote for a party based on a list of candidates proposed by the party. A number of seats (x) would be allocated to the party based on the proportion of votes that it won, and the first x names on the party's list would be elected.

[8] Compensatory seats would be allocated to parties that were able to win votes across multiple provinces, but that were disadvantaged at the provincial level precisely because their support was scattered and not concentrated. It was assumed that these seats would go to the more reform-oriented parties that had small pockets of support scattered around the country, versus the ethnic-dominated or organized Mujaheddin parties that would have strong support within provinces but not across the national territory.

[9] See Andrew Reynolds, "The Curious Case of Afghanistan" *Journal of Democracy,* April 2006; p. 105-107 for a similar description of the politics behind the decisions on the electoral law.

[10] The sessions were conducted by United Nations and IFES advisers. The Ministry of Justice's representative at the working group also participated.

[11] Karzai has been described as having "absolute power within his Cabinet room and no authority outside of it." This helps to explain the obsequiousness of his ministers, as well as the perception that he is only a "mayor of Kabul."

[12] Huntington, *Political Order*, p. 398. Huntington's entire chapter on parties and political mobilization is of enduring relevance. Also interesting is his observation that arguments against parties "are, in fact, less arguments against parties than they are arguments against *weak* parties" p. 405, emphasis in original.

[13] Dupree, *Afghanistan*, p. 650, footnote 17.

[14] A constant feature in the analysis of Zahir Shah's New Democracy era was that his failure to sign the political parties law was a key contributor to the demise of the era. In other words, he created a modern political structure but denied that structure one of the essential mechanisms for its functioning. Dupree discusses the issue in *Afghanistan*, pp. 649-650. Poullada notes that the student riots of the early 1960s "so frightened the timid king—who had to approve all laws—that he would not sign the law creating legal political parties, believing it would result in political chaos. In fact, legal political parties might have saved the situation by introducing party discipline and a loyal opposition, creating groupings around which moderates could rally." Leon B. Poullada, "The Road to Crisis, 1919-1980," in *Afghanistan: The Great Game Revisited*, ed. Rosanne Klass (New York: Freedom House, 1990) p. 52. Amin Saikal calls this refusal to sign the law a "fatal mistake"; see Saikal, *Modern Afghanistan: A History of Struggle and Survival* (I.B. Taurus: London, 2004) p. 155. Anthony Arnold also makes this point, noting that since the King's attempt to remove power gradually from his family to political parties "remained largely theoretical (e.g.,

the King never signed into law his own proposal for legalizing political parties), he has been accused, perhaps unfairly, of hypocrisy. It seems at least as probable that he simply did not have the political strength to abolish his relatives' prerogatives." See Anthony Arnold, "The Ephemeral Elite: The Failure of Socialist Afghanistan" in *The Politics of Social Transformation*, p. 37.

[15] This is all, perhaps, another way of saying what Barnett Rubin wrote in a preliminary note on the adoption of the 2004 Constitution: "It is not hard to show that ANY system of government cannot work in Afghanistan."

[16] For an electoral expert's take on the system in Afghanistan, see Reynolds, "The Curious Case of Afghanistan" p. 104.

[17] There is no shortage of reference books on electoral systems. One of the best organized, most concise and vividly written is Farrell's *Electoral Systems*. As Farrell describes, SNTV is currently used only in Jordan, Vanuatu, and partially in Taiwan. Curiously, it was used in Japan between 1948 and 1994—another Constitution that was greatly influenced by the United States, pp. 46-47.

[18] Under the Single Transferable Vote—considered by experts to be among the most representative, and endorsed by John Stewart Mill—voters have several votes which they rank according to their preferred candidate. If their top-ranked candidates are eliminated because they don't reach a certain quota, their lesser-ranked candidates are counted, until all votes are counted. See Farrell, *Electoral Systems,* pp. 121-152.

[19] Indeed, this is exactly what happened. See Chapter 15 below.

[20] The reserved seats option was advocated in January 2004 by, among others, Pippa Norris "Implementing Women's Representation in Afghanistan Electoral Law. Options for reserved seats" Harvard University, prepared for the Afghanistan Reconstruction Project.

[21] Vendrell later explained privately that the EU would not take a position against the U.N. and U.S.

[22] This was cited in Astrid Suhrke, "The Democratisation of a Dependent State: The Case of Afghanistan" FRIDE Working Paper 51, December 2007, p. 11. Suhrke quotes as the source of this anecdote Arthur Kent, "Cashing in on Karzai & Co." *Policy Options*, November 2007, p. 11.

[23] Reynolds, "The Curious Case of Afghanistan" p. 107.

[24] Suhrke, "The Democratisation of a Dependent State" p. 11.

[25] Andrew Reynolds and Andrew Wilder, "Free, Fair or Flawed: Challenges for Legitimate Elections in Afghanistan" Kabul, AREU, September 2004, p. 17.

[26] See pp. 96 and 97 above.

12
Applying the Law

The electoral law codified a new set of timelines for critical electoral events, such as the nomination of candidates, the definition of provincial boundaries, and the provision of population figures per province by the CSO (in order to apportion seats in the lower house). These timelines were set relative to the election date. That meant that if any of these events were delayed, the election would have to be delayed. At the time of the adoption of the law, the planning assumption was still that parliamentary elections would be held simultaneously with the presidential one, and that both would be held in June. Therefore, any missed deadline of the more complicated parliamentary process would also delay the simpler presidential election. Given the late passage of the electoral law, it was clear that elections could not be held in June, though this had yet to be formally acknowledged.

The adoption of the law therefore made everything suddenly urgent. The first deadline that had to be met was the decree on administrative boundaries (provincial and district), which the law required to be announced no later than 120 days prior to the election. Because of Ramadan and winter, and the potential need for a second round, the first half of October would be the last feasible moment in 2004 to hold the elections. If parliamentary elections were to be held in early October, then the decree on boundaries had to be issued in early June—within a week of the adoption of the electoral law. As previously noted, while the question of provincial boundaries was not contentious, the question of district boundaries was extremely complex and politically delicate.

The solution to the problem of districts was to fudge it entirely. On June 5, Karzai issued a decree stating that "in conformity with the provision of Article 11 of the electoral law and in preparation for the election of the Wolesi Jirga, 34 provinces of the country are recognized as electoral constituencies (the list of provinces and districts is attached)." The attachment, however, while listing districts, did not determine their boundaries. The decree carried another interesting feint:

it referred to "Wolesi Jirga" elections—the elections to the lower house. These elections were indeed based on provincial constituencies. The upper house, on the other hand, was partly made of representatives elected to District Councils. No district boundaries meant no District Councils; and no District Councils meant no indirect elections to the Meshrano Jirga. The wording of the June 5 decree already appeared to concede that district council elections would not be held and that the upper house would therefore not be constituted strictly according to the Constitution.

Two more decrees were also required immediately: a decree on population per province—to allow the apportionment of seats in the Wolesi Jirga—and a decree setting the electoral date. As noted, the law called on the CSO to provide the provincial population figures. As feared, the pre-census household survey was not yet completed, and the CSO, under pressure, had to improvise a methodology based on the unfinished census of 1979; historical population growth rates;[1] estimated adjustments due to war, refugee movements and maternal mortality rates; and the data emerging from the household survey where it was available.

This methodology had several obvious weaknesses. First, the incomplete 1979 census had only enumerated 67 percent of the population. It had tried to extrapolate the missing numbers with estimates based on a household survey conducted over the *previous* four years (between 1975 and 1979). Second, the household survey of 2003 and 2004 had not been able, for security reasons, to access five provinces at all, and had only partial access to another two.[2] Not surprisingly, the populations in all seven of these provinces were overwhelmingly Pashtun. As the chief adviser on population to UNAMA noted in an internal paper: "All that exists in reality are two imperfect data sets—the household listing date from 2003/2004 and the population estimates based on the census of 1979—upon which any estimates could be made." Since any estimates could be made, any estimates could also be challenged, adding political fuel to a statistical fire. The advisor noted that it would be important for the senior political figures in Afghanistan to be comfortable with the methodology. He further recommended that an "independent, world-class demographic expert" be recruited to separately audit the methodology and results.

This was a tall order for a UNAMA leadership that tended to finesse its way through political controversies, and for a president who was beginning to face his first electoral opposition. Both realized that the population figures would only matter if a decision were taken to hold parliamentary elections. This meant the question could be avoided as long as there was no decision on the parliamentary elections. The political sensitivities of agreeing on provincial population figures therefore became part of the argument against holding parliamentary elections in 2004. This issue now had to be resolved with finality.

The debate over the election date and the simultaneity of presidential and parliamentary elections had, up to now, been mostly restricted to the electoral experts and a few interested parties—such as the president and the U.S. ambassador. But with everyone's focus now on the electoral process, interest in this discussion widened.

The widening of the discussion would add incoherence and confusion to the decision-making process. The science of elections is not overly complex, but there are intricacies that do require a bit of study and understanding. Most foreign ministers and heads of government obviously do not have the time for such study. But even diplomats at the working level seemed disinclined to master the basics principles. This disconnect between technical knowledge and policy-making would ensure that the remaining decisions, like many that preceded them, would be made on the basis of hope or political desire, rather than reality and political pragmatism.

This effect began to exert itself on the two major unresolved questions: whether to hold parliamentary elections as well as the presidential election in the fall, and whether to conduct an out-of-country vote for Afghan refugees, especially in Pakistan and Iran. These two issues were, to a degree, hostages to each other. The complexities of *parliamentary* out-of-country elections were massive, probably insurmountable, and therefore undermined the case for out-of-country elections in general. On the other hand, a decoupling of presidential and parliamentary elections would make the case for an out-of-country presidential election more palatable. As these points were digested and discussed, practical election preparations had to continue in a state of great uncertainty about what actually had to be prepared, with the only certainty, again, being the need to have elections within months.

Patterns of Political Parties

With the electoral date and out-of-country voting issues still unresolved, the JEMB began to prepare for the nomination of candidates phase. Given the continuing uncertainty over parliamentary elections, procedures had to be adopted for both presidential and parliamentary candidates. This was yet another demonstration of how indecision at the political level complicated practical logistics; in this case, it forced the expenditure of resources on addressing hypothetical issues that resulted from an inability of decision makers to commit to the most rational and prudent course at the earliest opportunity.

As with the question of the delimitation of district boundaries, the JEMB Secretariat discovered that the provisions of the law on candidate registration could not easily be implemented. Article 44 (7) of the law required that the application of each presidential candidate include photocopies of 10,000 voter registration cards, and the application of each Wolesi Jirga candidate include photocopies of 500 registration cards. There were simply not enough photocopy machines in Afghanistan to meet this provision. In this sense, it constituted an unreasonable barrier to political entry (as Austin's electoral team had argued during discussions over electoral law). The fudging began again—the JEMB requested that the photocopies be replaced by signatures and that the law be modified by a decree to reflect this practical accommodation.

In most democratic systems, candidates are mobilized and supported by political parties. In a general sense, political parties require resources and organization and a certain amount of political space in which to form. In postconflict situations, resources are often controlled by former combatants, political space is limited, and the ideological or programmatic content of party platforms is distorted by the recent, violent past rather than by the hoped-for non-violent future.

This general observation applied to Afghanistan. An internal UNAMA analysis divided the 24 officially-registered parties into four main categories.[3] The largest category, accounting for ten of the parties, was labeled the "New Democrats." These were progressive parties that had mostly emerged in the post-Bonn period and supported the main planks of the Bonn Agreement: democracy, human rights, women's rights, and so forth. Their founders and members tended to have leftist backgrounds, and to have played a subdued role during the civil war, where politics had been dominated by various strains of Islamic parties. These parties were quite similar to each other and generally had limited popular backing—"not much support beyond the street where their office is located," as one UNAMA political officer described.[4]

The second largest group of parties, around five, was the "Royalists." These parties had been created by members of the old aristocracy who supported a continuation of the monarchy.[5] They were composed of moderate Pashtuns who generally supported Karzai (more as a Pashtun leader than as the face of the Bonn Agreement) even if they were increasingly disappointed with his performance, his perceived lack of loyalty to the King, and his apparent reluctance or inability to promote the interests of Pashtuns.

The third group, also composed of five parties, was the jihadis, which included both the minor jihadi groups from the Afghan resistance as well as the so-called "neo-Jihadis," who maintained links to the larger, established resistance parties while espousing a more moderate and less ethnically-tinted politics. The *major* jihadi groups still dominated Afghan politics, but they did not register as formal political parties.[6] This was, perhaps, because they assumed that people would vote based on the name recognition of their leaders rather than party affiliation, or that the association of their names with their parties was already fixed in people's minds, and therefore, the formation of actual parties was unnecessary.

Finally, there were four parties that were remnants of the Parchami and Khalqi communist factions that had launched the 1978 coup against Daoud. The historical legacy of communism in Afghanistan denied these parties much credibility. They were, furthermore, treated with a great deal of animosity by the jihadi parties, though to some extent the Pashtun dominance in the Parchami and Khalqi parties ensured that they retained some ties to Karzai's government. The post-communists generally supported Karzai and advanced a leftist, progressive agenda.

The formation of political parties was a tactical necessity for underdogs who needed to band together to gain support and organize voters. Established and known political figures did not need to be represented through parties. The electoral law, of course, provided no encouragement for their formation.

The Decision to Delay and Separate Elections

The question of the date of elections could no longer be avoided. As with the population figures, the law required the announcement of an election date 90 days prior to the election. For reasons described above, an early October election was the latest feasible moment in the year to hold an election. In other words, if no date was announced in early July, then it was unlikely that an election could take place in 2004, at least according to the letter of the law. There was a broad political consensus within the international community, joined by Karzai, that some sort of election had to take place in 2004 in order to preserve the magic of the Bonn process. As June ended and July began, and no election date had yet been set, the Bonn process reached its point of highest risk.

It was legally the JEMB's responsibility to set the date and the nature of the election—i.e. presidential alone or parliamentary as well. Needless to say, powerful political forces, Afghan and international, were also at work and had a large say in the decision. Once again, the positions taken by these forces were often at odds with compelling realities on the ground.

The JEMB decided to consult Afghanistan's registered political parties prior to making its decisions on the date and type of elections. During a meeting on June 16, of 19 attending, 13 recommended that one or both of the elections be postponed to 2005 (five parties had no point of view at all). This was a revealing and somewhat unexpected outcome. One of the main arguments within the international community for *not* postponing the parliamentary elections had been fear of a possible backlash among Karzai's opposition should the period in which he ruled by presidential decree be unnecessarily extended. Karzai himself had voiced this concern, stating that he did not want to govern without popular legitimacy any longer than necessary. The political parties, however, appeared to have a more realistic view of the situation and preferred to exchange time without power for time to adequately prepare their campaigns. Discussions with other actors—elders, religious leaders, and local leaders—emphasized the importance of completing the disarmament program before holding the elections. Again, these voices appeared to demonstrate a more realistic grasp of necessary electoral conditions than the international diplomatic community. Finally, the JEMB was, for its part, distressingly aware of the impediments to holding parliamentary elections in particular in 2004, and wanted to postpone them to 2005.

In New York, Security Council members grew increasingly anxious as the deadline for setting an electoral date neared. In some countries that were heavily involved in Afghanistan, a wearying public saw elections as a possible beginning of an exit from Afghanistan. Other governments, including the Bush administration, would themselves be subjected to elections before the end of 2004, and saw the holding of elections in Afghanistan as a vindication of their policies thus far. As a result of these pressures, the international press also became interested in the decision, and questions about the date of Afghan elections began to emerge at the U.N. press briefings in New York. Everyone could see the clock ticking; everyone knew that officially matters were in the hands of the JEMB; but nobody knew what would emerge from the JEMB and when.

On June 23, in Kabul, Arnault convened a meeting with the international members of the JEMB. He presented them with four options that he had prepared: (i) holding both elections in September 2004 (the preferred position decided at the Berlin conference); (ii) holding the presidential election in September and parliamentary elections in mid-November; (iii) holding presidential elections in

September and parliamentary elections in spring 2005; and (iv) holding both presidential and parliamentary elections in spring 2005. Of these, he considered only options (iii) and (iv) to be consistent with a legitimate electoral process. This was obviously a reversal of his earlier position, which had been in favor of holding the elections together in 2004. Arnault also told JEMB members that the decision on election timing, while formally a mandate of the JEMB, would have to be endorsed by the Secretary-General or the Security Council. He explained that he did not believe the JEMB had enough "weight" to convince political actors in Afghanistan to accept a decision of this importance. He argued that due to the surging numbers in the registration process, the U.N.'s prestige was then at its highest point, and it could provide the necessary backing to the JEMB.

Arnault sent the same set of options to the U.N. headquarters in New York, noting, as he had with the international JEMB members, his preferred options. He also requested the Secretary-General to take a decision on the options immediately—on the same day that the cable had been sent, given the imminent deadline. Secretary-General Annan immediately convened a meeting of his top Afghan advisors, including Brahimi (now serving as a sort of trouble-shooter at large), to discuss Arnault's options. Annan was leaving that evening on a trip to Africa, and therefore a decision could not be reached within Arnault's deadline, but one was made shortly afterwards. The Secretary-General and his *petit cabinet* endorsed the option of holding the presidential election in September and postponing parliamentary elections until spring 2005.

In a cable forwarding this decision, Arnault was requested to carry out further consultations with Afghan counterparts and the diplomatic community with a view to building a consensus around the Secretary-General's position. The cable also mentioned, for the first time, the possibility of having to postpone even the September presidential election, and asked Arnault to provide some benchmarks that, if not met, would make it necessary to suspend the election. Finally, the cable noted the importance of the responsibility of any change in the election date being shared with the government and the rest of the international community. The Secretary-General did not want the U.N. to be isolated on this mater, or be perceived as the sole decision-maker. The long-cited concerns of EAD—of assuming responsibility for a process over which it did not necessarily have control—were finally acknowledged at the highest level. But it was perhaps too late to matter.

Arnault quickly convened representatives of the diplomatic community in Kabul to obtain a consensus, as instructed, on what had become the Secretary-General's preferred option. The Europeans dragged their feet, still favoring the holding of both elections in September (among other things, this was considered the least costly option). Arnault cited the DDR benchmarks established in Berlin as a reason to push for separating the elections, arguing that delays in achieving these benchmarks had generated a climate of intimidation that would affect the results of local elections. In addition, after months of disregarding advice from his own staff that parliamentary elections would not be possible for technical reasons, Arnault also leaned heavily on technical arguments to buttress his case.[7]

If elections were to be held in September, the exact date had to be announced before the end of June in order to comply with the timelines of the electoral law. June, however, ended without consensus on separating the elections and without the announcement of a date. Reuters, on July 1, 2004, reported:

> The United Nations suggested on Thursday that Afghanistan's elections may have to be delayed beyond September, but said that a delay of a few days should not be seen as a major problem. "If elections are to be held as the Government has said in September, the election date must be announced 90 days before the vote—this Friday or Saturday," election officials said. Meanwhile, Said Mohammed Azam, spokesman for the UN-backed Joint Electoral Management Body, said that an announcement could not be expected on Friday, which is a holiday in Muslim Afghanistan, but insisted that the deadline would be met. Earlier, Manoel de Almeida e Silva, spokesman for the UN Assistance Mission in Afghanistan, told a news briefing that there was a continuing debate about the election date. According to de Almeida e Silva, the United Nations had concerns that had to be taken into account, including the integrity of the election operation, security for voters and candidates and conditions to ensure that the polls are free and fair.[8]

The following day, *The New York Times* reported that "United Nations officials and other diplomats fear that unless the warlords and their militias are disarmed, there will be intimidation and interference at the polls."[9] This reflected one of Arnault's arguments to the envoys.

Leaving aside the missed opportunities and the late hour of these statements, whose validity had been equally obvious months before, it was heartening to the electoral advisors that the United Nations was finally taking a public stand on the need for elections that were *credible* rather than simply *timely*. The position maintained up to then by Arnault—namely that the fact of meeting Bonn timelines had been the most critical factor in the success of the process—had finally begun to develop some nuances.

Not everyone was convinced, however. The jihadi parties were against a postponement of parliamentary elections and the U.S. government also continued to push hard for parliamentary elections to be held in the fall. Over the July 4 weekend, U.S. Secretary of State Condoleezza Rice called the Annan and urged him not to separate the elections. The issue was referred to Prendergast who, with briefing notes from EAD, responded to Rice with technical arguments explaining why it was simply not possible to hold parliamentary elections in the time available. This was a change from the habit of responding to such political demands with fanciful "plans." Reality had finally caught up to the political decision-makers.

That same weekend, in Kabul, Arnault met with Karzai and his cabinet. Karzai's ministers had, like Arnault, come to the conclusion that combined elections in the fall of 2004 would be impossible. As good politicians, they began to distance themselves from the question, arguing that the JEMB should be allowed to "substantially" *make* the decision, not just announce it, as Arnault had previously argued.

The international community was still divided. In New York, ambassadors continued their démarches to the Secretary-General, and to Under-Secretaries-General Guéhenno, and Prendergast, that joint elections should be held in the fall. Germany was among the most persistent advocates, arguing in part that holding separate elections would be a violation of agreement reached at the Berlin conference earlier in the year. They further argued that the registration process had generated a momentum that needed to be sustained, which could only be done by holding both elections in the fall. The argument had all the hallmarks of a diplomatic stretch, not least of which was the insouciant reversal of previous positions as if they had never been held. The registration project, previously seen as an example of U.N. electoral incompetence, had now become such an obvious success that the technical opinions of those most responsible for that success had to be discarded. After much back and forth, the final position of the German representative was that if elections were to be postponed, Berlin did not want to be ambushed by the announcement. This, at least, was not an unreasonable request.

Pakistan's position was even more difficult to address. Pakistan continued to maintain that elections had to be held together, and that Afghan refugees in Pakistan had to be able to vote. Pakistan's refusal to yield created an unprecedented post-Bonn division on the question of Afghanistan within the Security Council. Pakistan had no formal say over the eventual decision, but given its membership in the Council and the fact that it was a neighbor of Afghanistan, its concerns could not easily be ignored.

On July 8, Austin called EAD to say that the date would be announced by the JEMB around lunchtime in Kabul—early morning in New York. This did not happen. Instead, a cable arrived from Arnault saying that the JEMB had unanimously endorsed the case for separating presidential and parliamentary elections and that a formal announcement would be made in the next few days, after more international and domestic support had been mustered. Interestingly, Arnault also noted a discussion with the chief of the Afghan intelligence service, the National Directorate for Security (NDS) who reported that his informal polling suggested that most Afghans favored a separation. Bowing to the inevitable, U.S. Ambassador Khalilzad issued a statement that day in Kabul: "If the United Nations considers it [a separation of the presidential and parliamentary elections] necessary and the Afghans want it, the U.S. will support it."

The next day, the long-awaited announcement was made in Kabul by the JEMB: the presidential election would be held on October 9 and parliamentary elections would be postponed until 2005. At long last a date had been set for the 2004 presidential election, and a decision had been taken to hold off parliamentary elections until 2005. UNAMA had not informed New York, however, that the announcement would be made. In the end, the Germans, like everyone else, were ambushed.

Implications of Separation on Out-of-Country

The decision to separate the elections immediately re-opened the question of out-of-country voting. Arnault had informed New York in his July 8 communication that the Pakistani government had been opposed to the idea that refugees participate in the presidential election alone. Now that it was fairly clear that parliamentary elections would be postponed (the announcement of the decision was taken the day after the cable had been sent) he suggested that Pakistani authorities would understand that their opposition had become irrelevant. Unless the Pakistani government changed its position in the following three days, it would be impossible anyway to implement out-of-country registration and hence voting.

The first concern that struck U.N. Headquarters was Arnault's assertion that "no less" than 90 days were required for holding out-of-country elections. Previously, UNAMA had informed Headquarters, based on a proposal prepared by the International Organization of Migration (IOM), that the minimum time required to plan for credible out-of-country elections was 120 days. DPKO requested confirmation that this new minimum was truly a minimum. It also asked for UNAMA's assessment of the risks of beginning an out-of-country registration but not being able to complete it by October 9, when the rest of the country would be ready to go to the polls. Finally, headquarters asked for clarifications of Arnault's statement that the "entire exercise will have to be called off" if Pakistan did not drop its opposition to separating the elections. The statement implied that the presidential election would not be considered credible at all without refugee participation. In other words, after all the work involved in finally deciding on a realistic date for the Afghan elections, and all of the logistical, training, civic education, and legislation-drafting efforts undertaken to meet that date, *everything* now depended on Pakistan changing their long-standing and unrealistic position in the next three days.

Two days later, Pakistani diplomats informed the U.N. Secretariat that Pakistan's position was shifting—Islamabad could accept split elections as long as out-of-country voting was guaranteed for the presidential election. It was a shrewd tactic. Pakistan's position on holding the two elections together, even if both had to be delayed, had never really been tenable because it lacked support from anyone else. But by pushing its position to the brink, Pakistan's eventual concession seemed immense, making its request for out-of-country presidential elections in exchange seem correspondingly small. The JEMB therefore began to plan for out-of-country elections, based on the 90-day plan that Arnault had proposed.

On July 14, the Security Council received a briefing from the U.N. Secretariat on the decision to separate the elections. Key members had discreetly requested an "uncontroversial" briefing, so the Secretariat omitted the question of out-of-country voting in its briefing. In the "informal" discussion after the briefing, most Council members "regretted" but "understood" the JEMB decision to postpone parliamentary elections. Pakistan used its time to made a strong case for out-of-country elections. The Russian representative made a meandering statement about how the lack of broad consultation on this question had undermined the crucial role of the Security Council in Afghanistan. In the end, of course, the Council had not choice but to endorse the decision. In this way, the great questions of the date and type of elections, which had caused so much consternation, and whose resolution had been avoided for so long, ended with something of a whimper.

The DNA of Afghan Politics

Now that it was clear what race would be contested, the politics could begin to take shape. Electoral politics were completely new to the generation of post-Bonn leaders in Afghanistan, who were used to playing by more brutal and less transparent rules. The politics of the moment were therefore difficult to read. The landscape was littered with alliances and rivalries that had been formed, broken, and reformed during the civil war and before. Alliances were often tactical, designed to outflank rivals and advance personal interests, rather than to promote the sorts of ideological objectives that unite parties in democracies.[10] A full understanding of Afghan politics required a deep knowledge of family alliances, historical grievances, and all manner of secret deals made among Afghan factions as well as between them and outside patrons. Besides the U.S.' obvious interests, Iran, Pakistan, India and Russia, in particular, all had hands in the domestic political game. Finally there was the sheer anarchic spirit of Afghan politics that sometimes, to the outsider, appears to defy reason or even obvious self-interest.[11]

The Bonn Agreement had suspended to some degree, and for a brief moment, the resort to violence by Afghan politicians. But the achievement of political ends through violent means had shaped a generation of Afghan leaders. Even if they so far had accepted—or felt compelled to accept—the rules of the Bonn process, it was not certain that they would adhere to these rules in the long-term. In the early months of the Bonn process, the frightening accuracy of American airpower was fresh in people's minds and kept even the most bellicose leaders in a posture of cautious reserve. Brahimi's adroit diplomacy and sound advice to Karzai also kept enough of the main leaders sufficiently satisfied to hope that they could achieve their minimal interests through the process. But as time passed, and Afghans began to witness the growing inability of international forces to subdue the insurgency, not to mention the increasing number of incidents where U.S. bombs hit the wrong targets (for example, in June 2002, a Coalition bomb tragically killed dozens of civilians in Uruzgan) fears of U.S. military omnipotence diminished. The departure of Brahimi in early 2004 removed the factor of his subtle diplomacy and his trusted relationship with Karzai. With the upcoming election providing a major stake to contend for, many feared that some of Afghanistan's power brokers might break beyond the red lines of the Bonn Agreement.

Even in such extraordinary and unprecedented periods of politics as the one created by Bonn—where there is an opportunity for a society to fundamentally reorder itself—the essential DNA of a politico-cultural system is always a factor and often reasserts itself. This was famously noted by Tocqueville, who posited in *L'ancien Régime* that the French revolution had, for all of its upheavals, not fundamentally altered the structure of French politics. "Each time since [the revolution] that we wanted to destroy absolute power we have succeeded only in placing the head of Liberty on the body of a slave."[12] Marx, in frustration with the failure of the 1848 French revolution, referred in *The Eighteenth Brumaire of Louis Napoleon* as "world-historical necromancy": "The tradition of all the dead generations weighs like a nightmare on the brain of the living. And just when they seem engaged in the revolutionizing themselves and things, in creating something entirely new, [...] they anxiously conjure up the spirits of the past to their service [...]."[13]

If there were political laws in Afghanistan—or at least consistent principles derived from immutable elements of its political history—one of them was that a non-Pashtun could not rule the country. The emblematic demonstration of this principle was the nine-month reign in 1929 of the Tajik, Habib Allah Ghazi, better known by his nickname, "Bacha Saqao," or "the water-carrier's son." Habib Allah had seized Kabul, taking advantage of a general tribal uprising against the modernizing reforms of King Amanullah. He established a government but faced constant resistance from Pashtuns, who characteristically united against him. Eventually Nadir Shah, the father of the last King, Zahir Shah, wrested the capital and the government from Bacha Saqao. As Robert McChesney noted:

> Long maligned by the guardians of Muhammadzai history [...] as a bloodthirsty tyrant whose reign set Afghanistan back 'a hundred years,' in more recent times the figure of Habib Allah has been given a somewhat different gloss, as a representative of the underclasses in Afghanistan struggling against the oppression of Pashtun domination.[14]

Though the post-Bonn interim administration was led by Karzai, a Pashtun, Tajiks initially held the key ministries of defense, interior and foreign affairs. Furthermore, Karzai was increasingly perceived by Pashtuns as not effectively representing them. The Tajik triumvirate behind Karzai was perhaps as close as Afghanistan had been to the nine months of Habibullah's Tajik rule, certainly in Pashtun perceptions.[15]

We have seen already how the Emergency Loya Jirga and constitutional processes acted as valves to release political pressure within the system, and especially the pressure generated by the perception of Pashtun alienation. The elections, as the final defined step of the Bonn process, were the final opportunity for political positioning.

At the same time, many Afghan leaders might have had doubted that the elections would ever happen. The uncertain and generally nontransparent manner in which decisions had been taken during the election planning process must have subtracted confidence among the many not involved in the decision-making. Recent history also did not provide much confidence. Most Afghan leaders still remembered the brief attempt at peace in 1992, after the collapse of the Najibullah regime. Then, interim President Mojaddedi had relinquished power after his two-month term to Rabbani, as required by the Peshawar Accord.[16] Rabbani had failed to do the same when his six-month term was over. It would not have been unreasonable for an Afghan politician to assume that Karzai would attempt to delay as much as possible the holding of elections that might unseat him. This impulse, too, was part of Afghanistan's political DNA.

The unfortunately prudent distrust in Afghanistan's democratic future by the country's de jure and de facto power holders contributed to the worsening of security after the Emergency Loya Jirga in June 2002.[17] This deterioration at first had little to do with the insurgency that would later emerge. Rather, it took the form of increased factional fighting among subordinates of the larger faction leaders. Evidence of increasing political violence included the assassination of Haji Qadir on July 6, 2002, the attempted assassination against Karzai on September 5 in Kandahar, and an explosion in Kabul, also on September 5, that killed more than 30 people. The reasons for this acceleration of instability were most likely the fact that the losers at the Loya Jirga realized that they might not benefit from the Bonn process—in other words, they trusted less and less the pressure valve functions of the Bonn process. They were, in addition, perhaps emboldened by the international community's prolonged indecision over expanding ISAF beyond Kabul,[18] which was seen as a proxy for lack of international staying-power.

The north and southeast of the country were the most persistently problematic. In the north, the long-standing rivalry between General Dostum and General Atta was a constant source of tension. Both men unofficially controlled troops and arms. Local disputes between commanders over military posts and money frequently flared into protracted battles. After one of these battles, Arnault, while still DSRSG, successfully negotiated a ceasefire in Mazar-i-Sharif in May 2002, preventing an escalation of violence between Dostum's and Atta's forces. The agreement provided for a separation of forces to points equidistant from the city, and for the creation of a neutral security force. The first was accomplished, but the second was not, in part due to lack of financial support from the international community to create a 600-strong neutral police corps that was intended to stand between the rival armies.

In the southeast, Padshah Khan Zadran, a pro-monarchy tribal leader, had been threatening the area around Gardez, including parts of the provinces of Khost, Paktiya and Paktika, beginning in the spring of 2002. Zadran had been present at Bonn, had inked his name to the agreement, and had subsequently been named governor of Paktya province by Karzai. He quickly turned against the government, however, partly due to disappointment at the sidelining of the King and the monarchists early in the Bonn process. His defiance increased following the killing of his son by U.S. forces. Before the Bonn Agreement was concluded, Zadran had enjoyed American support in the hunt for Bin Laden. As was typical in those confusing days, someone at some point convinced the U.S. that Zadran's son was supporting the Taliban. Acting on this information, resulting in his death.[19] This set Zadran against the U.S. as well as the government. He launched a number of rockets against the city of Khost in the summer of 2002. In September, government forces backed by the U.S. attacked Zadran and pushed him from his position near Gardez, provoking a number of defections from his ranks. As Olivier Roy noted,

> Karzai's appointees might not have had personal power bases in the area, but their fellow tribesmen (the Wardak tribe in the case of Gardez and Governor Taj Mohammed Wardak, and the Taniwal tribe in the case of Khost Governor Akbar Taniwal) supported them against Padshah, while many Zadrans withdrew their support of Padshah for fear of losing influence.[20]

Zadran escaped, but was essentially defanged; this was something of a triumph for the government, which had enjoyed few such triumphs on the security front.[21]

Despite these worrying security developments, the evident advancement of the electoral process eventually had an impact on the decisions of the major warlords—especially Dostum and Ismail Khan who had, long after Bonn, exercised blatantly personalistic administrations in the areas they controlled. (The case of Ismail Khan is discussed in greater detail below.) The success of the voter registration process, the adoption of the electoral law, and especially, the setting of the electoral date, at last began to erode doubts that the elections would not be held. Increasing confidence that they would happen began to encourage political actors to get in the game, even if only as a hedge.

Karzai showed some unusual boldness during this period, and began to use the new political tools and incentives at his disposal to weaken the power of his main, armed rivals. On July 12, 2004, he issued a decree threatening to prosecute presidential candidates who failed to sever their links with armed groups—a requirement under the electoral law. This boldness was perhaps motivated by an incipient fear. Karzai was surely aware that the Bonn process was beginning to backslide with the deterioration of security. In addition, it was looking plausible, if not likely, that the election in the U.S. might be won by John Kerry. It was assumed that a consequence of a Kerry administration might be less robust U.S. support for Afghanistan than had been the case under Bush. In other words, Karzai might have recognized that his window of opportunity to strike against the warlords, while still being unconditionally backed by the U.S., was closing.[22]

Karzai followed his July 12 decree with another demonstration of political courage. When he submitted the papers for his own candidacy on July 26, his two vice-presidential candidates were Ahmad Zia Massoud (brother of the assassinated Panshiri commander, Ahmad Shah Massoud) and Abdul Karim Khalili, leader of the Hazara Hezb-i-Wahdat. It was an ethnically balanced ticket and a politically astute one.[23] What most observers noted, however, was who was *not* on the ticket—his defense minister, Mohammed Fahim Khan. Fahim had accrued significant power in post-Bonn Afghanistan. He was in the paradoxical position of being both one of the highest officials of the post-Bonn administration and one of its most significant potential spoilers. Fahim had used his position as Minister of Defense to avoid the disarmament of his own factions, combining in effect his personal and administrative capacities. For this, and for suspected corruption, he was increasingly criticized by the international community.

Karzai's decision not to include him on his ticket was described by the Pakistani journalist and Afghan expert Ahmed Rashid, as Karzai's "most momentous move since he accepted the job of interim president," and a "bold step against powerful warlords."[24] The move was certainly bold, probably wise, but definitely risky. Given the forces still directly loyal to him, a revolt by Fahim against Karzai was not inconceivable. Karzai had secured the backing of Ambassador Khalilzad prior to taking this decision, and therefore obtained a measure of confidence that the Coalition would repel any military move by Fahim.[25] There was no such move in the end, and Karzai's gamble paid off. Fahim's only retaliation was political—support for the candidacy of Karzai's long-time rival and Fahim's former colleague in the Northern Alliance, Yunis Qanuni.[26]

One surprise during the presidential nomination period was Dostum's decision to run for president. He announced his candidacy on July 22 in Mazar-i-Sharif to a crowd of 3,000, including tribal notables and other political leaders. His ear was surprisingly well-tuned to the value of democratic political theater and to the sensitivities of the population in the north. He billed the event a "convention" to nominate a "northern" candidate who could challenge Karzai.

Some of UNAMA's political officers offered a less cynical and equally plausible explanation of Dostum's candidacy. According to this version, it was the Uzbek elders and tribal leaders who pushed Dostum to run as a candidate with the expectation that he would gain at least a ministry in Kabul. This conformed to the old Afghan political view that it was important for each tribe or ethnicity to have a representative in Kabul—that ministry would then become *their* ministry, through which they would be able to assure a certain level of patronage and representation. For them, Dostum had the best chance of securing the most Uzbek votes and hence the optimal leverage for a powerful position after the election. This interpretation is fascinating in that it demonstrates some exercise of power from below, even in a political context defined by warlords. In other words, even if Dostum would have preferred to stay out of the electoral game in order to maintain his militia, his constituency had decided that the elections were the new political game and thrust him into it. Cynical on one level, it offered hope on another that the Bonn process was increasingly understood and internalized by Afghans.

Few doubted that Dostum would gain more than the approximately ten percent of votes that likely represented the Uzbek portion of the population. The bigger question was how serious he was about paying the normative cost of abandoning his militia in order to enter the electoral contest. How far would he go, and how much military weakening would he accept, to remain politically viable? And how much effort would be made to enforce the electoral law's provision on this question? Some experts thought that Dostum still saw himself as a "strong man" who could dictate a change of regime in Kabul. It was certainly a role he had played—more than once—in the past.[27]

Dostum's entry into the political game provided the first obvious test of Karzai's July 12 decree on the disarmament of candidates. Dostum's presidential bid became a proxy for the overall question of whether Afghanistan could move beyond warlordism. It also created a major dilemma for the JEMB—rejecting his candidacy if he refused to renounce control over his militia risked pushing him entirely out of the game, threatening the process. Accepting his candidacy while allowing him to retain control over his militia would, on the other hand, undermine the credibility of the election.[28]

The People's Reaction

On July 27, the JEMB released the provisional list of presidential candidates. Then began the difficult challenge of attempting to command respect for the law while accommodating, on the one hand, the political reality that some still had the power to ignore the law and, on the other, the growing popular demand for justice.

According to the electoral law, citizens had until July 31 to lodge complaints against those on the provisional list. During this period, 115 objections were launched against 11 candidates, with most complaints directed against Dostum and Khalili. The only complaints that the JEMB could legally consider were those pertaining to the specific provisions of the electoral law on candidate eligibility.[29] (Many Afghans had used the complaints process to allege human rights violations that had been committed in the past, which was the direct result of a lack of any formal process to deal with these violations.) The JEMB was responsible for vetting valid complaints, but did not have an investigative arm fulfill his task with any thoroughness. The commissioners decided therefore to submit the objections (with the names of the objectors redacted) to the ministries of foreign affairs, interior, defense, and finance, as well as the NDS (the domestic intelligence service), the Supreme Court, and diplomatic missions, requesting all of them to substantiate, if at all possible, the complaints alleged against the candidates. Most of these did not reply;[30] the Interior Ministry, however, sent a letter claiming that Dostum had exercised influence over military units, including ordering them to attack representatives of the central government in Faryab province in the recent past. As a result, the JEMB sent a letter to Dostum, affirming that it had:

> [...] given thorough consideration to the misgivings raised within the public, the statements given by the ministries and the circumstances surrounding the issue of military forces in Afghanistan and concluding that the most effective way to respond in a forward-looking way to allegations that your past military involvement could undermine your legal qualification to participate in the 2004 electoral process is for the units—corps and divisions, as the case may be—that were formally under your command to be immediately placed under the command of professional officers of the Afghan National Army.

Arnault properly and strongly supported this decision and urged Karzai to stand behind it.

While the Ministry had said nothing about Khalili and Ustad Mohaqeq, another Shia Hazara faction leader who was also contesting the election, the JEMB decided that, in light of the large number of complaints against them, and given the perpetually tense ethnic sensitivities in Afghanistan, it would be prudent to send identical letters to them. In practice—that is, in terms of effectively sundering Dostum's control over his militia units—the JEMB letter did not have a great effect. But it did have a symbolic impact that was more than negligible. The chairman of the JEMB, basing himself upon the law, had informed one of the most ruthless and effective military commanders in Afghanistan that he would have to comply with a measure presented by the JEMB if he wished to remain a candidate. More remarkably, in terms of symbolism, Dostum (and the others) *did* accept the conditions and go through the motions of complying with the order. Formally at least, the ex-Mujahhedin were playing the electoral game and the JEMB was showing that it could enforce its rules.

The final candidate list, presented by the JEMB on schedule on August 10, contained 18 candidates. The JEMB noted in its press release that on July 10, when the nominations period opened, 33 individuals had requested forms and 23 had filed nomination papers by the July 26 deadline. Following the evaluation of complaints, three candidates had been rejected for "failure to comply with the nomination procedures." A day before the announcement of the final candidates list, two withdrew, leaving 18 candidates to contest Afghanistan's first presidential election.

According to UNAMA's analysis, about a third of the presidential candidates were political newcomers. They were unknown to most Afghans in the provinces, yet had managed to rise to some level of prominence in the Kabul-based post-Bonn administration. About a quarter of the candidates were returned exiles attempting to reclaim political space they abandoned years before. The rest were mostly jihadis who had name recognition, financial support, an organizational structure, and a capacity to intimidate local electorates if necessary. Almost none of the candidates had the resources to mount a convincing nation-wide campaign. The exceptions were Qanuni, backed by Fahim, and Ahmad Shah Ahmadzai, the candidate of the radical Islamist leader Abdul Sayyaf.[31] The candidate who had the most resources, but also the most to lose—Karzai—had decided to adopt a posture of aloofness, staying above the political fray, acting in some ways more as a king than a candidate.

As the campaign period advanced, another issue began to assume a larger part of the political discussion. This was the competence of Karzai's administration. There was growing dissatisfaction with the inability of Karzai and his foreign backers to effectively address the insurgency and to deliver benefits of peace to the rural areas of Afghanistan. The corruption within Karzai's government was worsening. Because it was blatant and exercised particularly against the weak, it was increasingly apparent to the population outside Kabul. They increasingly sensed that the billions of dollars in aid—which were widely reported on the radio but not reflected in changes in peoples' lives—were being pocketed in Kabul. The temptation for opposition candidates to campaign against Karzai, rather than for *something*, led to several anemic attempts to unite behind a single opposition candidate. The laws of Afghan politics prevailed, however, and these efforts collapsed because no one could agree who would be the strongest opponent to Karzai. The opposition candidates, like the chieftains in Pazhwak's poem,[32] drew knives against each other in their attempt to control that intoxicating bag of Afghan soil.

Defanging the Warlords

In the late summer of 2004, with the campaign period underway, instability spread to the west of Afghanistan when fighting broke out around Herat as local commanders took on Ismail Khan, the powerful provincial governor. Khan had been the de facto emir of Herat ever since he wrested control of the city from the pro-Soviet government during a popular uprising in 1979. Hunted by the Communist government and later the Soviets, he melted into the countryside and waged a guerilla war against the Soviets throughout the occupation. After the Soviet withdrawal, he again seized control of the city, establishing it as his power base during the civil war. Like Massoud—and unlike most of the Mujaheddin leaders—he had, during his guerilla years, been able to establish an effective administrative apparatus as a resistance leader.[33] His area of influence included the former Soviet air base at Shindand, which was also Khan's home town. In March 1995, Khan lost a major battle against the Taliban at Shindand and was captured. He managed to escape to Iran, remaining there until 2001. After Bonn he was named by Karzai as governor of his home province. This formal appointment, however, merely ratified a political reality. Khan was Karzai's governor in name only. He responded to Kabul on his terms, not on the president's.

Herat, near the Iranian border, was one of Afghanistan's major trading centers, generating huge tariff revenues.[34] While these were officially state revenues, Khan had de facto control over them and gave to the central government what he wished, keeping the rest for himself and for Herat, though it was not obvious where one ended and the other began. This had consequences for Karzai's government in Kabul. Herat was the only province to earn more money for the central government than it would have been allocated. The revenues it owned undermined the extension of government everywhere else.[35]

Many considered Khan's control over Herat to be unchallengeable. More perceptive analysts, however, noted moves by the central government to weaken his control by appointing Kabul-friendly rivals to Khan as governors of surrounding provinces.[36] As early as the spring of 2002, some of UNAMA's political officers based in Herat had noticed that Ismail Khan's control over the region was not as absolute as most analysts and journalists believed. Furthermore, while Herat was generally considered to be well-administered, Khan was making fewer and fewer concessions to rivals, provoking further opposition to his governorship.

Karzai, in mid-2003, had managed to force Khan to choose between being governor of Herat or commander of the national army division stationed there (the 4th Army Corps and the 17th Division); at the time he was both. Khan chose the political role, and command of the two military units was transferred to rivals. The vice seemed to be tightening around Khan. In March of 2004, in a confusing incident, Ismail Khan's son (who was also Minister of Aviation) was killed by bodyguards of General Zahir, the new commander of the 17th Division. This led to a round of fighting in Herat, the deployment of the Afghan National Army to the western city for the first time, and a simmering tension in the city where Khan once reigned supreme. This tension erupted into violence again in mid-August 2004. In an apparently coordinated attack, fighting against Ismail Khan broke out in four provinces, ending with the capture of Shindand by Amanullah Khan, a former Taliban commander backed by Gul Agha Sherzai, Karzai's governor in Kandahar. Other fronts were led by the 4th Corps and the 17th Division. Ismail Khan reasonably sensed that this was a deliberate attempt to unseat him. Karzai's government, meanwhile, condemned the fighting as an attack against the state, but in fact was not unhappy to see Ismail Khan weakened. This fine line between the rule of law and the reality of Afghan politics continued to be negotiated for several more weeks. The two Khans, Ismail and Amanullah, maintained their standoff with the Afghan

National Army, which had stationed forces between their respective positions in Shindand.

In Kabul, Karzai decided to try to defuse the situation by offering Ismail Khan a ministerial position in Kabul, appointing a competent administrator from Kabul to govern Herat, and transferring the commanders who had attacked Khan to other positions in the central government. Ismail Khan refused this face-saving compromise. During the standoff, a spokesman for Dostum offered to send troops to assist Ismail Khan—a vestige of jihadi solidarity. This prompted the JEMB to send an immediate note to Dostum informing him that his spokesman's statements put Dostum's candidacy in potential breach of the electoral law, which prohibited threats of the use of force and incitements to violence. The note also said that Dostum's spokesman's statement suggested that the candidate had maintained links with "non-official armed forces," which he was supposed to have severed.

Increasingly isolated and militarily weak, Ismail Khan finally gave in. On September 11, 2004, Karzai announced the appointment of Ismail Khan as Minister of Mines and Industries and appointing a jihadi former ambassador to the Ukraine as governor of Herat.

The reaction in Herat to Ismail Khan's "appointment" was swift and violent. Shortly after noon, on September 12, a mob of several hundred began attacking the UNAMA offices in Herat with stones. They were able to drive a vehicle through the main gate and into the compound, where they set fire to a U.N. vehicle. U.N. staff in the compound immediately retreated to their bunker, from where they contacted the U.S. Coalition. U.S. forces took around 45 minutes to arrive, but were able to evacuate the 12 United Nations staff members from the compound. In the meantime, the mob ransacked the offices, causing extensive damage, and then turned on the adjacent offices of the UNHCR. The offices of the Afghan Independent Human Rights Commission (AIHRC) were also attacked, as were those of several NGOs. There were no casualties among the United Nations or other international staff, though 15 U.S. soldiers were wounded by the stone-throwing crowds.

During the attack, Ambassador Khalilzad had reportedly called Ismail Khan. Khan claimed he had no direct control over the mob but suggested he could contain the violence if his governorship was restored to him for ten days. Khalilzad held a hard but correct line, informing the governor that he would be held responsible for the violence and that if it continued it would affect his possible future in Afghan political life. At the same time, local elders visited Khan and urged him to accept the decision of the central government and take up the ministerial post. The mob eventually ebbed and then dispersed.

The incidents in Herat marked the end of Ismail Khan as a direct power player in Herat (though he maintained significant indirect authority.) UNAMA described the result as another major step toward defactionalizing Afghanistan—the previous steps being the non-inclusion of Fahim on Karzai's ticket and the pro forma separation of Dostum from his militia. The electoral process, and the political climate it had created, appeared to be gradually altering the political geography of Afghanistan, forcing old power brokers to recognize new political rules and abide by them.

In early September, a joint UNAMA-AIHRC report on the verification of political rights was released. [37] It took stock of the voter registration process, commenting that "massive popular involvement in the registration process has fulfilled one of the pre-conditions for the presidential election to be a genuinely democratic exercise." On the other hand, it noted the problems of "insecurity in those areas where extremist groups are bent on undermining by violent means a process that they fear; the information deficit, which exposes voters to manipulation and generates a climate of uncertainty for political parties; and the rule of local commanders over communities, which has the potential to distort the free expression of popular will." It also reported a lack of confidence among the public in the electoral process, in particular in terms of safeguards, and recommended that measures be taken to ensure that the safeguards that did exist well-understood by the public: "Clarity and transparency is key to dispelling such suspicions and allegations." It was, however, becoming late in the process to begin to insist on "clarity and transparency."

---

[1] For example, the CSO would assume a growth rate of about 1.6 percent per year for rural communities and 4.5 percent for Kabul, with medium-sized cities falling somewhere in between.

[2] The five inaccessible provinces were Helmand, Paktika, Zabul, Uruzgan and Daikundi. The two partially-accessed provinces were Kandahar and Ghazni.

[3] Thomas Ruttig suggests three main currents that "re-surfaced as the backbone of the emerging multi-party system, with the new democrats emerging as a new one" in a paper he wrote in 2006 for the Konrad Adenauer Stiftung. These currents were: (i) the political-religious (Islamic) current, made up of the mostly Sunni Mujaheddin parties based in Peshawar and the Shia groups based in Tehran during the anti-Soviet resistance (the so-called "Peshawar Seven" and Tehran Eight" respectively); (ii) the parties that stemmed from the PDPA and its Maoist offshoots; and (iii) the ethno-nationalist parties, of which Ruttig identifies at least three on the Pashtun side. See Ruttig, "Islamists, Leftists—and a Void in the Center" p. 17.

[4] Kit Spence would later refer to these as "vanity projects," see "Political Party Assessment in Afghanistan" National Democratic Institute for International Affairs, Kabul, Spring 2006, p. 11.

[5] King Zahir Shah, who had reigned between 1933 and 1973, when he abdicated after a coup by his cousin Daud, was still alive and had returned to Afghanistan from his Roman exile in 2002. The 2004 Constitution accorded him a special status as "Father of the Nation," but made no provisions for the extension of the monarchy beyond his lifetime (see Afghanistan Constitution, 2004, article 158). The king died in July 2007.

[6] One of them, Hekmatyar's Hezb-i-Islami was openly fighting the post-Bonn transitional administration.

[7] Around the same time, the AREU had issued a report on security in Afghanistan that made the following, relevant, complaint: "The nature of policy-making in Afghanistan has too often suffered from 'policy reductionism', where the nature and extent of the problem is simplified to make the problem appear more manageable." This was a fair description of how the electoral process had been handled so far by the policy-makers. See Michael Bhati, Kevin Lanigan and Philip Wilkinson, "Minimal Investments, Minimal Results: The Failure of Security Policy in Afghanistan" Kabul, AREU Briefing Paper, June 2004, p. 3.

[8] Reuters, "U.N. Suggests Afghan Election Delay Possible," 1 July 2004.

[9] Carlotta Gall, "Strife Reported to Delay Afghan Vote Again," *New York Times*, 2 July 2004.

[10] As Dorronsoro wrote of the mujaheddin period, "Relationships between commanders were generally characterized by competition arising out of personal rivalries, logistical issues, control over strategic positions, and humanitarian aid among other considerations." Dorronsoro's account also describes the rivalries between parties during the occupation, who fought against each other even while supposedly united in the overall aim of expelling the Soviets. See *Revolution Unending,* pp. 207-232.

[11] Rahman Pazhwak, an Afghan ambassador to the U.N. in the 1950s as well as a poet, wrote a poem of Alexander the Great's attempt to conquer Afghanistan, but from a characteristically Afghan perspective. In Pazhwak's poem, Alexander's anxious mother, the Queen of Macedonia, wrote him to ask why he was dallying in the land of the Afghans instead of moving on to India. Alexander replied that the answer was too complex for words—"not even Aristotle could understand." Instead he sent her five Afghan chieftains and, hidden beneath a saddle, a sack of Afghan soil. He told his mother to receive the Afghans on their first night as she would receive any king. She would find them courteous and honorable and knowledgeable on all the important subjects. Then he instructed her to convoke them again, on their second night, but this time to sprinkle some of the Afghan soil under the carpet before they arrived. The first meeting, Pazhwak writes, was "held with joy" and indeed the Afghan chieftains showed themselves to be men of culture, learning and wisdom. The second meeting, the poet describes, was something else:

And when it was time for the second meeting
The puzzling soil was scattered as instructed

When the chieftains of Ariana,
Those proud representatives of the Aryan race,
Stepped up to the palace's gate
They lost their normal state
By sensing the smell of their motherland's soil
Unsheathing their swords
They clashed each other with Afghan valor
Two or three of them fell in their own blood
And as they collapsed, you might say
The pinnacles of the sky collapsed
Or columns broke and ceilings were demolished
A thousand jars of wine cannot intoxicate the wine lovers
As a particle of dust intoxicates the patriots!
Oh what a commotion a handful of Afghan soil breeds
What a tumult of passion it creates!

This is on some level a disturbing parable of an irrational propensity to violence. It may be read, on another level, as an allegory for other known Afghan traits: competition among Afghans for foreign favor, and a willingness to sacrifice each other to impress the outside world. The many layers at which the poem can be read hint at the many layers of Afghan politics. (The translation was provided to me by an Afghan refugee professor in Peshawar in 1993. I am unaware of any published English translation.)

[12] Alexis de Tocqueville, *L'Ancien Régime et la Révolution,* 4th. ed. (Paris, 1860) p. 333, quoted in Albert O. Hirschman, *The Rhetoric of Reaction" Perversity, Futility, Jeopardy* (Cambridge and London: The Belknap Press of Harvard University, 1991) p. 50. Hirschman adds to Tocqueville's quote: "This amounts to saying (to use a very different, contemporary metaphor) that the changes which were introduced were 'merely cosmetic' and left the essence of things unchanged."

[13] Karl Marx, "The Eighteen Brumaire of Louis Bonaparte" in *The Karl Marx Reader*, Second Edition, Ed. Robert C. Tucker (New York: W.W. Norton and Company, 1978) p. 595.

[14] See Robert D. McChesney, *Kabul Under Siege: Fayz Muhammad's Account of the 1929 Uprising* (Princeton: Markus Wiener Publishers, 1999) pp. 1-2.

[15] According to Dobbins, when Karzai arrived in Afghanistan for the first time after the Bonn Agreement, Fahim, a Tajik, met him at the Bagram airport. Fahim, who was the Minister of Defense at the time, asked Karzai, "Where are your men?" Karzai responded, "You are my men." This demonstrated on Karzai's part a nice early instinct for both reconciliation and institutionalization; this promising instinct seems to have been subsequently overwhelmed. See Dobbins, *After the Taliban*, p. 104.

[16] Maley takes a more nuanced view, noting that the Council for Supreme Popular Settlement, the executive body of the Peshawar Accord, had endorsed Rabbani's remaining in office. It should be noted that Rabbani's opponents had boycotted the Council, claiming that Rabbani had manipulated it. Maley concludes, however, that the Council's "problem was actually a deeper one,

which would have exposed it to denunciation by whoever was disappointed by the outcome: as an unelected body, it could not claim to be representative." See Maley, *Afghanistan Wars,* p. 199. The semi-representativeness of the Emergency Loya Jirga can be seen as an attempt to correct this flaw of the Peshawar Accord.

[17] It is also worth noting that during this period the United States had not yet invaded Iraq (which would occur in March 2003) and had an undivided security focus on Afghanistan, though a thin one compared to what would come later. It was also not until August 2003 that a decision was taken to deploy ISAF units beyond Kabul. U.S. coalition units had been operating throughout the country from the beginning, but their focus was on counter-terrorism, not providing local stability or, in the much-maligned phrase, "nation building."

[18] From the beginning Brahimi had urged the expansion of ISAF beyond Kabul to provide a greater measure of security and demonstrate a firmer commitment to stability. It was not until August 2003 until the decision was made to expand ISAF. The actual expansion then took time; it was furthermore implemented incrementally. (See also in Chapter Two, footnote 6, Doronsorro's comment on the failure of the U.S. to insert ground troops in key areas in the aftermath of the fall of the Taliban.)

[19] A number of opponents to the Bonn process were the result of the unfortunate phenomenon whereby some tribes convinced the Americans that rival tribes were Taliban sympathizers. When the Americans attacked the rival tribes, those often joined the insurgency.

[20] See Roy, "Afghanistan: Internal Politics and Socio-economic Dynamics and Groupings" p. 8.

[21] Things changed again for Zadran in the fall of 2005, when he was elected to Parliament.

[22] It is interesting to compare this reaction with what occurred later: the election of Obama brought about the changed relationship that was feared under Kerry. Much has, of course, changed in the intervening half-decade. It is another interesting irony of history that John Kerry played a key role in the negotiation leading to a resolution of the 2009 electoral crisis described in the last chapter.

[23] The selection of Massoud was particularly astute. Massoud was the son-in-law of former President Rabbani, and his presence helped to split the Panshiri base that would have constituted Fahim's strongest support, had he decided to challenge Karzai. Massoud, who had been an ambassador for most of the civil war, could also be portrayed as part of the "new generation," and hence a symbol of the need for Afghan politics to move beyond "Jihadis" and warlords. Khalili was a Hazara and a Shia. Karzai's ticket thus superficially at least personified the hopes of the Bonn process: it was ethnically balanced, light on warlords, and generally forward-looking.

[24] Ahmed Rashid, "A Vote Is Cast Against the Warlords" *Far Eastern Economic Review,* Hong Kong: August 5, 2004. Vol. 167, Iss. 31, p. 12.

[25] Khalilzad issued a public warning to Fahim, saying that he had a "direct responsibility" for preventing violence.

[26] Qanuni, it will be recalled, bore a grudge against Karzai for the somewhat humiliating way in which he had been forced from the interior

ministry during the Emergency Loya Jirga, so as to break the Panshiri triumvirate over the ministries of defense, foreign affairs, and interior. It was, therefore, not surprising that he chose to oppose Karzai in the election; though his objective was probably less to become president than to build an opposition movement to Karzai. Karzai's popularity and backing by the international community at the time was such that even Qanuni must have known he could not win the election.

[27] Most notably in 1992. During the Soviet occupation Dostum's militia had sided with the occupiers. He continued to support the Najibullah regime after the withdrawal of the Soviets. When Naijbullah's regime collapsed in April 1992, facing Massoud's troops camped outside of Kabul in the north, and Hekmatyar's in the south, Dostum became a king-maker by ferrying some of Massoud's troops by helicopter into Kabul, winning the race for the capital. See Assem Akram, *Histoire de la Guerre d'Afghanistan* (Paris: Balland, 1996) p. 391. Dostum and his feared Jawzjani militia would later switch sides again, backing Hekmatyar, who by then had managed to secure sectors of Kabul lying south of the Kabul river.

[28] Dostum was not the only candidate with this problem, though he was the most powerful and the most obvious. Khalili and Mohaqeq were also accused of having links to militias.

[29] These were, according to Article 16(3) of the electoral law that "Candidates shall not: (a) Pursue objectives that are opposed to the principles of the holy religion of Islam and the word and spirit of the Constitution; (b) Use force, or threaten with, or propagate the use of, force; (c) Incite ethnic, linguistic, regional or religious tension and discrimination; (d) Create real danger to the rights or freedoms of individuals or intentionally disrupt public order and security; (e) Have non-official military forces ro be part of them; (f) Receive funds from foreign sources; (g) Receive funds from internal illegal sources. In addition, Article 13(2) required candidates to be qualified voters, and Article 13(1) required qualified voters to be "not deprived of any political and civil rights by an authoritative court."

[30] Two embassies did reply, however, stating that a presidential and a vice-presidential candidate held dual citizenship with their countries. One of the candidates resigned and the other renounced his non-Afghan citizenship.

[31] See Chapter Two, footnote 8.

[32] See footnote 12 above.

[33] See Rashid, *Taliban*, pp. 36 and 37.

[34] According to Olivier Roy, customs revenues exceeded USD 100,000 per day. See Roy, "Afghanistan: Internal Politics and Socio-economic Dynamics and Groupings" p. 9. Herat's importance had been further enhanced by a Pakistani ban on most exports through the Torkham border near Jalalabad—formerly a trading node that rivaled Herat. This meant that nearly two-thirds of imports into Afghanistan came from Iran through Herat

[35] Antonio Giustozzi, "'Good' State vs. 'Bad' Warlords?" p. 6. Giustozzi also quotes, on this subject, Barnett Rubin and Helena Malikyar, "The politics of center-periphery relations in Afghanistan" Center for International Cooperation, New York University, March 2003, pp. 30-33.

[36] See, for example, Giustozzi, "'Good' State vs. 'Bad' Warlords?" p. 9. Also, Roy, who noted in 2003 that, "At present, [Ismail Khan] has the support of the Shia population in Herat, embodied by the Afzali clan, but this is mainly due to the fact that he is currently supported by Iran. Hence Ismail Khan's power is less stable than it might appear, despite the fact that he controls a larger area of land than any other warlord in Afghanistan." See Roy, "Afghanistan: Internal Politics and Socio-economic Dynamics and Groupings" p. 9.

[37] The two organizations had agreed to release joint reports during each of the major phases of the election on the extent to which political rights were respected.

13
Countdown to Election Day

During the final preparations for the elections, the "co-responsibility" model functioned better than the electoral team had expected. In this sense, Arnault's approach had proven correct: it allowed Afghan buy-in and the use of Afghan knowledge without jeopardizing the process. Farooq Wardak and his team carried out commendable work, and became a small cadre of Afghan electoral managers who could eventually form the core of an all-Afghan electoral administration.

In the run-up to election day, a number of crucial decisions had to be taken under great pressure, and by UNAMA in particular. Most of these decisions were taken according to a political logic, and further strained Arnault's relationship with the electoral team.

However much these decisions could be criticized from the perspective of holding credible elections, Arnault's decisions reflected what was expected of him by key diplomats in Kabul, high-level officials in Karzai's government, and by his masters at U.N. headquarters in New York. It seemed that nobody really trusted a genuine election to deliver the results that everyone believed to be essential. Member states suddenly adopted surprisingly precise positions on a number of technical issues, while Afghan politicians, continued to play both inside and outside of the rules of the game. Arnault had to balance these factors and interests. It is understandable if he felt, in the heat of the electoral moment, that long-term democratic institutions were a luxury. The point was to get to election day, and get past it safely. The political logic was geared to the short term. Electoral logic was longer-term, but potentially risky in the short-term. It also required a sort of rules-based rigidity that was perhaps reckless in the chaotic Afghan context. Many of UNAMA's decisions, from this perspective, are understandable. But they did have their long-term costs.

Out-of-Country Voting

By mid-summer of 2004, out-of-country voting was the last major unresolved electoral issue. To recapitulate the situation at the end of July: In March 2004 the Security Council had adopted a resolution "encouraging" Afghan authorities to include refugees in the electoral process. On May 30, the JEMB had taken a decision that favored the inclusion of "refugees"[1] in Iran and Pakistan in the electoral process, but had set a number of preconditions that had not been met. UNAMA had in the meantime asked IOM to look into the practicalities of an out-of-country process. IOM originally said that at least 120 days would be required but, in early July, once the 120-day mark had been passed, the requirement had been reduced to 90-days. The JEMB decided to go ahead with out-of-country elections on the basis of IOM's 90-day plan. On July 12, the government of Iran signed a memorandum with the government of Afghanistan and UNAMA allowing preparations for Afghan elections in that country to proceed. On July 20, Pakistan signed a similar Memorandum of Understanding, and UNDP formally signed an agreement with IOM for the operation to begin.

By late July, therefore, the legal and financial conditions were in place to launch out-of-country operations. But 90 days was not a long time to set up the operation, for which no planning had taken place outside of IOM's hurried scenarios. In fact, a month earlier, in June, the JEMB logistics unit had taken a gamble that now proved to be very short-sighted. In order to save money,[2] and under the impression that out-of-country elections had become so unfeasible that a decision to hold them would never be taken, the logistics unit ordered only enough electoral kits for in-country voting. This was the first sign of the additional organizational burden and cost that out-of-country elections would impose on the in-country election.

IOM had selected an able and energetic electoral logistician, Peter Erben, to run the out-of-country operation. Erben was a former officer in the Danish army who had cut his electoral teeth during elections in Bosnia and Kosovo in the late 1990s, organized by the Organization for Security Cooperation in Europe (OSCE). He had also been involved with the logistics of the Emergency Loya Jirga in Afghanistan in 2003, working with Larry Sampler. Erben had a reputation for handling complex logistical exercises with competence and thoroughness, but also for running costly operations.

According to the various memoranda that governed the relationships between UNAMA, the JEMB, and IOM in the conduct out-of-country voting, IOM was to follow and implement all electoral rules and regulations established by the JEMB. UNAMA and the JEMB would provide registration materials, ballot kits, boxes, screens, forms, and seals, and was responsible for airlifting them from Kabul to designated destinations in Iran and Pakistan.

According to IOM's original 120-day plan, voter registration in Pakistan would begin at the latest seven weeks before election day and would be conducted according to the same procedures as in-country registration. Three hundred registration sites would be established, with two registration stations in each—one for women and the other for men. Most of the sites would be in the areas along the Pakistan-Afghan border, where the majority of Afghans in Pakistan were located, but a few sites would also be set up in Islamabad, Karachi, and Lahore. The sites would be open for three weeks, each one registering up to 4,800 voters. It would require the recruitment and training of 2,400 registration staff within several weeks.

This plan, submitted in early June, depended on preparations beginning immediately. The delays in taking decisions and signing Memoranda of Understanding meant that by the time the legal framework was in place, a month had been lost, and the 90-day operational plan had to be devised.

The main difference between the 120-day and 90-day plans was to revise downwards the amount of voters that could conceivably be registered in Pakistan. Out of the estimated 1.4 million eligible Afghans in Pakistan, under the 90-day plan it was thought that only about 400-500,000 would be able to be registered. (This presented an interesting little irony—if the main, but unstated, reason for advocating OCV had been to increase the number of Pashtuns voting and therefore the chance that Karzai would win, the accumulation of indecision and delay led to a situation where only around half a million Afghans in Pakistan could conceivably be registered, while 800,000 refugees in Iran—who were less likely to be Pashtun—had already been registered de facto through the *amayesh* cards.)

To make matters worse, the Pakistani authorities, who had insisted in the Security Council that Afghans in Pakistan be allowed to participate in the elections, appeared to be actively frustrating the operation at a bureaucratic level. Despite having signed the Memorandum of Understanding, they delayed the issuing of visas to the international IOM staff who needed to establish the regional offices, begin the recruitment of registrars, and carry out the myriad tasks required to set up the operation. By August 2, only three of the 30 requested visas had been issued. One interpretation of this odd recalcitrance, if it was indeed deliberate, could have been that Pakistan was still focused on ensuring refugee participation in parliamentary elections the following year,[3] and had resumed their tactics of brinkmanship to try to secure guarantees that this would happen, even at the cost of registration for the presidential election. In other words, they would release visas in exchange for a commitment to parliamentary OCV. An alternative theory was that Pakistan was trying to force a postponement of the entire presidential election, which would ensure that the presidential election would be held concurrently with the parliamentary elections the following year. This would have heightened the chance that refugees would be allowed to vote in both, which was Pakistan's original position. In other words, what had been conceded by Pakistan at the Security Council table was perhaps being regained by consular officers in the visa section.

Faced with continued delays stemming from Pakistan's non-cooperation, the international advisors in Kabul now believed that dropping out-of-country voting altogether was the lesser of the evils facing them. Nonetheless, Pakistan had done its political homework and had managed to establish, between Security Council Resolution 1536 and the Memorandum of Understanding, a strong political case against abandonment.

The only real option—apart from postponement—was to go back to the operational drawing board and reduce the concept to one that would fit within the even shorter time available, now that the timelines of the 90-day plan had been blown. Forced into this option, at the end of July, Erben proposed holding simultaneous registration and elections over a three-day period. Under this concept, registration sites would be open for three days prior to the election. Potential voters would arrive, face a "registration committee" made up of elders and respected Afghans, and, if determined eligible by the committee, would be presented with a "registration receipt" (obviously this would bear no photographs, fingerprints, or any other distinguishing data apart from, perhaps, a signature). On polling day—October 9—they would show their receipt, and vote. The advantage of this approach, Erben argued, was that the longer lead-time to prepare the registration would reduce the risk of logistical failure, and the shorter operational period when registration was actually taking place would reduce exposure to security threats. He estimated that 600-700,000 Afghans could be "enfranchised" through this method.

The disadvantage of the approach was that it stretched to the limit the idea of credible elections. The same concept had in fact been proposed several months earlier to the JEMB by Farooq Wardak. It had been quickly rejected at that time as insufficiently credible, for two reasons in particular. First, the system of both registration and polling was so different from what was being carried out in-country that it exposed it to charges of double-standards, with the ethnic question always looming in the background. In other words, it seemed to give one set of lax rules for Pashtuns, and another set of stricter rules for non-Pashtuns. Second, the process itself was riddled with opportunities for fraud.

Arnault sought the middle ground. He informed New York, that "in the refugee camps, the concept could work: indeed, at this stage the only real purpose of registration in Pakistan is to serve as much as possible to separate Afghans from non-Afghans. The camps by themselves fulfill this function, and while a three-day exercise would necessarily be quite perfunctory, the United Nations could state quite credibly at the end of the day that registration in the camps has captured—by and large—eligible voters." Arnault was perhaps trying to convince himself. To most others, it was obvious that this mechanism had nothing to do with credibility, but was a necessary logistical response to the need to get out of a very tight political corner. The real issue was not what the United Nations "could state quite credibly at the end of the day," but how to minimize the possible damage to the overall election that could be caused by such a "perfunctory" process.

In the meantime, the logistics unit of the JEMB Secretariat had to incorporate polling in Iran and Pakistan in their overall plans for election day. As noted, when they ordered the electoral kits, they had assumed that out-of-country operations would *not* take place. Once the decision had been made to go forward, they had to scramble to ensure that there were enough kits for the estimated 2.5 million additional Afghan nationals who would potentially be eligible to vote.

The Roots of the Indelible Ink Debacle

There are three general categories of materials required for elections: sensitive, non-sensitive, and what could be called infrastructural. The latter referred to the tables, chairs, and screens to ensure the secrecy of the vote. Sensitive materials were the ballots and the tabulation sheets that needed to be kept under tight security until the polling stations opened. Any breach could allow votes to essentially be manufactured. Non-sensitive materials were contained in the "electoral kits"—an assortment of stamps, stamp pads, pens, hole punches, forms and so forth. The kits also held a very important tool in the Afghan context—the indelible ink that all Afghans were told would prevent anyone who had registered more than once from voting more than once.

The process designed by the JEMB was as follows. When the voter arrived at the polling station, he or she would provide proof of registration. The voter would be handed a ballot stamped by a polling worker to show that it had been delivered. The voter's left thumb and cuticle would be marked with the indelible ink. Each voter would be required to show their left thumb before voting. If it was already marked, the voter would, at least, not be allowed to vote and, at most, be prosecuted for attempting to violate the electoral law.

There were three main options for applying the ink: a marker that was applied directly to the digit; a small wide-mouthed bottle filled with semi-humid sponges into which the voter dipped his or her thumb which, when removed, was covered with ink from the sponges; and a bottle with liquid ink and an applicator. On July 1, before a decision had been taken to go ahead with out-of-country voting, the JEMB had issued a decision specifying the polling materials that needed to be procured by UNDP. Among the materials was "Indelible Voter Ink: 25 percent Silver Nitrate." At that time, neither the quantity nor, more importantly, the form of application had been specified.

A Canadian company, CODE Inc., a well-established supplier of electoral materials, had been selected to supply the election kits. CODE had a "long-term agreement" with a U.N. body, the Inter-Agency Procurement Service Organization (IAPSO), which was the main procurement agent for UNDP.[4] CODE had also provided the registration kits, which had been an in-kind contribution of the Canadian government worth around $7 million. CODE did not actually *produce* any of the materials in the kits. It acted as a procurer and an assembler. It received the order of what was required, purchased the requirements from other vendors according to the specifications provided by UNDP, packed the items into individual kits, and then freighted the kits to Afghanistan. This entire process took a fair amount of time, which is why the JEMB Secretariat had decided to submit its specifications in early July.

In fact, even July was too late. In order to meet deadlines, the logistics section of the Secretariat had, on June 1, put in an order for 100,000 units of ink, specifying that the application form should be in dipping bottle with sponge insert. Given the expected 50,000 polling stations, the idea was to have two bottles for each station, allowing up to 1,000 voters to be accommodated. For reasons that will become important later on, the list also included 450,000 pencils to mark the ballots. At that point, there had not been enough materials ordered to fill the sudden need to hold out-of-country elections.

International politics and misplaced goodwill then intervened. During the second week of July—less than three months before the elections, and prior to the decision on out-of-country voting—the Indian election commission suddenly offered to supply Indian indelible ink markers as well as ballot papers. The immediate reaction of the international electoral advisors was to reject the offer. CODE was already busy assembling the kits in Canada according to the specifications provided by the logistics unit. Arnault, however, considered that it would be impolitic to reject the Indian offer. Using again the "strategies of the SRSG" clause in the terms of reference of the international JEMB members, he instructed them to approve the Indian offer. On August 17, a communication was sent by Austin to the Indian Electoral Commission requesting 50,000 indelible ink markers, specifying that the delivery should ideally be made by August 31 and no later than September 7. (The offer of ballot papers was rejected; printing of the required ballots was already underway in Canada.)

The ink offered by India came in the form of markers—not in the form of a bottle with either an applicator or a sponge. The perfect logistical storm began to gather. In mid-July, the training section needed to finalize its illustrated manuals, which had to be drawn, translated, and printed, to be able to train the trainers who would later train polling station workers. For some reason, logistics had not informed the training section that they intended to use pots. Since, earlier, the idea of using an applicator had been proposed, the training section assumed that applicators were being ordered and prepared their manuals accordingly.

On August 5, the Indian pens had still not arrived, yet the purchase order to CODE was suddenly amended. The JEMB Secretariat's logistics section requested that the pencils be replaced by permanent ink markers for voters to mark the ballots. This meant that not only were polling station workers being trained to use the only ink delivery system that was not available, but permanent markers that were virtually identical to the indelible ink markers supplied by the Indian commission were to be used to mark the ballots.

According to an investigation[5] carried out after the election: "All this had been done by the Logistics Department without any authority of the JEMB. As may be seen from the note of UNDP procurement officer, these articles were excluded/included under verbal instructions of the Chief of Logistics." Despite several investigations, logistics personnel were never able to adequately explain why these decisions were made and why they had not been communicated to the training unit.

The Indian markers arrived, finally, on September 14, three weeks before the election and two weeks after the ideal delivery date. The logistics staff immediately got to work, opening the voter kits supplied by CODE and replacing the pots with the Indian indelible markers. The reason for the exchange was that the pots would store longer, and could be used for the next year's election. No one seemed to have noticed how much the Indian indelible markers resembled the permanent markers that were to be used to mark ballots. Nor had anyone anticipated the confusion this might create once poll-workers—hardly literate in Dari or Pashtu, let alone in English—were confronted with the etymological distinctions between "permanent" and "indelible" markers.

The decision to hold out-of-country voting had been taken in the midst of this flurry of making and amending decisions, and accepting the Indian offer. The decision to conduct out-of-country voting meant that there was suddenly an insufficient number of Indian markers for both in-country and out-of-country elections.

The only solution was to use some of the pots that had been previously ordered. It would have been rational to use these pots only for the out-of-country exercises, given that training would be held later and in an accelerated manner, and this would allow at least a consistency of procedure for in-country voting. The out-of-country procedures for voting and registration were, after all, already different from those in-country. Erben, however, insisted on using the Indian markers, rather than the pots from CODE, because he considered them superior. Erben's stubbornness prevailed, and another logistical exercise began in order to ensure that kits with markers went to Pakistan and Iran, while within Afghanistan some polling kits would contain markers and others would contain pots. On October 3—six days before the election—a U.N. training officer in the northern province of Samangan wrote an email that reported ominously: "On checking the polling kits that we received in our province, we found that some of the kits [...] have indelible INK-POT instead of Marker. That might create some kind of confusion among the polling personnel. Could you please advise on the matter?"

After receiving a curt clarification from the logistics department, a message went out to all area managers and training staff: "Please be aware that some polling kits, instead of indelible ink markers, contain a jar with sponge. If this is the case, Identification and Inking Officer must request the voter to dip the left thumb into the Jar." Nothing in this bland correction hinted at the chaos that would occur on polling day as a cumulative result of this series of botched and hurried decisions, by both the political managers and the electoral specialists.

Final Preparations

As the out-of-country voting preparations and ink saga intertwined, preparations in Afghanistan were completed for the elections. By September 23, the identification of polling centers and stations was completed for all 34 provinces. There would be 4,893 polling centers comprising 21,924 polling stations, each station having separate voting facilities for men and women. GPS information had been provided for the majority of the polling centers and had been registered by the ESOC. Polling Center Supervisors were identified in all of the 34 provinces, and the recruitment and training of polling workers was well underway. A distribution plan for printed materials and training stationery was prepared in coordination with the logistics section to guide them in distributing the training materials to the provinces.

Meanwhile, at Kabul's international airport, dozens of cargo planes were arriving, ferrying in voting kits, ballots, ballot boxes, and everything else that would be required for the election. Once the equipment arrived, an immense and intricate logistical task was required to log the equipment, separate it according to where it needed to go, and then dispatch it by truck, fixed wing, or helicopter to the regional offices from where it would be further sent to the provincial capitals and, eventually, voting centers. In a relief to everyone, the JEMB Secretariat reported that all polling materials had been delivered by September 29. The logistics were in place.

A four-day training of 35 international and 80 national provincial trainers on polling and counting procedures was conducted between September 7 and 10 in Kabul. The participants—men and women—came from all of Afghanistan's provinces. The JEMB had decided, contrary to the practice during registration, to bring the national provincial trainers to Kabul to receive training directly from national trainers stationed in the capital. One of the lessons learned from the registration process was that a sizable number of registration staff, who had received training in the field, had been inadequately prepared.

Several last-minute political and operational decisions forced the procedures section to work overtime in the two weeks before the election. In early September, the JEMB decided that counting of ballots would take place in the regional centers rather than in provincial capitals. The primary factor behind this decision was that it allowed security to be concentrated around those centers. There was, of course, a trade-off between the security of the counting center versus the security of transporting ballots to the center. But the JEMB judged that, as counting was likely to be extended over weeks, it was better to risk problems that might occur during the day or two required for transport, than the vulnerabilities generated by an extended counting process carried out far from the eyes of observers. Counting in regional centers would make it easier for international observers and candidate agents to observe, and for JEMB staff to control the proceedings. Finally, it allowed for mixing of ballots, which added to the security of voters. (If ballots from a number of different stations were mixed before being counted, no specific area could be retaliated against for having voted for a given candidate.) Each regional capital would have several counting centers, depending on the number of provinces in the region. While the decision to count at the regional level made sense, its lateness meant that the counting procedures had to be extensively revised, retranslated, reprinted, and sent to the JEMB for approval, taking valuable time just weeks before election day.

Procedures also had to be changed once the Regulation on the Participation of Political Parties and Independent Candidates in the Electoral Process had been adopted. The final regulation was different from the draft from which the procedures department had been working. Again, changes had to be made in the training manual, the new procedures had to be translated, and the package had to be submitted to the JEMB for approval and dissemination.

Finally, the data center that had inputted the registration data began to set up and test the election results system. The idea was to be able to update, nearly in real time, the results of the election for the media. Fifty Afghan staff were trained to update the results as they came in, in batches of 10,000. The best news of all for the data center was that, as summer faded into fall, and a new chill began to creep into the high air of Kabul, the center was able to confirm in its weekly report that the air-conditioning of the main data entry hall had been "partially finalized."

The media center, which had cost around $5 million to build, was set up in a high school across the street from UNAMA's main headquarters. It was housed in a giant hall with massive screens in the neo-Orwellian style of the World Economic Forum. Banks of computers with internet access were available to journalists to file stories or, more often, surf the web while waiting for something interesting to happen. The hyper-modern hall gave a somewhat misleading image of how the elections were being prepared on the ground. As technicians tested the giant video screens, the slim, modern microphones, and the simultaneous translation booths, Russian jeeps crawled along unpaved, steep mountain passes, carrying trainers dressed in traditional clothes and wrapped in wool shawls to remote areas to haggle over the price of donkeys that would be used to take ballot boxes to even more remote areas.

Alongside the Media Center was an accreditation office that used digital cameras and plastic card printers to eventually provide 1,200 members of the media access to the center. This was a far more modern technique than the simple Polaroids, paper, and lamination that had been used to register Afghan voters. The international media began to arrive in Kabul to cover the historic event. The first big story was the highly publicized delivery of indelible ink provided by the Government of India.

Civic education and public information campaigns geared up for a final spurt of activity with instructions to "do what they can until the end." Radios broadcast messages about the election, and public information officers, armed with posters, flip-charts and giant sample ballots, fanned throughout the regions to remind people of the date of the election, its importance to their future, its rules, and how to vote. The main objective was to encourage as large a turnout as possible.

In a postconflict election, where the conferring of legitimacy on the government was as important as the result, turnout mattered a great deal. There was a fear among the internationals in the JEMB Secretariat that a low turnout would somehow stigmatize their own work. But perhaps the best public information tool of all was the proof, spreading around the country, that the election actually was going to happen, that President Karzai was submitting himself to the will of the people. Even in the remotest areas, materials had begun to arrive, and thousands of people were being hired and trained.

The funding travails that had made the implementation of registration so difficult had not, fortunately, affected the election process. The registration project had, in fact, come in under budget, allowing several million dollars to be advanced to the election project. The first cash deposits for the election—$12.5 million—had been received on June 17. The budget for elections was $102 million (including the $31 million for the out-of-country voting) and agreements by mid-June had been signed for an additional $19.7 million, while pledges amounted to $37.2 million. The total shortfall in elections funds committed or pledged therefore was just over $32 million. By the third week of September, nearly 80 percent of the budget had been provided in cash, and most of the rest had been pledged.

The final weeks were both routine and extraordinary. Extraordinary, because this was the moment when everything had to fall into place; it was the moment when suddenly the holding of elections in a place like Afghanistan began to become a reality. It was routine, however, in the sense that there were no more major decisions that needed to be made. The policy disputes of the past between the electoral team and Arnault's political team were no longer relevant. The difficulties and the rivalries were momentarily forgotten. What was done was done, and what was decided was decided. The work consisted in following through on the final details and implementing all the decisions that had been made. Everyone—those in the JEMB, the electoral team, UNAMA, the regional offices, the Coalition, the Afghan government, the international press, the donors—was now focused on election-day. The somewhat fantastical words agreed upon at Bonn nearly three years before were about to become a reality and almost within the equally fantastical deadline.

---

[1] A June 10, 2004 memo from the JEMBS' head of the Election Planning Unit to the JEMB pointed out that technically, according to the relevant conventions, a refugee was someone who "owing to a well-founded fear of being persecuted for reasons of race, religion, nationality, membership of a particular social group, or political opinion, is outside the country of his nationality, and is unable to or, owing to such fear, is unwilling to avail himself of the protection of that country ..." (1951 Convention relating to the Status of Refugees). Arguing that many Afghans in Pakistan may no longer be technically refugees, the Planning Unit proposed changing the wording to extend the franchise to "those Afghan citizens resident in Pakistan and Iran, who arrived during several periods beginning in 1979, and the adult children of those citizens." The proposal was not acted on by the JEMB.

[2] In the last week of June, the situation was as follows: The budget was $102 million, of which $12.5 million had been received in cash. Agreements had been signed for an additional $19.7 million and pledges were at $37.2 million. In other words, three months from the election, more than $32 million was still required and nobody had any idea where it would come from or when.

[3] Pakistan had sent, on 16 July, a Note Verbale to the Secretary-General stating their full cooperation and commitment to democracy in Afghanistan, but insisting on looking at ways to carry out parliamentary elections for refugees.

[4] IAPSO was set up as a self-financing arm of UNDP. Like many hybrid U.N.-private sector efforts, it ended up as the worst of both worlds. Instead of providing an efficient service based on a detailed knowledge of U.N. needs, it looked more like a cartel to which the U.N. paid a premium in order to limit its options for goods, which were procured at higher prices than they might have been through an open bid. Numerous suppliers complained about the opaque process by which companies were awarded—or, especially, not awarded—long-term agreements.

[5] This investigation, which was one of several, was not necessarily the most impartial. It was written in a highly defensive tone, and conducted by an Indian official seconded from the Indian Electoral Commission, who seemed anxious that no blame should be attached to his Government.

14
Polling and Counting

The UNAMA and the AIHRC Joint Verification Commission issued their third and final report on the verification of political rights in early October. Election day was a little more than a week away, and the report provided a final snapshot of conditions around the country. It focused its findings on the 30-day campaign period that had begun on September 7. During this period, it described a reassertion of Afghan historical patterns through the web of Western-style law and procedure that the electoral process had tried to knit. For example:

> Nearly all the candidates seem to rely on traditional means of extending their base of support by brokering relations and alliances with leaders representing other constituencies. The general assumption by most candidates is that people will base their electoral decisions on the guidance of local leaders, and therefore campaign efforts generally involve meeting with local leaders rather than appealing to the larger population.

The fear that large gatherings might present attractive targets to those who wanted to disrupt the election, and the expenses of running a campaign, were certainly additional factors that helped shape this tradition-oriented form of campaigning.

The most prominent candidate, Karzai, whose life had been threatened twice before while president, hardly left the palace during the campaign period.[1] He did, however, dispatch his two vice-presidential running mates to campaign for him. Three days before the election, one of them, Ahmed Zia Massoud, was attacked in the northeastern province of Badakhshan—the native ground of his father-in-law, the former President Rabbani. Five people were injured and one killed in the ambush, but Massoud escaped.

In the final days, candidates began to try to expand their appeal by holding more publicized meetings with larger crowds. UNAMA reported that the final ten days of the campaign had seen around 100,000 people participating in public rallies in support of one or another of the candidates. Another encouraging development that hinted at the possibility of politics beyond tribalism was that the major candidates also began to travel throughout the country, beyond the areas of their regional and ethnic bases. Candidates were increasingly campaigning outside Kabul, though mostly in the main population centers rather than in more isolated, rural areas. Campaigning was particularly intense in the north, where three candidates had established election committees and at least four had opened offices. Campaigning in the west had been limited while Ismail Khan had been Governor of Herat; his removal in September, however, opened unexpected political space. The first campaign rally took place on September 23. The structure of the electoral system was beginning to bequeath some form of mass politics.

Modern forms of political communication were increasingly used. The medium of choice was colorful posters—which were put up by supporters of candidates and often torn down by supporters of their rivals. Both public and private media attempted to communicate the platforms of the various candidates,[2] and Radio Television Afghanistan, the state broadcaster, allocated 20 minutes to each candidate to explain their positions. The JEMB, in collaboration with IFES, published a four-page newspaper in Dari and Pashtu with information about the election, the candidates, and their platforms.

The Joint Verification Commission also noted a number of cases of intimidation and abuse of authority by government officials. These cases did not seem to dampen the overall public enthusiasm for the coming election. As the commission noted, intimidation could be nullified as long as people had confidence that their vote would be secret. The commission then recommended that: "Every effort should be made to ensure that appropriate guarantees are in place so that, in spite of the limitations described in this report, the population can be confident that popular will [will] be effectively translated through the voting process."

The joint commission's report also suggested that electoral pressure had helped to significantly advance the disarmament process. The JEMB's August 10 request to the Ministry of Defense to appoint non-factional commanders in units affiliated with Khalili (one of Karzai's two running mates), Mohaqeq and Dostum had "created a new momentum in the DDR process." In the final two weeks of September, more than 3,000 men were disarmed, and nearly 2,000 heavy weapons were cantoned. Around 18,000 men in total had been disarmed since October 2003 when the program began, which meant that about 15 percent of the total soldiers demobilized came in the final two weeks of a program that had been going on, by then, for 44 weeks.

On the eve of polling, UNAMA reported to New York that rumors were rampant in Kabul of deals through which candidates would, at the last minute, drop out and back the stronger candidates in exchange for favors or positions in the government that they would likely form. Given Karzai's strength, most of these end-game rumors concerned him. On September 20, UNAMA reported that an agreement between Karzai and Qanuni was imminent, citing Karzai's astute selection of Ahmad Zia Massoud as one of his vice-presidential candidates as a key reason for Qanuni's willingness to concede his campaign. UNAMA's sources had jumped the gun, however. By polling day, 16 of the original 18 candidates—especially Qanuni—remained in the race, taking their chances with the voters.[3]

A number of statements were made by observers concerning the overall political environment and the campaign period as it entered its final days. The Free and Fair Elections Foundation for Afghanistan (FEFA), a local NGO set up specifically to monitor the election, issued a statement that the campaign up to then had been "mostly free and fair." On October 6, Arnault issued his own statement saying that: "It is with full knowledge of the difficulties that surround this exercise that we deem the degree of freedom and fairness adequate to allow the will of the Afghan people as a whole to translate at the polls, and the next president of Afghanistan to claim to represent the nation." This was a somewhat bold assertion, given that the election had not yet happened. Hedging his confidence somewhat, Arnault's two-page statement also acknowledged "the limitations that are bound to affect this election, including widespread lack of experience and understanding of democratic institutions; a lingering culture of violence inherited from the war; and violence or threat of violence by extremist groups." He concluded: "While we believe, therefore, that conditions exist for a good election, it is incumbent upon all of us to make polling day as free, fair and safe as possible."

Election Day

During the night before election day, electoral staff and police made the polling centers ready for the expected and hoped-for avalanche of voters, observers, media and candidate agents. The tables, chairs and locally-made voter screens, hung with green curtains, were set up overnight. Early in the morning, the voting kits and the sensitive materials were brought to the centers from provincial capitals. Centers in urban areas (and in Kabul there were frequently five-to-ten polling stations per center) had previously been secured with concrete barriers.

Specially-trained Afghan police controlled the entryways but were not allowed inside. Afghan and international Afghan JEMB staff nervously moved from room to room, ensuring that the stations were set up as described in the procedure manuals. At dawn, everywhere, things seemed to be going to plan.

At 6 a.m. in Kabul, the sky was unusually cloudy and the day was cold for that time of the year. One could almost feel the thickness of the clouds. Often in the capital, even in early winter, the clouds are quickly melted by the mid-morning sun. It did not seem that this would happen on election day. Even this would have its importance.

The polling centers opened on schedule at 7 a.m.. Crowds of Afghans—bearded men in turbans or modern dress; women in burqas or without—lined up in segregated queues. Polling centers set up in mosques, schools, ruined factories, and any other public buildings with walls and a roof began receiving thousands of men and women to cast their votes for the first time in their lives. The media deployed in great force, especially in the capital, to immortalize the historical moment—this beginning of a democratic dawn after 25 years of war, this culmination of a surprisingly successful Bonn process.

The Afghan electoral staff had done an excellent job. The kits were opened and the materials set up. The ballots were unsealed and set on tables. Security protocols had been respected to the last detail. The ritual of showing the empty ballot boxes to those observers and voters present when polling opened was performed with nervous solemnity. For good measure, the plastic ballot boxes were also transparent. Voters began showing up and following the process in surprising calm and order. As one local observer put it: "If you go [to] the bazaar, you can't believe it's the same Afghan who was standing in line [for the polls]."[4]

In that climactic moment—when the entire logistical and security capacities of the nation were focused on a single event—the intense work of 18 months came together. The voters provided their cards, the result of the painful and controversial registration process. They entered a room that was the same as thousands of other rooms around Afghanistan that day, each equipped with (almost) identical kits. They were instructed on procedure by the 125,000 trained Afghan poll workers who had been recruited, half of whom were women. They had been drawn to the sites by an intensive public information campaign. Finally the moment had come where the subjects-turned-citizens had a chance to exercise their citizenship in the most concrete way possible.

As the internationals moved through Kabul, from site to site, the silence was almost eerie. All non-official vehicles had been barred from circulating in order to reduce the possibility of vehicle-borne explosives.

The frightful Kabul traffic—an exhaust-breathing presence hiding within it the constant possibility of deadly violence—had vanished, replaced by a silent emptiness overhung by the thick clouds. For those who had known the city during the civil war, who had seen these same streets bearing tanks or trucks full of soldiers, or who had seen them stained with the blood of civilians killed by a stray rocket or mortar, the sight of Afghans lining up and waiting calmly to vote seemed almost a miracle.

The Afghan JEMB commissioners had abandoned their office in the center of Kabul for the day and moved to the UEC compound on Jalalabad Road. It was judged to be more secure and closer to the center of operations. They sat in the UEC conference room, surrounded by tea and biscuits, waiting for the first reports from the field. These initial reports contained good news: people were turning out to vote in large numbers, early. Media reported that in some areas, Afghans had purified themselves ritually and put on their best clothes, knowing that they might be killed while voting, but eager to vote despite the threats.

For the first half hour, electoral operations proceeded in this calm and quiet order, everything working according to plan. After that first half hour, a moment of rupture, a sense of agitation began to grow. There had been a few complaints—that someone had voted twice, that someone had been allowed to vote without a card, or that an obviously underage person had voted. But these had been easily addressed by the polling staff or the internationals, who explained that there was a complaints process and how to follow it. These complaints were normal, expected, and planned for.

At 7:45 a.m., however, the JEMB received a far more disturbing report—voters were claiming that the indelible ink from the indelible markers could be removed. Everyone understood, because of the strength of the public education campaign, that there was now no effective safeguard against multiple voting. The first report of the washable indelible ink was received as a text message from an observer; within minutes, the JEMB began to receive a flood of complaints about the ink.

Some technical background is required to understand what happened next. The ink is made indelible by the silver nitrate. Silver nitrate reacts to heat, which burns the ink into the skin. When the sun is shining, this is almost immediate; when there is no sun, because of thick clouds, for example, the ink can take more time to become fixed. Therefore, when it was washed, it appeared to fade even though it would re-emerge as a dark spot an hour later. But election day only had eight hours, and during the first third of these eight hours the clouds hung heavily over the city, preventing the silver nitrate from working immediately. In those hours, millions of Afghans had come to believe that the process had failed.

The reports of problems with the ink began in Kabul but soon were echoed from around the country. Crowds of Afghans felt cheated. Journalists took glee in broadcasting thousands of stories of men and women who, in front of the cameras, seemingly removed the ink from their fingers. In the second hour, the agitation increased. Complaints about multiple voting began to replace the complaints about the debility of the indelible ink. More and more Afghans emerged from polling stations, ran straight to a water pump, and seemed to wash the ink off their fingers.

Another major problem was, of course, the confusion between the markers with "indelible" ink and those with "permanent" ink. The worst fears, evoked by the electoral training officer in Samangan, had come to pass. It appeared that in many cases where the pens had been distributed instead of the bottles, the wrong pens—the ones to mark the ballots—had been used to mark the fingers of voters.

In station after station, the intensity of the protests rose. Some station managers, under intense pressure from voters, halted the process until the ink situation could be resolved. International members of the Secretariat, their fingers black like lepers' from multiple demonstrations, continued to insist that the bottles were perfectly fine, that the ink wasn't washing off. But voters stubbornly insisted that the process had broken down. It seemed that 150 million dollars and hundreds of thousands of man-days of effort were evaporating into a humiliating meaninglessness, disappearing like the supposedly faulty ink.

A sense of panic pervaded the JEMB and its Secretariat in face of the deluge of reports. Every mobile phone seemed to be ringing with the same bad news. Under the pressure, a new, ugly dynamic emerged within the group: the Afghan commissioners blamed the international advisers, Wardak blamed the Afghan commissioners, and the international advisers tried to mitigate the damage. Zakim Shah, the chairman, sank into his chair for a while and then left the building to go into the city and see the debacle with his own eyes. The old senator, Suleiman Yari, paced up and down the room, saying that this would have not happened if the Afghans had been responsible for the elections, demanding the name of the person responsible for purchasing the ink. The maligned international electoral team was left to correct the problem it had undeniably helped to create. It began collecting reports from the field, ordering and sending supplies to the areas where the ballots were running short, and dispatching instructions to the polling stations on how to properly use the ink.

At 9:30, the expensive new election media center got its first workout. Manoel de Almeida e Silva, Arnault's spokesman, opened the briefing with the picturesque and politically correct fact that the first person to have voted in the election was "a young woman, 19 years of age, in Islamabad. Her name is Muqadasa Siddiqi."[5] A representative of the Ministry of Interior then gave a briefing on the security situation which was, for the moment, remarkably calm.

Then, inevitably, De Almeida e Silva turned to the ink situation, which he described as a question of "great concern to the Electoral Authority, to the Electoral Secretariat, and to the United Nations." He invited Ahmad Baheen, the spokesman for the JEMB, and Farooq Wardak to read statements on the ink in Dari and English respectively. According to the statement, the JEMB had tested the ink and concluded that the problems were related to the application of the ink, not its quality, and that instructions had been issued to all provinces on how to apply it correctly.

> The Joint Election Management Body decided, one, to instruct that the election can move forward as scheduled and to continue to analyze reports during the course of the day, and two, to communicate this point to the polling staff, candidates, community leaders and the nation to congratulate the voters for their enthusiastic turnout on this historical day, and to request the patience of everyone as these additional instructions are put in place.

The journalists, comfortable in their ultra-modern media center, had found a better story than they anticipated. A number of questions were asked about the insufficiency of training or its poor quality and whether it would affect other aspects of the process—the handling of the ballot boxes, for example. "Don't you think that it casts a pall over the entire election that we can't get the ink issue correct and now we're having to fix that on the day?" one journalist asked. Wardak, Austin, and other hapless election officials were reduced to explaining that mistakes were inevitable, that it had been corrected, and that the election was running smoothly and enthusiastically in all other respects, especially security. Wardak, somewhat wistfully added, "I wish we had used a ballpoint for marking the ballot papers, so this is one lesson we have learned." The fate of the nation, once forced by a dentists' convention, now hung on a choice of writing implement.

Of course the journalist's question had been pertinent. The ink problem had begun to affect perceptions of the credibility of the process, first among voters, then, inevitably, among candidates. Early in the afternoon of polling day, the opposition candidates, headed by Qanuni, seized upon the issue as an excuse to denounce the entire election. They called for a boycott by their supporters. Individually they made a great show of not voting. In reality, the ink fiasco was an opportunity that had fallen into their laps to justify a decision they had already made. They had announced their intention to boycott two days before the election. But the ink gave them a solid, visible, convincing pretext to do so.

By the early afternoon, the clouds had disappeared, snow and rain were no longer an issue, the sun shone through, and the JEMB had issued several statements about the ink. The reports coming in from the field made it clear that the Afghan voting population considered the problems with the ink to be human error, not an attempt at fraud. The JEMB, after its initial hesitation and recriminations, had managed to correct the mistake and had, crucially, retained the confidence of Afghan voters.

The rest of the day proceeded smoothly. International and Afghan staff had performed well. The day did not see major security incidents.[6] More importantly the Afghan population had showed up in massive numbers to vote. The turnout was so high that at 4 p.m. the JEMB authorized a two-hour extension of polling in those centers in which people were still showing up to vote by the end of the afternoon. The closing of the polls lacked drama, which was perhaps the most dramatic conclusion to a day that had begun with such furor.

First Reactions to the Election

Throughout the day, Afghan voters had shown more composure than either the electoral commissioners or the presidential candidates. They largely ignored the boycott and continued to vote in large numbers. Even the agents of the opposition candidates remained in the polling centers rather than withdrawing in accordance with the boycott. When dusk gathered and the polling stations began to shut down, it seemed that the only people in Afghanistan who had not voted were the 15 candidates who ran against Karzai.

In Iran and Pakistan, Erben's IOM team also reported an absence of security incidents of any importance and of minimal intimidation. According to Erben in his report at the end of election day, 540,000 Afghans voted in the 1,578 Polling Stations (out of 1,657) in Pakistan that had reported by then. He projected a turnout of 75 percent, or 554,000 of the 738,000 registered.

There was a minor problem when several Afghans registered in Afghanistan tried to cast their votes in Pakistan. In Quetta, "due to a procedural error," there were indications that some of these, indeed, had been allowed to vote. Erben stated that a problem report would be attached to all ballot boxes where this might have happened. While, as in Afghanistan, security was better than expected, in one refugee camp near Peshawar, a small group of gunmen armed with Kalashnikovs had fired twice at police guarding a polling center the day before the election, and then threw three grenades, causing minor damage to the building. The police returned fire and the attackers fled. There were no election materials in the building at the time of the attack, and polling resumed after police had carried out their investigation.

In Iran, 1,126 polling stations were opened in 125 polling centers. On election day, Erben projected a participation of 260,000 voters. Since no registration was carried out, due to the existence of *amayesh* cards, there was no voter list and hence no total number of expected voters. Erben estimated the population of Afghans over 18 living legally in Iran as 500-600,000. He explained the lower-than-expected turnout as a result of polling centers being limited to urban areas, the short duration of the public information campaign, and the fact that it was a working day for many voters.

In Afghanistan, the first somewhat reliable reports estimated voter turnout at between 60 to 80 percent. The electoral team was happy with these numbers. They worried that a turnout much above 85 percent would suggest, given the likelihood of significant multiple registration, that there had been widespread multiple voting as well. A figure below 80 percent supported the hypothesis that real turnout was high but that the multiple voting had been contained.

Despite this success, the ink fiasco lingered within UNAMA and the recriminations hardened. "This is a catastrophic failure of training," Arnault argued during a heated meeting with his electoral experts late in the afternoon of polling day. The causes of the catastrophe were not, however, limited to training. The decisions that Arnault had forced the JEMB—to accept out-of-country voting and India's ink—had also contributed, and perhaps more directly, to the problem.

Even with this, Arnault's anger was understandable. Earlier in the afternoon, on what everyone had hoped would be a day of congratulation and relief, Arnault had been forced instead to receive a very upset Qanuni. The candidate expressed his outrage at the ink fiasco and said that he and the other opposition candidates would not recognize the election results. He pressed three demands on Arnault as conditions for ending the boycott. First, he wanted to re-open voting the next day in Panjshir province (the locus of his political support), where he claimed that turnout was low due to early snowfall. Second, he asked for the appointment of an independent international panel to investigate all voting irregularities, not only the ink. Third, he requested that the opposition candidates who had boycotted the election should be themselves allowed to vote in a public, televised event.

The demands were discussed between Arnault and his advisors, including some from the electoral team. Again with a mediator's mindset, Arnault began probing ways in which it would be acceptable to re-open voting in the Panshir. He convened a conference call with the heads of the regional offices to discuss the issue.

The regional office head responsible for Panshir province reported that turnout had indeed been low (around 20 percent compared to an estimated 70 percent elsewhere in the country), but he attributed this to a suspected high multiple-registration rate and to the fact that a large segment of the Panshiri population lived in nearby Kabul and probably voted there. In addition, he noted that the snow that Qanuni had complained about had begun falling very late in the day and was unlikely to have affected turnout. Arnault asked the heads of other regions if there were any reasons for which they would recommend reopening polling—the thought being that if re-opening polling in the Panshir for a good reason could be balanced by reopening polling in a Pashtun area for an equally good reason, then nobody would suspect that the decision was actually being taken to placate one of the candidates. The regional office heads, including the one who covered Panshir, unanimously advised against re-opening voting, arguing that this would cast unnecessary doubt on the process. They were joined by the electoral advisors, who contended that none of the usual factors that would ordinarily result in a re-vote were in place, and it would be impossible to conceal that an additional day of voting in Panshir was anything other than a sop to Qanuni.[7]

Qanuni's proposal to convene a panel to examine irregularities was less controversial. The advice from election experts was that the panel, if convened, should conduct an investigation into all complaints on behalf of the JEMB, but should not conduct an investigation independent of the JEMB, nor should it conduct an investigation *of* the JEMB itself.[8] In other words, the line would be maintained that the investigation was carried out according to the legal provision of the law, for which the JEMB already had procedures, and had already set up an investigative unit. The electoral team also expressed the fear that a delay of the process caused by the investigation would provide additional opportunities for tampering with ballot materials—or would create suspicions thereof. Politically, this would distract from the overall positive perception of the process by the voters and would seem to give official sanction to the politically-motivated complaints by the boycotting candidates.

The final demand—allowing the boycotting candidates to have a public, ceremonial vote, was not discussed at any great length. Some of Arnault's political advisors argued that this should be allowed to happen as a means of reconciling the losing candidates to the result of the election, allowing them to "save face". The electoral team advised against the separate "ceremonial" vote for the boycotting candidates. They argued that the JEMB had conducted a massive campaign to tell people that there would be only one chance to vote, that the rules would be the same for all, and that they should take the opportunity to participate in their nation's future even at the risk of their lives. It would send a hypocritical message to hold, several days later, a special and very public election in which the boycotting candidates were allowed a second chance to vote. It undermined every message that the electoral process had tried to send; it suggested to all Afghans that there were indeed different rules for those who risked their lives to vote and those who held political power but had scorned the process. Given that the 15 votes could not even change the result, it was as politically meaningless as it was symbolically perverse.

Arnault argued that it was essential to the legitimacy of the process for the opposition to recognize the results. The electoral experts countered that there was no compelling reason for them not to recognize the results, even if they did so petulantly. Apart from the ink, there had been few reported irregularities, and the first indications were that Afghans had turned out in massive numbers. The logic of democracy should prevail over that of extra-institutional deal making, and losers' petulance was an acceptable price to pay to reinforce the logic of democracy. The BBC, in fact, was already reporting a growing popular backlash against the boycott.

Late the next morning, Arnault convened the diplomatic community for a closed briefing. He informed them of the three demands the opposition had made and his decisions. He said first, that balloting would not be reopened anywhere. Second, he would create an independent international panel to investigate all complaints (not just of the ink fiasco); candidates would have until 6 p.m. the next day to submit complaints relative to specific ballot boxes. This meant, he explained, that counting would not begin until morning of the following day—in other words, four days after election day. Finally, he said that candidates who boycotted would have a chance to vote the following afternoon in a public ceremony.

To the electoral team, Arnault's capitulation to the election's losers was disheartening, both because it undermined what had been achieved and because it seemed politically unnecessary. Arnault clearly differed on the question of the political necessity of these concessions. He believed that Ismail Khan's attack on the UNAMA compound in Herat had occurred because Khan felt he had lost face. A similar loss of face by the protesting candidates could lead to more instability as well as, perhaps, attacks against UNAMA. But these fears did not hide the fact, poignantly stated by one UNAMA electoral expert, that "We told the voters to turn out on election day and brave the thugs. They did. But when it came our turn to brave the thugs, we couldn't."

A press conference was scheduled for 3 p.m. to announce the creation of the international investigative panel and the decision that the JEMB would be "amenable" to giving the former boycotters a chance to vote if they wanted. As soon as the latter decision was announced, the first question from the press was, not surprisingly, "does that mean their supporters can vote, too?" The answer, of course, was no. But the question underlined the arbitrary nature of the decision. The fact that it was so quickly asked made clear that the decision would be seen as a capitulation to the powerful.

In the meantime, one of UNAMA's political officers had canvassed the candidates who had not voted to see if they wished to participate in the ceremonial ballot. Only one was interested. In the meantime, Arnault had decided that this particular transgression of the electoral law should take place at the offices of the JEMB that very afternoon, rather than publicly.[9]

Despite Arnault's concessions, the opposition was still unsatisfied in the first days after the election. The ink fiasco, the boycott, and ongoing complaints of the opposition cast a shadow over the counting process and heightened tension around it. It was difficult now for UNAMA's electoral experts to quell the opposition's discontent with technical explanations, as they were seen as being responsible for having caused the problems. Arnault's political officers were similarly too associated with the process to be effective advocates. Sensing the delicacy of the situation and the palpable rise of political tension, Robert Barry, a former U.S. diplomat and the head of the OSCE Election Support Team,[10] offered to make a public statement, based on his team's observations, to shore up the overall credibility of the elections. The day after the election, the OSCE issued a statement declaring the complaints of the boycotting candidates to be unjustified and supporting the JEMB's integrity:

> Based on reports from our own teams as well as information provided by the European Union election experts, domestic monitors and delegations from a number of countries, we concur with the Joint Election Management Board [sic] that the candidates' demand to nullify the election is unjustified. [...] It is clear from the reports of our own teams and others that there were irregularities on election day, including but not limited to the issue of indelible ink. Afghanistan's Electoral Law describes how to deal with such complaints. [...] October 9 was a historic day in Afghanistan, and the millions who came to the polls clearly wanted to turn from the rule of the gun to the rule of law. If their aspirations are to be met, disputes about the validity of election results should be dealt with as the law provides.

This statement, coming as it did from an independent observer, helped to shift the debate from the complaints of the losers to the overall credibility of the process.

Other international monitoring groups also began issuing public statements. The European Union Democracy and Election Support Mission[11] had dispatched around 120 representatives of European Union embassies to polling stations as "special guests" (they were not technically "observers" but fulfilled the same function). On October 9, the Dutch foreign minister, speaking in his capacity as the representative of the European Union Presidency, said he was "encouraged by the fact that polling day proceeded calmly and that no major security incidents occurred." He also noted that "there were certain technical problems, in particular with regard to indelible ink," and encouraged "a full and independent investigation of any complaints and an assessment of the extent to which any irregularities may have affected the integrity of the process."

Meanwhile, the European Union's Special Representative in Afghanistan—still Francesc Vendrell—issued a comprehensive and typically frank assessment:

> Reports from witnesses of the voting process, including the EU Democracy and Election Support Mission, indicate that the Afghan people were overwhelmingly able to cast their votes freely in an environment devoid of intimidation or violence. [...] Notwithstanding the most unfortunate problem with the application of the indelible ink, which, in the heat of the moment, may have prompted several of the Presidential candidates to prematurely question the validity of the entire voting process and call for a halt to the vote, our impression is

> that the call came too late in the day to have had serious impact on the voters, most of whom had by then already cast their vote or were unaware of, or unwilling to pay heed to it.

The most detailed and arguably incisive of the early assessments was a private one, on October 10, prepared by Robert Kluyver, an ex-UNAMA staff member who was then supporting the Free and Fair Elections Foundation for Afghanistan (FEFA). FEFA had deployed 2,000 trained local observers in 100 of Afghanistan's approximately 400 districts. It was the largest deployment of observers, as well as the least experienced. Kluyver's verdict, based on the reports received from FEFA's teams, was harsh. He described the election as a "success for the Afghan people and failure for the Afghan government and the international community." He argued that "most problems can be attributed to JEMB's faulty organization and training," and stressed reports of bias in the filling of electoral positions, of electoral staff being unaware of procedures, and of the occurrence of numerous logistical problems. These criticisms overestimated the ease of training 120,000 Afghans, often in remote areas, who were for the most part illiterate, and who had never before in their lives seen an electoral process. But given the unquestionable responsibility of the logistical department of the JEMB Secretariat in the ink fiasco, Kluyver's criticisms were otherwise well-founded. They would be generally echoed by other organizations, including the final FEFA report, and those of the various international organizations that had sent representatives to monitor the election.[12]

Another observation that could immediately be made was the lack of significant security incidents. Not a single violent death was reported on election day, no serious attacks had been made against the 5,000 polling centers, and there were very few reports of voter intimidation. Given the number of attacks during the registration process, and the many who had been injured and killed in the lead-up to the election, the almost freakish calm on the day surprised everyone.

As for the Afghans themselves, a poll conducted by the International Republican Institute revealed that 82 percent of respondents said the election was "free and fair" and 97 percent said that the complaints raised by opposition candidates would not affect the outcome. The reliability of this poll can be questioned—while 17,000 people had been polled in 177 locations, coverage was badly skewed by security and geographical constraints—but even after adjusting for these factors, it remained a highly positive verdict.[13]

Establishment of the Impartial Panel of Election Experts

These first impressions about the process were interesting and informative, but information everyone wanted to know was who won? Immediately after the election, ballots began to be transported—by truck, helicopter, and donkey—to the regional centers for counting, During that time, UNAMA's political team moved quickly to assemble the international panel of experts that Qanuni had exacted. After rapid consultations with international partners, three international experts, two of whom had previous link with the JEMB, were selected. Those two were Staffan Darnolf, head of the IFES assistance project to the JEMB, and Craig Jenness, head of the IOM operation in Iran under Erben. While both were recognized experts in elections, it was almost even more important that they were both physically nearby and could begin work almost immediately. The international stakeholders agreed that the European Union nominate the third panelist, but the EU had no one immediately available. After several days of searching, the EU nominated David Mathieson, a former information technology specialist who was, at the time of his appointment, the interim director of the United Kingdom Electoral Reform Society.[14] Darnolf and Jenness were able to begin work in Kabul on October 11, the day that the JEMB formally requested the United Nations to nominate a panel; [15] Mathieson arrived three days later. Although the panel was mandated to supplement the work of the JEMB complaints unit, it quickly moved to establish itself as a final arbitrator of the election results.[16]

The sense of dismay at the appointment of the panel was palpable among the electoral team. Long bruised by its combats with Arnault's political officers, the international electoral experts now felt that the UNAMA's political office was attempting to assume credit for an operation that was increasingly seen as successful, while channeling responsibility for what went wrong exclusively to them. It was not lost on them that Arnault's politically-driven and delayed decisions on OCV and on accepting the Indian ink were partly responsible for the one visible stain on the process.

Their dismay was heightened by the fear that the successes of the election risked being diminished by UNAMA's post-election decisions. The panel's focus on irregularities, they felt, would distract from the overall positive impression left by the election once the ink issue had faded to a minor point in the public's eye. The existence of the panel would in addition give excessive and unreasonable credence to accusations of fraud by the opposition. Finally, and more practically, the electoral team feared that the panel's work would postpone the start of counting and raise additional suspicions that ballots were being manipulated.

Arnault began to justify that final concern when he requested the JEMB to delay the counting until the panel "recommended" that counting could begin. The ballot papers, arriving continually at the regional counting centers, began to accumulate. The workflow was paralyzed by, on the one hand, Arnault's request to wait for the panel's green light, and on the other the panel's meticulousness before making its decision. Arnault's political desire to have the panel quickly clean up the mistakes of the electoral team was beginning to conflict with the panel's own intent to assiduously discharge its terms of reference—it's members, after all, were electoral experts as well, with reputations to defend. Independent bodies have consequences. Austin was informed by the panel that it needed to see all the complaints that had been registered at the polling stations, whether resolved or not. [17] This meant that 22,500 tamper-evident bags would have to be opened, exposing highly sensitive materials like the voter tally sheets, which were essential to corroborating the count. It amounted to a corruption of the entire purpose of the tamper-evident bags. In the meantime, the holding of ballot boxes overnight in the centers was already prompting candidate complaints. The idea of the panel had been born around the question of the ink, but the panel itself clearly saw its role as far more expansive.

The JEMB issued a deadline of 6 p.m. on October 12—more or less 24 hours after the announcement of the creation of the panel—for additional complaints to be submitted. Forty-three complaints were received, on the basis of which the panel recommended that boxes from 10 polling centers be quarantined. This amounted to about 50 boxes and affected mostly the provinces of Ghazni, Kabul, Logar, and Wardak. The panel, dissatisfied with this meager crop of additional complaints, on its own extended the deadline for further complaints for an additional 48 hours, until 6 p.m. on October 14. Now UNAMA, the panel, and the JEMB were all playing visible roles; it was less and less clear who was actually responsible for the process.

The actual opening of ballot boxes and mixing of ballots could not begin until the panel's deadline, in order not to risk opening boxes that might subsequently have to be quarantined. Nonetheless, on the morning of October 14, before its deadline expired, the panel finally "recommended" that counting could proceed.

The Five Stages of Counting

The counting process had five stages. First, the sensitive materials were "checked-in" by the polling center supervisors and moved to a secure storage area. There was insufficient room to count all the ballots simultaneously. A system had to be set up to allow the orderly count of some of the ballots while ensuring the security of those ballots that could not be counted. Not all ballots arrived simultaneously; the timing depended on remoteness of the polling center and the mode of transport.

The second stage was "reconciliation." In this stage, the number of ballots from each box were counted to ensure that they tallied with the number of ballots recorded as delivered on the polling center return form. If the totals did not match, there would be a recount. If, after the recount, the discrepancy was less than two percent, the ballots were counted. If it was greater than two percent, the counting center manager had to initiate an investigation. If there was no satisfactory explanation for the discrepancy, the manager reported the facts to the Regional Coordinator who in turn informed JEMB headquarters. The ballot papers would be returned to the ballot box, the box would be resealed, the new seal numbers recorded, and the box returned to the "quarantine station" until additional instructions were issued by the JEMB.

The third stage was "mixing." Here, the ballots from batches of ten reconciled boxes were mixed together in preparation for the actual count. During the count, the fourth stage, the ballots were first sorted per candidate and then tallied and recorded. Finally, in the fifth stage, the results were reported to the tally center in Kabul where they were inserted into a database and periodically (several times per day) projected onto a screen in the Media Center, where the public and journalists could begin to follow the emergence of a winner.[18]

The formal five-stage process was an attempt to insert as much order as possible into what would clearly be a chaotic process. Despite the setting aside of rooms in each center for the ballots of each province, and marking lines in tape on the floors of the large warehouses to keep the counting operations for each province separate, entropy inevitably intervened. During the transport of ballots from the polling stations to the regional centers—trips of several hundred kilometers at times—boxes were sometimes separated from the sensitive documentation that belonged to them. Prior to counting, boxes and documentation had to be reunited within the increasingly cramped spaces where materials from each province were stored. As this reordering happened, additional boxes continued to arrive. This was a physically challenging and mentally mind-numbing process. It took place against a backdrop of uncertainty inspired both by the panel's sudden but authoritative recommendations and the growing political tension arising from the chaos of incoming materials that for the moment had nowhere to go. It was also becoming clear, and disheartening, that counting would continue several weeks longer than initially expected. This raised the possibility, if there was no winner in the first round, of not having sufficient time to organize a second round.

The counting process of any election, no matter how well organized, generates tension. This is the moment when voter trends begin to emerge and candidate agents—particularly those of losing candidates—become particularly vociferous. Their natural instinct is to try to salvage through the complaints process what their candidates might have lost through votes. The centralization of the counting also allowed the concentration of political agents, which had its drawbacks as well as its benefits. The political agents were the least trained of electoral actors, being even less informed than domestic observers of the procedures that applied to the count. They did not always have a sense of what the boundaries of correct behavior were. In addition, they bore the pressure of making sure their candidates received as many votes as possible. Complaints that arose during counting were, therefore, high in number and sometimes intimidating in form. Not all JEMB staff reacted correctly to complaints, which were often in the form of provocations and accusations of bias. As the process proceeded, the temperature inside the centers rose, creating a political hothouse charged, as always in Afghanistan, with the menace of violence.

The international panel, having launched the counting process, then decided it would carry out two types of investigation. First, it would conduct specific investigations of complaints filed before the first deadline of October 12. There were 20 such cases, and they had resulted in the quarantining of a number of ballot boxes. In these cases, the panel was able to actually examine the evidence directly. The evidence quickly revealed that, if the lack of Afghan electoral experience had sometimes been demonstrated in the poor management of polling centers, that lack of experience was also sometimes evident in the crude attempts to rig the election. One of the most frequent problems encountered during the counting process was that ballots were carefully stacked and then folded into neat piles before the box was sealed, allowing far more ballots to be cast than the box was designed for, but demonstrating clearly that the boxes were stuffed. No ballots would naturally fall into such neat piles.

The second investigation track was that of "general or thematic" issues raised by the candidates. There were 661 allegations filed by candidates that were investigated under this category. The pattern of these allegations was interesting: only 7.6 percent (50) were related to the ink problem and 13.5 percent (89) to the "general polling station procedural issues." Nearly half of them (300) were related to "allegations of bias and intimidation"—these complaints were the most subjective and hardest to prove and tended to be from the losing candidates.[19] One of the inevitable things about elections is that such complaints can be both the cause and the consequence of electoral defeat.

Into the tense environment of investigations and postponed counting, another concern was introduced. Ramadan, the Muslim month of fasting, began the week after the election. During Ramadan, Muslims allow nothing to pass their mouths between sunrise and sunset—not food, not water, not cigarette smoke. Out of courtesy, the internationals, sequestered in the counting centers with Afghan JEMB staff and political agents, either tried to respect their Afghan colleagues' religion by not eating or by eating minimally and discreetly. The net effect of the fasting period was to slow the counting while quickening tempers, both political and splenetic. Afghan staff either stopped working early in the afternoon or demanded that the JEMB provide them with *iftar*—the fast-breaking meal at dusk. No one had anticipated this request while preparing the budgets, though this was a hardly satisfying response to the hungry and impatient counting center staff.

Meanwhile the internationals, who were ultimately responsible for adjudicating complaints inside the counting center, felt increasingly threatened by the political party agents. The initial euphoria of election day had been marred by the debacle of the ink. Now the ink had provided every political agent with a reason to be skeptical of the conduct of the election, especially of the internationals who were supposed to guarantee a professional process. The internationals who had worked on the elections for the past year or, in some cases, two, were exhausted. They wanted the election to be over so they could go home for a winter break. The political agents and international panel members, on the other hand, had just begun to play their designated roles and were inspired and energetic. The longer the counting went on, the more the complaints multiplied, which delayed the counting, and generated more complaints. The process began to appear perpetual, acting on the minds and moods of the increasingly tired and the increasingly hungry JEMB staff.

With the results from counting being updated almost constantly, the candidates began to take stock of their positions. On October 18, nearly 20 percent of the votes had been counted. Karzai was well ahead with 62 percent, followed by Qanuni with 19 percent and Dostum with just over eight. The geographic patterns were also clear: Karzai was strongest in the cities and the Pashtun belt, while Qanuni, Dostum, and Mohaqeq had gained the most votes in the areas where their respective ethnicities were most densely populated.

As these results emerged, Qanuni's position alternated between accepting the results and challenging them. In the same day he would reassure UNAMA that he would accept the results of the count, but would appear later at a press conference accusing UNAMA and the JEMB as being biased. His party agents continued to aggressively submit complaints at the counting centers. Dostum, on the other hand, showed himself far more inclined to accept the results. He had probably never expected to win. But for him, the results legitimized his claim to be the true representative of the Uzbek population, and washed away some of the stigma of his former warlordism. At same time, they gave him political capital which he could use to claim a prominent position in the new government.

UNAMA maintained a constant line in response to the complaints—it insisted that the process must run its course and reminded all political actors that the complaints mechanism, including the international panel which was in regular contact with the candidates, was functioning properly. The observer reports supported UNAMA's position. They described a flawed process but one whose flaws were far more the result of expected inexperience than of intentional fraud.[20]

Certifying the Count

Arnault was surely as exhausted with the process as the members of the electoral team. He bore the heavy weight of responsibility for the decisions that had been taken, and few had been easy. He was the focus of the anger of the losing candidates, as well as of the expectations of Karzai himself and of the international community that Karzai emerge victorious. Under the building tension of the moment, the mutual overall objectives of Arnault and his electoral experts were once again overshadowed by the mutual antipathy of the main protagonists. Arnault began to blame his international experts for the delays in counting. On October 26, two weeks after counting started, he convened a meeting with his electoral and political advisors. That same day, the final ballot box had been emptied for counting and about 95 percent of the total votes had been counted. According to preliminary figures, Karzai was winning with 55 percent and Qanuni was in second place with 16 percent. This was the outcome that most in the international community had hoped for—a victory of over 50 percent by Karzai, thereby avoiding the dreaded runoff, and a convincing distance between Karzai and the next highest vote-getter, which would diminish the force of the loser's argument that, were it not for fraud, he would have won.

The purpose of the October 26 meeting was to decide how and when the final results would be certified. Even though most of the counting was completed, the JEMB still had to consider reports of fraud before it could issue a final certification. Normally, if votes affected by proven fraud are less in number than the difference between the winning and second-place candidate, then they are not considered to be decisive. There was, nonetheless, a need to reach this determination, and that depended on the conclusions of the international panel. Arnault requested clarification from Austin and his team on when the JEMB was likely to pronounce the results. A JEMB international commissioner replied that a number of reports still had to be finalized—including the report of the independent panel of international experts. Once they were completed, they had to be translated and considered by the JEMB before it could issue its final certification. The likely date for this was expected to be on or about November 5. A few other participants in the meeting noted favorably that this would place the inauguration, according to the Constitution's 30-day provision, on December 5—three years to the day of the Bonn Agreement, a rather felicitous coincidence.

Arnault, however, wanted an earlier certification. He said the JEMB was moving too slowly. The Afghan people had endured a year of the electoral process and they needed closure. Afghanistan, he added, was "not a country that has had 2,000 years of institutions;" the political situation was fragile and could not last much longer with the uncertainty of not knowing who the president was.

Arnault's arguments were not unfounded, but the sense of frantic urgency with which they were delivered led some in the electoral team to believe that Khalilzad had leaned on him to ensure that the election results were formally announced before the U.S. presidential election, which was on November 2, or exactly a week away. President Bush, the day before Arnault's meeting, had hailed the Afghan elections in a campaign speech, noting that "freedom is on the march" in Afghanistan. The U.S. election was expected to be close and some analysts thought that good news from Afghanistan could tip the scales in Bush's favor.

But ultimately the delays were far more the result of the decision to create the international panel, rather than indolence on the part of the JEMB. The need to appoint the panel and receive complaints had postponed the start of the count; the ongoing work of the panel was now postponing certification. The JEMB's only fault was that of taking seriously the measures that Arnault had implemented. This last act of the election, therefore, perfectly encapsulated the tension that had run through the entire process. It epitomized the conflict between creating competent institutions and laying a solid groundwork for future political development, and the need for political expediency where processes were created to complete the Bonn process "on time," not only to appease Afghan political actors who relied on the calendar as a means of gauging the sustainability of the process, but now to benefit outside stakeholders—in this case the American President, who saw the achievement of the process as part of his own political legacy. Such processes, devoted to such purposes, would inevitably be characterized by a certain superficiality.

The meeting broke up with the usual dissatisfactions, the usual sense that one side did not understand the other, and the usual confusion over whether the internationals were there to help the Afghans or to help themselves. For Arnault, it seemed, his electoral experts had once again let him down. For the electoral experts, Arnault's reaction deepened their feeling of being unfairly blamed for everything that had gone wrong and not given any credit for what had gone well.

Kidnapping of International Electoral Staff

Two days after the tense meeting in Arnault's office, a car carrying three international U.N. electoral staff was stopped by men in police uniforms on a Kabul street. It was morning and they were on their way to work at the central region counting center on the western outskirts of the city. The internationals were forced out their vehicle and made to lie on the road, Kalashnikovs pointed at their heads. Once subdued, they were transferred to another vehicle and driven away. The whole incident had taken a few minutes. The U.N. driver, left behind, reported the incident to the JEMB Secretariat.

News of the kidnapping spread rapidly through the electoral team and through the rest of the United Nations and then the international press. The security procedure in such cases was to declare a "white city," in which all staff members are to return to their guest houses and account for themselves through a radio check. White city had been used before, during suicide and rocket attacks, but this was the first time in Afghanistan that United Nations staff had been kidnapped. The phenomenon was well known, however, from Iraq. This was a time when videos of humiliating captive statements, and often beheadings, were leading the headlines. The entire momentum of the electoral process now came to a terrible halt. Electoral staff were escorted to their homes in military convoys and waited nervously for further news, especially the names of the kidnapped.

At first it was believed that the kidnapping was directly related to the election. All three were staff of the JEMB Secretariat. Two of the three kidnapped—Shqipe Habibi and Annetta Flanigan—had worked together at the counting center in Kabul. A UNV who had been working with them, Amandine Roche, later published in France her journal entries from her year in Kabul. In her entry of October 13, she describes threats made against Habibi by opposition political agents.[21] Habibi, a Kosovar, had survived war in her own country and was not easily intimidated. The political agents, according to Roche, drew their fingers across their throats, a universal sign of threat, but one that engendered a very real and specific fear in the context of the times. "You work for Karzai and you'll pay for it," the agents reportedly said. Flanigan, a Northern Irish lawyer who had worked in the training section, was nearby and tried to calm tempers. She explained to the political agents that they could fill out complaint forms if they were unhappy with the way the counting was proceeding, stressing that the code of conduct for candidate agents did not permit the making of threats. The third kidnapped staff member, Angelito Nayan, from the Philippines, did not work in the counting center but had worked on the elections.

On the day the kidnapping happened, Roche describes being questioned by U.N. security officials: "You worked closely with these three during the counting. Did you notice anything strange?"

"Yes. We had a number of disputes with candidate agents. They accused us of being pro-Karzai and favoring his re-election."

"Why didn't you ever report that you had felt threatened?"

"Because we've received this sort of threat every day for a year. We didn't pay any attention to them anymore."[22]

As the day wore on, speculation continued. Finally, a group contacted a press agency and said they had carried out the kidnapping. They said they were allied to the Taliban and demanded the liberation of all Taliban prisoners in Guantanamo Bay and in Afghanistan as well as the departure of international forces and the United Nations. If the group's message was to be believed, the kidnapping had nothing to do with Karzai's opponents. This was far worse.

UNAMA, the Electoral Secretariat, and the international community in general focused on resolving the kidnapping, which lasted three weeks. At the same time, the electoral process had to move forward. On November 1, the international panel completed its report. The 70-page document contained a detailed analysis of the election's flaws, its methodology for addressing them, and its recommendations for avoiding them in the future. The executive summary concluded as follows:

> In summary, this was a commendable election, particularly given the very challenging circumstances. There were shortcomings, many of which were raised by the candidates themselves. These problems deserved to be considered, to ensure the will of the voters was properly reflected, and to help shape improvements for future elections. The Panel concludes, however, that these concerns could not have materially affected the overall result of the election.

This was, for better or for worse, the classic definition of a flawed but fair election: one where the flaws did not affect the outcome. The panel had fulfilled Qanuni's request: it had been international and independent, it had carefully examined all of the complaints, and it had provided a report whose comprehensiveness could not be denied.

The panel's report allowed the JEMB to finally certify the election result on November 3. Karzai was declared the winner with 55.4 percent of the vote; Qanuni came in second with 16.3 percent; Mohaqeq was third with 11.7 percent; and Dostum was fourth with ten percent. The rest of the candidates received no more than 1.5 percent of the vote. In the end, Karzai won 80 percent of the out-of-country vote in Pakistan and 44 percent in Iran. The out-of-country results gave Karzai about 560,000 additional votes. Even without out-of-country voting, however, he would have won the election with over 50 percent.

The certification could not have been more anticlimactic for the electoral team, especially those who were closest to their kidnapped colleagues. By then, the dreaded videos of the captives had already appeared, with a masked militant by their side holding a Kalashnikov. The *mise-en-scène* had been borrowed from Iraq, it was understandable to fear that the end would be the same.

In the meantime, significant international expertise was brought in to help the Afghan security forces find the kidnappers.[23] Scotland Yard, the U.S. Coalition, ISAF, and UNAMA endeavored first to block off the general area where the captives were thought to be held, and then more and more narrowly define that area. Incoming intelligence began to suggest that the kidnappers were not themselves Taliban, but a criminal gang that had been sub-contracted by an extremist group to carry out the kidnapping.[24] If this was true, it was presumed that the next move of the gang would be to physically deliver the hostages to the extremists who had contracted them, hence the importance of sealing the area as much as possible. The internationals of UNAMA and the electoral team were finally united. Vendrell's old civil affairs officers worked their own networks to try to glean intelligence and ensure that the captives were not taken from the city. Arnault dedicated himself fully to helping organize the effort, speaking regularly with the families of the captives and deploying the full resources of the mission to their release.

Roche, in her published diary, compellingly portrays the sense of panic, fear, helplessness and uncertainty during this time—the paranoia and the utter fatigue of constantly feeling oneself to be a potential victim. A rumor had begun to spread amid the electoral team that the kidnappers possessed a list of 25 electoral workers whom they wanted to kidnap. Suddenly the drivers or house staff with whom one had joked for a year—or even helped with school money for their children or to buy a generator for their house—became objects of suspicion. How much money would it take for them to give away a location, a routine, or a travel route? For the more pessimistic and historically-minded, it recalled the fate of the English cantonment in the first Anglo-Afghan war (1839-1842) when, after two years of living unmolested in the shadow of Bibi Maru, amid dinner parties of "champagne, hock, Madeira, sherry, port, claret, sauterne, not forgetting a glass of curaçao and maraschino," the Afghans suddenly turned on the English, leading an ordnance officer to note in his journal: "The unwelcome truth was soon forced upon us, that in the whole Afghan nation we could not reckon on a single friend."[25]

In reality, the Afghans rallied visibly to support the kidnapped United Nations staff, from King Zahir Shah to the United Nations cleaning staff. Many Afghans called ISAF with leads. Hundreds rallied in Kabul to demand the release of the kidnapped internationals. A group of women offered to place themselves in the custody of the kidnappers instead of the internationals.

In the meantime, by triangulating mobile telephone calls, the security cell set up to deal with the kidnapping was able to narrow down the area in which the captives were held. On 21 November, a team of U.S. special forces conducted a search operation in Western Kabul that resulted in several explosions. These occurred approximately a mile away from where the kidnappers were being held. The kidnapped later described hearing the explosions and wondering whether their proximity would shorten or lengthen their lives. The fact of a U.S. raid so close to the safe house rattled the hostage-holders, however, who were faced with a quick decision to either kill or release the hostages. The next day the UNAMA kidnap team was contacted with the news that the hostages would be released. The day after that, 23 November, the team was instructed to position themselves at the Bagh-e-Zanana—the "women's garden" in the center of Kabul—and wait for the hostages. The hostages had been given a stolen car and told which direction to drive in. They were duly met at the gardens and returned quickly to one of the U.N. compounds.

The conclusion of the election, the certification of results, hardly registered in the minds of those who had worked the hardest to make it happen. The need to begin preparing for the much more complicated parliamentary elections lay ahead, and the trauma of the kidnapping remained vivid. Nobody really noticed that those words written on that paper back at Petersburg castle, words written in haste and in ignorance, had been made real, had been converted into history. For the first time ever, this remote and fractious people had had a direct say in choosing their leader.

---

[1] On 16 September, he attempted to meet with local leaders in Gardez, south of Kabul, but the visit was aborted when a rocket was fired at his helicopter.

[2] Though a report conducted by the JEMB Media Commission noted that Karzai received by far the largest amount of coverage—around 35 to 40 percent.

[3] Two candidates had dropped out, expressing their support for Karzai.

[4] Quoted in International Crisis Group, "Afghanistan: From Presidential to Parliamentary Elections," Asia Report No. 88, Kabul/Brussels, November 23, 2004, p. 9.

[5] Because Pakistan is in a time zone one-half hour ahead of Afghanistan's, polling began in Pakistan before Afghanistan.

[6] There were some security incidents like the intimidation and attacks by Mohaqeq supporters in Parwan, a rocket attack from the Pakistan border, Qanuni's supporters' attacks on individuals who did not support the boycott, and stoning incident against a polling center in Ghor. In Bamyan three individuals in possession of 10 voter cards each were arrested by the Afghan police. Overall these incidents had no impact on the elections.

[7] Factors such as catastrophic events that would prevent access to polling stations, the destruction of polling stations, or the lack of preparation of polling stations.

[8] Some among the electoral team even argued that the panel should restrict itself to investigating the international role in the ink problem.

[9] In the end, the "special vote" did not take place—it was rumored that Ambassador Khalilzad had prevailed upon the belated democrat to not exercise the special voting option offered by UNAMA. That evening, Qanuni gave a press conference—after meeting with Khalilzad—in which he said that everything had been a big misunderstanding and he had never called for a boycott.

[10] The Organization for Security and Cooperation in Europe (OSCE) did not sent a full observation team, but an Electoral Support Team whose purpose was "to engage actively with the U.N., election administrators, candidates and the media, using extensive experience in observing and administering elections, to improve the process."

[11] None of the international organizations could send, for security reasons, a sufficient number of observers to describe these missions as "electoral observation." Normally, observation requires the ability to cover a statistically meaningful percentage of polling stations and to ensure balanced regional coverage. Security fears in general prevented the numbers, and security fears about the south prevented the balance. Hence the various neologisms such as the EU's "Democracy and Electoral Support Mission" and the OSCE's "Election Support Team." It is also possible that these groups took the political decision not to send full-fledged observation missions to avoid having to make negative comments on an election that few expected would meet "international standards."

[12] Interestingly, Kluyver minimized the ink problem, calling the two separate ink delivery mechanisms "ill-conceived," but noting that "it actually might not have been a problem (if multiple voting didn't result) but was jumped upon opportunistically by opposition candidates to justify the call for a boycott."

[13] Nonetheless the exit poll predicted the outcome of the election within five percentage points. In that respect at least, it was far more accurate than the exit polls that would take place a few weeks later in the United States.

[14] In a minor irony, given the debate over Afghanistan's electoral law in the spring, the Electoral Reform Society was created to advocate the replacement of the United Kingdom's first-past-the-post system with a proportional representation system.

[15] The JEMB statement of 11 October on the panel read as follows: "The JEMB had extended discussions yesterday, 10 October, regarding the difficulties and irregularities on Election Day and protests lodged by candidates. In order to further enhance the transparency and legitimacy of the election, the JEMB decided to request the United Nations to identify an impartial panel of international electoral experts to fully investigate these protests and present recommendations to the JEMB for its adjudication. This panel's work will supplement the work already underway by the JEMB's existing Complaints and Investigations Unit. The panel members that have been nominated by the United Nations are Mr. Craig Jenness, a former Canadian diplomat and experienced jurist who has been involved in numerous elections over the last decade, and Mr. Staffan Darnolf, an election administration specialist from Sweden who has also served on election teams in postconflict environments in the Balkans and Africa for the European Union, the United Nations, and IFES over the last decade. The United Nations has requested the European Union to assist with the identification of another expert who would be readily available to serve as a third member of the panel. His or her name will be announced shortly."

[16] The creation of the panel can be seen to be the first in a series of such independent verification mechanisms. The concept was repeated in the December 2005 Parliamentary elections in Iraq. Also, in 2005 the Security Council established a High Representative for Elections to verify the credibility of the Côte d'Ivoire elections (which did not happen until 2010). Verification teams were also established by the United Nations for the 2007 elections in Timor Leste and Nepal.

[17] It should be noted that the quality with which these complaints were resolved was highly uneven. Local observers, notably the 2,000 trained Afghan electoral observers working for FEFA, noted that many poll workers did not know the rules very well and were not able to explain their rulings effectively. In other words, how deep into the complaints process the panel should go was one of political judgment, and required weighing the pros and cons of delaying the count and lending credence to what were, as most recognized, politically motivated complaints.

[18] Since the Media Center had been installed inside a school, it actually had to close before all of the results were counted and announced.

[19] The pattern of complaints submitted at polling stations, and included in the Tamper Evident Bags, was somewhat different. First of all, there were only 173 such complaints across the country, perhaps indicating that few people knew of this avenue of protest. Of these complaints, nearly half (70) were about the ink, where as only 10 percent (14) concerned intimidation or partisan poll personnel. There were more complaints (17), in fact, about the lack of food and water at the polling stations.

[20] Impartial Panel of Election Experts,Final Report of Impartial Panel of Election Experts Concerning Afghanistan Presidential Election 2004, Kabul, 2004.

[21] Amandine Roche, Le vol des colombes: journal d'une volontaire en Afghanistan, (Paris: Robert Laffont, 2005) p. 260.

[22] Roche, *Vol des colombes*, p. 268.

[23] A selective impression from the inside of the workings of this effort can be gleaned from Matthew J. Morgan, *A Democracy is Born* (Westport, CT: Praeger Security International, 2007) pp. 92-116.

[24] It was later determined that the group was the Jaish-ul-Muslimin, then based in Quetta. According to a report written afterwards by the team of UNAMA and ex-UNAMA Afghan experts (essentially the civil affairs officers who had initially been recruited by Vendrell), it had contracted a local criminal group to carry out the kidnapping in order to raise its profile in the Arab jihadi donor community. The gang apparently adopted rather quickly an autonomous plan, encouraged by the prospect of ransom money. The same lure led to internal rivalries within the Jaish-ul-Muslimin at the same time.

[25] See Meyer and Brysac, *Tournament of Shadows* (New York: Basic Books, 2006) pp. 91-97.

15

The 2005 Parliamentary Elections

The separation of the parliamentary elections from the presidential one in 2004 avoided a likely electoral failure, but prolonged by a year the intense stress of elections on the political environment and on the U.N. itself. The international team that had just implemented the presidential election had learned a great deal about holding elections in an environment as particular as Afghanistan's. They were also aware, both from experience in other elections and from logical deduction, that the parliamentary elections would be far more complex logistically than the presidential. There would be thirty-four ballots instead of one, thirty-four counting centers instead of eight, thousands of candidates instead of twenty-one, a worsening security situation, and the implementation of the dreaded SNTV voting system. At the same time, the presidential elections had proven that elections could be held in Afghanistan and that Afghans were enthusiastic about voting. It had provided an array of lessons that could already be applied to the planning of the parliamentary elections. Those who were involved hoped that the knowledge gained in 2004 would compensate for the additional complexities presented by the parliamentary election. This was an opportunity to allow the democratization of Afghanistan take a decisive and consolidating step forward.

Even while the presidential ballots were still being counted, the international election team began planning the parliamentary elections. On 23 October, they held a day-long brainstorming session at the Kabul Intercontinental Hotel. The meeting took place during the very brief pause between election day and the kidnapping, at a time when counting was proceeding in a fairly orderly manner and a calm end to the election appeared imminent.

The ink debacle weighed heavily on the planner's minds. It was difficult to say whether the team had been incredibly lucky or incredibly unlucky. However much Arnault's decisions on out-of-country voting and on accepting the Indian ink had contributed to that disaster, the root cause was a procurement mistake for which the JEMB Secretariat, and especially its international professionals, had to accept the lion's share of the blame for what could have been a total disaster.

While the presidential elections had shown how quickly a logistical error could turn into a political crisis, the real fear for those thinking about the parliamentary elections was that the nature of SNTV contained the seeds of multiple potential political crises. The team returned to the possibility of trying once more to revise the law, now that Karzai had been elected and that the time pressure had somewhat abated. The U.N.'s criticisms of SNTV that had been provided in the first half of 2004, when the law was being debated for the first time, were echoed by the international observers during the 2004 election. The report of the European Union Democracy Support Mission report was unequivocal:

> There is widespread dissatisfaction at the choice of SNTV system for parliamentary and local elections. The system is wholly inappropriate for the development of a representative and effective parliament as it is likely to result in a lower house that is fragmented and which could be easily dominated by powerful individuals with the support of a minority of the popular vote. Urgent consideration should be given to adopting a more suitable electoral system for Afghanistan following immediate consultation with national stakeholders and international advisers.[1]

Momentum for amending the electoral law therefore seemed to be increasing in late 2004. Apart from President Karzai and a few political opportunists within his circle who were more concerned with gaining the President's favor than with the future of parliamentary democracy in Afghanistan, few saw the virtues of SNTV.

The moment was also opportune to attempt another change. Absent a legislature, all laws were still enacted by presidential decree. Once the National Assembly was elected, its members might be reluctant to change the system that elected them. The best moment to push for a revision was therefore before the parliamentary elections took place. As the debate evolved, however, Karzai found an unexpected ally in The Asia Foundation.[2] The Foundation's Regional Director for Elections and Political Processes, Tim Meisburger, drafted a memo defending SNTV that was widely circulated in Kabul. Meisburger's memo argued that:

> Usually, in the selection of PR as an election system is the perception that it is an effective tool for facilitating peaceful transitions and stable political outcomes in postconflict countries. Typically in a postconflict democratizing country the competing factions (warlord, militias,

> armies) will morph into political parties. Using proportional representation as an incentive, negotiators can then offer each faction or party a share of power in the new government proportional to the area or population they control. This works quite well for the faction leaders, who more or less share the spoils, but it may not be the most appropriate system to encourage sustainable and representative self-government.[3]

This was a somewhat skewed way of understanding the workings of PR. It over-emphasized the "engineering" aspect of the electoral system by stressing what "negotiators can offer"—which is not at all the point of an electoral system, let alone an election. At the same time, it underestimated the incentives within the system for political actors to negotiate with each other, and in particular to encourage reaching beyond local or tribal blocs for support. The memo compounded these misunderstandings with a crudely mechanistic analysis of Afghan politics that exhibited a number of Charles Tilly's "pernicious postulates". Tilly has argued[4] that these postulates, such as defining societies—or in this case, armed factions—as homogenous units, in the way that Meisburger does in his memo, occluded a proper understanding of political processes. Another "pernicious postulate" was that societies evolve according to fixed stages, much as Meisburger suggests that "typically in a postconflict democratizing country the competing factions [...] will morph into political parties." The memo's forced conclusion could only be upheld by an over-simplification of Afghanistan's political realities, as follows:

> The introduction of proportional representation may be particularly inappropriate in Afghanistan, where one of the primary objectives of the transition is to weaken the power of the informal militia leaders. In a proportional system each militia band will form a party, and if that party were to win fifty seats in the National Assembly, the militia leader will retain control of all of them. In contrast, in an SNTV system the same party might again win fifty seats, but each representative would be an independent operator directly accountable to his or her constituents–rather than the party leader–and able to form cross party alliances in their interest. The militia leader, instead of directly controlling fifty seats, would control just one.[5]

It was simplistic to think that a militia leader, because he was the head of a party, would command the loyalty of everyone elected under his party banner. Defection, betrayal, and realignment are the eternal features of the Afghan power game, whether it is played on the field of battle or on in politics.[6] In fact, if Meisburger's premise were accepted, it would be the single strongest argument *for* PR, rather than against it. The advocates of PR never expected that Afghan parties would actually act as cohesive blocs, in a modern parliamentary fashion, only that the existence of parties might, on some issues, encourage a development towards that sort of party discipline. On the question of party formation, the memo conceded SNTV's weaknesses:

> It's true that SNTV will weaken the power of the parties in Afghanistan, but if the parties are not democratic, are in fact informal militia groups in sheep's clothing, that may not be a bad thing. To be successful in the SNTV parties will have to change, will have to appeal directly to voters, and will become more democratic and accountable. To maximize the number of seats they win parties will have to develop a grassroots organization, again enhancing their accountability and representativeness.[7]

What this argument ignores is that the political dynamics in Afghanistan were made up of more than just "militia groups." They included, in many areas, tribal dynamics which were not always articulated through armed factions. Furthermore, if Meisburger's assumption that all political parties in Afghanistan were power-hungry militias was true, they would be better off by intimidating voters than by developing "a grassroots organization." The memo concluded that "the advantages of the SNTV far outweigh its disadvantages. It will provide more effective representation and democratic accountability, help build democratic political parties and a vibrant political culture, and weaken the power of informal militia groups."[8]

Meisburger's memo is interesting in hindsight as an intellectual dissent to an issue on which there was otherwise a general consensus among experts. And even if, as argued above, the reasoning behind this dissent was badly flawed, it was probably not decisive in the failure to reform the electoral law prior to the parliamentary elections. In the end, it was Karzai's ongoing resistance to political parties that prevented any serious reform from being addressed before the window of opportunity closed.[9]

Revising the Institutional Arrangements

Another re-evaluation was underway in UNAMA itself. Arnault, burned by the logistical failure of the ink and frustrated by the inefficiencies of U.N. intra-agency cooperation, decided to radically alter the way electoral support would be delivered. His first move was to replace

Austin with Peter Erben, as his chief electoral advisor, during the winter lull.

Throughout the OCV process, Peter Erben had shown himself to be a competent logistician and manager. He had proved able to easily adjust his plans to meet diminishing deadlines. The easy manner in which Erben had shifted his minimum definition of an effective out-of-country organization from 120-days to 70-days was emblematic of his ability to accommodate political masters, or, put less charitably, his ability to prioritize the accommodation of his political masters over the credibility of an electoral process. This was not missed by Arnault, who had felt pestered and undercut throughout the previous year by apparently metaphysical statements from his electoral team about credibility, sustainability, and institution-building. These issues would be less likely to distract Erben, who would focus on delivering the event and on time. The insistence that the JEMB actually be empowered to play its role would no longer impede the necessity of taking rapid decisions or the acceptance of decisions dictated by the political managers of the process. No longer would a perceived concern about implications on credibility force the delay of a deadline. No longer would anyone stress the point that a body that was formally independent should be empowered to act independently. If elections were a purely logistical exercise that had to take place within a constricted timeframe, then nobody was better than Erben at delivering them.[10] This would come, however, at a high financial cost—Erben was known for incurring high budgets. And, if Austin and his team were correct about the importance of institutions, and that a concern about credibility was not merely metaphysical, then event-driven elections could exact a high political cost as well.

Justifying himself with the recommendations of numerous international evaluations of the elections,[11] Arnault decided to "streamline" the electoral operation under a single United Nations agency. He requested UNOPS to implement all aspects of the electoral operation (previously UNOPS had only been responsible for supporting the AIEC). All staff on UNDP contracts, including most of international UEC staff, therefore received an abrupt letter informing them that their contract with UNDP would be terminated and that they were free to apply to vacancies with UNOPS. It seemed like a summary dismissal, and it rubbed hard salt into the wounds already created by the battles of the previous year. Whether it was intended or not, it had the effect of causing many experienced staff to leave in frustration and disappointment. Arnault then ensured that the United Nations, over the objections of EAD in New York, hire Peter Erben and his team to organize the parliamentary elections, effectively dismissing Austin.

Austin's team had not been perfect and no one, least of all its members, would dispute that mistakes had been made. It sometimes seemed paralyzed by the complexities that Afghanistan threw at it. But in many ways its inefficiencies were not merely paralysis, but a result of its position that an election is more than a series of logistical events, and that if the various processes that together make an election are treated with sufficient attention, the results of the election could be trusted and would have a political value. For all its weaknesses, the obstacles the team faced were never sufficiently understood by those that stood judgment over it—neither Arnault and his political team, nor the *mauvaises langues* of the international community, nor the donors who thought that Afghans and suppliers would work on credit. Replaced by Erben and his team, they left for other elections, leaving behind a job half-done, and feeling a bit like Sir Walter Scott's "breathing man": "Unwept, unhonored, and unsung."[12]

EAD and the Parliamentary Elections

The end of 2004 and the beginning of 2005 was a busy time for the Electoral Assistance Division in New York as well. With the Afghan presidential elections completed, world attention turned to the Iraqi elections scheduled for January 2005.

As noted above, Perelli, had been dispatched by the Secretary-General to Iraq in early 2004 to make a technical assessment, demanded by Ayatollah Sistani, of whether elections could be held by June of that year.[13] Practically everyone at United Nations headquarters expected her to return with the obvious verdict that elections were simply not possible in Iraq at that time, and would not be possible until peace had been restored. This outcome was not only expected given the sharp deterioration of security in Iraq, but was desired by the United Nations' senior management. Most staff at U.N. headquarters felt strongly that the U.S. had walked into Iraq not only deaf to the counsel of the "international community", but disdaining and maligning it. As James Traub later wrote, the United Nations' "political officials, many of whom viewed the war as a raw exercise in American power, had no wish to wrap the effort in the UN flag."[14] This was even more true after the bombing of the U.N. offices in Iraq on August 19, 2003, which killed 21 United Nations staff-members. Furthermore, the U.S.-instigated investigation into the oil-for-food scandal, which began to heat up in January 2004, and seemed directly targeted at Kofi Annan and his inner circle,[15] only deepened the sense of personal animosity between the Bush and Annan administrations. Relations between the United States and the United Nations had, it seemed, sunk to the level of a tribal vendetta. So when the U.S. was suddenly confronted with Sistani's opposition to their plans to transfer power, and the U.N. was placed in a position where it could assist the U.S. out of their predicament in Iraq, few in the U.N. wanted to make that escape particularly easy.

Nevertheless, it is the fate of the Secretariat to do what the Security Council resolves, and Security Council resolution 1511 of October 2003 called on the United Nations to "strengthen its vital role in Iraq, including by providing humanitarian relief, promoting the economic reconstruction of and conditions for sustainable development in Iraq, and advancing efforts to restore and establish national and local institutions for representative government." Annan's top policy-makers, however, balked at providing anything more than the minimum required to avoid U.S. criticism. Furthermore, ceilings for United Nations staff presence in Iraq following the Canal Hotel bombing made it difficult for the United Nations to do anything more than the bare minimum, even had it wanted to.

There was therefore surprise and dismay among the U.N.'s upper management when Perelli returned from her second visit to Iraq in June 2004 with a technical verdict that elections *could* be held eight months after three essential conditions were fulfilled: the creation of an independent electoral commission, the setting aside of funds for the election, and the adoption of an electoral law. This was not only far from what the mandarins on the 38th floor of the U.N. Secretariat building had wanted to hear, it was also a political wager of immense audacity. No one thought elections could be held in Iraq under the conditions that then prevailed, or that were likely to prevail eight months hence, with or without an electoral law, or budget, or institution. Perelli's verdict seemed to obtusely ignore the violent realities that were then the top of every day's news cycle.

Her subsequent approach to the Iraqi elections brought out what her enemies disliked most about her: a bureaucratic stubbornness exhibited in her persistent requests to the U.N. to raise the staff ceiling in Iraq for election staff, a self-righteousness demonstrated in her claim to be doing the right thing by the Iraqi people and in redemption of de Mello's death, an impression of political infallibility as she argued that elections could be held despite the daily bloodshed, and the usual reliance on a small inner circle of trusted advisors to implement the election. Worst of all, she was dragging the institution back to Iraq, where it had no wish to go. All this drove against the cautious grain of the institution and added fuel to the arguments of her growing number of detractors.

Perelli's immediate supervisor and former defender, Kieran Prendergast, the Under-Secretary-General for Political Affairs, now began to lend his ear and his support to complaints of the many enemies she had accumulated in her half-decade in the Secretariat—complaints that had always been there and that he had previously dismissed. In a sad twist of fate, Perelli's main champion in Prendergast's office, his Special Assistant Rick Hooper, had been killed in the Canal Hotel bombing while visiting Baghdad for a few weeks in August 2003.

On December 28, 2004, in the middle of the winter holidays, between Christmas and the New Year, and a few weeks before the crucial Iraqi elections, Perelli was informed by an email from Prendergast that he had ordered a "management review" of EAD as a result of complaints from within her division. The review was to be carried out by a Geneva-based firm, MANNET, which DPA often used for human resource consulting.

MANNET's initial report, delivered in March 2005—after the surprising success of the elections in Iraq that Perelli had managed to organize despite opposition within the bureaucracy—was a damning indictment of Perelli's management of EAD and of her character. The report, which quickly found its way into the press,[16] described a pattern of abuse of power, misuse of funds, favoritism, and sexual and workplace harassment. It inevitably led to a decision by Prendergast to launch an investigation against her. The investigation led to a decision in November 2006 to dismiss Perelli on the grounds of sexual harassment and professional misconduct. It is rare for anyone to be terminated by the United Nations, let alone a woman for sexual harassment. The locks on Perelli's office door were changed, and she was escorted out of the Secretariat building by uniformed U.N. security personnel, just as Iraq prepared for a second successful election (its constitutional referendum).

The consequence of EAD's leadership crisis for Afghanistan was that it disarmed the division from playing an assertive role in setting policy for the parliamentary elections. This role began with the selection of the head of the electoral operation. Perelli's weakness meant that Arnault was able to conduct his own negotiations with Peter Erben over the conditions of his employment with UNAMA.[17] Erben, and his management team, immediately deployed itself to Afghanistan, retaining few of the experts who had worked under Austin, but hiring a large number of new international staff, many of whom had worked with Erben in the Balkans. Erben's budget for the 2005 elections was $150 million, more than had been spent on the registration and presidential election combined. Unlike the presidential election, where the funding came in unpredictable fits and starts, virtually all of the funding required for the parliamentary elections was provided up front—the donors, at least, appeared to have learned something from 2004. There was no need for the agonizing decisions that had faced Austin's team at the beginning of the registration process.

Arnault's insistence that UNOPS be the sole implementing entity, eliminating the complicated arrangement in 2004, where UNOPS, UNDP, and UNAMA all had responsibilities for different parts of the process, streamlined operational decisions and saved time. This allowed the complex election to be planned within the deadlines. At the same time, it removed some levels of accountability, which would lead to unimagined and damning consequences. The new implementation model worked as follows: Arnault instructed Helseth, the head of UNOPS, to give Erben what Erben said he needed for the election. Erben's shopping list was long, and he hedged his logistics with money. Anecdotes abounded about spending decisions, such as the purchase of simultaneous translation equipment before it was discovered that there were no available simultaneous translators. Ballots were ordered in such precautionary quantities—and flown in from Austria and the United Kingdom in a convoy of Boeing747s and Ilyushins—that, in the end, given the relatively low turnout, millions of dollars worth of unused ballot papers had to be shipped to Pakistan to be incinerated, also at significant cost.[18]

It was clear a few months into the parliamentary process that the rate of spending was such that the initial budget would be surpassed. Erben informed donors that the budget should include a ten percent contingency factor. This was noted by donors, but not acted upon. As election day approached and passed, the project began to run out of money. The high costs of the international salaries meant that each passingday added to the financial deficit.[19] A quick decision had to be made: halt everything until the additional funds required for the project were provided, or continue in the expectation that they would eventually be provided. The second option was technically not legal according to United Nations rules, since a project cannot spend money that it doesn't have. But since money is fungible, cash assets are frequently lent from one project to another and repaid once funds are provided to the borrowing project. The books are then balanced through accounting when the projects are over. The only requirement is that the funds required for both projects are paid in full. Donor representatives in Kabul strongly pushed the United Nations to continue electoral operations, promising that they would pay whatever the overrun would be at the end of the project. The political process was, as always, a priority. The rest was just accounting. In the end, the cost overrun was around $15 million, which UNOPS had covered with money from other projects..

As far as donors were concerned, the entire electoral process dictated by Bonn was now, finally, considered to be complete.[20] A parliament had been directly elected for the first time in Afghan history. Speeches were made, congratulations were issued, backs were slapped, and, of course, the books were closed on the election. The Erben team quickly folded its operation and left the country, leaving behind a three-month, $5 million "capacity building" project design, which was essentially a quick and dirty diversion to cover their hasty retreat. The question of the cost overrun was not addressed. The extra $15 million had to be swallowed by UNOPS.[21]

Electoral, Security and Political Developments Resulting from the Parliamentary Elections

The legacy of 2005 began to stamp itself on the direction of Afghanistan's democratization and institutional development. The immediate consequence of the financial deficit was lack of sufficient funds to sustain an independent election commission that "will have the high integrity, capacity and resources to undertake elections in an increasingly fiscally sustainable manner by 20 March 2009," as had been agreed by the Afghan government and its international backers in a conference held in London in early 2006, and codified in the Afghanistan Compact.[22] Normally, a large electoral operation would be followed by long-term capacity building-project that would work with the electoral institution between elections to ensure that the succeeding election would require far less international support. This was done, for example, quite successfully in East Timor. Donors, however, were reluctant to spend more money on a follow-up capacity-building project because they knew that whatever funds they provided would have to go first to paying back the $15 million debt. For nearly a year virtually nothing happened with the commission. Many of the national staff who had gained experience in Afghanistan over the previous two years drifted away because there was no money to pay them.[23] Vehicles and equipment began to disappear. The entire structure that had been built up over the previous three years essentially deflated.

This should prompt a closer look at the way donor decisions are taken. Arnault's desire to streamline operations and Erben's extravagance were one thing. But in the end they had delivered what donors wanted: elections held on time and whose results were "good enough" to be politically accepted. What is incomprehensible is that, having made that bargain, they should throw away a $300 million dollar investment for the sake of $15 million in overspending. It is as if, for want of financing to finish the final three stories of a skyscraper, its financers decided to tear the entire structure down rather than put up the remaining capital to complete it. This attitude is nonsensical when dealing with a piece of infrastructure, and tragic when applied to the fate of a country.

In addition to donor fatigue, the consolidation of democratic institutions was hindered by Afghan bureaucratic complexities. The staff of the electoral commission had been almost entirely funded by the international community. When the parliamentary elections were over, it became necessary to establish the commission as a national institution. One of the new parliament's first tasks was to create and fund the commission. This also meant that the electoral staff needed to become Afghan civil servants. The Afghan Civil Service Commission, however, resisted the transfer of election staff onto the civil service rolls because many of them did not have the education requirements established by the commission. The unique and specialized experience they had gained counted for nothing. After much discussion, the Civil Service Commission finally gave in and agreed to accept the electoral staff on an exceptional basis. In the 18 months it took for this to happen, many of the most qualified Afghan election workers—including four of the 11 department heads—found work elsewhere. Similarly, those initial 18 months would have been ideal to use for additional training, before planning would have to begin for the 2009 presidential election.

The second effect of the 2005 elections was political. The fact that so many political figures perceived to be responsible for much of the country's miseries over the previous decades were elected to parliament created an initial disappointment among votes, along with the many allegations of fraud that accompanied their election. Since the process was so rushed—especially the vetting of candidates and the civic education campaign—most of the so-called "warlords" ended up in parliament instead of continuing to be marginalized. This was to a degree expected; it echoed the political decision at the Emergency Loya Jirga to include these figures because to exclude them could turn them into spoilers. But voters saw the result as excessive. Few efforts had been made, as with Dostum the previous year, to demonstrate that participation in parliament was not a right that stemmed from the power they held. On the contrary, it required political responsibility and some demonstrations of commitment to the democratic political order.

The electoral law contained provisions to prevent those who had been convicted of crimes against humanity and those who had connections with armed groups from running. But the parlous situation of Afghanistan's judiciary meant that no Afghan had ever been convicted of crimes against humanity, and the process of determining who had links with armed groups was susceptible to manipulation, including by President Karzai who resisted efforts to disqualify his allies who he wanted to see in parliament.

Of the more than 2,800 candidates for the lower house, only 34 were formally barred from running because of links to armed groups.[24] The International Crisis Group reported, "That such questionable personalities were able to contest the polls caused consternation and confusion."[25] The process itself was seen as riddled with fraud by voters, deepening their cynicism. The trend line of optimism that had been rising until the end of 2005, tipped downwards once the new parliament assembled. Hossain Ramuz, an Afghan who worked with the National Democratic Institute and later with the Afghan Independent Human Rights Commission, divided the post-Taliban period into two phases: "a phase of 'optimism about a developing party pluralism' (2001-2004) and a phase of disillusionment."[26]

In early 2006, coincidentally or not, the Taliban insurgency began to gain significant ground, increasingly denying territory to the government and international aid agencies and denying hope to ordinary Afghans. In Kabul, the political class became increasingly involved in petty but venal politics, where the best administrators were driven out. Karzai, lacking now either the sound advice he used to receive from Brahimi and Khalilzad, began to rely increasingly on his tactical aptitude for balancing rivals, shuffling a number of mediocre and corrupt ministers through his ministries and governorships. The policy described earlier of gradually removing or weakening the worse of them was slowly abandoned. At the same time, the robustness of the narco-economy abetted an explosion of corruption within the police and government, causing an even greater loss of trust in the government. This development provided both material resources and political justifications for the new insurgents.[27]

And what of the politics that emerged from the parliamentary elections? Given the debate over the electoral law, it is worthwhile to examine the results of the parliamentary elections and the effect of SNTV. In terms of effective representation, Andrew Reynolds pointed out in a post-election article that:

> When judging the relationship between votes and seats in the Wolesi Jirga, it is important to stress that the candidates elected are not those for which a majority of Afghan voters cast their ballots. Just over two million of the more than six million votes (32 percent) were cast for winning candidates, and thus four million votes (68 percent) were cast for candidates who lost. The extent of this "wasted vote" is remarkably high; in comparison, only 5.3 percent of votes were wasted in the January 2005 Iraqi elections, and less than 1 percent in South Africa's first democratic election in 1994.[28]

If the major flaw of the Bonn Agreement was that the initial political settlement was not representative, and the major function of the Bonn process was to gradually provide that representation, then the SNTV system, because it structurally worked against representation, undermined the entire point of having elections.

Furthermore, the UNAMA electoral team's fears about the instability of the system were largely borne out, as Reynolds also demonstrated:

> The first seat in each region was won with an average of 11.5 percent of the vote, and the last seat was taken with an average of just 5.7 percent. In Kabul province, more than 400 candidates competed for 33 seats, and the last seat went to a candidate who received only 0.5 percent of the vote. SNTV indeed caused the lottery effect we had predicted, especially in the larger districts. On average, there were only 864 votes between the lowest-polling elected candidate and the highest-polling (male) runner up. Such tiny margins brought into dispute the results in areas tainted by vote fraud and campaign manipulation.[29]

There were some positive political developments from the election, as well. The first was that political parties played a more important role than expected. As Andrew Wilder wrote in his comprehensive analysis of the 2005 parliamentary and provincial council elections, "given the unpopularity of political parties, candidates officially affiliated with a registered party did remarkably well in the elections."[30] He goes on to note that 88 candidates elected to the Wolesi Jirga, or 35 percent, were formal members of parties.[31]

Parties were the primary vehicle of political organization for non-Pashtun groups especially. In the north, 79 percent of candidates were affiliated with parties, and in the Hazara-dominated Central Highlands 88 percent were. In the Pashtun-dominated south, however, only 32 percent of candidates were affiliated with parties. Instead, the main vehicle of political organization was the tribe. Wilder documents a number of interesting examples of tribal groups deciding among themselves to limit the number of candidates representing them in order to ensure that their (the tribe's) votes were not diluted. The ease with which political actors grasped the main features of the system and used them to their advantage was a positive development in that it suggested that electoral politics could function in even the most conservative parts of the country.

The third positive surprise was the strong performance of women candidates. According to Wilder, 19 Wolesi Jirga candidates won seats "in their own right," that is, without needing the quota that was part of the electoral law.[32] This was a particularly impressive result given that women had far more constraints on their campaign activities than men. Wilder theorized that "voting for female candidates was a protest vote against the many unsavory male candidates."[33]

Unfortunately, despite these glimmers of politics being played by the rules and yielding positive results, there was also a great deal of power being exercised outside the rules, through fraud and intimidation. As Wilder notes:

> The unsavory reputations of a large number of newly elected WJ members are tarnishing the image of the WJ before it has even convened. [...] According to one well-informed analysis, the newly elected [National Assembly] will include 40 commanders still associated with armed groups, 24 members who belong to criminal gangs, 17 drug traffickers, and 19 members who face serious allegations of war crimes and human rights violations.[34]

Before concluding this analysis of the results delivered by the SNTV voting system, some consideration must be given to the other side of the debate. If there were arguments in favor of SNTV, they were not the positive arguments of Meisburger—that SNTV would be a good system for Afghanistan's political development—but negative arguments: that it would be the least bad system. The proponents of PR, after all, based their arguments on an uncertain wager. The wager was that, at this very early stage in Afghanistan's democratic development, the requirement for parties under PR would force the creation of real parties. Furthermore, the parties that would be created would be cross-ethnic and national, rather than localized ethnic coalitions.

While we have seen that party-affiliated candidates did better than expected, the number of these candidates was so low that it is impossible to extrapolate, from their positive performance, a general conclusion that a party-based electoral system would have set Afghanistan on a clearer path to representative democracy. The good performance of parties in the election demonstrated that they were not as demonized as many had thought before the election. It did not establish, however, that political parties were strong enough to be genuinely representative, or developed enough to mobilize and organize broad support. We will never know whether Karzai was right about political parties being so distrusted and so weak that an electoral system could not be built around them. Even if his stance was taken for the wrong reason—a historical distaste of political parties masking his own fear of creating an organized opposition—it is quite possible that political parties were not sufficiently developed to sustain a PR system, and furthermore that the incentives of a PR system would have been insufficient to force their development in the short time before the first parliamentary elections. A case could be made, after all, that SNTV was the least-bad option for Afghanistan.[35] Unfortunately, the decision was never taken on the basis of an real debate on the positives and negatives of the system.

The New Parliament

On December 19, 2005 the new parliament convened for the first time. It was the first popularly elected parliament since the New Democracy experiment in the 1960s, which had ended in a coup, then engendered another coup, an invasion, a civil war, the Taliban theocracy, and the Bonn process. And while much had changed in the world—and in Afghanistan—since 1960, the Parliament that convened at the end of 2005 faced many of the same structural challenges that its predecessor had.

There were several common features between the new Parliament and the parliament of the 1960s. Both had feeble formal powers compared to the strong executive. Both contended with a state apparatus that was not evenly extended over the territory of the country. The state did not have the capacity to enforce legislation adopted by the parliament, which would likely lead parliamentarians to take their legislative roles less seriously. Both parliaments were formed by members who had little experience with parliamentary procedures and techniques. And in both Parliaments these members were elected mostly on the basis of local issues and local standing. In 1960 the King had refused to sign a political party law. In 2005, while a political party law was on the books, the electoral system did not encourage the formation of parties and those candidates with party affiliations had not even been able to indicate them on the parliamentary ballots. One major difference between the two Parliaments was, of course, the significant presence of women in 2005.

In the 1960s, these structural problems impeded the drafting, negotiation and adoption of legislation. Instead, parliament seized upon one of the few unambiguous powers available to it: the power to question government ministers and officials. As Robert Newell noted in 1972, "During its first six years the parliament has frequently demonstrated its ability to be an effective critic. Its committees have embarrassed officials on several occasions with disclosures of incompetence, corruption and various forms of favoritism."[36] It was unable, however, to do much else. In the 1969-70 session, parliament passed only one piece of legislation.

The ineffectiveness of the government in the 1960s took its toll. Ultimately, inability of the new constitutional institutions to effectively address the very real problems of Afghans—including a famine in 1972 in which approximately 100,000 died—led to an acquiescence to, or even welcome of, a 1973 coup by the King's cousin, Mohammad Daoud. The 1973 coup ended the King's reign and his ten-year "new democracy" experiment. In the meantime, paralysis inside the parliament had fostered a polarization of political forces outside. Parties on the communist left and on the Islamic right formed and strengthened, especially in the universities. Confronted with each other, they radicalized. Daoud's destruction of monarchical legitimacy made it harder for the weakening center to hold. The simmering political forces eventually exploded, launching the series of historical tragedies that Afghanistan has faced in the decades since. The 2005 parliament was of course the crowning achievement of the agreement that had been designed to put all of these political genies back into their bottle.

Despite the initial cynicism with which Afghans greeted the new parliament in 2005, in its first year it proved to be surprisingly progressive and responsible. Parliamentary sessions were broadcast on national television, and the image of former armed enemies debating the future of the country with some sophistication gave a brief, new sense of hope. Once members of parliament began to understand the powers that they possessed, and the inherent rents available to them, the body became increasingly ineffective. At the same time, very little international support was provided to ensure that parliamentary functions could take place. There was a lack of competent legislative drafters and a lack of resources to help its members remain in contact with their constituents, which undermined the legislature's credibility.

There has unfortunately been little research on how Afghanistan's parliament has functioned since 2005; the researchers' lack of interest is due most likely to the perceived lack of importance of the body itself. For most of its first sitting, it has been a docile branch of government, more docile even than its predecessor in the 1960s. The largest bloc in the Parliament was pro-government and generally was able to act in support of Karzai.[37] To the extent that members or parliament "are ideally perceived as having the ability to bring resources to their community from the national government and international community"[38]—in other words, more representatives of economic interests rather than political interests—then it was entirely rational for members to maintain good relations with the president. As a result, unlike again in the 1960s, the president was hardly challenged on legislation, budgets or cabinet nominations.[39] Finally, the parliament was prolific in adopting legislation, some of which was blatantly self-serving, such as the 2008 law extending amnesty to "all political groups and belligerent parties who were involved in a way or another in the armed conflicts before the establishment of the Interim Administration." This docility and token-oppositionism would, however, begin to change in its final year, after the second presidential election in 2009.

The institutional weakness of the parliament was reflected in an even more pronounced way on the provincial councils, which had also been elected in 2005. The councils' powers were not clearly defined in the Constitution, and the resources provided to them were even fewer than those provided to the national legislature. In mapping this legislative structure, where those who most directly represented the people were provided with the feeblest support, the weaknesses of Afghanistan's democratic design became apparent. The top-down approach ensured that one man in Afghanistan, the president, would hold effective powers that were in fact greater than those enumerated in the already strongly presidential Constitution. Liberal democracy requires not only elections, but also the separation of powers to ensure that no branch becomes so strong that it can undermine the others. The inattention to this basic fact left the executive branch in a position of great strength, which it used when it came time for the President's own re-election in 2009.

---

[1] EU DESM Final report of the 9 October Presidential Elections, p. 7.

[2] As noted in Chapter 3, The Asia Foundation had received millions in U.S. government funding to support the logistics of the Emergency Loya Jirga of June 2002, where Karzai had been elected head of the Transitional Administration, and the presidential elections. TAF unpretentiously described its contribution to the process as "TAF and Global Risk are providing invaluable advice and assistance to the JEMB Secretariat." The value was difficult to

quantify—the cost, at $15 million, wasn't. (http://www.asiafoundation.org/pdf/Afghan_globalfactsheet.pdf.)

[3] "PR vs. SNTV. Election Systems in Developing Democracies," Tim Meisburger, The Asia Foundation, November 18, 2004.

[4] Charles Tilly, *Big Structures, Large Processes, Huge Comparisons* (New York: Russell Sage Foundation, 1984) p. 11. Tilly argues that "In the analysis of social change, we cling loyally to ideas built up by nineteenth-century intellectuals. Intellectuals formed these ideas in their astonished reaction to what they saw going on around them: unprecedented concentrations of population, production, capital, coercive force, and organizational power. They formed ideas treating increasing differentiation as the master process of social change, ideas of societies as coherent but delicate structures vulnerable to imbalances between differentiation and integration, and other ideas connected to them." Tilly, *Big Structures*, p.2. There is little more remote from Afghanistan's historical experience than the political, economic, and social transformations that occurred in the west in the nineteenth century.

[5] Meisburger, "PR vs. SNTV."

[6] In the relatively peaceful 1970s, the Afghan communists could not avoid splitting into separate factions, the Khalq and the Parcham, which roughly broke down on Durrani-Ghilzai Pashtun lines. In war, the constant shifting of alliances among and within mujaheddin parties ensured a very stable "balance of power" that ensured no one prevailed.

[7] Meisburger, "PR vs. SNTV."

[8] Ibid.

[9] See Reynolds, "The Curious Case of Afghanistan" pp. 110-111 for a slightly more detailed account of the attempt in early 2005 to reintroduce a PR system. According to Reynolds, Karzai had been open to changing the system following sustained lobbying by the international community. He ultimately dissuaded, however, by the fear that charismatic non-Pashtuns would benefit disproportionately from a list system.

[10] An article written by Peter Erben and his associate, Ben Goldsmith, was revealing in this regard. Erben and Goldsmith present a checklist of processes determining a "successful election." If one removed the word "Afghanistan" from the text, one would hardly know where the election described was taking place or the political, ethnic, cultural and organizational realities that had posed so many specific and unique problems. It describes an approach based on process, rather than a country-specific approach that recognized that individual steps in that process might be more or less important in different contexts. See Erben and Goldsmith, "What Constitutes a Succesful Election? The Case of Afghanistan's National Assembly and Provincial Council Elections" in *Every Vote Counts*, eds. Richard W. Soudriette and Juliana Geran Pilon (Landham, MD: University Press of America, 2007) pp. 47-61.

[11] Many of these evaluations underestimated the extent to which numerous early bureaucratic impediments that presented themselves in the early stages of the process, were in fact resolved during the process.

[12] Sir Walter Scott, "The Lay of the Last Minstrel." *The Poetical Works of Sir Walter Scott*, ed. Horace E. Scudder (Boston: Houghton Mifflin, 1900) p. 74.

[13] See Chapter 9.

[14] Traub, *Best Intentions*, p. 190

[15] Michael Soussan provides a vivid personal take on the spreading scandal. See Michael Soussan, *Backstabbing for Beginners: My Crash Course in International Diplomacy* (New York: Nation Books, 2008).

[16] The story was widely reported. Two particularly thorough articles were Judith Miller, "Review Finds Abuses by Management at the U.N.'s Election Monitoring Office," *New York Times*, March 30, 2005, and Maggie Farley, "U.N. Elections Chief Accused of Harassing Staff, Misusing Funds," *Los Angeles Times*, March 30, 2005. The Miller article quotes a U.N. official noting that the report stems from differences over Iraq: "Although her boss, Prendergast, declined to comment, the report refers to a 'very public dispute' between the two that U.N. staffers say has its roots in their disagreement over how involved the U.N. should be in Iraq."

[17] Erben and his top advisors insisted on not being hired as U.N. staff, but as a "management team," hired directly from the Washington-based International Foundation for Electoral Systems (IFES).

[18] Erben insisted on the highest quality "safety paper" for the ballots. Unfortunately, most of the risk of fraud came not from the possibility that ballot papers would be forged, but from the lack of oversight at the polling station. In the end, Erben's pricey paper ballots were diligently marked for a given candidate and folded, several at a time, and neatly stacked in the ballot boxes by unscrupulous polling station managers.

[19] A major drain on the projects financing was the drawn-out counting process which required the presence of international staff to be extended far longer than originally anticipated.

[20] In fact, two major processes set in the Bonn Agreement remained to be completed. One was the holding of a census, and the other were the district assembly elections called for in Afghanistan's constitution. The willingness to declare victory led these details to be ignored.

[21] UNOPS' Afghanistan head, Helseth, was eventually fired from UNOPS. An internal UN investigation alleged that he had used hundreds of thousands of US dollars for his personal use, which he denied. In June 2009, Secretary-General Ban Ki-moon asked the United States to conduct a criminal probe into these allegations and waived his immunity. See Colum Lynch, "Ex-U.N. Official Spent Development Funds on Luxury Items, Probe Says" *Washington Post,* March 27, 2009, and Lynch, "U.N. Seeks U.S. Probe of Alleged Misuse of Afghan Aid" *Washington Post,* June 11, 2009. It is quite possible that the probe resulted from the overspending of UNOPS funds on the 2005 elections.

[22] The Afghanistan Compact was a series of benchmarks covering security; governance, rule of law and human rights; economic and social development; and counter-narcotics, agreed to by the Afghanistan Government and about fifty supporting governments at the London Conference on Afghanistan in January 2006.

[23] This problem was compounded by the need to shift staff members of the IEC from UN contracts to Afghan government contracts, a process that was frustrated by lack of cooperation from the Civil Service Commission. The

Commission, as is often the case in Afghanistan, had its own view about who should get jobs in the IEC, and these views often had little to do with the experience of applicants.

[24] The question of vetting candidates was one of the most difficult of the post-Bonn period and deserves much more comment than can be provided here. It could have been a moment where the policy of accommodation began to be reversed. In the end, this moment was not seized, and the policy of accommodation accelerated. See, for technical details of the vetting process, International Crisis Group, "Afghanistan Elections: Endgame or New Beginning?" Asia Report No. 101, Kabul/Brussels, July 21, 2005, pp. 17-18.

[25] International Crisis Group, "Afghanistan's New Legislature: Making Democracy Work" Asia Report No. 116, Kabul/Brussels, May 15, 2006, p. 4.

[26] See Ruttig, "Islamists, Leftists—and a Void in the Center" p. 18. To be fair, according to Ruttig, Ramuz credits the beginning of disillusionment not with the parliamentary elections themselves but with the decision to adopt the SNTV system, as a result of which political parties "reduced their activities and the internal reform mechanisms failed. As a result, Islamist parties became 'even more conservative and authoritarian'; none held a public congress."

[27] Amin Saikal, writing about Afghanistan in the twentieth century, said that "The patronage of a foreign power (or powers) proved akin to drug addiction." Paradoxically, in the post-Bonn period, for the insurgents drug addiction became increasingly akin to the patronage of a foreign power. See Saikal, *Modern Afghanistan*, p. 6.

[28] Reynolds, "The Curious Case of Afghanistan" p. 112.

[29] Ibid., p. 112 and 113.

[30] Andrew Wilder, "A House Divided? Analysing the 2005 Afghan Elections" Kabul, Afghan Research and Evaluation Unit, December 2005, p. 10.

[31] Andrew Reynolds has essentially the same data, but interprets it differently: "In the runup to the parliamentary elections, SNTV was expected to retard the development of a stable party system by causing political fragmentation, thereby making national legislation the business not of ideologically coherent political parties but of regional warlords and religious fundamentalists. The election outcome gave credence to each of these concerns. Only 16 percent of the more than 2,700 candidates were from registered political parties; these candidates won less than a third of the seats in the Wolesi Jirga." See Reynolds, "The Curious Case of Afghanistan" p. 113. Reynolds' own statistics back up Wilder's point: candidates affiliated with parties were disproportionately elected. The International Crisis Group adopted a middle position, reporting that 12 percent of candidates were affiliated with parties, and 14.5 percent of winners were "'officially' affiliated." The Group concluded that, "This suggests that a tie to a political party did not hurt a candidate's chances, as had been widely suggested by the executive." See International Crisis Group, "Afghanistan's New Legislature" p. 7.

[32] Wilder, "A House Divided?" p. 13.

[33] Ibid., p. 14.

[34] Ibid. See also the ICG, "Afghanistan's New Legislature" p. 6.

[35] It is worth noting that even proponents of PR for "new democracies," such as Arend Lijphart, also argue that "the Latin American model of presidentialism combined with PR legislative elections remains a particularly unattractive option." Afghanistan's presidentalist system could easily be said to fall into this category. See Lijphard, "Constitutional Choices for New Democracies" in *Global Resurgence of Democracies,* p. 167,

[36] Newell, *Politics of Afghanistan*, p. 175.

[37] See M. Hassan Wafaey and Anna Larson "The *Wolesi Jirga* in 2010: Pre-election Politics and the Appearance of Opposition" Kabul, Afghanistan Research and Evaluation Unit, June 2010, p. 3.

[38] See Noah Coburn, "Connecting With Kabul: The Importance of the *Wolesi Jirga* Election and Local Political Networks in Afghanistan" Kabul, Afghan Research and Evaluation Unit, May 2010, p. 3.

[39] The main exception being the rejection by the Wolesi Jirga in 2007 of Karzai's nominee for Foreign Affairs, Dadfar Rangin Spanta. As a sign of the president's strength, however, he appointed Spanta regardless of the rejection. While Spanta was able to carry out his functions, Karzai's peremptoriness towards parliament precipitated a minor constitutional crisis. See John Dempsey and J. Alexander Thier, "Resolving the Crisis over Constitutional Interpretation in Afghanistan" Washington, D.C., United States Institute of Peace, March 2009.

16
Reckonings: The 2009 Presidential Election

The 2009 Afghan presidential election was a perfect political storm that severely stressed the structures of the Bonn process and came very close to breaking them. Had that been allowed to happen, Afghanistan in 2009 might have looked very much like it had 1992, when the political consensus broke down and led to civil war. A new civil war would, however, have taken place in the midst of an ongoing insurgency, leaving the international forces in Afghanistan with no clear state to support and no obvious faction to back. As unhappy as the outcome of the 2009 election was for those who had higher hopes for Afghanistan, it was in fact the least bad outcome of an extremely perilous situation.

A sober analysis of the election and the crisis it begat became difficult following the public and bitter controversy between the head of UNAMA, Kai Eide, and his political deputy, Peter Galbraith. Anyone who followed the well-covered 2009 election in the western press would come away with the impression that Eide had forged such a close relationship with President Karzai that he decided to overlook—and even cover up—significant fraud in the elections in order to allow Karzai to continue in office.[1] They would have also come away with the impression that Galbraith, acting more virtuously, had tried to prevent that fraud and was fired by the U.N. Secretary-General for refusing to be complicit with the fraudulent election. This narrative was cemented through a series of self-serving editorials that Galbraith placed in the U.S. press after being sacked by the U.N. Secretary-General in September 2009. His version has been accepted at face-value by journalists covering the issue. As always, the issue was more complex and the real story leant itself less to the caricatures of heroes and villains that emerged from Galbraith's editorials, and more to the difficult realities of politics in Afghanistan, and burden of its post-Bonn democratization effort.

In the same spirit of revealed bias that I have tried to maintain throughout this book, my own role in the events that followed must be established. I was the head of the Afghanistan team at U.N. headquarters, working for DPKO and backstopping UNAMA. In that capacity, I had worked closely with Eide after his appointment in the spring of 2008. Eide had asked me to join him in Kabul as his Special Assistant in early 2009. Of course I accepted. We got along well on a personal level; professionally I admired the energy he had applied to strengthening the mission, as well as the strategic vision he had articulated for UNAMA and the international community. Most of all I appreciated the respect he had for Afghans and their sense of dignity. In the dispute that would break out between Eide and Galbraith, I was fully on Eide's side. What follows is very much an explanation of the thinking behind the policy position that Eide took, based on an analysis of the situation we were confronted with in 2009. Many of these complexities were the *reductio* of decisions that had been taken long before, during the holding of the 2004 and 2005 elections.

Much had changed in Afghanistan between 2005 and 2009. First, the security situation had deteriorated dramatically. According to the U.N.'s Department of Safety and Security (DSS), the first six months of 2009 saw the highest month-on-month levels of security incidents since 2001. There were, for example, 849 incidents per month compared to 626 in the same timeframe the previous year. These trends were the extension of a consistent month-on-month rise in security incidents since 2001.

Second, Karzai's government had begun to bleed legitimacy among the Afghan people and the international community. Karzai's policy of shuffling incompetent and corrupt power-holders through ministries and governorships, rather than trying to sideline or even arrest the worst of them, had by early 2009 brought neither stability nor state effectiveness.[2] As a result, during Karzai's first administration, despite hundreds of millions spent on "capacity building" by the international community, Afghanistan became *more* corrupt—falling from 117 on Transparency International's list of most corrupt countries several years ago to the second most corrupt in 2009.[3]

Blatant and growing corruption undermined Karzai's standing with his two main constituencies: the Afghan people and the international community, the latter which was losing soldiers at an increasing rate to bolster a government that was becoming more and more difficult to defend publicly. Popular frustration with Karzai's government was exploited by the Taliban, particularly in Pashtun areas, bolstering the popularity of the insurgents as the government's legitimacy declined.[4]

In UNAMA, Jean Arnault completed his long stay in Afghanistan in early 2006. His replacement was a German politician from the Green Party. Thomas Koenigs, who had previously headed a small U.N. human rights mission in Guatemala. Koenigs had no prior experience in Afghanistan, nor in running a large mission. His influence over Karzai and Karzai's ministers during his two years in Kabul was minimal. UNAMA appeared to enter a period of drift just as Afghanistan continued its slide towards instability. Koenigs' political deputy (the function Arnault had had relative to Brahimi) was a young Canadian diplomat, Christopher Alexander, who had previously been his country's ambassador to Kabul for many years. That Koenigs and Alexander had somewhat differing views on UNAMA's role and the future of Afghanistan, as well as a far strong network of Afghan and international contacts, did not contribute to the overall coherence of the mission. Koenigs left in December 2007, replaced in March 2008 by Eide, a Norwegian diplomat. Eide, as his country's ambassador to NATO for the previous several years, had followed Afghanistan closely and knew most of the main figures in the Afghan government. To address the general perception of UNAMA's lack of direction, the mission's mandate was "strengthened," on paper at least, also in March 2008 through a Security Council resolution.[5]

There had been changes at U.N. headquarters in New York as well. Perelli was replaced as Director of EAD by Craig Jenness nearly a year after her dismissal, during which time the division had been led by an interim director, but not an electoral expert, from within the Department of Political Affairs. Jenness had worked for Erben as head of the Pakistan out-of-country voting effort in 2004, and immediately afterwards had headed the independent panel that Arnault had created to examine the allegations of fraud.

Perelli, some months after her dismissal,[6] was hired as the Executive Vice-President of IFES, the Washington-based electoral foundation that had been the vehicle for the management contract for Erben and his team in 2005. In an odd professional resurrection, Perelli would visit Afghanistan on IFES' behalf in mid-2009—IFES had again been given a large contract by USAID to provide electoral assistance. She would end up prolonging her stay until long after the election was over, and played a critical role in helping to resolve the post-election crisis, working closely with Eide.[7]

In the years between 2006 and 2009, donors did not pay a great deal of attention to electoral support in Afghanistan. After several years in which elections had dominated the agenda, and hundreds of millions of dollars had been spent, a predictable fatigue set in. A small UNDP-run project was eventually established in October 2006, entitled ELECT (Enhancing Legal and Electoral Capacity for Tomorrow), which mostly focused on technical options for a new voter register. Very little support was provided to the Independent Election Ccommission (IEC) after the 2005 elections (in 2009, the AIEC was commonly referred to as the IEC, and will be henceforth in this text). Apart from supporting the IEC, another missed opportunity for electoral development in the post-2005 period was, as Scott Worden points out, the failure to "launch a comprehensive civic-education campaign designed to teach voters, candidates, political parties, polling workers, and civil servants what it means to participate in a democratic system and what roles they need to play to create a fair process that returns fair results for all."[8]

As the 2009 electoral date approached, it became clear that ELECT would have to be significantly expanded to provide the technical support that would be required by the IEC. The structure and extent of the U.N.'s support for the 2009 election was defined by an EAD Needs Assessment Mission conducted in late 2007, led by Jenness. The mission's recommendations took several months to be endorsed, and it was only in the early summer of 2008 that ELECT was finally retooled and given the resources it would need to support the Afghan commission. As before, the election would have to be almost entirely financed by the international community, with UNDP as the main channel, because the Afghan government had made no budgetary provision for holding elections. EAD and UNDP selected an Australian expert, Margie Cook, to head the strengthened ELECT project and act as the lead electoral advisor to the Afghan Independent Election Commission. Cook had co-written the UNDP evaluation of the 2004 and 2005 election, so she was not unfamiliar with the challenges and complexities of organizing elections in Afghanistan.

While the U.N. would provide a great deal of support to the Afghan commission, the 2009 elections were supposed to be the first run by an entirely Afghan institution. This fact was widely hyped, but was also misleading. Had an institutional approach been adopted earlier, the commission would have been staffed by the same Afghans who had been through two previous elections, learning how to conduct them alongside international experts. Instead, the aftermath of the 2005 election had put a brake on institutional development; there had been significant staff turnovers since then. While the 2009 election was the first Afghan-run election, most of the individual Afghans running it were involved in elections for the first time. The formal role of the U.N. was to provide technical support to the commission.[9] This was the sort of mandate that would normally be applied to a far-more experienced and capable electoral commission than the one that existed in Afghanistan in 2009. In this mismatch between Afghan capabilities and international mandates, which was in effect yet another mismatch between political fiction and reality, lay the roots of the frustration and incomprehension that would follow.

U.S. Policy during the 2009 Election

The policy of the United States, as the most important international presence in Afghanistan, would also have a significant effect. Many of the actions of Afghanistan's politicians during the election were reactions to perceptions of U.S. policy, rather than to the incentives of the electoral rules. Galbraith's somewhat unorthodox appointment to UNAMA was itself perceived as an element of this policy. Following the decision of Alexander to resign from UNAMA in early 2009, a selection process was initiated to replace him. This process was fairly well advanced when Richard Holbrooke was appointed as President Barrack Obama's senior advisor on Afghanistan and Pakistan. Holbrooke took an immediate interest in UNAMA's political deputy position, and proposed Galbraith as a candidate. Holbrooke and Galbraith had a well-known and longstanding relationship of trust. The appointment of Galbraith was eventually accepted by the U.N. Secretary-General, and was announced in March 2009.

The issue was not handled by Holbrooke's team in a way that would establish confidence between Eide and his new deputy. Just as Galbraith was being described in the Washington press as a member of Holbrooke's team in Kabul, along with the new U.S. ambassador and the new Commander of ISAF,[10] Holbrooke was reported as making negative comments about Eide in the press. The *London Times* reported that "a 'U.S. diplomatic source said that Mr. Holbrooke considered Mr. Eide 'useless and ineffective.' 'Galbraith is a much stronger personality, he's a bigger name, from a bigger country and he is going to carry more weight,' the official said."[11] The cumulative effect of this media strategy was to raise the suggestion among many in Afghanistan that Galbraith was working for Holbrooke more than for Eide.

Galbraith, for personal reasons, was not able to deploy to Kabul until early June. By that time electoral preparations were well-advanced. Eide and his team had taken a number of measures to attempt to level the political playing field. Everyone recognized that the stakes of the election were extremely high. Karzai, running for re-election, faced significant popular dissatisfaction. Furthermore, the areas where he expected to find his electoral—and ethnic—base were also the centers of the insurgency. It was not clear at all if people would be able to vote in large numbers in these areas because of poor security and the intimidation threatened by the Taliban.

The U.S., in addition, had recently been particularly critical of Karzai's leadership. As the *Washington Post* reported, "top administration officials thought that increasing pressure on Karzai would lead him to take meaningful steps to reduce corruption and improve governance. The officials also hoped to encourage potential rivals to run against Karzai by sending a clear signal that he was no longer Washington's man. [...] 'He was sure," [a Washington official] said, 'that Washington wanted him to lose.'"[12]

This strategy quickly became incoherent. Were the public statements against Karzai by American officials intended to force an improvement in his behavior as a leader? Or were they signals to other Afghan political actors that Karzai was no longer the favored U.S. candidate, and that Washington would therefore welcome and support any credible rivals who presented themselves? The manner in which the strategy was implemented blurred these two questions. Since they were mutually inconsistent, this blurring led to a fatal political confusion. Kabul was rife with rumors that Holbrooke had encouraged a number of other candidates to run against Karzai. Interestingly, instead of pushing the reform-minded candidates, such as Ashraf Ghani, Zalmay Khalilzad (the former U.S. ambassador), and Ali Ahmad Jalali (former interior minister), to select a single leader from among themselves, whom the others would support, thereby creating a powerful opposition ticket, Holbrooke was said to have encouraged several different candidates, each believing they were Washington's favorite. As Elizabeth Rubin reported in the *New York Times Magazine*:

> The new U.S. ambassador, Karl Eikenberry, barely a month into his term, made a point of showing up at news conferences with other presidential candidates, including Ghani and Abdullah. […] The American tactic seemingly worked. Afghans began talking overnight about how the Americans had adopted a new candidate — either Ghani or Abdullah.[13]

The administration's strategy had three results: it spread the field of candidates widely (more than 40 registered) reducing the chance that Karzai would get 50 percent of the votes and increasing the chance of a second round; it did not yield a credible candidate who could truly contest Karzai; and it made Karzai suspicious about every move the U.S. made with regard to the elections. Whenever the U.S. claimed it was attempting to level the playing field, Karzai saw them tilting it against him. For example, when ISAF carried out last minute military operations in Helmand province, ostensibly to secure the area to allow people to vote, Karzai claimed that these operations were designed to scatter voters likely to support him. Given the publicly-emphasized association between Holbrooke and Galbraith, Karzai and his team interpreted UNAMA positions expressed through Galbraith in the same manner.

Eide had undoubtedly developed a close working relationship with Karzai. After the doldrum years under Koenigs, when UNAMA had lost much influence with Karzai and his government, Secretary-General Ban Ki-moon's first instruction to Eide had been to establish a relationship of confidence with the Afghan president. Eide had used this relationship to try to influence Karzai positively across a range of issues during the first year of his mandate in Afghanistan. The inherent inconvenience of Eide's position was that he could not reveal where he had been successful because that would end his influence with the president. Where he had failed, however, was always apparent to all. It was therefore easy to portray Eide's failure to influence Karzai on any given issue as an *unwillingness* to do so. During the election process, this was depicted by Galbraith as a conspiracy.

Political Fantasy and Political Responsibility

The elections were held on August 20, 2009 against the politically-poisoned background just described. The organizational preparations of the elections had faced some of the now-familiar bureaucratic obstacles, but overall they took place with relatively little drama. Unlike in 2004, election day in 2009 saw a very high number of low-intensity incidents. The day had initially appeared calm, but when all of the security reports were compiled, it emerged that it had been one of the most violent days since Bonn, at least in terms of the number of security incidents that had occurred. It was also immediately clear, from the reports submitted by UNAMA political officers, that significant and unsubtle fraud had taken place across the country. The fraud was so blatant that it would require a policy response if the credibility of the election, and elections in general in Afghanistan, was to be saved. The question of what that response should be immediately divided UNAMA. One camp, led by Galbraith, favored making public statements about the fraud. The other camp, led by Eide, considered that it was the role of the electoral institutions to determine the extent of the fraud and to correct it, and furthermore that public statements made on the basis of unofficial reports would undermine UNAMA's ability to support those institutions. The controversy was bitter, became public, and called into question everything that had been done so far for electoral democracy in Afghanistan.

It was inevitable that, in 2009, the elections were more likely to reflect the prevailing situation than to fundamentally change it. Had stronger institutions been put in place over the previous years, the electoral process might have contributed to state-building. As it was, the failure of state-building helped to doom the election. This should have been easily understood by those analyzing Afghanistan's political situation. Instead, once again, many attributed a sort of political alchemy to the electoral event. When that failed—when the elections were not manifestly "free and fair" and when, especially, they did not result in a victory over Karzai—the deep disappointment of those who believed that Afghanistan could only improve if Karzai was removed once again yielded to political fantasy. As one of Galbraith's supporters in UNAMA put it in September 2009, the electoral crisis offered the opportunity of pressing "the reset button," as if in a country that wears its history as heavily as Afghanistan does, the past could be erased and forgotten, the mistakes of the international community forgiven, and all the players could return to the squares they had occupied on September 12, 2001 and start over.[14]

The only real option—the best of an unappetizing menu—was to allow the process to reach its conclusion while keeping it within three essential boundaries: the Constitution had to be maintained, the institutions of democracy had to be preserved as much as possible, and the idea of democracy had to not be totally discredited among Afghans. If these could be achieved, then work could begin once the election was over to correct the flaws of the democratization effort over the previous years. This was an emotionally unsatisfying conclusion to those who were frustrated with Karzai's leadership, and who chafed at seeing him elected despite so much fraud, much of it clearly orchestrated by him or on his behalf. But it was the only politically mature way to proceed. Any other approach risked real chaos.

The counter-argument against this position was superficially convincing: the Constitution was severely deficient, the institutions of democracy—particularly the Independent Election Commission (AIEC)—were clearly biased towards Karzai, and Afghans had already lost faith in democracy. The problem was that even if all of the above were true, there was still no better alternative to sticking with the Constitution that existed and trying to rescue the process such as it was through the institutions that existed. The conditions that had prevailed in

2003, when the Constitution was formulated, simply did not exist anymore. Re-opening a constitutional debate would probably have led to political deadlock, stripping away the only scaffolding that continued to hold together non-Taliban Afghan political leaders.

By 2009, it was too late and counter-productive to take such a doctrinaire position on electoral purity. Habits had been formed, incentives had been created, too many lapses had been tolerated, and now the consequences had to be faced. There were four essential themes from the preparations for the 2004 elections that had particular consequences for the 2009 elections. These were: first, the focus on elections as a political event rather than democratization as a process of institutionalization; second, insufficient—and insufficiently judicious—pressure by the international community on Afghan political actors, Karzai in particular; third, an uneven quality of electoral advice; and fourth, the dissonance between the political goals of the international community and the resources required to achieve those goals. All of these combined in 2009 to create a unique situation that required unique remedies.

The Failure of Institutionalization

By treating elections as events that take place every few years, rather than necessary but insufficient conditions of democratization, the need to develop electoral institutions was short-changed by Karzai's government and by the international community. In 2009, as in the previous electoral cycle, the immense logistical challenges of holding elections in Afghanistan were overcome in an admirable fashion—an achievement overlooked or minimized by those whose exclusive focus was fraud. The problem was not the hardware of the election but its software. The central institution, as we have seen, was the AIEC, which was technically unprepared and politically not trusted by Karzai's opposition given that Karzai himself appointed all of the commissioners.

The electoral law, adopted in 2005, that governed the 2009 election granted the president the sole authority to appoint members of the AIEC. As the ICG pointed out in June 2009, "...the IEC has been appointed solely by the president and its perceived partisanship is a major potential shadow over the legitimacy of the 2009-2010 elections—something that donors should have been far more vocal about before making funding commitments."[15]

The U.N. might have led the effort to be "far more vocal" but did not when this pressure might have been exerted. Koenigs did not have sufficient standing in Afghanistan to do so, and U.N. headquarters did not push this issue either. Previously, EAD used the requirement for a request for U.N. assistance as a form of leverage. The request was followed by a Needs Assessment Mission, which would propose the conditions under which assistance would be provided. The opportunity to set conditions for assistance might have been used to insist on a more credible electoral commission. The strategy was not guaranteed to work because, in the end, the international community wanted to see elections take place and knew that they would not without international support. Therefore, an insistence on too many conditions might have backfired. On the other hand, some concessions might have been gained, and at the very least Karzai might have been sensitized to the problem of appointing a commission that would oversee his own re-election. (Of course, the way the international community allowed the appointment of Farooq Wardak in 2004 to run the JEMB Secretariat had already sent a signal of ambivalence on this point.) Finally, it would have signaled that the U.N. was not necessarily going to provide unconditional support to a process about which it had evident qualms. But these qualms were not made evident at the time.

The obvious deficiencies and biases of the AIEC forced Eide to push for an Electoral Complaints Commission (ECC) structure that was particularly robust and that would need to be prepared to play a potentially corrective role relative to the IEC—as indeed happened. Eide's'decision to create a robust ECC overrode the objectives of Cook and the UNDP electoral team, which favored a weaker institution. The origins of the ECC lay in the commission hastily created after the 2004 election. In essence, the ad hoc measure demanded by Qanuni after 2004 was institutionalized and enshrined in the revised law that governed the 2005 elections. According to that law, the ECC was to be composed of five commissioners, three of whom were named by the SRSG (though formally appointed by Karzai). The other two were to be Afghans, one named by the AIHRC and the other by the Supreme Court. Given the real independence of the Human Rights Commission, this body was one that Karzai could not hope to influence.[16]

The process of forming the ECC, which came to play such an important role in resolving the electoral crisis, merits a brief parenthesis. In December of 2008, Eide had asked his Deputy for political affairs at the time, Chris Alexander, to provide international candidates for the commission. Alexander did not provide a list of ECC candidates until February. The list he provided contained only one international name—Grant Kippen, a Canadian expert of some experience who had been on the commission in 2005 and would eventually chair it again in 2009. Kippen was already in Kabul as an advisor to IFES, and was working on the problem of designing an appropriate ECC, based on his experiences five years earlier. The rest of the names were Afghans or Afghans with other citizenships.

Alexander's view was that the law could be read as saying that "internationals" could be Afghans, and that this was in fact the better option. Eide disagreed with this interpretation of what was, in the end, a rather clear provision of the law. He furthermore advised that, given the perceptions of partiality by the Karzai-appointed IEC, it was especially important that the ECC have strong international commissioners and as robust a presence across the country as possible. Kippen had strongly pushed this position as well, but it was not shared by Margie Cook, the head of the ELECT project.[17] Unfortunately, funding for the ECC was to come through ELECT, and Cook's suspicions of a strong ECC led her initially to deprioritize support for the institution that would become critical.[18]

Normally EAD, with its roster of electoral experts, would have provided names of prominent experts to serve as complaints commissioners. Given the initial preference for Afghans to sit on the Commission, this did not happen until very late in the process. In May, two additional names were finally provided. EAD offered Maarten Halff, a U.N. electoral officer with previous experience in Afghanistan (he had been the legal advisor on the JEMB in 2004, and Arnault's special assistant in 2005). Kippen proposed Scott Worden, an American who worked at the U.S. Institute for Peace, and who had worked as a legal advisor for UNAMA on electoral issues in 2005 and part of 2006. It did not help that all three international commissioners were from Western countries that were heavily involved in Afghanistan, a fact that would later feed Karzai's suspicions that the true motives of the international community were to unseat him.

In early September, when it became clear to those at the IEC that to continue to exclude votes based on fraud triggers would likely bring Karzai below 50 percent, the ECC faced its great test. Prior to the election, the IEC had adopted procedures, with advice from ELECT, such that any ballot box that contained more than 600 votes (the maximum number of ballots allocated to a station) or 90 percent for a single candidate was to be presumed fraudulent and the votes rejected. The rejection of these votes, as ballot boxes came in from the southern provinces, were inexorably reducing Karzai's percentage of votes from an initial high of around 56 percent. Facing the prospect that the rest of the ballots from the south would bring that below 50 percent, the IEC suddenly claimed that it had no legal authority to remove votes from the initial results (ignoring the fact that it had already removed a significant number of votes). Based on this surprising legal finding, the IEC announced on September 7 that it was abandoning the triggers, fixing Karzai's total at 54.6 percent in the preliminary count.[19]

The ECC immediately took the bold but necessary decision to order the IEC to conduct an audit of all votes in the preliminary results that fell under certain criteria that closely matched the IEC's original triggers. In essence, by this order, it reinstated the triggers. The courage of this position is worth highlighting. It was a direct institutional challenge to Karzai's authority, but solidly rooted in the law. It was also a challenge by the ECC to the IEC, which by its September 7 decision had revealed clearly its bias. The IEC, reluctantly, complied, though this required a great deal of cajoling and mediation by Eide. The IEC's acceptance of the ECC order avoided an immediate crisis. Nonetheless, it was essential now to ensure that the IEC and the ECC cooperated on establishing the terms of the audit. Given the state of tension in the country, and the breakdown in trust between Karzai and the international community, any decision by the internationally-dominated ECC that was not accepted by the Afghan IEC could be delegitimized as a violation of Afghan sovereignty. The IEC was, after all, a body created by the Constitution whereas the ECC was merely the product of the electoral law. The negotiation over the terms of the audit took many weeks with, again, Eide working behind the scenes to bring it to a successful conclusion.

The completed audit resulted in Karzai's vote dropping to 48.3 percent and the vote of his closest rival, Abdullah Abdullah, rising from 28 to 31.5 percent. The fact that the IEC, which had abandoned its triggers, accepted the de facto reinstitution of its triggers through the audit, was a major achievement. At the same time, that the internationally-dominated ECC had taken decisions bringing Karzai below 40 percent was fraught with danger. It took Karzai several weeks, staring into the constitutional abyss, before accepting to face a second round (this is described in greater detail below). The outcome was the result of the formal functioning of electoral institutions, but it was not a demonstration of effective institutional-building: an internationally-dominated body, of course enshrined in Afghan law, had to correct the blatant, partisan failure of an Afghan institution.

For the international community, which had again spent hundreds of millions of dollars on an Afghan election, the ECC's audit order and the agreement between it and the IEC on a methodology saved the election from descending into total farce. For international journalists, many of whom had covered Afghanistan for years and who were frustrated with Karzai, the parrying of what was seen as an attempt to steal the election was a great story. But in order to maintain the Manichaean narrative inspired by Galbraith's self-justifying op-eds from late September on, artful elisions were required. "Eide" was still covering up fraud on behalf of Karzai, while "the UN-backed" ECC, removed more than a million votes on suspicions of fraud.[20] The result was that Eide was criticized in the western press for abetting fraud in favor of Karzai[21] and at the same time lost the confidence of Karzai for having consistently defended the institution that removed his's fraudulent votes.

The ECC's correction of the IEC was the most concrete and dramatic manifestation of the costs of deficient institutionalization. There are a number of other institutions that are required for the effective functioning of democracy: political parties, civil society, justice institutions, security institutions, and an effective state apparatus. Little progress had been made since 2005 on developing any of these. A more exhaustive history of the 2009 elections might focus on how the lack of effective justice meant that many candidates were allowed to present themselves who might otherwise have been tried for criminal activities; how the failure of security institutions, in particular the police, contributed to making August 20, 2009 the most violent day in post-Bonn Afghanistan;[22] and how the lack of political parties and civil society organizations greatly diminished the breadth of information available to voters in order to form their electoral decisions.[23]

Karzai's Campaign Strategy

The 2004 election was essentially the popular ratification of Karzai's status as interim president. Both Karzai and the international community seemed to see the election in that way. Both were correct in that Karzai was the most popular candidate the election did reflect the popular will.[24] But in the ensuing five years Karzai had lost popular support. The degree to which Karzai himself acknowledged this was difficult to ascertain. Were his blatant attempts to ensure his own re-election including through fraud a sign that he felt he could not win a fair election? Were they the instincts of a politician who did not want to leave anything to chance?[25] Or were they a sign that he never really understood what elections were about? He had been given a great deal of leeway by UNAMA in 2004, when the entire international community wanted to see a Karzai victory. As a result he had never really been provided with what might be called an electoral education.

Apart from controlling the key electoral institutions, Karzai opted for a campaign strategy similar to the one he had used in 2004—a strategy that was ultimately undemocratic. His method of interacting with the electorate was not to appeal to the interests of voters or groups of voters, but to make deals with civil war-era power brokers who ostensibly could control blocs of votes.[26] This helped explain Karzai's decision to select Mohammed Fahim Khan as his First Vice-President—the same Fahim whom he had rejected under pressure from Brahimi and Khalilzad in 2004, as well as his rapprochement with Dostum just before the election. Interestingly, this tactic was less successful than it had been in 2004, suggesting that democratization efforts had achieved something over the past years, and that voters were willing to vote beyond their ethnic blocs, or for candidates other than those considered to be "their" strongmen. This is demonstrated by the relative successes of Abdullah and Bashar Dost, who finished second and third respectively, and neither of whom was considered to be a dominant leader of their respective communities. Abdullah's votes came from Tajik-dominated areas, despite the fact that Fahim was arguably a more powerful Tajik leader and certainly possessed a greater capacity to intimidate. Similarly, Bashar Dost, a member of parliament who ran his campaign from a tent across the street from the parliament building, won a large number of Hazara votes despite the fact that both of the main Hazara leaders had pledged their support for Karzai.

It is sadly telling that in the years between 2004 and 2009, Afghans had demonstrated that they understood how electoral processes could help them signal their political preferences, including their dissatisfaction with their leadership, while in the same time period the major donors providing assistance to Afghanistan had gradually lost their effectiveness in exerting influence over that same leadership. The president, in particular, had learned how to play the international community against itself. And the international community had set for itself, in the years between 2005 and 2009, other priorities besides the institutionalization of democracy. Karzai had read their disinterest accurately, and by the time they became interested again, his habits had already been formed. He had become immensely skillful at the tactical co-optation of leaders of powerful Afghan factions. Where this policy was exercised maladroitly, for example in Kandahar, where the Ghilzai's were largely excluded in favor of his own Durrani, and in particular Popalzai, tribesmen, he left the security problem that resulted to be handled by international forces. There was little room in this tactical game for a strategic vision of state-building, let alone one that was based on strengthening institutions.

The Defects of the Constitution

Another unfortunate legacy of the early transition period that had to be faced in 2009 were the technical defects of the Constitution concerning the electoral provisions. The consequences of the carelessness of these provisions will continue to bedevil every election held until the Constitution is amended; amendment will surely have other costs, to be paid most likely in the coin of human rights. The 2009 electoral process, from beginning to end, highlighted the parlous effects of the Constitution's electoral provisions.

The constitutional requirement to hold elections in the spring had generated a political crisis even before the process started, and had profound political implications as the process continued. According to the letter of the Constitution, the presidential term expired on May 21 and elections had to be held 60 days prior to that date. As discussed in Chapter 6, this timeframe for holding elections was unfeasible in Afghanistan for reasons of weather and geography. In mid-2008 the international community, the IEC, and Afghan political leaders had to again find a way of setting a realistic date for holding elections without causing a constitutional crisis. Again, the solution had to be political, because there was no way of holding summer elections without starkly contradicting one of the least ambiguous provisions in the Constitution. In August 2008, an agreement was reached between the IEC, the president's office, and the parliament to hold elections on August 20, 2009. In early 2009, however, Qanuni, now the Speaker of the lower house of parliament, threw a clever spanner in the works. While not challenging the agreement that elections be held on August 20, he maintained that Karzai's presidency would not be legitimate after May 22, the date set in the Constitution for the end of the presidential term. In other words, there would be a gap of several months where Karzai would not be the president, and would therefore not possess the formidable powers of incumbency. The local media was full of proposals to address the interregnum. The most popular were either that the First Vice-President should assume interim powers or that a caretaker government should be set up under the Speaker of the upper house, who was Mojaddedi.[27] None of these were clearly constitutional; then again, neither was the extension of Karzai's mandate. In fact, the only clear constitutional provision was declaration of a state of emergency, but this was something that everyone wanted to avoid for both proper and selfish reasons.[28]

In the end, Karzai resorted to a tool that he had used in the past—securing a decision from the pliable and loyal Chief Justice of the

Supreme Court (also a Karzai appointment) affirming that the presidential mandate was legitimate until the certification of the results of the next election. Prior to this, Karzai's first vice-president, Zia Massoud, declared that he would not support Karzai if he remained in power after May 22. Massoud resigned after the Chief Justice issued his ruling. This moment was the nadir of Karzai's political authority. Never, since his instauration at Bonn, had his hold on power been as uncertain as in February 2009, with his constitutional legitimacy seriously questioned and one of the top figures in his government essentially declaring his lack of confidence in him.

Another major problem presented by the Constitution was the requirement for a second round to be held if no candidate gained a majority in the first round, and especially the absurd provision that this second round should be held two weeks after first-round results were certified. The logic of a two-round system is based on preventing a minority candidate from being elected among a large field in the first round, and encouraging coalitions of political parties to align themselves around a preferred candidate in the second round.[29] Given Afghanistan's ethnic makeup, the chances of the first occurring were minimal. Given its current state of political development, in particular the lack of political parties, the second was almost impossible.[30]

The 50 percent barrier to election created a volatile state of political instability following the announcement of the IEC and ECC audit. The growing probability that Karzai would not win outright in the first round altered the calculations of the main players. The long process of adjudicating complaints and implementing the audit, with no established deadline for its completion,[31] brought to mind Arnault's frustration in 2004, when he exclaimed that Afghans did not have the patience to wait forever to know who their president would be. As the 2009 crisis wore on without any sign of an imminent result, banks reported that money was flowing out of the country as those with means began to protect their assets. Applications for visas at several regional consulates rose precipitously, in preparation for emergency flight. The lurking memories of 1979, 1992, and 1996, which had each seen a significant exodus of Afghans, encroached upon the present. More immediately, the constitutional requirement for holding the second round within two weeks of certification meant that the IEC had to order the printing of second-round ballots (because their printing and transport would take much longer than two weeks) long before it was officially announced that Karzai had won less than fifty percent of the votes.

The fact that the audit yielding this result had been ordered by the internationally-dominated ECC fueled the president's suspicions that the international community was interfering in the election result. Karzai's bitterness at what he perceived as outside interference to bring him below the threshold undoubtedly contributed to his dangerous brinksmanship that followed. He was not entirely wrong about this. In a meeting with President Karzai just after the election, Holbrooke had reportedly informed the president that he would not be considered legitimate if he won on the first round.[32] An anonymous "senior U.N. official" had unhelpfully stated the same to the *Guardian* of London, days after the election, saying that "there would be 'no real legitimacy if Karzai claims to have won on the first round'."[33] This contributed to the standoff that occurred after the audit results had been announced, when Karzai refused to accept a second round, insisting that he had won more than 50 percent according to the IEC's preliminary figures.

This game of political chicken was the most dangerous moment of the entire process. U.S. Senator John Kerry happened to be visiting Afghanistan at the time and was drawn into several long meetings with Karzai and a team of his ministers who exhaustively reviewed the audit methodology. In another twist in the tale, the audit had been partly designed by Carina Perelli, who was still in Kabul, representing IFES, and Carlos Valenzuela, perhaps the U.N.'s most brilliant and experienced electoral expert, who had been brought *in extremis* from the Democratic Republic of the Congo[34] to also assist in designing the audit. Perelli and Valenzuela, along with the ECC Chairman Kippen, were also called to the palace several times to explain and defend the audit methodology. Karzai evidently explored every possible option before finally, on October 20, accepting the necessity of a second round. This was the moment when he stepped back from the political abyss into which he had been staring, while his countrymen had been holding their breath. Karzai's announcement that a second round would be held on November 7 was greeted with pre-planned messages from world leaders praising his statesmanship. This was praise, in essence, for the statesmanship of not deliberately throwing his country into premeditated chaos.

The electoral provisions within the Constitution have other problems that remain unaddressed. Not least of these is that district boundaries have yet to be set, meaning that no District Council elections have taken place. As in the previous cycle, the constitutional requirement that one-third of the upper house be made up of representatives elected at the district level remains unfulfilled. Finally, there is also Afghanistan's punishing electoral calendar, which requires 13 elections in a 20 year cycle.[35] This provision is not directly relevant to this discussion, but is a reminder of the overall poor decisions on the electoral provisions of the Constitution.

The Quality of International Technical Assistance

Questions concerning the quality of electoral advice in 2009 were brought to the front pages of the world's newspapers, following Galbraith's allegations that the U.N. had not done enough to prevent fraud. In the numerous editorials he drafted following his dismissal by the U.N. Secretary-General, Galbraith essentially repeated the same three claims: that the U.N. had allowed "ghost polling stations" to be opened, that it had not leaned sufficiently on the IEC to reverse its decision to include votes suspected of being fraudulent, and that it had withheld information on fraud from the IEC and the ECC. In other words, the international community had failed in its assistance role.

The last claim was easily disproven, and UNAMA later documented the information that it had provided to both bodies and when it had provided it (though it is true that Eide had qualms about this information being misused).[36] The allegation, with its innuendo of "cover up", was far more dramatic than the facts. The information collected by UNAMA staff members on election day was for the most part anecdotal, incomplete, and useless to both bodies as proof of fraud. It had been collected by political affairs officers who were not necessarily familiar with the rules of the elections or observation methodologies, and who at times substituted their subjective views for what was appropriate according to the electoral law.[37] The quality of this information was sufficient for the purpose it was intended: to provide a contextual snapshot of how the election had gone, and to help in planning future operations. The implied suggestion by Galbraith that it was sufficiently robust to invalidate votes goes against every standard of electoral practice, not least the clear U.N. policy that it should not monitor elections in which it also provides technical assistance.

The question of ghost stations was more serious and here Galbraith had a legitimate point. The IEC had originally announced, as a planning figure, its intention to open approximately 6,900 polling stations. The number and location of these stations was based on the standard exercise of dividing the estimated electorate by the number of voters each station could accommodate and situating the resulting number of stations such that each voter had a more or less equal chance to vote.

The reality of conflict-riddled Afghanistan, however, was that many of the polling stations whose locations resulted from this theoretical exercise would be opened in areas that were known to be highly insecure, if not under Taliban control. Most of these areas were in the Pashtun-dominated south. This created a dilemma with no clear-cut solution: on the one hand was the risk of disenfranchising Pashtun voters by making polling stations less accessible to them; on the other the risk of opening stations where there was so little security that neither observers nor candidate agents could be present. In the latter case, these polling stations could—and in many cases did—become "ghost stations," in other words they existed on paper but did not actually open. Since no one would notice if these stations opened or not, corrupt electoral officials could simply not bother moving materials to where they should be opened and instead stuff the boxes unseen and return them to Kabul to be counted. There were a number of reports from the 2005 election where boxes never reached their designated location, but were instead kept in the offices of provincial governors or chiefs of police and stuffed there without ever being seen by a voter. It was more than plausible to presume that this would occur again.

Galbraith's diagnosis was correct, and in fact it was shared by Eide and others. In the weeks prior to August 20, numerous meetings were held between the IEC, the national security institutions,[38] UNAMA, ISAF, and ambassadors from the main troop contributing countries to reach a clear decision of which polling stations could be secured. The IEC maintained its position that it had determined polling station locations according to criteria of equitable representation. The IEC argued that if the security agencies determined that some locations could not be secured, then it would remove the stations. The IEC, in other words, shifted responsibility to the security institutions for a fundamental electoral issue.

The national security institutions of course all reported to Karzai. The heads of these institutions furthermore adopted an expansive notion of what could be secured. There were multiple motives for this. They might have been willfully closing their eyes to probable fraud; they might have been unwilling to admit how much of the country they were not able to control; or they might have been trying to allow as many Pashtuns as possible to vote to avoid disenfranchisement. The situation was complicated by the fact that a number of military operations were being conducted up to the day before the elections in order to secure as much of the country as possible on election day. But this made it unclear what areas actually would be secure on election day, creating an additional bias against closing some stations.[39]

The outcome of this long series of meetings was to eliminate around 700 of the initial 6,900 planned centers. Galbraith argued that 400 more should be eliminated. His was a minority position, however, even among international ambassadors. There was thought to be a real possibility that stations could open, and there was a clear interest in giving the benefit of the doubt to Pashtun voters whose sense of political alienation was already considered to be fueling much of the insurgency.[40]

Given the facts available at the time, this was not an unreasonable compromise. Furthermore, the result *had* to be a compromise. The international community did not control the IEC or the security institutions. It had the power to persuade and even to threaten to withdraw support, but short of stopping the entire election at that point—which not even Galbraith advocated—a negotiated solution had to be found The U.N., in particular, was constricted by its mandate to support Afghan institutions, rather than ditcate to them. The international community in general was trapped by its own rhetoric of "Afghanization;" and ISAF was limited by its need to preserve its relationship with the Afghan security institutions.

One of the factors that weighed on the thinking of the international community when these decisions were being taken was the fact that there were a number of "triggers" to indicate whether fraud had occurred at any given polling station. In other words, the risk of fraud in ghost stations would be mitigated by systems to catch fraud when the tally sheets reached the IEC headquarters in Kabul. For example, any tally sheet where more than 600 votes were recorded, or where more than 90 percent of the votes were for a single candidate, was to be withheld from the preliminary results.[41] These triggers, which were accepted by the IEC, provided a safeguard against whatever blatant fraud might be committed at the ghost stations.

Here, the ironic transparency of the 2009 election must be highlighted. Unlike in 2005, the IEC had taken the decision to post the results of the election online, polling station by polling station. Rather than the "cover-up" alleged by Galbraith, the problem was that so much of the fraud was so blatant that it could be inferred by anyone looking at the IEC data online. The IECs pro-Karzai bias, or perhaps its *fear* of not delivering for Karzai, was equally conspicuous when the commission took the blatantly pro-Karzai decision on September 8 to abandon the triggers and include all votes in its preliminary tally. The ECC then took the correct measure, which was to order an audit of all votes that met the original IEC triggers. In other words, the process worked. But it was a messy process that was difficult to explain to an international media that had seized on both the tabloid soap opera of the Galbraith-Eide feud and the newsworthy story of massive fraud being committed by Karzai while foreign troops were dying in the name of his regime.

Galbraith had successfully spun a media narrative of being the unheeded hero—of having proposed measures to mitigate fraud which had been rejected by Eide. Apart from the measures to reduce "ghost stations," which Eide had taken on board, Galbraith's only proposals were to "force" the security ministries to do what they would not do in terms of accepting the impossibility of securing 400 polling centers, and "force" the IEC to do what it would not do in terms of not abandoning its triggers. But where would this "force" come from? In one of his many articles, Galbraith claimed that Eide had overruled his efforts to "tell them [the IEC] to hold an honest election"[42]—as if a good talking-to were all it would have taken to set the IEC straight. But Eide had worked long enough in Afghanistan[43] to understand that head-to-head confrontations with Afghans generally only hardened their positions and weakened the bargaining position of the international community.[44] Galbraith himself admitted in public that after his attempt to "urge that the IEC stick with its established procedures," the "Afghanistan Permanent Representative [to the United Nations] threatened to have me expelled from the country."[45] The recent debate over official corruption in Afghanistan demonstrates this dilemma very well: as important an issue it is for the U.S., and as many resources as it puts into Afghanistan, neither public nor private political pressures have worked to effectively reduce the problem.

One measure that was hardly considered, by Galbraith or anyone else, was to count the ballots at regional or provincial centers, as had been done in 2004 and 2005 respectively, rather than at the polling stations. International observer groups, however, had recommended that counting should be done at polling station levels. For some reason, the observers believed that the risk of manipulating ballot boxes while they were being transported to provincial or regional centers was greater than the risk of fraud being committed at the polling station itself, where there were few observers or party agents, and that observation at thousands of polling centers would be easier than at 34 provincial counting centers.[46]

Ironically, the international community's efforts to ensure a credible election began to look, for Afghans, like international interference in their election. The Afghan political class, in particular, who observed closely the positions of the members of the international community, saw these positions as efforts to affect the results in highly specific ways.[47] This overall perception unfortunately undermined one of the big achievements of 2004, which had been the embrace by Afghans of the electoral process as their own. Now, elections increasingly appeared as a foreign imposition whose ultimate design was to control Afghans.

Insufficient Resources

The final theme carried over from 2004 to 2009 is the unwillingness of the international community to apply resources equal to its stated ambitions. Here, at least, one crucial lesson had been learned: the travails of funding that the 2004 team had to endure were not repeated again for the electoral event. In both 2005 and 2009 sufficient funds were provided up front to properly plan and implement the elections. Unfortunately, because of the lack of institutional continuity and capacity-building, the cost of each election kept rising.

A constant—and large—component of this cost was the lack of a reliable voter register. The 2004 register, as bad as it was, had been updated for 2005, but using essentially the same very basic technology. A pilot project funded by the United Nations Democracy Fund (UNDEF) explored several options for biometric registration. Disagreements within the Afghan government over which ministry should house the register prevented further progress. Between 2005 and 2009 there had also been discussions on establishing a civil register from which a voter register could be extracted. A civil register is a feature in most European countries. It essentially contains the essential details of each citizen and resident of the country. For the initial investments in carrying out a civil registration to pay off, however, an administrative apparatus must be in place across the national territory to register births, deaths, marriages, coming-of-age to vote, and other changes in civil status. This administrative apparatus does not exist in Afghanistan and, in all likelihood, will not exist for years or generations to come.

Looking back at the significant transformations in Afghanistan over the past eight years—transformations that have yielded both positive and negative changes—one is struck by two conclusions: the utter lack of progress made in building democratic institutions despite the hundreds of millions of dollars spent on democratic processes, and the holding of now four national elections (including the second parliamentary elections in 2010); and the fact that the enduring disconnect between the citizens of Afghanistan and their government—precisely what democratization efforts were supposed to mend—is one of the biggest factors behind the growth of the insurgency. Many discrete electoral tasks had been done well, and the key electoral events had been held, but they did not seem to add up to democratization.

---

[1] See Peter Galbraith, "Excerpts: Galbraith's Letter to U.N. Secretary-General," *New York Times*, October 1,2009.

[2] The Mujaheddin leaders had no administrative experience beyond running their parties, or *tanzims*. But these parties were essentially mini-rentier sub-

states: they were patronage based and loosely organized; their goals were securing support from outside patrons in order to combat the Soviets while at the same time fighting rivals within Afghanistan. Many of these rivalries continue to dominate political activity at the expense of state-building long after the civil war was over.

[3] Samuel Huntington has argued that "Corruption in modernizing society is thus not so much the result of the deviance of behavior from accepted norms as it is the deviance of norms from the established patterns of behavior." He adds, "The conflict between modern and traditional norms opens opportunities for individuals to act in ways justified by neither." See Huntington, *Political Order*, p. 60.

[4] The Taliban-led insurgency began as a reaction by a small group of defeated fighters to a specific government that it felt had been imposed from outside. Its ranks were swelled, however, in large part by those who were motivated by the *lack* of governance, as well as by the corruption within whatever government existed. The ground that has been lost will not be recovered easily. A highly worthwhile study that documents this point is Stephen Carter and Kate Clark, "No Shortcut to Stability: Justice, Politics and Insurgency in Afghanistan", Chatham House, December 2010.

[5] Security Council Resolution 1806(2008).

[6] Perelli contested her termination by the U.N. The first level of appeals for U.N. staff members exonerated her and recommended reinstatement or full compensation. The Secretary-General rejected this advice. The case is, as of this writing, pending before the final level of appeals, whose decision is binding.

[7] In an even stranger twist of fate, Peter Galbraith was responsible for bringing her to Kabul. They had worked together in East Timor and in Iraq. One of Galbraith's first acts upon arriving in Kabul was to ask IFES to send her to Afghanistan to evaluate the status of preparations. Once the crisis began, however, she rejected Galbraith's "megaphone diplomacy" approach to dealing with the fraud, as described in greater detail below, and backed (and even informed) Eide's approach.

[8] Scott Worden, "Afghanistan: An Election Gone Awry," *Journal of Democracy,* July 2010, Vol. 21, No. 3, p. 17.

[9] In 2006 and 2007, the Security Council simply renewed UNAMA's mandate on the basis of recommendations set out in a February 2006 report of the Secretary-General. It was not until March 2008, when the Security Council, considerably alarmed by the deterioration of the situation in Afghanistan, redrafted UNAMA's mandate in fairly specific terms. The mandate for elections read as follows: "support, at the request of the Afghan authorities, the electoral process, in particular through the Afghan Independent Electoral Commission (AIEC), by providing technical assistance, coordinating other international donors, agencies and organizations providing assistance and channelling existing and additional funds earmarked to support the process." (Security Council resolution 1806 (2008) This language was essentially renewed in the 2009 mandate.

[10] The appointment of Galbraith was portrayed in the U.S. media as part of the U.S.-driven civilian surge, and his presence in UNAMA as part of President

Obama's new team in Kabul. See for example, James Bone and Tom Coghlan, "US strengthens diplomatic presence in Afghanistan," *London Times*, March 17, 1009; Matthew Lee and Anne Gearan, "Officials: U.S. Prepares Civilian 'Surge' in Afghanistan to complement higher troop levels," Associated Press, March 18, 2009; Warren P. Stroebel and Jonathan S. Landon, "Obama's Afghanistan 'Surge': diplomats, civlian specialists" McClatchy, March 18, 2009; and Karen DeYoung, "Civilians to Join Afghan Buildup; 'Surge' Is Part of Larger U.S. Strategy Studied by White House," *Washington Post,* March 19, 2009.

[11] James Bone, "Peter Galbraith will take key UN role in Afghanistan 'civilian surge,'" *London Times*, March 26, 1009.

[12] Rajiv Chandrasekaran, "A Softer Approach to Karzai," *Washington Post,* November 20, 2009. See also, Joshua Partlow and Karen DeYoung, "US Looks to Reduce Reliance on Karzai," *Financial Times* (London) August 14, 2009.

[13] Elizabeth Rubin, "Karzai in his Labyrinth" *New York Times Sunday Magazine*, August 9, 2009, p. 44.

[14] This instinct for fantasy manifested itself in Galbraith's proposal to cancel the election results entirely and replace Karzai with an Afghan technocrat such as Ashraf Ghani, who was more palatable to the West. See James Glanz and Richard A. Oppel, "U.N. Officials Say Americans Offered Plan to Replace Karzai" *New York Times*, December 16, 2009, an article that to my experience is largely accurate. Galbraith, however, denied this account in a letter to the *New York Times* dated 28 December 2009. In a modern version of the Vietnam-era logic of destroying the village in order to save it, the argument here was that it was necessary to cancel the elections in order to justify the millions of dollars that had been spent on them and the lives of foreign soldiers who had died trying to make them safer.

[15] International Crisis Group, "Afghanistan's Election Challenges," Asia Report No. 171, Brussels, 24 June 2009, p. 9.

[16] Indeed, the AIHRC representative on the Commission played a highly courageous role, withstanding threats and pressures, and perhaps compromising his future career in government in Afghanistan, to uphold the integrity of the election.

[17] In an interesting twist, the need to quickly reinforce the capacity of the ECC as the extent of fraud and the number of complaints became known, forced IFES to play a much larger role than intended. IFES was providing support to the process under the U.N.'s coordination mandate. The fact that it could hire staff much more rapidly than UNDP meant that it was essential to ensuring that the ECC had the capacity to meet expectations of it. Perelli, then the Executive Vice-President of IFES, found herself in Afghanistan during the electoral crisis in Kabul, working closely with Eide's office on both strengthening IFES and advising on the audit process. Carlos Valenzuela, who had been her most trusted operator during her EAD days, was brought in temporarily by the U.N. from his position as head of the electoral unit in the U.N. mission in the Democratic Republic of Congo to help with the audit.

[18] Some close to the situation later spoke of a sort of electoral "Stokholm syndrome," a shorthand description for a situation where UNDP ELECT's

managers opposed a robust ECC because they feared ECC criticism of the IEC would end up reflecting badly on them.

[19] Here one is reminded of Austin's email to Wardak in February 2004, warning of pressures "from those who may seem to have the power to ruin you or to make your life much better." See Chapter 9.

[20] The auditing of the ballot boxes, rather than a recount, was a highly unusual process. It was required, however, by the amount of time that a recount would take, pushing the process into the winter months, and by the nature of the fraud. A recount would not reveal much about ballot stuffing. Interestingly, the election results after the fraudulent votes had been "cleaned" by the audit reflected the results of two pre-election polls carried out by the Washington-based International Republican Institute (IRI). These polls had yielded at least three surprising—or at least not obvious—results: Karzai obtaining less than 50 percent; Bashardost, the Hazara reformist candidate gaining around 10 percent; and Ashraf Ghani obtaining less than two percent. All of these results were reflected in the post-audit figures, after the fraudulent votes had been "cleaned" from the preliminary results.

[21] The International Crisis Group, in a report at the end of 2009, actually called for the dismissal of Eide, positing that "if UNAMA's credibility is to be restored, Eide must step down." The report was basically a reflection of Galbraith's version of the dispute. The ICG, in writing the report, spoke to none of Eide's main electoral advisors. This was the first time the ICG had ever called for any head of a U.N. mission to step down. See International Crisis Group, "Afghanistan: Elections and the Crisis of Government," Asia Briefing No. 96, Kabul and Brussels, November 25, 2009. Eide protested to Louise Arbour, the president of the ICG, and presented a letter cataloging the report's numerous misstatements of fact, to no effect.

[22] Violence in this case is measure by the U.N.'s tracking of security "incidents," which include threats. The insurgency seemed to have taken a conscious decision not to cause significant amounts of bloodshed. For example, there were no suicide bombers in polling stations. But it did demonstrate its strength by the large number of low-level incidents, and its breadth by the geographic distribution of these incidents. Its capacity for intimidation was especially obvious in the south, where the insurgents were able to suppress voter turnout.

[23] This point is essentially valid. It was true, however, that many candidates were able to wage a campaign on ideas. Also, unlike in 2004, where there was a candidate for each major ethnicity, and voters tended to vote for the candidate of their own ethnicity, the 2009 election was much less ethnically based, a point that Karzai made when he finally accepted the second round.

[24] See Chapter 10, footnote 14.

[25]Ashley Tellis, a Senior Associate at the Carnegie Endowment for International Peace, made this point during a hearing on Capitol Hill at which Galbraith was also testifying. "What we saw in this election was essentially Karzai behaving as a rational politician, understanding that his power base in the south would not be able to exercise their suffrage because of Taliban intimidation. He did what a rational politician in the state of nature would do; he

cooked the books to win the elections." Hearing of the National Security and Foreign Affairs Subcommittee of the House Oversight and Government Reform Committee of Subject: "Afghan Elections: What Happened and Where Do We Go from Here?" Chaired by Representative John Tierney (D-MA), November 19, 2009. One is also reminded here of John Kenneth Galbraith's remarks on the plight of South Vietnam's President Diem: "The desire to prolong one's days in office has a certain consistency the world around and someday somebody should explain this to the State Department with pictures." John Kenneth Galbraith, *Ambassador's Journal: A Personal Account of the Kenndy Years* (Boston: Houghton Mifflin, 1969) p. 267.

[26] The prevalence of voting blocs in Afghanistan are well described by Noah Coburn and Anna Larson, "Voting Together: Why Afghanistan's 2009 Elections were (and were not) a Disaster," Kabul: Afghanistan Reconstruction and Evaluation Unit, November 2009, pp. 10-16.

[27] Mojaddedi was a widely respected figure in Afghanistan. He had played a similar role in 1992, heading a caretaker interim government according to the Peshawar Accord for two months and handing over power to Rabbani when his allotted time was over.

[28] Article 143 of the Afghan constitution states that, "If due to war, threat of war, serious rebellion, natural disasters, or situations similar to these protecting the independence or nation's survival becomes impossible by following the provision of this Constitution, the President in confirmation of National Assembly shall declare a state of emergency in some or all parts of the country." While conditions in Afghanistan might have objectively justified the declaration of a state of emergency, such a state also allowed the president to place restrictions on rights of assembly and other rights that are somewhat important for the holding of a democratic election. The selfish reasons for the opposition to oppose a state of emergency was that it would reinforce Karzai's powers, rather than diminish them.

[29] Pascal Perrineau and Dominique Reynié, *Dictionnaire du Vote*, (Paris: Presses Universitaires de France, 2001) pp. 303-304. On the other hand, supporters of the two-round system argue that, in Afghanistan, a split Pashtun vote could result in a non-Pashtun candidate being elected by a plurality, with possibly destabilizing consequences. One of the fears in 2009, however, when President Karzai failed to obtain a majority in the first round, was that non-Pashtuns, sensing the President's weakness, might band together behind the non-Pashtun opposition candidate, Abdullah Abdullah. The fact is that Pashtuns are likely to be a plurality in Afghanistan, not a majority, and this is true whether there is a one- or two-round system.

[30] As another example of the hodge-podge nature of the Afghan electoral system, the parliamentary system of SNTV was based on the lack of political parties, but the two-round majority system for electing the president presumes the existence of effective political parties that can realign themselves according to common political interests.

[31] A more exhaustive study of the 2009 elections will have to provide a detailed account of the decisions taken by the ECC. It soon became clear that the complexity of the process overwhelmed their capacity. The normal function

of an electoral complaints mechanism is to establish in this circumstance whether a second round is required. The initial approach taken by the ECC, however, was to try to determine the legitimacy of each and every vote—an exercise with no political value that would have taken months.

[32] See Ian Pannell, "U.S. Envoy 'in Angry Karzai talks'," BBC News, August 27, 2009.

[33] See Jon Boone and Daniel Nasaw, "Cloud Hangs over Legitimacy of Afghanistan Election Result," *The Guardian* (London) August 23, 2009.

[34] Perelli and Valenzuela had worked together for many years. In particular, Valenzuela had been hired by Perelli when she was still the director of EAD to run the Iraq election in January of 2005. Given this long relationship, Perelli was instrumental in convincing Valenzuela to come to Kabul from the DRC.

[35] The separation of presidential from parliamentary elections in 2004 actually reduced the periodicity of elections in the first *15* years. With the separation, only eight elections were required in the first fifteen years—this is, of course, assuming that district council elections are held, which so far have not been.

[36] Eide refuted these allegations in a press conference in Kabul held on October 11, 2009, whose trasncript is still available on the UNAMA website (www.unama.unmissions.org).

[37] For example, in several instances UNAMA observers stated that they had seen obviously underage voters voting. When they had intervened to protest this, the IEC staff had said that since they had valid voter cards, they had to be allowed to vote. The IEC staff members were, in fact, correct about this. For reasons discussed earlier, it may well have been true that underage voters were allowed to register. But the subjective opinion of a UNAMA monitor over someone's age could not overrule their right to vote if they held a card.

[38] The Ministry of Interior, the Ministry of Defence, and the National Directorate for Security.

[39] While international forces were avidly trying to clear Pashtun areas where the population was more likely to support Karzai, Karzai was accusing international forces of destabilizing areas where people were more likely to vote for him.

[40] Galbraith later argued that the fraud had vindicated his position. The fact is that fraud also occurred where security forces and observers were present. Fraud also occurred on behalf of candidates other than Karzai.

[41] In a tribal society like Afghanistan, it is entirely possible that 95 percent of a voting area would vote for a single candidate. The recording of 600 votes would be highly unusual, however. This was the number of ballots provided to a station, but included overage in case any given station was deluged with voters. The number of voters expected in each polling station, however, was 540. There were a surprising number of stations returning exactly 600 ballots, and these accounted for much of the fraud.

[42] Peter Galbraith, "Karzai was Hellbent on Victory. Afghans Will Pay the Price," Guardian.co.uk, 2 November 2009.

[43] In contrast, for example, to Galbraith, who had no experience in Afghanistan when he arrived in early June 2009. Between Galbraith's

appointment in March and his departure in mid-September, he had spent a total of eighty days in Afghanistan.

[44] Eide was also affected by an experience several months earlier, in late June, when UNDP ELECT had asked him to request the Chairman of the IEC not to go ahead with the sacking of a provincial electoral commissioner. UNDP ELECT believed that the provincial commissioner was doing an effective job, but that Ludin wanted to replace him with someone more pliable. Eide raised the issue with the Chairman of the Electoral Commission, Azizullah Ludin, but it had no effect. Ludin later claimed that he had no intention of replacing the commissioner, but once he had been asked not to by the SRSG, he went ahead and did it to "demonstrate his independence." Ludin's story on this is not very credible, but his rationalization is a good example of Afghan argumentation in such situations, and the ability to use the rhetoric of the international community against itself. On a larger scale, the difficulty of getting Afghans to cooperate with one's own intentions was highlighted in an excellent *Washington Post* article on Karzai's inauguration. The article essentially proves the point that while Eide's "softly-softly" approach is easy to criticize, it achieves better results than a publicly confrontational approach. See Chandrasekaran. "A softer approach to Karzai."

[45] See Galbraith, "Excerpts."

[46] Richard Atwood, an expert who worked on both the 2005 elections under Erben and was an advisor during early preparations for the 2009 election, makes the valid counter-argument that in 2005 it had actually been very difficult to prevent fraud in the counting centers, where local power-brokers could effectively "capture" a warehouse and intimidate staff, political agents, and observers (personal correspondence). On the other hand, one of the 2009 ECC commissioners, Scott Worden, also questions the decision to count at the polling station. "By placing polling stations in remote areas that were threatened by violence and could not be observed, election planners gave corrupt officials an open door." Scott Worden, "Afghanistan: An Election Gone Awry," p. 20.

[47] AREU published some stunning conclusions on this after the 2009 election: "While opinions were mixed on the role of figures like Karzai and Abdullah, and institutions such as the IEC, there was almost uniform condemnation of the role of the international community, both on election day and in the period following. Alarmingly, almost every respondent interviewed after the IEC's announcement of a planned second round vote mentioned the role of the international community in manipulating the electoral process (the decision was widely reported as made under international pressure)." Noah Coburn, "Losing Legitimacy? Some Afghan Views on the Government, the International Community, and the 2009 Elections," AREU Post-Election Brief 2, Kabul, November 2009.

17
Logistics, Politics, and Transitions

We return in these final pages to the nexus of logistics and politics—to the link between elections as a logistical exercise and their practical effect in generating political change through expanded political participation. The 2004 and 2005 elections in Afghanistan and Iraq, and the failure of "democracy" to immediately implant itself led, in the United States in particular, to an implosion of confidence in democratization. This was in part an almost chemical reaction to the euphoria at the generally successful electoral *events* in those two countries in 2004 and 2005. But because the expectations were unrealistically high, the disappointment was fatally deep. A further misreading of the lessons from these processes will, in all likelihood, lead to the jettisoning of much that worked, much that can be learned from, and much that can be built upon.

For those who had been advocating for Afghanistan an institutional rather than an event-driven perspective, the sudden lamentation among policy-makers and commentators that "elections do not make a democracy" sounded a belated false note. Electoral events were never intended to "make" a democracy. Democracy can only be made through a continual process of institution-building and a gradual regularization of the rites of democracy—a long-term process for which the first elections were only a small step. Furthermore, these early events were only contributory if a number of less dramatic parallel processes were tended with equal care and attention. As Huntington has argued, "the problem is not to hold elections but to create organizations."[1] The desiderata of postconflict elections is not necessarily their results—in other words, who won—but the fact that objects of rule and misrule begin to transformed into citizens by the rites of registration and voting. Similarly, the protagonists of violence begin to be constrained by the rules of politics. While many definitions of democracy focus on the procedures that deliver periodic and transparent elections, Charles Tilly's wider definition is perhaps more pertinent: "a regime is democratic to the degree that political relations between the state and its citizens feature broad, equal, protected and mutually binding consultation."[2] Elections only have meaning if they are followed by repeated signals that the act of becoming a citizen, of participating in politics, is translated into some desired effect on the lives of at least the majority of citizens at least some of the time.

For example, the biggest problem with the 2005 Afghan parliamentary election was not necessarily that the elected parliament was full of "warlords." As Olivier Roy wrote perceptively several years prior to that election: "What has been identified as the main problem of state building in Afghanistan, the role of warlords and commanders, the weakness of the state and the fragile ethnic balance, is also an expression of the resilience of a common Afghan political culture, which could be reshaped toward something closer to a modern state."[3] The inclusion of warlords may even have been necessary, if not inevitable. But with the conduct of elections appearing more and more as impositions from outside, they lost their connection with the "common Afghan political culture." In this sense, the dynamic of hope that had been built up through the participatory processes from the Emergency Loya Jirga, through the Constitutional Loya Jirga, to the presidential elections began to unravel. As flawed as these earlier processes were, they had allowed people to participate in politics in ways they never had before, and they perceived that their voice, through their representatives, was being heard at levels where crucial decisions were being made. But the combination of warlords acting like warlords in parliament, and the perception that elections were driven from outside, became fatal to the legitimacy of formal power.

Finalizing these pages in the shadow of the 2010 parliamentary elections, it is sobering to watch the democratization debate begin its sad traverse from the position that elections are not a sufficient condition for democracy to the conclusion that in Afghanistan elections undermine democracy.[4] As Afghanistan's second democratic experiment steadily regresses to its point of departure—which seems increasingly likely to be a renegotiation of power arrangements, this time involving the Taliban—holding elections increasingly served only one purpose, which was to keep the Constitution alive. Whatever the flaws of that document, it remains the only glue really uniting Afghanistan's political class—and a thin glue at that. Not to have held elections would have been to effectively break the political arrangement that had prevented the country from sliding into total civil war. And so elections were held, despite the greatly deteriorated security situation and the manifest weaknesses of the Afghan institutions responsible for organizing and securing them. Elections have now become little more than a means of securing and freezing in place a fragile political settlement, rather than an instrument to expand political representation.[5] In this inversion of the role of elections, once can sense the great disappointment of Bonn.

Understanding Transition

For those who advocated a democratization process, the disappointment of Bonn is that it appears to prove that democratization is impossible. What is increasingly ignored in discussions of elections and democratization is the notion of political transition—a process that is more complex and longer-term than the notion of transformation that was apparently desired from the early elections in Afghanistan and Iraq. It is a particularly American oversight that is perhaps rooted in the remarkable stability of the U.S. political system itself, and the fact that in the early years of American independence political transition and transformation took place almost invisibly. As Hannah Arendt noted, "the act of foundation, namely the colonization of the American continent, had preceded the Declaration of Independence, so that the framing of the Constitution, falling back on existing charters and agreements, confirmed and legalized an already existing body politic rather than made it anew."[6]

In other words, the Constitution was a ratification of a pre-existing political consensus. In postconflict societies such as Afghanistan, the constitutional and electoral processes were part of a consensus-*building* effort, an effort that is rife with rivalry and jockeying for position, and is inherently unstable. The historical American insulation from radical politics, however, has consequences for the American understanding of these long and difficult processes. As Louis Hartz has written, "the psyche that springs from social war and social revolution is given to far suspicions and sidelong glances that the American liberal cannot easily understand."[7]

Modern electoral assistance theory is largely rooted in the transitions from authoritarianism to democracy that took place on the Iberian peninsula in the 1970s and in Latin America in the 1980s. The conceptual frameworks that emerged from the study of these transitions included much more than the holding of elections: the liberalization of society, the establishment of independent institutions (electoral and judicial in particular), free markets, settling "accounts with memory,"[8] and other measures that both establish a political framework for the future and deal with a very real, very recent, and very traumatic political history. Students of these frameworks also paid great attention to the sequencing of different events as well as the need to set the "rules of the game" for all political actors. These considerations, applied to a proper understanding of each individual context, are the difference between "electoralism" and nurturing a real political transition.[9]

An implicit but infrequently recognized function of postconflict elections, especially where there is no democratic tradition, is the demystification of democracy. As the elections in Afghanistan and Iraq clearly demonstrated (and in fact as turnout figures in almost all postconflict elections demonstrate) people do not need much persuading to seize the chance, when offered, to participate in the shaping of their government. This desire is especially fervent after a long period in which people have been voiceless and often defenseless. The case of the Timorese, in 1999, who knew they were risking mass deaths to vote for independence, is but one demonstration. Postconflict voting populations may, however, harbor suspicions about how that process works and who is conducting it. This requires developing processes that are transparent, easy to understand, and self-evidently logical and credible. These processes must also not be so complex or expensive that subsequent elections will inevitably fall short, making democracy seem like a gift from outside rather than the exercise of a fundamental political right.

Transitions from conflict have different dynamics than transitions from authoritarianism, but much can be, and has been, borrowed from democratic transitions in Europe, Latin America and the former Soviet Union in recent decades. The early proposal by EAD to draft a one-time electoral law, for example, was intended to allow a negotiation among the main parties of the "rules" of the electoral game, and thereby to establish confidence long before the election began. The work that was put into creating a JEMB that could actually be independent was intended to build an institution that could credibly referee the rules, once these rules were decided upon through a political consensus. In fact, a salient feature of postconflict situations is that in the best of cases electoral institutions form a sort of scaffolding for the entire transition process, or short-term proxies for the sorts of durable institutions that liberal democracies require.

For example, the electoral law is often one of the first postconflict laws, not only to be adopted, but to be implemented. Its implementation, furthermore, must be of a sufficient standard as it will be put to the test, and passing that test is crucial to the entire transition. This is not necessarily the same for other early postconflict legislation, on which the stakes are smaller. One can adopt a law on commercial contracts, but no one will be surprised, and the transition will not be greatly affected in its early stages, if that law is not scrupulously applied. In the same vein as the electoral law, the independent election commission is one of the first bodies to be created with an independent and neutral character after years of conflict.[10] Intensive civic education campaigns serve as proxies for a free press (though without championing any positions or candidates). Adherence to the "rules of the game" force former armed factions and other political groups to act like parties; measures such as codes of conduct or provisions in the electoral law that prohibit candidates from maintaining links with armed groups provide both incentives and sanctions to encourage this development. These early initiatives then provide a latticework along which indigenous liberal institutions can develop and grow, as long as there is follow-up and the process is nurtured as a real transition, not as a series of procedures leading up to an event in which the political context of that event is ignored or assumed away. All of this, however, requires more vision and persistence than the international community is often willing or able to provide, and often more maturity and magnanimity than local actors can muster, especially when they begin to understand that they face no real penalties.

Was It All a Big Mistake?

The perceived failures of the electoral processes in Afghanistan and Iraq led some to conclude that the holding of any elections at all was a mistake in itself, that some societies are simply not "ready" for democracy. In this despair is lost Amartya Sen's subtle observation that "a country does not have to be deemed fit *for* democracy; rather, it has to become fit *through* democracy."[11] But becoming fit *through* democracy requires the navigation of many pitfalls by all actors, domestic and international, as well as a sense of realism that is often defeated by an understandable lack of patience. One of the basic tensions of any transition is, as Perelli wrote, "balancing what is desirable with what is achievable. All shades of gray are found in the murky middle: the realm of the lesser evil."[12] Or, as another Galbraith wrote, "Politics is not the art of the possible. It consists in choosing between the disastrous and the unpalatable."[13]

Holding elections in 2009 in Afghanistan was the lesser evil; anything else would have been worse for the country. The method through which the electoral crisis was resolved was superior to all other options in terms of retaining as much as possible of the democratic idea and the electoral institutions. But in 2009 the requirement was to make the best of a situation that was the result of many years of short-sighted decisions that had consistently favored the event over the process, and the momentary political need over the need to build effective institutions. In 2009, the election was a rescue operation, not a consolidation of institutions.

The future for Afghans now seems to increasingly resemble their past. Many recalled that the Soviets had also used the concept of "democracy" as a justification for their occupation of Afghanistan.[14] It was said that the Soviets had promised a democracy that would bring food, clothes, and shelter. But instead of food it gave bullets; instead of clothes, the burial shroud; and instead of shelter, the tomb. Many Afghans have begun to ask themselves the same question about democracy again, and are finding the same answers.

Democracy is, as is often said, the only self-correcting political system. The flip-side of that is that, in the end, everyone involved also shares some blame for its failures. The previous pages have attempted to account from a somewhat personal vantage for the share of the international community in the effort to democratize Afghanistan. But the international community was only half the story. This account awaits correction, and perhaps complement, from the other side—the Afghans.

---

[1] Huntington, *Political Order*, p. 7.

[2]Charles Tilly, *Democracy* (New York: Cambridge University Press, 1997) pp. 13-14.

[3] Roy, "Afghanistan: Internal Politics and Socio-economic Dynamics and Groupings" p. 10. The question of the *state* itself has been perhaps insufficiently discussed in this study. Obviously the existence of a state capable of implementing decisions arising from consultation is crucial. Unfortunately, the building of such a state apparatus was the task that should have taken place between 2004 and 2009, a time period only touched upon in this book. One of the main reasons that such a state apparatus was not built had to do with the governing style of President Karzai, partly discussed in Chapter 15, as well as the general lack of coordination among the international community and its failure to focus on institutions. The complete reasons for this failure are far more complicated, however, and will hopefully be the subject of many dissertations to come.

[4] See, for example, *The Economist,* "Not Exactly a Ringing Endorsement: Another Year, Another Rigged Vote," London, September 23, 2010, vol. 396, which describes the 2010 parliamentary elections as "a vote to set democracy back" and quotes Dr. Abdullah, the 2009 runner-up, as saying that "Democracy is already damaged." See also Dan Murphy, "Are Afghanistan Elections Hurting Democracy?" Christian Science Monitor, Global News Blog (csmonitor.com/world), September 21, 2010, and Aryn Baker, "Afghan Elections: Corruption Could Again Thwart Democracy," *Time*, New York, September 21, 2010.

[5] Though, as Coburn and Larson have documented, at the local level elections do serve to reconfigure patterns of representation. See "Voting Together."

[6] Hannah Arendt, *Between Past and Future: Six Exercises in Political Thought* (Cleveland: Meridian Books, 1963) p. 140.

[7] Louis Hartz, *The Liberal Tradition in America* (San Diego: Harcourt Brace, 1991) p. 7

[8] This is a somewhat poetic phrasing of what in Afghanistan has been referred to as the need for some mechanism to address the crimes of the past, in particular committed by many of the "warlords" who now have seats in parliament. It is not an accident that in 2008 Parliament adopted an amnesty law that essentially prevents such a process from happening.

[9] See in particular Samuel P. Huntington, *The Third Wave: Democratization in the Late Twentieth Century* (Norman, OK: University of Oklahoma Press, 1991), which comprehensively discusses these transformations. Tilly's *Democracy,* published more recently, examines the process of democratization and "de-democratization" with a fuller set of data—discussing patterns in earlier European democratization as well as later efforts in post-Soviet Central Asia. Most interesting, for the discussion of Afghanistan, is his description of the fits and starts of Swiss democratization and state-formation. Switzerland in the late eighteenth century shared a number of characteristics with Afghanistan, including its landlocked and mountainous geography, its decentralized politics, its religious split, and the various interests of stronger neighbors in its stability or instability (see pp. 51-79). There, too, according to Tilly, the process was long and uncertain.

[10] Frequently, human rights commissions and national reconciliation commissions are also created, but they have a longer time in which to perform their tasks and gain trust.

[11] Amartya Sen, "Democracy as a Universal Value" *Journal of Democracy* vol. 10.3 (1999) p.4.

[12] Carina Perelli, "The Paradoxes of Elections and Transitions: When is a Nation Ready for Elections?" in *Every Vote Counts*, eds. Soudriette and Pilon, p 41.

[13] John Kenneth Galbraith, *Ambassador's Journal*, p. 312.

[14] According to Paul Robinson and Jay Dixon, the Soviet concept of "national democracy" emerged as a result of the confluence of the post-Stalin thaw and the opportunity presented by newly-decolonized—but not necessarily communist—countries that nonetheless found the socialist economic model attractive: "Previously the idea had been that the communist party would force the pace of development. Now, the concept of national democracy permitted progressive forces of any class, not just the proletariat, to initiate the process of freeing post-colonial economies from imperialism." See Paul Robinson and Jay Dixon, "Soviet Development Theory and Economic and Technical Assistance to Afghanistan, 1954-1991," *The Historian*, vol. 72, no. 3, Fall 2010, p. 605.

Bibliography

Abootalebi, Ali Reza, *Islam and Democracy: State-Society Relations in Developing Countries 1980-1994*. New York: Garland Publishing, Inc., 2000.

Adamec, Ludwig, *Dictionary of Afghan Wars, Revolutions, and Insurgencies*. Landham, MD: Scarecrow Press, 1996.

Akram, Assem, *Histoire de la Guerre d'Afghanistan*. Paris: Balland, 1996.

Allan, Nigel J.R., *Tribe and Village Agrosystems in the Hindukoush*. Syracuse, NY: University of Syracuse Press, 1979.

Amin, S. H., Law, *Reform and Revolution in Afghanistan*. Glascow: Royston Publishers, 1993.

Arendt, Hannah, *Between Past and Future: Six Exercises in Political Thought*. Cleveland, OH: Meridian Books, 1963.

Baker, Aryn, "Afghan Elections: Corruption Could Again Thwart Democracy," Time, New York, September 21, 2010.

Barry, Michael, *Le Royaume de l'Insolence: La Résistance Afghane du Grand Moghol à l'Invasion Soviétique*. Paris: Flammarion, 1984.

Bennett, Christina, Wakefield, Shawna, and Wilder, Andrew, "Afghan Elections: The Great Gamble," (AREU: Kabul, November 2003).

Bhati, Michael; Lanigan, Kevin; and Wilkinson, Philip. "Minimal Investments, Minimal Results: The Failure of Security Policy in Afghanistan." Kabul: Afghan Research and Evaluation Unit, June 2004.

Bierce, Ambrose, *The Devil's Dictionary*. New York: Dover Publications Inc., 1958.

Bjornlund, Eric C., Beyond *Free and Fair: Monitoring Elections and Building Democracy*. Washington, D.C.: Woodrow Wilson Center Press, 2004.

Bone, James, "Peter Galbraith will take key UN role in Afghanistan 'civilian surge,'" The Times (London), March 26, 1009.

Bone, James and Coghlan, Tom, "US strengthens diplomatic presence in Afghanistan," The Times (London), March 17, 1009.

Boone, Jon and Nasaw, Daniel, "Cloud Hangs over Legitimacy of Afghanistan Election Result," The Guardian (London), August 23, 2009.

Bradsher, Henry S., *Afghan Communism and Soviet Intervention*. Oxford: Oxford University Press, 1983.

Burns, John, "Afghan Professionals Fleeing Rule by Clerics," New York Times, 7 October 1996.

Camus, Albert. *The Rebel: An Essay on Man in Revolt*. Translated by Anthony Bower. New York: Vintage International, 1991.

Carter, Stephen and Clark, Kate Clark, "No Shortcut to Stability: Justice, Politics and Insurgency in Afghanistan", Chatham House, December 2010.

Chandrasekaran, Rajiv, "A softer approach to Karzai," Washington Post, 20 November 2009.

Noah Coburn, "Losing Legitimacy? Some Afghan Views on the Government, the International Community, and the 2009 Elections," Kabul: Afghanistan Reconstruction and Evaluation Unit (Post-Election Brief 2), November 2009.

Coburn, Noah, "Connecting With Kabul: The Importance of the Wolesi Jirga Election and Local Political Networks in Afghanistan." Kabul: Afghan Research and Evaluation Unit, May 2010.

Coburn, Noah and Larson, Anna , "Voting Together: Why Afghanistan's 2009 Elections were (and were not) a Disaster." Kabul: Afghanistan Reconstruction and Evaluation Unit, November 2009.

Coll, Steve, *Ghost Wars*. New York: The Penguin Press, 2004.

Crewes, Robert D. and Tarzi, Amin, eds., *The Taliban and the Crisis of Afghanistan*. Cambridge: Harvard University Press, 2008.

Dempsey, John, and Thier, J. Alexander, "Resolving the Crisis over Constitutional Interpretation in Afghanistan." Washington, D.C.: United States Institute of Peace, March 2009.

De Tocqueville, Alexis, *L'Ancien Régime et la Révolution*, 4th. ed. Paris, 1860.

DeYoung, Karen, "Civilians to Join Afghan Buildup; 'Surge' Is Part of Larger U.S. Strategy Studied by White House," Washington Post, March 19, 2009.

Diamond, Larry and Plattner, Marc F., eds, *The Global Resurgence of Democracy*. Second Edition. Baltimore and London: Johns Hopkins University Press, 1996.

Dobbins, James F., *After the Taliban*. Dulles, VA: Potomac Books, 2008.

Donini, Antonio; Niland, Nora; and Wemester, Karin, eds., *Nation-building Unraveled? Aid, Peace and Justice in Afghanistan*. Bloomfield, CT: Kumarian Press, 2004.

Dorronsoro, Gilles, Revolution *Unending: Afghanistan, 1979 to the Present*. New York: Columbia University Press, 2005.

Dupree, Louis, "The New Republic of Afghanistan: the first twenty-one months," Special Paper, Afghanistan Council of the Asia Society, New York, 1976.

Dupree, Louis, "The Democratic Republic of Afghanistan, 1979", American Universities Field Staff Reports, Hanover, NH, 1979.

Dupree, Louis, *Afghanistan*. Princeton: Princeton University Press, 1980.

The Economist, "Confounding the doomsters," London, July 24, 2004, vol. 372.

The Economist, "Not Exactly a Ringing Endorsement: Another Year, Another Rigged Vote," London, September 23, 2010, vol. 396.

Eliot, T.S., *The Complete Poems and Plays: 1909-1950*. New York: Harcourt, Brace & World, 1971.

Elklit, Jorgen and Svensson, Palle, "What Makes Elections Free and Fair?" Journal of Democracy, vol. 8, 1997, pp 32-46.

Esposito, John, and Voll, John O., *Islam and Democracy*. Oxford: Oxford University Press, 1996.

Evans, Anne; Manning, Nick; and Osmani, Yasin, *A Guide to Government in Afghanistan. Kabul*. The World Bank and the Afghanistan Research and Evaluation Unit, 2004.

Evans, Martin and Phillips, John, *Algeria: Anger of the Dispossessed*. New Haven and London: Yale University Press, 2007.

Evans, Peter, *Embedded Autonomy: States and Industrial Transformation*. Princeton: Princeton University Press, 1995.

Fairfield, Roy P., ed., *The Federalist Papers*. Second Edition. Baltimore: Johns Hopkins University Press, 1981.

Farley, Maggie, "U.N. Elections Chief Accused of Harassing Staff, Misusing Funds," Los Angeles Times, 30 March 2005.

Farr, Grant M. and Merriam, John, G., eds., *Afghan Resistance: The Politics of Survival*. Colorado: Westview Press, 1987.

Farrell, David M., *Electoral Systems: A Contemporary Introduction*. New York: Palgrave, 2001.

Fischer, Jeff, "Elections and Peace Operations: Analysis and Case Studies, 1989-2000." Washington, D.C.: IFES Center for Transitional and Post-conflict Governance, 2005.

Franks, Tommy. *American Soldier*. New York: Regan Books, 2004.

Galbraith, John Kenneth, *Ambassador's Journal: A Personal Account of the Kennedy Years*. Boston: Houghton Mifflin, 1969.

Galbraith, Peter, "Excerpts: Galbraith's Letter to U.N. Secretary-General," New York Times, October 1, 2009.

Galbraith, Peter, "Afghanistan Votes, the U.N. Dithers," The New York Times, October 28, 2009.

Galbraith, Peter, "Karzai was Hellbent on Victory; Afghans Will Pay the Price," Guardian.co.uk, November 2, 2009.

Gall, Carlotta, "UN Representative Warns That Afghan Peace Is Fragile," New York Times, February 24, 2003.

Gall, Carlotta, "With Future Charted, U.N. Envoy Departs," New York Times, January 6, 2004.

Gall, Carlotta, "Strife Reported to Delay Afghan Vote Again," New York Times, 2 July 2004.

Gall, Carlotta, "At Border, Signs of Pakistani Role in Taliban Surge," New York Times, 21 January 2007.

Ghani, Ashraf, "Afghanistan xi. Administration," *Encyclopaedia Iranica*, Vol. I, 1985.

Ghani, Ashraf Lockhart, Clare, *Fixing Failed States: A Framework for Rebuilding a Fractured World*. Oxford: Oxford University Press, 2008.

Giustozzi, Antonio,"'Good' State vs. 'Bad' Warlords? A critique of State-Building Strategies in Afghanistan", Crisis States Programme Working Paper no.51, October 2004.

Giustozzi, Antonio, *Koran, Kalashnikov, and Laptop: the Neo-Taliban Insurgency in Afghanistan*. New York: Columbia University Press, 2008.

Giustozzi, Antonio, *Decoding the New Taliban: Insights from the Afghan Field*. London: Hurst & Company, 2009.

Giustozzi, Antonio, "Between Patronage and Rebellion: Student Politics in Afghanistan." Kabul: Afghanistan Research and Evaluation Unit, February 2010.

Glanz James and Oppel, Richard, A., "U.N. Officials Say Americans Offered Plan to Replace Karzai," New York Times, 16 December, 2009.

Goldwin, Robert A., and Schambra, William A., eds., *How Democratic Is the Constitution?* Washington and London: American Enterprise Institute for Public Policy Research, 1981.

Goodwin-Gill, Guy S., *Free and Fair Elections: International Law and Practice*, new expanded edition. Geneva: Inter-Parliamentary Union, 2006.

Gopalakrishnan, R., *Geography and Politics of Afghanistan*. New Delhi: Concept Publishing, 1982.

Gregorian, Vartan, *The Emergence of Modern Afghanistan: Politics of Reform and Modernization, 1880-1946*. Stanford: Stanford University Press, 1969.

Guerra, Claudio Lopes, "Should Expatriates Vote?", *Journal of Political Philosophy*, vol. 13, issue 2, June 2005.

Hanafi, Jamal, "Editing the Past: Colonial Production of Hegemony Through the Loya Jerga in Afghanistan," *Iranian Studies*, vol. 27, issue no. 2, June 2004.

Hartz, Louis, *The Liberal Tradition in America*. San Diego: Harcourt Brace, 1991.

Hirschman, Albert O., *The Rhetoric of Reaction: Perversity, Futility, Jeopardy*. Cambridge and London: The Belknap Press of Harvard University, 1991.

Huntington, Samuel P., *Political Order in Changing Societies*. New Haven: Yale University Press, 1968.

Huntington, Samuel, *The Third Wave: Democratization in the Late Twentieth Century*. Norman, OK: University of Oklahoma Press, 1991.

Impartial Panel of Election Experts, Final Report of Impartial Panel of Election Experts Concerning Afghanistan Presidential Election 2004, Kabul, 2004.

International Crisis Group, "The Loya Jirga: One Small Step Forward?" Kabul and Brussels, Asia Briefing No. 17, May 16, 2002.

International Crisis Group, "The Afghan Transitional Administration: Prospects and Perils," Asia Briefing No. 19, Kabul and Brussels, July 30, 2002.

International Crisis Group, "Afghanistan's Flawed Constitutional Process," Asia Report No. 56, Kabul and Brussels, June 12, 2003.

International Crisis Group, "The Problem of Pashtun Alienation," Asia Report No. 62, Kabul and Brussels, August 5, 2003.

International Crisis Group, "Disarmament and Reintegration in Afghanistan," Asia Report No. 65, Kabul and Brussels, September 30, 2003.

International Crisis Group, "Afghanistan: From Presidential to Parliamentary Elections," Asia Report No. 88, Kabul and Brussels, November 23, 2004.

International Crisis Group, "Afghanistan's Elections: Endgame or New Beginning?" Asia Report No. 101, Kabul and Brussels, July 21, 2005.

International Crisis Group, "Afghanistan's New Legislature: Making Democracy Work," Asia Report No. 116, Kabul and Brussels, May 15, 2006.

International Crisis Group "Afghanistan's Election Challenges," Asia Report, No. 171, Kabul and Brussels, June 24, 2009.

International Crisis Group, "Afghanistan: Elections and the Crisis of Government," Asia Briefing No. 96, Kabul and Brussels, November 25, 2009.

International IDEA, *Electoral System Design: the New International IDEA Handbook*. Stockholm: 2006.

International IDEA, *Voting From Abroad: The International IDEA Handbook*. Stockholm and Mexico City: 2007)

Inter-Parliamentary Council of the Inter-Parliamentary Union, Declaration on Criteria for Free and Fair Elections, Paris, 26 March 1994.

Kakar, Hasan Kawun, *Government and Society in Afghanistan: The Reign of 'Abd al-Rahman Khan*. Austin: University of Texas Press, 1979.

Kent, Arthur, "Cashing in on Karzai & Co.," Policy Options, November 2007.

Khalilzad, Zalmay, "Lessons from Afghanistan and Iraq," Journal of Democracy. Vol. 21, No.3, July 2010.

Klass, Rosanne, ed., *Afghanistan: The Great Game Revisited*. New York: Freedom House, 1990.

Lee, Matthew and Gearan, Anne, "Officials: U.S. Prepares Civilian 'Surge' in Afghanistan to complement higher troop levels," Associated Press, March 18, 2009.

Lynch, Colum, "Ex-U.N. Official Spent Development Funds on Luxury Items, Probe Says," Washington Post, March 27, 2009.

Lynch, Colum, "U.N. Seeks U.S. Probe of Alleged Misuse of Afghan Aid," Washington Post, June 11, 2009.

Macintyre, Ben, *The Man Who Would Be King: The First American in Afghanistan*. New York: Farrar Straus Giroux, 2004.

McChesney, Robert D., *Kabul Under Siege: Fayz Muhammad's Account of the 1929 Uprising*. Princeton: Markus Wiener Publishers, 1999.

Maley, William and Saikal, Fazel Haq, *Political Order in Post-Communist Afghanistan*. Boulder: Lynne Rienner, 1992.

Maley,William, ed., *Fundamentalism Reborn*. New York: New York University Press, 1998.

Maley, William, *The Afghanistan Wars*. New York: Palgrave Macmillan, 2002.

Maley, William, *Rescuing Afghanistan*. Sydney: UNSW Press, 2006.

Maley, William, "Afghan Elections: From the Sublime to the Ridiculous?" (Paper presented at Indiana University, 13-14 November 2009, unpublished.)

Margesson, Rhoda, "Afghan Refugees: Current Status and Future Prospects," Washington, D.C., Congressional Research Service, 2007.

Marsden, Peter, *The Taliban: War, Religion and the New Order in Afghanistan*. London: Zed Books, 1998.

Martin, Ian, *Self-determination in East Timor: The United Nations, the Ballot, and International Observation*. International Peace Academy Occasional Paper Series. Boulder and London: Lynne Rienner, 2001.

Matinuddin, Kamal, *The Taliban Phenomenon*. Oxford: Oxford University Press, 1999.

Meisburger, "PR vs SNTV. Election Systems in Developing Democracies," New York, The Asia Foundation, November 18, 2004.

Melia, Thomas O., "Afghan Perspectives on Democracy: A Report on Focus Groups in the Kabul Area on the Eve of the Emergency Loya Jirga," Washington, D.C., National Democratic Institute for International Affairs, May 28, 2002.

Mernissi, Fatema, *Islam and Democracy: Fear of the Modern World*. Translated by Mary Jo Lakeland. Cambridge, MA: Perseus Publishing, 2002.

Meyer, Karl E. and Brysac, Shareen Blair, *Tournament of Shadows*. NewYork: Basic Books, 2006.

Miakhel, Shahmahmood, "The Importance of Tribal Structures and Pakhtunwali in Afghanistan: Their role in Security and Governance" (unpublished).

Miller, Judith, "Review Finds Abuses by Management at the U.N.'s Election Monitoring Office," New York Times, 30 March 2005.

Moore, Barrington, Jr., *Social Origins of Dictatorship: Lord and Peasant in the Making of the Modern World*. Boston: Beacon Press, 1967.

Morgan, Matthew J., *A Democracy is Born*. Westport, CT: Praeger Security International, 2007.

Müller, Joachim, ed., *Reforming the United Nations: The Quiet Revolution*. The Hague: Kluwer Law International, 2001.

Murphy, Dan, "Are Afghanistan Elections Hurting Democracy?" Christian Science Monitor, Global News Blog (csmonitor.com/world), September 21, 2010.

Newell, Richard S., *The Politics of Afghanistan*. Ithaca and London: Cornell University Press, 1972.

Newman, Edward and Rich, Roland, eds, *The UN Role In Promoting Democracy: Between Ideals and Reality*. Tokyo: United Nations University Press, 2004.

Norris, Pippa, *Electoral Engineering: Voting Rules and Political Behavior*. Cambridge: Cambridge University Press, 2004.

Norris, Pippa, "Implementing Women's Representation in Afghanistan Electoral Law. Options for reserved seats," New York, Center on International Cooperation (New York University) Afghanistan Reconstruction Project, [undated].

O'Hanlon, Michael E., Sherjan, Hassina, *Toughing It Out in Afghanistan*. Washington, D.C.: Brookings Institution Press, 2010.

Omrani, Bijan and Ledwidge, Frank, "Rethinking the Durand Line: The Legality of the Afghanistan-Pakistan Frontier," Rusi Journal, Vol. 154, No.5, October 2009.

Pannell, Ian, "U.S. Envoy 'in Angry Karzai talks'," BBC News, August 27, 2009.

Partlow, Joshua and DeYoung, Karen, "US Looks to Reduce Reliance on Karzai," Financial Times (London), August 14, 2009.

Paz, Octavio, *Alternating Current*. Translated by Helen Lane. New York: Arcade Publishing, 1990.

Perrineau, Pascal and Reynié, Dominique, *Dictionnaire du Vote*. Paris: Presses Universitaires de France, 2001.

Pipes, Daniel, *In the Path of God: Islam and Political Power*. New York: Basic Books, 1983.

Planhol, Xavier de, *Les Nations du Prophète*. Paris: Editions Fayard, 1993.

Poullada, Leon B., "The Pashtun Role in the Afghan Political System," Occasional Paper Number One, New York, The Afghanistan Council of the Asia Society, 1970.

Powell, Bingham G. Jr., *Elections as Instruments of Democracy: Majoritarian and Proportional Visions*. New Haven and London: Yale University Press, 2000.

Power, Samantha, *Chasing the Flame: Sergio Vieira de Mello and the Fight to Save the World*. New York: The Penguin Press, 2008.

Przeworski, Adam; Stokes, Susan C.; and Manin, Bernard, eds., *Democracy, Accountability, and Representation*. Cambridge: Cambridge University Press, 1999.

Rashid, Ahmed, *Taliban: The Story of the Afghan Warlords*. London: Pan Books, 2001.

Rashid, Ahmed, "A Vote Is Cast Against the Warlords", Far Eastern Economic Review, Hong Kong: August 5, 2004. Vol. 167, Issue 31, p. 12.

Rashid, Ahmed, *Descent Into Chaos: The United States and the Failure of Nation Building in Pakistan, Afghanistan and Central Asia*. New York: Viking, 2008.

Rashid, Ahmed, "In Afghanistan, Let's Keep it Simple," Washington Post, 6 September 2009.

Ratner, Steven R., *The New U.N. Peacekeeping*. New York: St. Martin's Press, 1995.

Reilly, Benjamin, *Democracy in Divided Societies: Electoral Engineering for Conflict Management*. Cambridge: Cambridge University Press, 2001.

Reuters, "U.N. Suggests Afghan Election Delay Possible," 1 July 2004.

Reynolds, Andrew, The Architecture of Democracy: Constitutional Design, Conflict Management, and Democracy. New York: Oxford University Press, 2002.

Reynolds, Andrew and Wilder, Andrew, "Free, Fair or Flawed: Challenges for Legitimate Elections in Afghanistan," Kabul, Afghan Research and Evaluation Unit, September 2004.

Reynolds, Andrew, "The Curious Case of Afghanistan," Journal of Democracy, Vol. 17, No. 2, April 2006.

Robinson, Paul and Dixon, Jay, "Soviet Development Theory and Economic and Technical Assistance to Afghanistan, 1954-1991," The Historian, vol. 72, no. 3, Fall 2010, p. 605.

Roche, Amandine Roche, *Le Vol des Colombes: Journal d'une Volontaire en Afghanistan*. Paris; Robert Laffont, 2005.

Rose, Richard, ed. *International Encyclopedia of Elections*. Washington: CQ Press, 2000.

Roussel, Frédéric Roussel, Caley, Marie-Pierre,"Les 'Manteqas': Le Puzzle Souterrain de l'Afghanistan" (photocopy).

Roy, Olivier, *The Failure of Political Islam*. Translated by Carol Volk. Cambridge: Harvard University Press, 1994.

Roy, Olivier, "Le Mouvement des Taleban en Afghanistan", Afghanistan Info. No. 36. Geneva, February 1995 (photocopy).

Roy, Olivier, *Islam and Resistance in Afghanistan*. Cambridge: Cambridge University Press, 1995.

Roy, Olivier, "Afghanistan: Internal Politics and Socio-economic Dynamics and Groupings," WriteNet Paper, March 2003, ISSN 102-8429.

Rubin, Barnett R., *The Fragmentation of Afghanistan: State Formation and Collapse in the International System*. New Haven: Yale University Press, 1995.

Rubin, Barnett R. and Malikyar, Helena, "The Politics of Center-periphery Relations in Afghanistan," New York, Center on International Cooperation, March 2003.

Rubin, Barnett R., "Crafting a Constitution for Afghanistan," Journal of Democracy, Vol. 15, No. 3, July 2004.

Rubin, Elizabeth, "Karzai in his Labyrinth," New York Times Sunday Magazine, 9 August 2009.

Ruttig, Thomas, "Islamists, Leftists—and a Void in the Center: Afghanistan's Political Parties and where they come from (1902-2006)," Konrad Adenauer Stiftung, [undated].

Ruttig, Thomas, "The Other Side," Afghanistan Analysts Network, Thematic Report 01/2009, Kabul, July 2009.

Ruttig, Thomas, "How Tribal Are the Taliban? Afghanistan's Largest Insurgent Movement between its Tribal Roots and Islamist Ideology," Afghan Analysts Network, Thematic Report 04/2010, Kabul, June 2010.

Sachedina, Abdulaziz, *The Islamic Roots of Democratic Pluralism*. Oxford: Oxford University Press, 2001.

Saikal, Amin, *Modern Afghanistan: A History of Struggle and Survival*. London: I.B. Taurus, 2004.

Santa-Cruz, Arturo, International Election Monitoring, Sovereignty and the Western Hemisphere Ideal: The Emergence of an International Ideal. New York and London: Routledge, 2005.

Sartori, Giovanni, *The Theory of Democracy Revisited*. Chatham, NJ: Chatham House Publishers, 1987.

Schaefer, Brett D., "Time to Reign in the U.N.'s Budget", Heritage Foundation's Backgrounder, No. 2368, Washington D.C., February 3, 2010.

Schneider, Cornelia, "The International Community and Afghanistan's Constitution," Peace, Conflict and Development: An Interdisciplinary Journal, Vol. 7, July 2005.

Schofield, Victoria, *Afghan Frontier: Feuding and Fighting in Central Asia*. New York: Palgrave Macmillan, 2003.

Scott, Sir Walter, *The Poetical Works of Sir Walter Scott*, ed. Horace E. Scudden. Boston: Houghton Mifflin, 1900.

Sen, Amartya, "Democracy as a Universal Value", Journal of Democracy vol. 10, No. 3, July 1999.

Sisk, Timothy D., *Islam and Democracy: Religion, Politics and Power in the Middle East*. Washington, D.C.: United States Institute of Peace Press, 1992.

Smith, Michael G., with Dee, Maureen, *Peacekeeping in East Timor: The Path to Independence*. Boulder and London: Lynne Rienner, 2002.

Smith, Wilfred Cantwell, *Pakistan as an Islamic State (Preliminary Draft)*. Lahore: Shaikh Muhammad Ashraf Publisher, 1951.

Soudriette, Richard and Geran Pilon, Juliana, eds., *Every Vote Counts*. Lanham, MD: University Press of America, 2007.

Soussan, Michael, *Backstabbing for Beginners: My Crash Course in International Diplomacy*. New York: Nation Books, 2008.

Spence, Kit, "Political Party Assessment in Afghanistan," Kabul, National Democratic Institute for International Affairs, Spring 2006.

Stroebel, Warren P. and Landon, Jonathan S., "Obama's Afghanistan 'Surge': diplomats, civilian specialists", McClatchy, March 18, 2009.

Suhrke, Astrid, "The Democratisation of a Dependent State: The Case of Afghanistan," Madrid, FRIDE Working Paper 51, December 2007.

Tadjbakhsh, Shahrbanou and Schoiswohl, Michael, "Playing with Fire? The International Community's Democratization Experiment in Afghanistan," International Peacekeeping, vol. 15, No. 2, April 2008.

Tanner, Stephen, *Afghanistan: A Military History from Alexander the Great to the Fall of the Taliban*. New York: Da Capo Press, 2002.

Thier, J Alexander, ed. *The Future of Afghanistan*. Washington, D.C.: United States Institute of Peace, 2009.

Tilly, Charles, *Big Structures, Large Processes, Huge Comparisons*. New York: Russell Sage Foundation, 1984.

Tilly, Charles, *Democracy*. New York: Cambridge University Press, 1997.

Tilly, Charles, *Democratization*. New York: Cambridge University Press, 2007.

Traub, James, *The Best Intentions: Kofi Annan and the UN in the era of American World Power*. New York: Farrar, Straus and Giroux, 2006.

Tucker, Robert C., ed., *The Karl Marx Reader*, Second Edition. New York: W.W. Norton and Company, 1978.

United Nations, *The Blue Helmets: A Review of United Nations Peace-Keeping*. Third Edition. New York: United Nations Department of Public Information, 1996.

Veron, Chantal, "Nous sommes commes morts," Les Nouvelles d'Afghanistan, Paris, No. 76, 1st trimester, 1997.

Wafaey, M. Hassan and Larson, Anna, "The Wolesi Jirga in 2010: Pre-election Politics and the Appearance of Opposition," Kabul, Afghanistan Research and Evaluation Unit, June 2010.

Weiner, Myron and Banuazizi,, Ali, eds., *The Politics of Social Transformation in Afghanistan, Iran, and Pakistan*. Syracuse, NY: Syracuse University Press, 1994.

Weisman, Steven, "U.S. Aides Hint Afghan Voting May be Put Off," New York Times, 16 February 2004.

Wilder, Andrew, "A House Divided? Analysing the 2005 Afghan Elections", (AREU: Kabul, December 2005).

Worden, Scott, "Afghanistan: An Election Gone Awry," Journal of Democracy. Vol. 21, No. 3, July 2010.

Yousaf, Mohammad and Adkin, Mark, *Afghanistan: The Bear Trap*. Havertown, PA: Casemate, 1992.

Index

About the Book

Scott Seward Smith focuses on Afghanistan's 2004 presidential election—the first popular election ever held there—as he explores the painstaking attempt by the United Nations to develop democratic institutions in the country.

Smith thoroughly describes the personalities, policies, bureaucracies, and external factors that shaped the faltering transition process from 2001 through 2009. He also points to the missed opportunities that contributed to the flawed elections of 2009. Arguing that the failure to give sufficient weight to the importance of institution building led to the crisis of confidence and the resurgence of warlord politics that we see today, he sheds light not only on what has gone wrong in Afghanistan, but also on the prospects for Afghan democracy.

Scott Seward Smith, a consultant on elections and democratization, was formerly senior political affairs officer and Afghanistan team leader in the UN Department of Peacekeeping Operations.